Time Out

1000

Great Holiday Ideas

timeout.com

Edited by Chris Moss

Published by Time Out Guides Ltd, a wholly owned subsidiary of Time Out Group Ltd.
Time Out and the Time Out logo are trademarks of Time Out Group Ltd.

© Time Out Group Ltd 2010

10 9 8 7 6 5 4 3 2 1

This edition first published in Great Britain in 2010 by Ebury Publishing
A Random House Group Company
20 Vauxhall Bridge Road, London SW1V 2SA

Random House Australia Pty Limited 20 Alfred Street, Milsons Point, Sydney, New South Wales 2061, Australia
Random House New Zealand Limited 18 Poland Road, Glenfield, Auckland 10, New Zealand
Random House South Africa (Pty) Limited Isle of Houghton, Corner Boundary, Road & Carse O'Gowrie,
Houghton 2198, South Africa

Random House UK Limited Reg. No. 954009

Distributed in USA by Publishers Group West
1700 Fourth Street, Berkeley, California 94710

Distributed in Canada by Publishers Group Canada
250A Carlton Street, Toronto, Ontario M5A 2L1

For further distribution details, see www.timeout.com

ISBN: 978-1-84670-175-7

A CIP catalogue record for this book is available from the British Library

Printed and bound by Firmengruppe APPL, aprinta druck, Wemding, Germany

The Random House Group Limited supports The Forest Stewardship Council (FSC), the leading international forest
certification organisation. All our titles that are printed on Greenpeace approved FSC certified paper carry the FSC
logo. Our paper procurement policy can be found at http://www.rbooks.co.uk/environment.

Time Out carbon-offsets all its flights with Trees for Cities (www.treesforcities.org).

Contents

Introduction 11
About the guide 13

Holiday ideas 1-99

24 hours around the world 14
Shopping trips 19
Epic rail journeys 21
Turkey's romantic getaways 22
Camping heaven 26
Adventure! 28
Ferry nice breaks 31

Ideas from the expert:
  Latin American boutique gems 34

Stag dos 36
Classically cultural Italy 36
African safaris 38

Holiday ideas 100-199

Best European beaches 40
Sunny Cyprus 45
Classic boutique hotels 48

Ideas from the expert:
  Great walks in the UK 51

Alternative camping in Britain 52
Fabulous film locations 55
Foreign food: Cookery schools 59
Ultimate ski holidays 62
Time Out's 21st-century
  European Grand Tour 64

Holiday ideas 200-299

Ten natural wonders of the world 66
Brilliant beaches in the British Isles 70
Five hen dos 73
Boutique Spain: inland 75

Ideas from the expert:
   Top ten South-east Asia 77

Only here for the beer 79
Learn the lingo:
   Foreign-language courses 79
Ten inspiring island refuges 81
Wine cities and regions 83
Which Greek island? 86
Where the hell is it? 89

Holiday ideas 300-399
Once-in-a-lifetime blowouts 92
Mexico on the beach 96

Ideas from the expert:
   Exciting short breaks 100

On the road: Five unforgettable
   US drives 103
Easy Africa 105

Irish idylls 107
Ten UK campsites 108
From St Pancras International
   train terminal to... 110
Fabulous food festivals 112
New Zealand wonders 114

Holiday ideas 400-499
A room (and table) with a view 116

Ideas from the expert:
   Ten glorious gaycations 120

Ski-free snow fun 121
Modern travelogues
   to inspire 123
I want to ride my bicycle 124
Self-indulgent wellness breaks 128
Boutique Spain: coast 130
Clubbing destinations 133

At ***DoSomethingDifferent.com*** we believe what you do on holiday is more important than how you travel, where you stay or what car you rent.

Enjoy a fun-filled circuit across grassy tracks and sandy slopes aboard a 4-wheeled dune buggy before switching to an ATV Quad Bike.

Dune Buggy and ATV Experience

Experiences starting from ONLY £15

VIP Space Shuttle Launch

This once-in-a-lifetime experience takes you to the Kennedy Space Center and the closest authorised viewing site for the launch of Space Shuttle!

Over 1500 experiences worldwide

Take to the skies on a breathtaking hot air balloon flight and savour the spectacular views and peaceful serenity of the morning sunrise.

Orlando Balloon Flight

Volunteering projects 135
Beyond the Eurozone 137

Holiday ideas 500-599

Man-made wonders 140
Ten things to do in London
  for under a tenner 144

Ideas from the expert:
  Great holidays for single parents 146

Wilderness lodges 147
The Gulf: Dubai and beyond 149
Rural refuges in the UK 151
Cute Alpine villages linked
  to vast ski areas 153
Wicked winter sun 155
Classic America 157
Coach holidays 160
Best stopovers 161
Brilliant budgeting ideas 163
Far Eastern journeys 164

Holiday ideas 600-699

Ten best worldwide road trips 166
Gourmet Britain 170

Festivals, parties, carnivals 172

Ideas from the expert: Ten ideas
  for a worthwhile gap year 176

Thailand for all budgets 177
Five alfresco dining spots 179
Edgy escapes 180
Failsafe honeymoons 181
Animal magic 184
Ten cheap or free things
  to do in New York 187
Original (or quirky)
  UK weekend breaks 188

Holiday ideas 700-799

New boutique hotels 192
Cool cruises 195
Holiday camps in the UK and Europe 197
Eight things to do in Croatia 199
Diving and snorkelling 201
Family-friendly holidays worldwide 202

Ideas from the expert: Exotic
  spots in which to tie the knot 205

Creative breaks 206

Whatever your carbon footprint, we can reduce it

For over a decade we've been leading the way in carbon offsetting and carbon management.

In that time we've purchased carbon credits from over 200 projects spread across 6 continents. We work with over 300 major commercial clients and thousands of small and medium sized businesses, which rely upon our market-leading quality assurance programme, our experience and absolute commitment to deliver the right solution for each client.

Why not give us a call?

T: London (020) 7833 6000

www.CarbonNeutral.com

UK heritage trains 207
Ten singles holidays 208
The best of Portugal 210
Argentina and Chile 212
Cities for foodies 214

Holiday ideas 800-899

Perfect places in Morocco 216
Villas in beautiful
  European settings 219
Watersports 221
Grand Indian hotels 223
Eco-friendly holidays 225

Ideas from the expert:
  Destinations for disabled travellers 226

Worldwide yoga retreats 227
Central Asia: Silk Road holidays 227
Europe's second cities 229
The best of Egypt 231
The other Caribbean 233
World's safest places
  (for the travel-anxious) 234
Amazing all-inclusives 235
Where to go when 238

Holiday ideas 900-999

Tropical paradises 240
Awe-inspiring Australia 244

Ideas from the expert:
  Ultimate globe-spanning trip 246

Themed thrills worldwide 247
Ten useful websites 249
The perfect weekend in Paris 251
Spectator holidays 254
Middle Eastern promises 256
Stay for free... well, almost 257
Coastal retreats in the UK 259
And now for something
  completely different... 263

Holiday idea 1000

See the ultimate sunset 266

Maps:
  Great Britain & Ireland 268
  Europe 270
  The Americas 272
  Rest of the world 274
Planning your trip 276
Advertisers' index 280

Get the local experience

Over 50 of the world's top destinations available.

Introduction

Welcome to the ultimate list of holiday ideas: a thousand trips, breaks, journeys, voyages and escapes to set your imagination flying. Your first journey should probably be to somewhere quiet to browse our suggestions – head for the kitchen table with a glass of wine, into the garden with a marker pen or to your favourite café. It's time to travel!

This book is not meant just as a guide to the practical bits of planning and paying for a trip but, rather, an inspiring whirl around the planet. A thousand ideas means a thousand rich possibilities: from wicked winter sun destinations to budget British breaks, from diving holidays to dining out around the world, from boutique hotels in Spain to rockets to the moon (we kid you not). It's all laid out in easily digestible bites so you can pick and choose, mix and match – and tick away to your heart's content.

You probably love lavish coffee-table photo books, travel stories, travelogues, history, features, dreamy poems... so do I. Here at Time Out we produce quite a few of those, as well as our full-colour, intensively researched city guides. Why, then, a book full of lists? Well, for one thing, to save you the donkey work. There are so many travel websites, so many travel brochures, and – especially felt by we journalists and guidebook publishers – so many PR firms and tour operators bombarding us all with suggestions, packages and offers. This book is a distillation of the very best inspirational ideas.

But the main purpose is to give you a sense of the variety of travel experiences on offer. In 25 years of travelling – about 15 of them as a travel journalist – I've been to six of the seven continents and about a third of the 200-odd countries. It sounds like a lot, but it doesn't feel it – not yet. Compiling this list, with the help of Time Out travel gurus, guide editors, writers and researchers, I realised how much more I still have left to explore. Next time someone delivers that old yawn of a comment about 'the world is becoming uniform and monotone, every place like the next', make them flick through *1,000 Great Holiday Ideas*. We trust the cooking, shopping, eating, sailing, language-learning, heli-skiing, whale-watching ideas we have unearthed will enlighten the travel-weary (or armchair-bound) sceptic.

How to use the book? Easy: open it wherever you like and browse. It really is that sort of book. Riffle, skip, hop, compare, pick at random, shuffle ideas, and then get online or on the phone to talk to the expert tour firms we recommend throughout. If you want a bit of structure, see the contents pages or flick through the index maps in search of your favourite corner of the world.

But, actually, who needs structure? There's enough of that when you get to the travel agent, the airport, and the bank. Just indulge in this selection box of ideas for the moment and check where you've been, where you're heading, where you really want to go, and where you never dreamed of going... until today.

Chris Moss, Editor
travel@timeout.com

Time Out Guides Limited
Universal House
251 Tottenham Court Road
London W1T 7AB
Tel + 44 (0)20 7813 3000
Fax + 44 (0)20 7813 6001
Email guides@timeout.com
www.timeout.com

Editorial
Editor Chris Moss
Deputy Editor Anna Norman
Proofreader Tamsin Shelton

Managing Director Peter Fiennes
Editorial Director Ruth Jarvis
Business Manager Dan Allen
Editorial Manager Holly Pick
Assistant Management Accountant Ija Krasnikov

Design
Art Director Scott Moore
Art Editor Pinelope Kourmouzoglou
Senior Designer Henry Elphick
Graphic Designers Kei Ishimaru, Nicola Wilson
Advertising Designer Jodi Sher

Picture Desk
Picture Editor Jael Marschner
Deputy Picture Editor Lynn Chambers
Picture Researcher Gemma Walters
Picture Desk Assistant Ben Rowe
Picture Librarian Christina Theisen

Advertising
Commercial Director Mark Phillips
International Advertising Manager Kasimir Berger
International Sales Executive Charlie Sokol

Marketing
Sales & Marketing Director, North America
& Latin America Lisa Levinson
Senior Publishing Brand Manager Luthfa Begum
Art Director Anthony Huggins
Marketing Intern Alana Benton

Production
Group Production Director Mark Lamond
Production Manager Brendan McKeown
Production Controller Damian Bennett

Time Out Group
Chairman Tony Elliott
Chief Executive Officer David King
Group Financial Director Paul Rakkar
Group General Manager/Director Nichola Coulthard
Time Out Communications Ltd MD David Pepper
Time Out International Ltd MD Cathy Runciman
Time Out Magazine Ltd Publisher/MD Mark Elliott
Group IT Director Simon Chappell
Marketing & Circulation Director Catherine Demajo

The Editor would like to thank the following Time Out Guides staff: Ruth Jarvis for overseeing the project, Anna Norman for her rigorous copy editing, Will Fulford-Jones for tips on the USA and cycling sections, Holly Pick for her help with the map index, and Jael Marschner and Peter Fiennes; from Time Out magazine, thanks to Arts editor and foodie Nina Caplan, Gay editor Paul Burston, Clubbing editor Kate Hutchinson, Food & Drink editor Guy Dimond, Shopping & Style acting editor Dan Jones, staff writer Natasha Polyviou for Cyprus information and chief sub Chris Bourn for help with the theme parks and paradise islands categories; thanks to the following freelance writers: Claire Boobbyer, ski guru Dominic Earle and Kate Miller; from the Time Out International network, thanks to David Plant, publisher of *Time Out Croatia*, and the *Time Out New York* team, editor of *Time Out Abu Dhabi* Jonathan Wilks and editor of *Time Out Dubai* Jeremy Lawrence. Thanks also to the following researchers: Joseph Armson, Seb Brixey-Williams, Jessica Donati, Clare Gittins, Monika Greenfield, Josh Heller, Jessie Lieberson, Jennifer Lipman, Pat Yale and Yolanda Zappaterra. In the travel trade, I'd like to thank Brian Seaman at Tourism for All, Manuel Diaz Cebrian and the Mexican Tourist Board, Accessible Travel & Leisure, Ian Bradley at TravelPR, Genevieve McCarthy of Cellartours of Spain, Caroline Phillips of Explore, Laura Rendell-Dunn at JLA, Vladi Prevratska at HF and Jenny Myddleton at Original Travel; finally, thanks to Bob Greig of Only Dads and Only Mums.

Cover photography by Alys Tomlinson; Ben Rosenzweig; Champagny en Vanoise/Christian Tatin; Christmas Island Tourism Association; Elan Fleisher; Getty Images; Greg Gladman; iStock; Jade Mountain Resort; Karl Blackwell; Olivia Rutherford; Orient Express; Shannon Mendes; Space, Ibiza; Tourism Australia; Thailand tourism; Vintage Vacations.

Contents pages photography by Champagny en Vanoise/Christian Tatin; EXPLORE; Featherdown Farm; Gardel Bertrand/Hemis.fr; Heloise Bergman; Intrepid Travel; iStock; Jade Mountain Resort; Jael Marschner; Karl Blackwell; Las Vegas News Bureau; Sam Robbins; Tourism Authority of Thailand; Tricia de Courcy Ling; www.exodus.co.uk; www.imagesofholland.com; Patrik Rytikangas; Rod Edwards; Wanaka Skydive.

Photography by pages 3, 14/15 Getty Images; 11, 23, 86, 87, 88, 91, 99, 104, 125, 126, 138, 140, 160, 166/167, 206, 215, 232, 233, 244, 264 iStockphoto; 13 The Dominican Republic Ministry; 16, 84, 219, 262 Jonathan Perugia; 17 Karl Blackwell; 19 Ben Rosenzweig; 20, 92/93, 116/117, 240/241, 266/267 Photolibrary.com; 21 Northern Territory Tourism; 24 EXPLORE; 29 www.exodus.co.uk; 30 Harry Baumert/ Des Moines Register; 37, 111 Olivia Rutherford; 38 Tribes Travel; 39 African Horseback Safaris; 40/41 Gemot Westendorf/Sylt Marketing; 43 imagesofportugal.com; 44 www.discover-sardinia.com; 45 Duncan Cox; 46/47 Louisa Nikolaidou; 54 (top) Henry Elphick; 54 (bottom) Sam Robbins; 57 Utah Office of Tourism; 58 South Dakota Tourism; 59, 65 Jitka Hynkova; 63 SkiJapan.com; 64, 165 Fumie Suzuki; 66/67 Tourism Australia; 69 Brian Adams/Travel Alaska; 70 Britta Jaschinski; 71 James Gordon; 73, 158 Elan Fleisher; 75 Karl Blackwell; 79 Rob Greig; 82 Vanuatu Tourism Office; 95 Private Islands Inc.; 101, 150 (left), 238 Jael Marschner; 102 Graz Tourismus; 106 (top, bottom) Namibia Tourism; 106 (middle) Ute von Ludwiger; 112, 130, 131 Turespaña; 115 www.coromandel.com; 121, 234, 251, 252, 258 Heloise Bergman; 122 The Border Inn; 123 Weissensee; 133 Michael Kirby; 142 Oliver Knight; 145 Andrew Brackenbury; 146 Jackie Lewis/Mango holidays; 154 Christian Tatin; 155 Markus Greber; 156 The Dominican Republic Ministry; 159 Las Vegas News Bureau; 163 The Landmark Trust; 173 David Bowen; 175 Andrew Bannister; 176 (right), 277 Rob Greig; 178 Tourism Authority of Thailand;179 David Loftus; 185 Nina Bailey; 188, 189 Alys Tomlinson; 195 www.imageandcommerce.co.uk; 199 Marijo Bandi/Croatian Touri; 200 Filip Horvat; 201, 210 Shutterstock; 211 Lydia Evans; 213 Marc van der Aa; 214 Ben McMilan; 216/217 Getty Images; 220 James Mitchell; 227 Jane Airey; 231 Dick Gillberg; 243 Tamsyn Williams; 254 www.americaasyoulikeit.com; 255 ROLEX/Carlo Borlenghi; 265 Wu Hong/eps/Corbis.

The following images were provided by the featured establishments: pages 26/27, 34, 35, 49, 50, 51, 52, 53, 61, 77, 80, 85, 97, 98, 100, 109, 119, 120, 124, 128, 134, 136, 146, 148, 150, 152, 162, 164, 169, 170, 174, 176 (left), 180, 183, 186, 191, 192/193, 194, 197, 198, 203, 204, 205, 208, 223, 224, 226, 228, 237, 246, 247, 248, 256, 261.

About the guide

Our 1,000 Great Holiday Ideas are divided into 114 categories that we hope you will find useful. The categories are listed in the contents list on pages 4-9. To futher help you choose the holiday that's right for you, we've plotted all the destinations in the book on a set of maps (pages 268-275) to allow you to browse by location, and used symbols to indicate which entries are best suited to particular needs and interests, such as active breaks, eco-friendly and beach destinations. These symbols are explained in the list below.

In addition, there's a section called Planning Your Trip at the back of the book, starting on page 276, where we list useful addresses, telephone numbers and websites and share some invaluable money-saving tips.

Key to symbols

£ Budget ideas. We've used this symbol to indicate when a holiday is suitable for people on a tight budget or represents relatively good value within a non-budget category.

City breaks. This symbol is awarded when a holiday is primarily an urban break or when one or more worthwhile cities feature in a tour.

Beach paradises. The beach icon is used to indicate classic beach holidays, as well as places included for other reasons that also have great beaches.

Natural highs. The tree symbol denotes holidays where the natural environment or wildlife feature heavily.

♡ Romantic destinations. We've applied this symbol to destinations that are traditionally romantic, and also for holidays that offer plenty of seclusion and privacy.

Family-friendly. This symbol is used to flag up places that are particularly suitable for children, along with those geared to family-centred activities.

Sport & active. This symbol denotes holidays devoted to active pursuits such as hiking, watersports and skiing, and locations that are convenient for them.

Short breaks. We have used this icon to flag up holidays that can be taken as short breaks (of up to four days) by readers based in the UK, or a short flight away.

Party places. Destinations that are especially renowned for nightlife, festivals or carnivals have been identified with this symbol.

Wonders of the world. This icon has been applied to holidays based around or convenient for the world's most astonishing sights – whether famous archaelogical sites, awe-inspiring man-made structures or natural wonders of the world.

Eco-friendly. This symbol indicates when a destination listed is renowned for being particularly environmentally aware or when a holiday involves conservation activities.

1 Sunrise over Mount Fitzroy

Towering Mount Fitzroy – at 3,405 metres the highest mountain in Argentina's Parque Nacional Los Glaciares – looks awesome in any light. But when the warm, orange light of sunrise strikes the sheer granite walls of the main peak and neighbouring pinnacles, it's just breathtaking. Known in the native Aonikenk language as 'Chaltén' or 'smoking mountain', the massif is often hidden in a swirl of cloud, but if the sky and sun are on good behaviour, you'll soon have your memory card rammed with photographs.

2 9am... Breakfast at the Wolseley, London

The Wolseley, housed in a 1920s luxury car showroom in London's Piccadilly, is an opulent European-style café with a reputation as a place where the unlisted can sit beside A-listers and enjoy equal attention. As well as the please-all menu, the ten types of specially imported tea and famous Viennoiserie displays, Londoners come for the experience of having what is usually such a familiar repast in such grand surroundings. Breakfast here isn't a meal, it's a ceremony.
020 7499 6996/www.thewolseley.com.

3 11am... Take in some art at New York's Museum of Modern Art

MoMA contains the world's finest and most comprehensive holdings of 20th-century art, including a superb collection of photography. The Midtown museum, recently reopened after a big renovation and expansion in the early 2000s, is now a beautiful place to while away a morning.
+1 212 708 9480/www.moma.org.

4 High noon in California's Death Valley

Travel, sometimes, is about extremes, being tested, experiencing tastes, spaces and temperatures that are far removed from your daily routine. The 3,000-square-mile stretch of parched desert in California and Nevada known as Death Valley – the lowest, driest and hottest location in North America – is just such a place. Venture out into the salt lake at Badwater, or just let the mirages form as the mercury rises; Death Valley holds the record for the highest reliably reported temperature in the Western hemisphere: 134°F (56.7°C) at Furnace Creek in 1913.

5 6pm... Shibuya intersection, Toyko

Can a road junction be sexy? Well, not if you happen to be trying to cross Piccadilly Circus on a workday. But Tokyo's Shibuya crossing is different; located in front of Shibuya Station, it allows pedestrians to cross the entire intersection at once, by stopping traffic in all directions. It's also become a place where new youth trends are spawned, and is surrounded by streetwear and fashion shops. The Starbucks overlooking the crossing is one of the world's busiest, and gives a great view of the swarms of people below.

6 7pm... Stroll La Passeggiata, Rome

Many cultures take the air around dusk, but the Italians invented the evening stroll or *passeggiata*. This 'little walk' is taken between 5pm and 7pm, when everyone turns out in their best clothes to stretch their legs, say hello to

3: MoMA, New York

friends and neighbours and, above all, to be seen *'fare la bella figura'* (or 'cutting a beautiful figure'). An essential part of the day for anyone living the dolce vita, the *passeggiata* ticks all the romantic boxes, especially when performed in Rome: you can take in the fountains and the palaces and the ancient ruins as you wander along and you gently work up an appetite for a late dinner of delicious pastas and wines.

7 *8pm... Sip a cocktail at the Copacabana Palace, Rio de Janeiro*

We've all had a decent caipirinha in a local bar – minty, zesty, zingy even – but hardly a fully Brazilian moment. So how about having one on the terrace of Rio de Janeiro's most iconic hotel? The Copacabana Palace on the eponymous sweeping curve of beach is a stucco-fashioned glory opened in 1923 when Rio was the place to be for the world's glamour set. The new Bar do Copa, decorated by the South African architect Graham Viney, is right by the pool and expert mixologists are on hand to get your evening going with a shake and a stir.
+55 21 2548 7070/www.copacabanapalace.com.

8 *9pm... Dine at dusk at Poseidon, Istanbul*

Turkish cuisine is up there with French and Chinese for complexity, history and tastiness. Istanbul's sunset over the Bosphorus is sublime. So combine the two at Poseidon, consistently rated top of the fish restaurants in Istanbul. Every detail of the dining experience has been perfected: the decor is pleasant and calm; the mezze selection is impressive; and, on ordering a mixed platter for you and your friends, you'll be presented with a generous serving including regional mini-fish such as hamsi and sea bass. Expensive, but worth it. In the summer months, make sure to reserve a table near the water.
+212 263 38 23.

9 *Midnight... Move those limbs at the Barghain nightclub, Berlin*

Marlene, Bowie, Einsterzende, Eno, U2... Berlin has long loved its music and is arguably the dance capital of Europe. Berghain is a strong contender for best club in the city, if not the

5: Shibuya intersection

continent. In basic terms, it's a techno club in a former power station, but it has to be experienced to be fully understood. Even non-fans of the genre fall head over heels in love with the relaxed atmosphere, interesting mix of eccentrics, well-thought-out design details, fantastic sound system and sexually liberal attitude. Panorama, with its smaller dancefloor and Wolfgang Tillmans artwork, is open all weekend; the more intense Berghain part of the venue is only open on Saturdays.
www.berghain.de.

10 *Night-time... See the stars at Utah's Natural Bridges Park*

Because the world's first dark-sky park, Natural Bridges, is small, rather remote and not close to other parks, it's not heavily visited, despite being near many great, lesser-known spots such as White Canyon, Cedar Mesa, Grand Gulch Plateau and the La Sal Mountains. Natural bridges are formed by running water and tend to be found within deep canyons. That's the blurb; here's the knowledge: the night sky in this particular park is so special that the International Dark-Sky Association designated it the world's first great dark-sky place in 2007. This is one to head for to stargaze, dream and switch off.

15: Tokyo

11-20

Shopping trips

11 Currency conversions in Damascus

£ ▦

All the great Arabian cities have souks (Arab markets), but few can compare with those at Damascus and Aleppo. The former is a maze of alleys and courtyards that all lead to a grand arcaded thoroughfare full of artisan perfumers, veil and headdress boutiques, wedding shops, coffee bean traders, jewellers – you name it. Be sure to pause for rest at famed ice-cream parlour Bakdash. Aleppo's souk is, if anything, even more impressive, and the network of alleys and arcades goes on for an amazing 14 kilometres. Haggle hard and you'll come away with quality Persian carpets, olive oil soaps and antiques – all at bargain prices – and a great fridge-magnet of unsmiling but much-loved president Bashar Al Assad. Unlike in Moroccan cities and Cairo, Syrian shopkeepers do not hassle passers-by.

12 Get star-studded in New York

▦

Forget Fifth Avenue – welcome to the Upper East Side consignment stores. Rich traders and bored housewives leave their impulse buys, often with four or five figure tags still on, at these boutiques, and get half of whatever they sell for in return. You'll get change from £100 and make everyone hate you at work.

13 Be delirious in Dubai

▦

Shopaholics need not apply – they may never return. The largest mall in Dubai, simply called the Dubai Mall, has four times as many shops as the Westfield centre in London, Europe's largest urban mall. Bargain-hunters can escape the glitz at the vast gold souk, which sells the stuff in every hue, style and colour, often by weight.

14 Keep it real in Rome

▦ ◁

For mountains of second-hand designerwear, bargain high-street styles, crockery and even chickens, head to the Sunday market at Porta Portese. Don't be intimidated by Neapolitans shouting in dialect (not even the Romans understand them) and it's never too late to bargain. Leave fancy watches and cameras at home.

15 Get technical in Tokyo

▦

World-famous for discount consumer electronics, the central district of Akihabara has also become a haven for animation geeks. Find everything from spanking new high-tech gadgets to black and white animated porn. Chain stores throughout the city now offer electronics at similar prices, but probably aren't half the fun.

16 Be slick in Sydney

▦ ☌

Australian brands have now invaded the world's great shopping cities, so it's only fair to include one Aussie destination here. The shopping streets winding through Sydney's heart have become a home to slick,

12: New York

sophisticated outlets; if you're after those sexy surfers, make sure you hit the Bondi Beach boutiques for swimwear first.

17 *Get chic in Copenhagen*

Always reinventing the wheel, or at least the chair, the Danish capital is the ultimate destination for design. Shoppers in search of the perfect lampshade, as well as budding craftsmen, will find inspiration at every corner. If holidaying en famille, leave your raucous teens on Strøget, the longest pedestrian shopping street in Europe – a mile of trends, styles and street artists.

18 *Go marketing in Thailand and Cambodia*

£

Along the border, between skirmishes and disputes, thriving markets have sprung up on either side and are a melting pot of nationalities. Permanent establishments and impromptu pick-ups sell everything from local foodstuffs to designer clothes. Best known is the Ban Khlong Luek Border Market, born after the war when enterprising Cambodians began trading UN donated clothing.

19 *Sample some vinyl in Manchester*

Manchester's Northern Quarter rivals London for retro boudoirs, as innovative traders redefine the experience of vintage shopping with classy displays, refreshments and hosted events. Music-lovers should head to 'Vinyl Valley' to explore the 30-odd independent record stores specialising in a variety of genres.

20 *Join the avant-garde in Antwerp*

For must-have unique accessories, head to Belgium's coolest city. Home to the Antwerp Six – six avant-garde designers who graduated from Antwerp's Royal Academy of Fine Arts in the 1980s – the fashion district, clustered in and around Nationalestraat, is top-end, glamorous and tasteful. For a more eclectic mix of boutiques and streetwear stores, head to Kammenstraat.

29: Bullet train, Japan

21-30

Epic rail journeys

The railway is not as vital to travel as it was 100 years ago, but in some countries there are lines that are as magnificent for their sheer scale and engineering prowess as they are for the views they offer through the window. Passengers choose trains because they allow them to indulge – at least away from the likes of the TGV and AVE high-speed networks – in a slower, more social and very human mode of transport. When planning an epic railway holiday, you can either try to go it alone, using local services (which may involve some inconveniences and discomfort, and, in places such as India, marathon queuing sessions) or book a charter through a railway specialist such as **Great Rail Journeys** (www.greatrail.com), **Rail Europe** (www.raileurope.co.uk) or **Ffestiniog Travel** (www.festtravel.co.uk).

30: Ghan railway, Australia

21 USA Coast to Coast
£ ♤

Route *New York-Washington-Chicago-Denver-Grand Junction-Durango-Flagstaff-Grand Canyon-Los Angeles-San Francisco.*
Time needed *20-25 days.*
In the early months of his presidency, President Obama told Americans how a new high-speed railway network would change travel in America; this marked a radical move away from the dominance of cars and planes. Ride from east to west like the cowboys who fought for the frontier on an odyssey through five of the nation's most important cities, taking in the prairies of the Mid-West, the Rockies, Arizona, Monument Valley and the Grand Canyon.

22 The Orient Express
♡

Route *London-Paris-Munich-Vienna-Budapest-Belgrade-Sofia-Istanbul.*
Time needed *8 days.*
You may have heard of a very posh train, properly called the Venice Simplon-Orient-Express – that runs between Venice and Paris and is as fancy as it is expensive. Sadly, the original Paris-Istanbul/Damascus Orient Express no longer runs, so we suggest the above itinerary with stops in Munich for beer, Vienna for coffee and Sofia because none of your friends have been.

23 Trans-Siberian Express
▥ ♤

Route *London-Brussels-Cologne-Warsaw-Moscow-Vladimir-Yekaterinburg-Novosibirsk-Irkutsk-Vladivostok.*
Time needed *16-18 days.*
The Big Red Railway runs to Moscow time, but crosses seven time zones extending over 9,000 kilometres. Whether for natural beauty, a cultural odyssey or the longest vodka party of your life, all train buffs should experience the epic ride once in their lifetime. Contact Russia Experience for details (0845 521 2910, www.trans-siberian.co.uk).

An alternative route for this trip is to head south after Irkutsk on the Trans-Mongolian railroad to see Mongolian capital Ulaanbaatar and Beijing, China.

24 London to Marrakech
▥

Route *London-Paris-Madrid-Algeciras-Ceuta-Chefchaouen-Marrakech.*
Time needed *10-14 days.*

There are several good services between Paris and Madrid (including the luxury Trenhotel). After these great city breaks, head to Andalucia for *jamón*, flamenco, sunshine and bullfights; from Algeciras you can make side-trips to the Costa de la Luz and sherry region. Cross into Africa via Ceuta (or travel from Tarifa to Tangier). Discover the meandering medina of Chefchaouen before continuing to beautiful, chaotic Marrakech.

25 Across Canada in winter

Route *Vancouver-Jasper-Winnipeg-Toronto-Niagara Falls-Quebec-Halifax.*
Time needed *17-18 days.*
Take in three of Canada's biggest cities, the Rockies, the central plains, Jasper National Park, Niagara Falls, French Canada and Nova Scotia, including Halifax – the first British town in Canada, founded in 1749 – on the country's superb trains. Some have see-through roofs so you can ogle the mountains and big skies.

26 South Africa overland

Route *Johannesburg-Pretoria-Mkhaya Reserve-Durban-Bloemfontein-Ripon -Oudtshoorn-Cape Town.*
Time needed *14-16 days.*
Ride from north to south on the luxurious Rovos Rail line through grasslands to haunting plains. Chase lions, elephants and antelope at the largest park in Swaziland, and discover the hideouts of some of the world's endangered species. In Cape Town, tour the country's finest wine-producing regions and drink as much as you like on this car-free odyssey.

27 Arctic semi-circle

Route *Stockholm-Ostersund-Arctic Circle -Narvik-Trondheim-Geiranger-Bergen-Oslo.*
Time needed *14-15 days.*
Spend a day in the Gamla Stan (old town) of Stockholm before riding through forests and lakes to Ostersund. Enter the wilderness of Lapland and then the Arctic Circle, travelling round fjords and beneath looming cliffs to the port of Narvik. See the fjord of Geiranger, set against snowy peaks and waterfalls, then ride to fairytale Bergen, finally winding up in the elegant Norwegian capital.

28 India's grand railways

Route *Mumbai-Ellora Caves-Udaipur-Ranthambore-Jaipur-Delhi.*
Time needed *10 days.*
Get your fix of history – 1,000 years of Buddhist and Hindu heritage – and see the Indian tiger's last home in the wild, on this trip from Mumbai to Delhi. Highlights include ancient monasteries and the artworks of the Ellora and Ajanta caves, the Amber Fort of Jaipur and the Taj Mahal. Travel in luxury aboard the Deccan Odyssey, which has ensuite loos and a spa.

29 Japan's bullet trains

Route *Tokyo-Hiroshima-Miyajima-Kyoto -Nagoya-Mishima-Hakone-Tokyo.*
Time needed *14 days.*
High-speed luxury meets slow-changing culture. See Tokyo's ancient temples and markets, Hiroshima's memorials, the shrines of Miyajima Island and take time out at old Kyoto – Japan's capital for over a millennium. From Nagoya, take in the 'Japanese Alps' and untouched villages and springs of Hakone at the foot of Mount Fuji. End as you began, in Tokyo.

30 Sydney to Alice Springs

Route *Sydney-Melbourne-Adelaide-Alice Springs-Uluru (Ayers Rock).*
Time needed *14-17 days.*
Start with Sydney's Opera House, nightlife and beach buzz, before travelling on to Melbourne for nature reserves and scenic beauty outside the city. From Adelaide, take the famous Ghan railway through Australia's vast red centre to Alice Springs. End at the sacred Aboriginal sandstone rock site of Uluru.

31-40

Turkey's romantic getaways

Four hours away and full of incredible scenery, culture and cuisine, Turkey is the hot choice for couples. Get away from the summer crowds at these secluded love nests.

31: Istanbul

31 *Istanbul*

🖼️♡

Spread over seven hills and surrounded on three sides by water, Istanbul is stunning. The audacious architecture measures up to the city's natural charms: Ottoman minarets crown a skyline constructed on Byzantine foundations, while ferries scoot between Bosphorus suburbs of wooden villas. Sultanahmet – with the holy trinity of Hagia Sophia, Topkapi Palace and the Blue Mosque – provides the eye candy, but for the food of love you need to escape this overpriced enclave. Hit the heights of the rooftop restaurants of Beyoglu as an alternative.
Stay at *Ansen Suites (+90 212 245 8808/ www.ansensuites.com); Ibrahim Pasha Hotel (+90 212 518 0394/www.ibrahimpasha.com); Sarnic (+90 212 518 2323/www.sarnichotel.com).*

32 *Islamlar & Kalkan*

💧♡

With its swimming clubs carved into the cliff and yachts bobbing on the sea, Kalkan has a certain old-school glamour. The restaurants are smart and the patrons even smarter, but if

you're pouted out, head to the hills – the picturesque mountain village of Islamlar is a short drive away. Here you'll find elegant villas, fruit trees and olive groves, and a teeming trout stream hopscotching down the hill. For about a tenner, you can eat the fish along with breads and mezze at one of the many restaurants.
Stay at *Kalkan Regency, Uzüm Evi, Narli Ev (020 8605 3500/www.exclusiveescapes.co.uk).*

33 *Bozcaada*

🍷♡

There are not many places left along the coast that retain their original architecture, but Bozcaada is an island, and the cute little stone houses of the town have managed to weather both the years and Turkey's tourism boom. The castle here is fatally photogenic, and the fish restaurants lively and fun. Toss in a couple of decent cafés and Greek-style tavernas, sprinkle with soft sandy beaches, and the recipe is complete. The ferry-crossing from the mainland is short and sweet.
Stay at *Rengigul Konukevi (+90 286 697 8171); Kaikias Hotel (+90 286 697 0250); Katina Hotel (+90 286 697 0242).*

39: Cappadocia

34 *Kalekoy*

♨ ♡

Snuggling up to Kas and overlooking the Bay of Kekova, Kalekoy's beauty comes from its isolation – this small village is connected to the mainland only by a rough track and is visited mainly by excursion boats that return to base long before the sun sets. When night falls you and a handful of locals will have the place to yourselves. With waterside fish restaurants, Lycian tombs, a Byzantine castle, beautiful blue sea and no cars, Kaleköy is the perfect cliché but still a joy to visit. The pensions are quite ordinary, but they're pleasant enough and boast striking views of the bay.
Stay at *Mehtap Pansiyon (+90 242 874 2146); Olive Grove (+90 242 874 2234); Kale Pansiyon (+90 242 874 2111); Simena Pansiyon (+90 532 779 0476).*

35 *Assos*

♨ ☾ ♡

Assos proper, down in the harbour, is half a dozen old stone houses-turned-hotels right on the waterfront. Behramkale, a hillside village, is a straggle of stone cottages struggling to make it to the top of the hill, where the Temple of Athena gazes across at the Greek island of Lesbos. Both are gorgeous. During the day the stallholders who line the path up to the temple are a pain, but they go home at dusk, whereupon the village reverts to the classic rural idyll. For boutique comforts, choose Behramkale; for proximity to the water, Assos.
Stay at *Biber Evi (+90 286 721 7410); Yildiz Saray (+90 286 721 7025); Hotel Assos Kervansaray (+90 286 721 7093).*

36 *Alaçati*

♨ ♡ ⚘

Alaçati is one of Turkey's most fashionable resorts, with a clutch of boutique hotels and gourmet restaurants in converted stone houses that were, until eight or so years ago, virtually abandoned. It's a surfing haven, although the rollers come ashore four kilometres away from the centre. Don your glad rags to dine out and expect to blitz your credit card for rooms and food. Pricey (by Turkish standards), but worth it.
Stay at *Alaçati Tas Otel (+90 232 716 7772); O Ev Hotel (+90 232 716 6150); Lale Lodge (+90 232 716 6108).*

37 *Safranbolu*

♡

To step back into Turkey's Ottoman past, explore Safranbolu. Spend your days strolling around the cobbled streets of a townscape that has hardly changed since the 19th century, and then go for a soak in the lovely Cinci Hamami (Turkish bath), which is two centuries older than that. Weekends see prices rise and the streets fill with out-of-towners, but weekdays are blissful.
Stay at *Havuzlu Asmazlar Konagi (+90 370 725 2883); Gul Evi (+90 370 725 4645); Cesmeli Konak (+90 370 725 4455); Selvili Kösk (+90 370 712 8646).*

38 *Kaleiçi*

♡

If your idea of romance relies on an injection of history, then a stay in Kaleiçi, the old part of Antalya above the harbour, might fit the bill. Pick your hotel carefully – the best are those located farther from the harbour, close to Memerli Parki. Not only is there a lot to see and do inside Kaleici itself, but you're also within a tram ride of the Antalya Museum, one of the best in the country. What's more, it's easy to organise excursions to all sorts of Roman ruins in the surrounding area.
Stay at *Minyon Hotel (+90 242 247 1147); Tütav Turk Evi Otelleri (+90 242 248 6591); Villa Perla (+90 242 248 9793); Tuvana Hotel (+90 242 244 4054).*

39 *Cappadocia*

☾ ♡ ⚘

The only thing crazier than Cappadocia's rock formations are the many uses to which the locals have put the caves – frescoed churches, private homes, wineries, even complete underground cities. Once famed for its backpacker pensions, Cappadocia now has more boutique hotels than anywhere in the country outside of Istanbul and Bodrum; most are inside cave complexes. For those of a more romantic bent, bathing in a cave-cut hamam rates pretty highly too, while the best way to see the extraordinary landscape is by hot-air balloon.
Stay at *Serinn House, Urgüp (+90 384 341 6076); 4 Oda Cave House, Urgüp (+90 384 341 6080); Les Maisons de Cappadoce, Uçhisar (+90 384 219 2813); Anatolian Houses, Göreme (+90 384 271 2463).*

40 *Mardin*

♡

Of all the once-troubled towns in the east to have emerged into the recent glare of tourism, Mardin, with its honey-coloured houses tumbling down the hillside, has to be the finest. The market has a buzz, there are old churches and medreses, and there's even gourmet food to be had at the lovely Cercis Murat Konagi. Be sure to book ahead.
Stay at *Erdoba Konaklari (+90 482 212 7677); Artuklu Kervansarayi (+90 482 213 7353); Tatlidede (+90 482 213 2720).*

41-50
Camping heaven

41 Camping Les Romarins, French Riviera

ℛ ⚲ ♡

+33 4 93 01 81 64/www.campingromarins.com.
Above the millionaires' yachts basking in the harbour of Cap Ferrat sits a peaceful

retreat in the rugged hilltops. Below lies the Mediterranean panorama of medieval villages, while the swanky towns of Monaco and Nice are only a short drive away. One of the world's most romantic drives, along the winding Moyenne Corniche, is carved into the coastal cliffs.

42 Greystoke Mahale, Lake Tanganyika, Tanzania

ℛ ⚲

www.greystoke-mahale.com.
Set on the white-sand beaches fringing Lake Tanganyika, cocooned in rolling forests, Greystoke Mahale is a campsite of swish *bandas* (thatched huts) in a remote corner of Africa. Guests can read online about the local chimps, which they are likely to meet during treks into the jungle, home to nine species of primate and many other exotic creatures.

43 Longitude 131, Uluru, Australia

⚲ ♡

+612 8296 8010/www.longitude131.com.au.
In this primeval land of ancestral legends, camping need not be as severe as the scorched

43: Uluru, Australia

landscape. This luxury campsite of raised tents, electric blinds and air-conditioning will come as a relief to overheated visitors, with spectacular views of the sacred sandstone rock of Uluru, and tours of the wilderness of Uluru-Kata Tjuta National Park.

44 Camping La Fresneda, Matarraña, Spain

○ 🌿

+34 978 85 40 85/www.campinglafresneda.com.
Taste Spain on a walking holiday in this valley of olive and almond groves. Locally cured hams, olive oil pressed on site and freshly-made and subtly seasoned cheeses are just the start of the sensory adventure. A natural hot spring rock pool, prehistoric paintings and ancient villages are among the treasures to be discovered for hikers.

45 Camping des Glaciers, La Fouly, Switzerland

○ 🌿

+41 27 783 17 35/www.camping-glaciers.ch.
Postcard beauty organised by the Swiss – life surely couldn't be much more perfect.

Go to La Fouly for glorious Alpine meadows, scented wild flowers and pristine rivers, and white puffs of cloud drifting at the tips of the glaciers overhead. If you're feeling dreamy, wake up with a hair-raising walk along the rocks beneath the 14 waterfalls of the Gorges du Durnand. The campsite has good facilities for families, including a games room for the kids.

46 Camping Strasko, Novalja, Pag Island, Croatia

🏊 ○ 👪

+385 53 661 226/
www.turno.hr/en/campsite_strasko_croatia.html.
The Dalmatian coast's azure bays, rocky cliffs and friendly people are well known. Pag Island offers all this with a touch of Ibiza, as open-air parties play music 24 hours a day, all summer long. Young campers will love it for the dancing, but parents will find plenty of facilities for entertaining children: lots of sports events and competitions are organised by the staff. Peaceful bays and shaded sites under Dalmatian oaks are also at hand.

47 Bellavista, Lake Garda, Italy

☼♡👫⛵

+39 464 505644/www.camping-bellavista.it.
Camp by Italy's most magnificent lake,
against a setting of limestone mountains.
The site is perfect for watersports, in particular
windsurfing and sailing. Once you have
fulfilled your quota of getting wet, take a
ferry day trip to some of the other towns
surrounding the lake, such as Sirmione,
Bardolino and Garda.

48 Taupo Motor Camp, New Zealand

☼⛵

+64 7 378 8559/www.taupoholidaypark.com.
Hiring a camper van is the best way to travel
around this outdoorsy country and there are
plenty of motor camps to park-up in to enjoy
the sights. Taupo Motor Camp is close to Lake
Taupo, one of the most famous lakes on the
North Island, and boasts a range of activities,
from bungee jumping to whitewater rafting
to skydiving.

49 Park Grubhof, Salzburgerland, Austria

☼⛵

+43 6588 8237/www.grubhof.com.
Plenty of fresh mountain air and snow-capped
Alpine scenery are on offer at this campsite
on the banks of the River Saalach. The pitches
are sizeable and shade is given by ancient
chestnut trees. Embark on steep mountain
walks up the Loferer and Leoganger Steinberge
mountains for memorable views. If high-
altitude hiking isn't your thing, visit the
quaint villages of St Martin and Lofer,
or cycle to the famous Krimml waterfalls.

50 Poros Beach Camping, Lefkada, Greece

🚴☼

+30 26450 95452/www.porosbeach.com.gr.
Greece may not be the country that first
springs to mind for camping, but this peaceful,
pretty 70-pitch site (there are 40 bungalows too)
in a beachside village on Lefkada is ideal for
getting into the laid-back rhythms of Greek
island life. Tuck into fresh yoghurt and
honey, crisp salads and souvlaki, or take a
boat trip around the seven surrounding
islands, which include Kefalonia.

51-60
Adventure!

51 *Go cycling in India*

🚴☼⛵

Discover the back roads of Kerala on a cycling
holiday along the north coast, and experience
village life through homestays. You pedal under
canopies of coconut trees, through tea and spice
plantations, past waterfalls, down into valleys
and along crescent-shaped beaches. Out of the
saddle you can trek through the stunning
Periyar National Park to see herds of elephant,
sambar deer and myriad bird species.
Fitness level *Moderate. There is an average of 26
kilometres of cycling a day – 240 kilometres over
nine days, in hot conditions.*
Duration *15 days.*
Group size *12 to 16.*
When to go *Oct-Dec.*
Who goes there? *Explore (0845 013 1539/
www.explore.co.uk).*
DIY? *Bikes can be hired in Kerala but the
homestays could prove more difficult to arrange.*

52 *Kenya and Tanzania: on safari and up Kilimanjaro*

☼⛵

See the 'Big Five' and climb up the highest
mountain in Africa. This 16-day trip is pretty
full on. You visit national parks: Lake Nakuru,
to see the teeming flamingo population and
rare white rhinos; and Masai Mara, to witness
wildebeest and zebra skipping from lions
and hyenas. You meet the Maasai warriors
and get the opportunity to take a dawn
balloon ride over the African plains. The
tour then crosses the Tanzanian border
to begin the ascent up Mount Kilimanjaro;
be prepared for six days of strenuous
walking, with full porterage, to reach the
summit, but you will be rewarded with
breathtaking views.
Fitness level *Tough, involving several days
at high altitude.*
Duration *16 days.*
Group size *4-12.*
When to go *Dec-Feb.*
Who goes there? *Exodus (0845 863 9600/
www.exodus.co.uk).*

DIY? *Both the safari and the climb would be impossible without a local guide. A safari could be arranged on arrival in Kenya, but slots for Kilimanjaro climbs get booked up quickly.*

53 *A hill tribe trek in Thailand*

Experience a tribal adventure in Northern Thailand, trekking through lush jungle terrain and visiting local villages to see the brightly woven crafts and handmade silver jewellery. You stay in local village huts where a warm welcome and copious amounts of rice wine await you every evening. You get to rest your limbs when you climb aboard a wooden raft to float down the river in Erawan National Park; here you can see the famous Bridge on the River Kwai and spend the night on a floating raft house. Malaria pills are strongly recommended for this trek.

Fitness level *Easy.*
Duration *15 days.*
Group size *10-15.*
When to go *Jan-Mar to avoid the rainy season.*
Who goes there? *STA Travel (0871 230 0040/ www.statravel.co.uk).*
DIY? *Straightforward. Fly to Bangkok and head to Chiang Mai by bus; hill treks can be booked from there.*

54 *A great American bike ride*

If you are a two-wheeled adventurer, why not take part in one of the great American cycle rides? Every year thousands of cyclists travel across America taking in all the pleasures of the open road but also experiencing the outdoors free of the confines of a car. The RAGBRAI (Register's Annual Great Bicycle Ride Across Iowa) starts in July, BRAN (Bike Ride Across Nebraska) pedals off in May and BRAG (Bike Ride Across Georgia) begins in June. All are non-profit bike rides.

Fitness level *Moderate; some training is required.*
Duration *Around one week.*
Group size *Hundreds, if not thousands, of people take part.*
When to go *May-July.*
Who goes there? *Visit www.ragbrai.org, www. bran-inc.org and www.brag.org for more information.*
DIY? *Easy. You can hire a bike and ride the routes yourself any time of the year, but you will miss the group atmosphere.*

55 *Glacier hiking in New Zealand*

Want to feel like an explorer? Scale the ice and climb the famous South Island Fox Glacier,

52: Mount Kilimanjaro

walking through ice tunnels, deep into caves and up sheer walls of electric blue mountain ice – always with pickaxe in hand and crampons on foot. Learn about the formation of the glacier from tour guides who offer half- and full-day hikes. Get there by flying to Queenstown then driving five hours to reach the glacier.
Fitness level *Easy to moderate; no training is required but you should be relatively fit.*
Duration *6-7hrs.*
Group size *5-10.*
When to go *Nov-Apr.*
Who goes there? *Fox Glacier Guiding (+64 3 751 0825/www.foxguides.co.nz).*
DIY? *Not without previous ice-climbing experience and the right gear.*

56 *Rafting in North Wales, UK*

The Tryweryn is the perfect river for year-round adrenaline junkies. The white water, controlled by a dam near Bala, is flowing when other British rivers are dry. The national whitewater centre, Canolfan Tryweryn (say that after a few drinks), developed the first commercial whitewater rafting operation in the UK.

Fitness level *Anyone can do it, but there are some Grade III sections, so you have to be brave!*
Duration *You'll get four runs down the Tryweryn so allow a full day.*
Group size *Up to 7.*
When to go *All year round, but May-Aug are best for water conditions.*
Who goes there? *Canolfan Tryweryn (01678 521083/www.ukrafting.co.uk).*
DIY? *Are you serious? Go only with a qualified tillerman. Places can be limited so book early.*

57 *An Antarctic cruise*

Adventure? Exercise? Well, you might stretch your jaw muscles gawping at the wonders on parade in this most pristine of continents. You kick off with a crossing of the Drake Passage, the tempestuous sea between Argentina and the Ice. Then the islands and bays of the Antarctica peninsula gather round your ship and you enter a world of cute penguins, surreal icebergs, magnificent humpback whales, evil leopard seals and awesome albatrosses. Cruises are expensive, but all your food and excursions are included.

54: RAGBRAI bike ride, USA

You will take many, many photographs and you will never forget your voyage into this unique environment.

Fitness level *Anyone can do this.*
Duration *10-20 days.*
Group size *90-100 on the smaller, expedition cruises.*
When to go *Nov-Mar.*
Who goes there? *Peregrine Adventures (0844 736 0170/www.peregrineadventures.com).*
DIY? *Tricky. You can fly down to Ushuaia and haggle for a ride on an outgoing cruise with empty cabins. If the ships are full, bad luck.*

58 *Walking China's Great Wall*

Why not meander along the bricks of one of the most famous structures on earth? Enjoy the beauty of the Badaling section of the Great Wall, by far the most photographed; travel to the Mutianyu section, even more beautiful and with fewer tourists; work out on the Huanghuacheng and Jiankou section, where there are steep peaks and broken bricks. Mountaineering gear, food and water is needed, as water is unavailable on the wild sections. Tours start in Beijing and end in Shanghai with visits en-route to the Terracotta Warriors in Xi'an.

Fitness level *Moderate – the wall is challenging and steep in parts.*
Duration *9 days.*
Group size *6+ with a tour leader.*
When to go? *Sep-Oct to avoid the peak season.*
Who goes there? *On the Go (020 7371 1113/ www.onthegotours.com).*
DIY? *Fairly easy. Some sections of the wall are free to visit, and taxis and accommodation can be booked from Beijing.*

59 *Torres del Paine trek, Chilean Patagonia*

Escape to Chile's most spectacular national park, Torres Del Paine, on the southern edge of the Patagonian ice cap. The park is a wonderland of snow-capped mountains, granite peaks, beautiful waterfalls, glacier-fed lakes, virgin forests and open pampas. The tour begins with a drive from El Calafate in Argentina across the frontier to Chile to trek to the base of the mighty Torres, to the stunning Grey Glacier and between the impressive granite walls of the French Valley.

Fitness level *Moderate; no specialist skills required but the trek is strenuous in parts.*
Duration *7 days.*
Group size *2+*
When to go *Oct-Apr.*
Who goes there? *Journey Latin America (020 8747 8315/www.journeylatinamerica.co.uk).*
DIY? *Yes, but solo trekking in the park is not allowed. There is an entrance fee into the park and camping charges range from free to the equivalent (in pesos) of a few pounds.*

60 *Kayaking in Iceland*

Adventure combined with peace and quiet. In Iceland, you can kayak past icebergs miles away from anybody and with only the silence of the wilderness and the cracking of brash ice and glaciers calving into the sea. Three national parks can be visited, including Europe's largest, Vatnajokul, to see eerie landscapes of grey desert and ice caps.

Fitness level *Previous kayaking experience required.*
Duration *10 days.*
Group size *10.*
When to go *May-Sept.*
Who goes there? *Discover the World (01737 218 8010/www.discover-the-world.co.uk); the company can also arrange short, cheap kayaking trips if you are making your own way to Iceland.*
DIY? *You can easily make your way out there but kayaking in the remote wilderness is dangerous without supervision.*

See *Time Out Adventure!* for more ideas.

61-69

Ferry nice breaks

61 *Bilbao, Spain*

Although it's not the most scenic of cities, Bilbao is the gateway to Northern Spain. Check out the Guggenheim art gallery – inside is less impressive than outside – before continuing on to foodie capital San Sebastián and the cradle of Basque culture, the village of Guernica.

Go with *P&O from Portsmouth (08716 645 645/ www.poferries.com). Voyage: 35hrs.*

Book it, pack it...

... we've got the perfect holidays for thrill-seekers.

62 *Guernsey*

⌚

Head to Britain's nicest island and buy a locally brewed ale with Guernsey pounds in one of St Peter Port's lively pubs. The capital is still a busy little hub, framed by tiered gardens and criss-crossed by worn steps and hidden alleys. Don't miss the fresh Guernsey ice-cream.
Go with *Condor from Portsmouth (01202 207216/ www.condorferries.co.uk). Voyage: 7hrs.*

63 *Capital and coast, The Netherlands*

▦ 🏊

Get a Stenaline ferry to the Hook of Holland, for quick and easy access to the country's main cities. Catch the train to the Hague, the Dutch seat of government; take in the historic houses of parliament and the Peace Palace, and do a tram ride before heading to the North Sea resort of Scheveningen for some kitesurfing and sunworshipping (and, if you want it, naturism). Rotterdam, Haarlem and Amsterdam are also all within easy reach of the Hook and the Hague.
Go with *Stenaline from Harwich (08705 70 70 70/ www.stenaline.co.uk). Voyage: 6hrs 55mins.*

64 *Zeebrugge, Belgium*

🦪

Zeebrugge looks on to the beaches of the Belgian coast, and is only a drive away from Bruges, Oostkamp and Northern France. It's an interesting town in itself and the huge wholesale fish market means the local restaurants serve up fresh catches every lunchtime. The Seafront Zeebrugge maritime theme park is full of pirate-themed exhibitions and interactive gizmos for the kids, as well as historical displays for adults.
Go with *P&O from Hull (08716 645 645/www. poferries.com). Voyage: 13hrs 45mins (overnight).*

65 *Dublin, Ireland*

▦ ⌚

It's hard to avoid the clichés of Guinness and folk bands in this city, so why not embrace them and head to the Guinness Storehouse museum – pull a pint and then sip another one while enjoying views of the city from the Gravity Bar. After dark, head to Temple Bar for a knees-up.
Go with *Irish Ferries from Holyhead to Dublin Ferryport (08717 300 400/www.irishferries.com). Voyage: 2hrs.*

66 *Fishbourne, Isle of Wight*

🦪 ♨ ⌚

The tiny village of Fishbourne is the arrival point, and lies between the yachting hub of Cowes and Victorian Ryde. The Isle of Wight is the best ferry option for those seeking a peaceful break – breathe in fresh air while gazing at the Needles and the colourful sands of Alum Bay.
Go with *Wightlink from Portsmouth (0871 376 1000/www.wightlink.co.uk). Voyage: 40mins.*

67 *St Malo, Brittany*

🦪

If you fancy searching in rock pools for sea creatures and collecting fresh mussels for dinner, then St Malo is for you. A town by the sea, it's a handsome, stone-walled place filled with restaurants, bars and shops.
Go with *Brittany Ferries from Portsmouth (0871 244 0744/www.brittany-ferries.co.uk). Voyage: 12hrs.*

68 *Lerwick, Shetland*

♨ 🏊

Shetland isn't just full of small ponies, it has lots of trout too. In fact, the island has an array of watery activities from fishing to scuba diving to surfing, as well as plenty of wildlife and dramatic landscapes. Although it's a long slog to get there – an overnight ferry from Aberdeen to Lerwick– the change of pace from bustling city life to idling island life makes it well worth it.
Go with *North Link from Aberdeen (0845 6000 449/www.northlinkferries.co.uk). Voyage: 12hrs (overnight)*

69 *Esbjerg, Denmark*

▦

Denmark's fifth largest city is built around one of the country's most important North Sea harbours. Take a trip to the Fisheries & Maritime Museum to learn about its history before taking a look at the city's newest landmark – four chalky white giants, by Svend Wiig Hansen entitled *Man Meets the Sea*. Stroll around one of Esbjerg's parks to see wild deer and roe.
Go with *DFDS Seaways from Harwich (0871 522 9955/www.dfdsseaways.co.uk). Voyage: 18hrs 15mins.*

Ideas from the expert

70-79

Journey Latin America's Sarah Bradley reveals ten Latin American boutique gems.

70 Casa Aliso, Quito, Ecuador (+59 3 2 252 8062, www.casa aliso. com), a welcoming and beautifully restored former family home, is located in Quito's quiet, leafy residential district of La Floresta. It has just ten rooms, each individually decorated, which face the front or back garden, or are located on the upper floor around a marble and iron staircase. Walls throughout have been painted by local artists. Other facilities include a cosy breakfast room and living room with a library and fireplace. While you're there, visit Otavalo market, go downhill biking on Cotopaxi volcano and relax in the thermal springs at Papallacta.

71 La Passion, Cartagena, Colombia (+57 5 664 86 05, www.lapassionhotel. com), an eclectic and beautifully converted old Republican-style house, is located inside the walled historical *barrio* of Cartagena. The interior has been thoroughly revamped, with minimalist decor, bold colours, painted cement or tiled floors, and dabs of Moorish and Arabic influence. There are eight spacious rooms surrounding a central patio; all are different but each has a plasma TV/DVD, MP3 player and ensuite bathroom. Two of the suites are enormous and have balconies overlooking the street as well as huge, free-standing marble bathtubs within the living area. Hotel facilities include a patio bar, games room, lounge, jacuzzi and lovely rooftop terrace with large infinity pool. Must-dos in Cartagena include visiting the Rosario Islands, taking a salsa lesson and doing a walking tour of the colonial city, renowned for its turbulent history of pirates and forts. To get there, fly to Bogotá and take a domestic flight to Cartagena.

72 An exclusive boutique property, Inkaterra La Casona (0800 458 7506, www.inkaterra.com/en/cusco), in Cusco, Peru, has an illustrious past. Built on the site of the palace of Inca-founder Manco Capac, the 16th-century mansion was the home of prominent Spanish conquistadores and this affluent colonial past is reflected in the design and furnishings of the hotel. It stands on a quiet, historic plaza close to Cusco's principal attractions. Facilities have been refined with contemporary touches: the 11 suites and junior suites have sitting rooms with open fires and extra-large free-standing tubs in the bathrooms. The property is part of the Inkaterra hotel group, recognised as a leader in sustainable tourism in Peru. From here, you can visit Machu Picchu by train or on foot, explore the fortress of Sacsayhuaman, and go whitewater rafting on the Apurimac. Fly to Lima and take a domestic flight to Cusco.

73 Mansion Dandi Royal (+54 11 4361 3537, www.mansiondandiroyal.com) is located in the district of San Telmo in the Argentinian capital of Buenos Aires, the home of tango. This elegant former mansion recreates the romance of the 1920s' golden era of dance, incorporating a tango school with renowned instructors. Next door there's an authentic ballroom where tango performances take place twice weekly. Guest rooms are quaint and charming, many adorned with murals or retaining their original features. Being an old building, guest rooms do differ. Dandi rooms are quite small, while the newer, more spacious Royal rooms either have an internal window or no window at all. There is a breakfast room and a roof terrace with a small pool. Just about all residents go to a tango show or take tango lessons at some stage, and even non-tangophiles should visit the nearby district of La Boca, famed for its football team, and soak up the café culture in trendy Palermo Viejo.

74 Casas Brancas (+55 22 2623 1458, www.casasbrancas.com.br) is a small, friendly boutique hotel perched on a bluff with fine views over the bay at Búzios, Brazil. All 32 individually decorated rooms have air-conditioning and private bathrooms. The hotel is well placed for those who want to make a boat trip to one of the bay's tropical islands, and the town centre is within walking distance for a good selection of restaurants, bars and boutiques. Take a schooner to several tropical bays and hidden coves, and go snorkelling or surfing. Fly to Rio de Janeiro then drive for three hours north, or take a bus.

75 Casa Higueras (+56 32 249 7900, www.hotelcasahigueras.cl/es), a converted mansion in Valparaíso, Chile, has a great location on a lovely hillside and is close to the city's restaurants and bars. There are 20 bright, airy rooms, all with cable TV/DVD and private bathroom, and some also have a small terrace. The main difference in the rooms is the size and the view: some look out to the hills and some over to the bay. Facilities include a restaurant, first-floor swimming pool, sauna and jacuzzi, and a roof terrace with splendid bay views. Visit Pablo Neruda's house, take a boat to Isla Negra or simply wander around the streets and enjoy the seafood. To get there, fly to Santiago de Chile then take a bus; Valparaiso is about a two-hour drive away.

76 Mexico City's Casa Vieja (+50 2 7832 7903, www.casaencantada-antigua.com) is a small, exclusive, highly individual boutique hotel in a quiet street near Chapultepec Park, in the upscale neighbourhood of Polanco. Its ten rooms and suites are each named after, and decorated in, the style of a Mexican artist, and all come with jacuzzi, sound system and a dining area. There is also a rooftop restaurant shaded by tropical plants. Visit the pyramids of Teotihuacán, which pre-date the Aztecs, take a boat trip on Xochimilco lake and buy food from the boats passing by, and see both the National Museum of Anthropology in Mexico City and Frida Kahlo's house-museum, La Caza Azul (the Blue House), in Coyoacán.

77 Casa Encantada (www.casaencantada-antigua.com), in picturesque Antigua, Guatemala, is an elegant and intimate colonial-style hotel on a bustling little street ten minutes' walk from the main plaza. It has ten rooms and one rooftop suite, each with a ceiling fan, four-poster bed, minibar and small bathroom. There's also an attractive rooftop patio-bar with volcano views, plunge pool and cosy living room area with a fireplace. Climb Pacaya volcano with a guide, visit the market town of Chichicastenango and explore Antigua's colonial architecture. Fly to Guatemala City then take a bus or taxi to Antigua (a 45-minute drive).

78 Turtle Inn (+501 523 3244, www.blancaneaux.com) in Placencia, Belize, is one of three exclusive hotels in the region owned by film director Francis Ford Coppola. It lies behind a small sandy beach three kilometres from the main village of Placencia. The dining area is a vast open thatch-roofed construction with hardwood floors and a bar. Beyond this are 19 large, thatched individual cabins dotted around a deep, central pool, each with its own secluded garden and outdoor shower. All are designed with impressive attention to detail: hand-carved hardwood furnishings, plush armchairs, huge ornate doors, grand comfy beds and luxurious bathrooms. Kayaks and large bikes are available for hire, and scuba diving, snorkelling and fishing excursions can be organised from the dive shop, along with a variety of land-based trips. Or just relax on the beach. To reach it, fly to Belize City then take a domestic flight to Placencia, or go by road (about four hours' drive).

79 Canal House (507 228 1907, www.canalhousepanama.com) in Panama City is a homely hotel in the historic Casco Viejo area of the city. It's a lovely old building with large wooden staircases and just three individually designed rooms: one is a double room with en suite bathroom; a second has a living room with a private bathroom; and a third has two bedrooms and one bathroom. There is a dining room, various lounge areas and a small roof terrace with nice views. The Canal House has been awarded the prestigious Green Globe award; it is the first hotel in Panama to achieve this certification accolade for its standards of sustainability. At some stage, do a half- or full-day transit on the canal, see the tropical birds in the Soberania National Park and visit enchanting Taboga Island.

■ **Journey Latin America** 020 8747 8315/ www.journeylatinamerica.co.uk.

71: La Passion, Cartagena

80-84

Stag dos

Brno **80**, the Czech Republic's second city, offers fairytales and vineyards, but it's arguably also the mud-wrestling capital of Europe. Punters get the chance to vote on whether the wrestlers should fight naked or in underwear, and then watch them fight in a tub full of foam before the stag is thrown in for the last round. See www.chillisauce.co.uk for further details.

For something a little more relaxing, consider a beach-based stag do in **Barcelona 81**, Spain. Even if the drunken stag party fails to impress the sexy Spanish chicas at first, a few days hanging out on the beach and a taste of the vibrant nightlife on offer should unleash the Latin lover within. And if it doesn't, there are watersports, skydiving, karting, scooter tours and, of course, strippers. For even more ideas check out www.maximise.co.uk.

Stags with a weird Russian fetish or fondness for sado-masochism can get the whole party banged up in a former Soviet prison in **Riga**, Latvia **82**. Add a little night-time surprise and arrange a 3am cell raid by guards – although be warned that the only thing likely to be drilled are a bunch of press-ups. See www.chillisauce.co.uk

For something a little closer to home, consider a trip to **Newcastle-upon-Tyne 83**, where nightclubs and women wearing tiny hot pants in Arctic conditions are only a small part of the attraction. See www.stagnightsout. co.uk for a mind-boggling array of activities to wrap around a solid strip-club package; from scuba- and skydiving to paintball and dogs (of the four-legged variety).

If you're after something less conventional, however, head over to **Tallinn 84**, Estonia, where run-of-the-mill strippers can be replaced by hot medieval lesbians. Watch them undress in a tavern that has, according to local lore, known how to float a sailor's boat for a very long time. Play with guns and go karting during the day. Check out www.redsevenleisure.co.uk for more information.

85-94

Classically cultural Italy

85 Rome

For more than 2,000 years history has unfolded in the loud, vibrant capital, where ancient streets always seem to lead eventually to tratorria and trendy bars. Ancient monuments, palaces and churches – and those fountains – are around every corner.
Stay at *Teatro di Pompeo (+39 06 6872812/ www.hotelteatrodipompeo.it), built into the Roman theatre's ruins.*

86 Florence

Home to Botticelli's *Venus*, the marbled Duomo and bathed in frescoes, Firenze is the city that gave us the Renaissance. Go out of season and you'll queue less for the masterpieces and for dinner.
Stay at *Palazzo Galletti (+39 055 3905750/ www.palazzogalletti.it), and enjoy the on-site spa.*

87 Siena

Once a thriving medieval Italian city, Siena's exquisite monuments are as integral to the town's spirit as its fiery passions. During the summer months, visitors can see the explosive Palio horse races in the main piazza, which trace their roots back to 12th-century rivalries.
Stay at *Il Chiostro del Carmine (+39 0577 223476/www.chiostrodelcarmine.com), a restored monastery with modern comforts.*

88 Venice

Perhaps the most photogenic of all Italian cities, Venice's palaces are built over and in the water. The impossibly beautiful, car-free city has immense wealth in culture and art, paid for by patrons who benefited from the city's control over shipping routes from the East.
Stay at *La Calcina (+39 041 520 64 66/www. lacalcina.com), away from the mobs of tourists.*

89 Pisa

Away from the leaning tower, the town's palaces, museums and medieval sites, on both sides of the River Arno, make it a worthy escape in summer from the crowds in nearby Siena and Florence.
Stay at *the conveniently located Hotel Bonanno (+39 050 524030/www.grandhotelbonanno.it).*

90 Milan

Fashion and factories are culture too. The commercial heart of Italy, what Milan lacks in historic sites and alleys it makes up for in designer shops, glamorous bars and celebrity-filled clubs.
Stay at *the Town House Galleria (+39 02 89058297/www.townhousegalleria.it), in a palace above Prada, where your personal butler will organise your tickets to La Scala.*

91 Naples & Pompeii

Not for the faint-hearted: brave the chaos to ogle the architectural glory of Southern Italy's finest palaces and churches, all made more beautiful by the distressed pastel façades. Take a day trip to the Roman town of Pompeii, buried in AD 79 by nearby Vesuvius.
Stay at *Hotel Cimarosa (+39 081 556 7044/ www.hotelcimarosa.it), and ask for a view of the sea.*

92 Amalfi Coast & Capri

Carved into cliffs slashing into the sea, the stunning towns of Positano, Amalfi and Ravello live up to expectations. Bathe in crystalline waters, take the ferry to Capri and relax with limoncello, a sweet but potent lemon liquor.
Stay at *Hotel Amalfi (+39 089 872 440/ www.hamalfi.it), the best three-star hotel in town.*

93 Tropea & Calabria

Medieval towns built into the rocks along the sandy coastline draw visitors to ruggedly beautiful Calabria's historic sites as well as to its beaches.
Stay at *Tropea at Il Convento (+39 347 509 0576/ www.ilconvento.com), an old convent set into the cliffs, overlooking the sea.*

94 Agrigento, Sicily

Rule by Asians, Europeans and Africans over the centuries has given Sicily eclectic architectural riches and a distinguished fusion cuisine. Visit the ancient Greek ruins of the Valley of the Temples, and recover with a plate of the island's cream-filled cannoli pastries.
Stay at *Terrazze di Montelusa (+39 0922 28556/ www.terrazzedimontelusa.it), a restored palazzo at the heart of the historic centre.*

95-99
African safaris

95 Gorilla tracking in Uganda with Acacia Safari

+256 414 253597/www.acaciasafari.co.ug.
Over half the world's mountain gorillas live in the Bwindi Impenetrable National Park. The ancient rainforest is also home to 11 other primates, magnificent birdlife and

97: Kenya

96: Horseback safari, Botswana

luxuriant flora. Groups limited to six are taken to observe one of four gorilla groups tracked by rangers and protected by strict guidelines to ensure they are not disturbed while going about their daily activities in the jungle.

96 Horseback riding in Botswana and South Africa with Aardvark Safaris

01980 849 160/www.aardvarksafaris.co.uk.
Ride from the Dinaka Game Reserve in South Africa to Botswana on horseback, where you can spend four nights on the banks of Kipling's 'great grey-green, greasy Limpopo River'. Close encounters with the 'Big Five' – and even the elusive leopard – are likely.

97 The beasts of Kenya with Tribes

01728 685 971/www.tribes.co.uk.
From the great wildebeest migration of Masai Mara, to the exotic creatures of the Rift Valley Lakes (see flamingos, hippos and crocodiles), to the sheer beauty of the palm-fringed coastline, Kenya's safaris have always been among the most popular. Ethical operators ensure your visit benefits indigenous tribes,

who organise many of the tours and may also provide the accommodation.

98 Three-country adventure with Wild About Africa: Botswana, Namibia and Zambia

020 8758 4717/www.wildaboutafrica.com.
The Okavango Delta in Botswana is the largest inland delta in the world. Its vast water networks are home to crocodiles and hippos, while lions and cheetahs hunt on its plains. Spend the first six days here, before travelling to the Mahango game reserve and the villages of Caprivi in Namibia. End at the mighty Victoria Falls in Zambia.

99 The wilderness of Gabon with Farside Africa

0131 315 2464/www.farsideafrica.com.
Impress your friends and go to central Africa where wildlife tourism is still in its early stages and vast areas of the region are uninhabited. From the Dzanga-Sangha Reserve to a cruise down the Rembo Ngowe River, get close to elephants, track gorillas and join the Pygmies on hikes to learn about their fascinating culture.

100-119

Best European beaches

100 *Kampen, Sylt, Germany* This white-sand beach, with its backdrop of red cliffs and its bracing air, is on the fashionable North Sea island of Sylt. Go native and grab yourself a Strandkorb (giant wicker beach chair).

101 Es Trenc, Mallorca

Three kilometres of unspoilt beach backed by natural dunes provide a habitat for sea thistle and pine and tamarind trees. The protected strip has sugar-cube white sand, clear water, and, at one end, a naturist area in which to bare all.

102 Valencia, Spain

Just a short taxi ride from Spain's third city is a long, golden stretch of sand lined with tavernas serving top-notch paella. When you tire of soaking up the rays, head into town for culture, bar-hopping and some great boutiques.

103 Priaia del Fuoco, Italy

This romantic beach is hidden away at the end of the Capo Vaticano coast, the tip of the bunion on the toe of southern Calabria. Accessible only by boat or by a very precipitous path, this rocky cove has pashmina-soft sand and steep shelving, and is gently lapped by aquamarine waters.

104 Pentrez Plage, Brittany, France

With its rock pools, foaming surf and acres of white sand, this is the kind of beach you visit to kick footballs, hunt for crabs and fly kites.

105 Baska Voda, Croatia

The Blue Flag Baska Voda beach, which sits in the lee of the pink-hued Biokovo Mountains, is one of Croatia's undoubted hotspots. The Krka National Park and the island of Hvar, with its cool harbourside bars and superb architecture, are all within easy reach.

106 Sagres, Algarve, Portugal

This fine undeveloped beach is backed by orange cliffs, with impressive rollers attracting surfers from all over. The small town of Sagres is the gateway to the Alentejo – Portugal's agricultural heartland – and the wild scrub of the Costa Vicentina Natural Park.

107 Mondello Lido, Sicily

Near the small fishing village of Mondello on the Mediterranean, lies Mondello Lido, just nine kilometres from Palermo, Sicily's vibrant capital. Its wide white sandy beach runs for two kilometres from Monte Pellegrino to Monte Gallo. Mondello's bars, cafés, nightclubs and hotels line the shore.

108 La Manga del Mar Menor, Spain

Europe's largest salt-water coastal lagoon – known locally as the Little Sea – offers warm, shallow waters and beautiful sandy beaches for families with young children.

109 Golden Sands, Bulgaria

The soft golden sand here is reputed to be the best in Europe. The resort was built in the late 1950s and sits less than 16 kilometres away from the city of Varna, a resort town filled with lots of good-value hotels and camping spots. Golden Sands has received numerous awards for its environmental awareness; the water and beach are closely monitored for toxins and there is solar-powered transportation on offer.

110 Turquoise Coast, Patara, Turkey

This 19-kilometre stretch of soft-sanded Mediterranean coastline is flanked by huge mountains of sand; a nesting area for the endangered loggerhead turtle, it has remained undeveloped thanks to its national park status.

111 Myrtos beach, Kefalonia, Greece

Perhaps the most dramatic of all the Ionian beaches, this is a huge sweep of white limestone pebbles, set in a deep, wide bay. Viewed from the road above, it forms the perfect crescent that you might recognise from the covers of countless guidebooks.

112 Maspalomas, Gran Canaria

Gigantic wind-sculpted sand dunes form a stunning backdrop to this wonderful stretch of

106: Algarve, Portugal

golden sand, divided into four areas – the largest of which is popular with families.

113 *Pinarello, Corsica*

Craggy coves, herb-scented slopes and white sands are the natural draws of the bay at Pinarello. With a handful of seafood restaurants, an old church and a couple of jetties stretching into the clear water, this is small-scale, idyllic Mediterranean beach life.

114 *Erimoupolis, Crete, Greece*

Lying at the very northern tip of Eastern Crete, tucked between rugged rocks and an ancient cemetery, Erimoupolis is named after the 'abandoned town' of Itanos, the ruins of which you have to pass on your way to the beach.

115 *Chia, Sardinia*

A slice of the Caribbean a little closer to home, with towering dunes, crystalline waters flanked by juniper trees and traces of the ancient Phoenician city of Bithia, on which Chia now stands.

116 *Sesimbra, Portugal*

An atmospheric fishing port an hour's drive from the capital. Although not undeveloped, Sesimbra is still authentic, its long beachfront lined with cafés and restaurants where sardines sizzle on charcoal grills. The south-facing shoreline is safe for swimming, and there is an old harbour where fish is sold at daily auctions.

117 *Ramla Bay, Gozo, Malta*

A half-hour ferry ride from the main island, Gozo is steeped in Roman history; the fiery orange sands of Ramla Bay are hidden away at the bottom of a fertile valley.

118 *Grand Plage, Biarritz, France*

The two casinos (the Barrière and the Bellevue), tuxedoed waiters, waterfront fashion boutiques and ageing hotels remind you that Biarritz is a veteran resort as well as a hub for young surfers: find a pitch on the Grand Plage (Big Beach) alongside moneyed French bathers and tuck into Basque cuisine at lunchtime.

115: Chia, Sardinia

119 *Sopot, Poland*

Is the water cold? Yes, it's absolutely Baltic. But Sopot, one of three coastal cities in the Tri-City area (aka the Polish Riviera), has long been the beach to be seen at for tourists from Poland and Germany. Beer gardens and vodka bars line the main street of Monte Cassino, while volleyball nets decorate the bleached white sands – and the air temperature is often in the high 20s.

120-129
Sunny Cyprus

120 *Head for the hills*

The holy trinity of sun, sea and sand is the draw for most visitors to Cyprus, but venture into the island's interior and a radically different, relatively overlooked side of the country emerges. A holiday in the Troodos Mountains is recommended for anyone in search of a laid-back break beneath the shade of cedars and pines, interspersed with walking, cycling or easygoing sightseeing.

Make your base a traditional house, such as the charming, eco-conscious Spitiko tou Archonta (+ 357 9952 7117, www.spitiko3 elies.com), which also offers Cypriot cooking demonstrations using seasonal ingredients.

121 *Party barefoot*

Agia Napa, once the clubbing destination of the eastern Med, still attracts a respectable crop of big-name DJs, but the fresh new summer clubbing scene centres around the Elysian combination of beach and bar. Give the lairy mainstream joints a wide berth and make for Guaba (www.guababeachbar.com) on Agia Varvar beach in Amathountos, Lemesos; the grassroots beach bar keeps the music and drinks flowing from the morning till the wee hours.

122 *Capital pleasures*

The island's capital has only recently emerged as a tourist destination, thanks in no small part to the international interest attracted by the historical opening of the Green Line, the UN-controlled zone separating the Republic of Cyprus in the south from the Turkish-occupied north. Spend the day in the capital, Nicosia, exploring the labyrinthine, beguiling streets of the old town within the ancient Venetian walls, then make your way to the Shacolas Tower Museum & Observatory (corner of Ledras & Arsinoes) for panoramic views across both sides of the last divided capital city in Europe.

123 *Go with the grape*

More than 50 boutique wineries are dotted across the Troodos Mountains, and a day sampling the fruits of their toils is thoroughly recommended. Ideal places in which to pop the cork are the Krassohoria (meaning 'wine villages'), where you can check out the Agia Mavri Winery in Kilani, Lemesos (+357 25 470 225) and its award-winning white muscat. Don't leave without a bottle of sweet Commandaria, the oldest-named wine in the world and a splendid after-dinner tipple.

124 *Take a late-summer dip*
£₨

Cyprus's geographical location in a ray-catching corner of the Mediterranean makes it a failsafe target for end-of-the-summer sun-seekers. The country's most alluring beaches – sugary shores lapped by translucent waters – are in the south-east, in the area around Agia Napa and Protaras. May and September are the best times to go, when the crowds have thinned out but it's still warm enough to swim and tan. Follow the locals and flip-flop down to Konnos beach, a bijou bay at the foot of the spectacular cliffs at Cape Greco.

125 *Indulge in imaginative taverna dishes*

Sidestep the ubiquitous and underwhelming tourist trap tavernas and seek out one of the mushrooming number of small-scale operations offering more creative takes on traditional dishes. At Mageirion to Elliniko (Votsi 8-10,

Ktima), a picturesque eaterie secreted away in the old quarter of Paphos, you can look forward to a table crowded with little-seen plates inspired by the traditions of Greek-era Constantinople, such as yaourtlou chicken and pera kebab. All served to a thrice-weekly soundtrack of live rembetika – a Greek version of the blues.

126 *Explore untouched wilderness*

Communing with nature for many visitors means nothing more than lounging on the beach. For those with more adventurous appetites, the Akamas peninsula in the west of the island offers mile after mile of scenic, untamed wilderness studded with craggy Aleppo pines, circled by kestrels and visited by the odd elusive snake. Active types can have a field day trekking or cycling over rocky off-road tracks; joining a tour with a company like BikeTrek (Aliathon Holiday Village, Kato Pafos, +357 26 913 676) is a sound idea if you're at all nervous about venturing into the unknown.

127 *Find your sea legs*

In Latsi, a small community near Akamas, you can hire a motorboat and set off on a solo trip round the picturesque peninsula with no more than a quick lesson and a wave goodbye from the hire company. Powering along the coast from Latsi to the Blue Lagoon for a spot of snorkelling, dolphin-watching and sea turtle-spotting is an exhilarating experience. A driving licence is all that's needed, and four hours' hire of a 40-horsepower boat costs €83 – not bad for a memorable outing if you have a fellow sailor or two. For more details, contact Latsi Watersports Centre (+357 26 322 095, www.latchiwatersportscentre.com).

128 *Have an old-school spa treatment*
£

Get properly pummelled with an old-school massage at the spruced-up Omeriye Hamam (+357 22 460 570/22 750 550), the most luxurious Turkish baths on the island. The

124: Konnos beach, Cyprus

spa offers seven steam rooms at different temperatures, plus indulgent treatments like body wraps and a chill-out space on lush divans. Perfect for winding down after a day's sightseeing, and it won't break the bank at €18.

129 *Take a hike*

Keen walkers have dozens of nature trails to choose from in Cyprus, with distances to suit all abilities and energies. Cedar Valley in the mountains is bisected by the European long-distance walking path (E4) to the peak of Mount Tripylos. A picnic area with majestic views serves the less active. Alternatively, the Kalidonia trail (Caledonian Falls) in Platres offers a not-too-taxing trek along a refreshing stream – getting your feet wet is a welcome treat in the warmer months.

130-139
Classic boutique hotels

Boutique wasn't born yesterday. Long before the muted tones and potted grasses took over so-called designer bedrooms and lobbies, hotel architects and interior designers were trying to provide their guests – who tended to be richer in the olden days – with a luxurious home from home. Here are ten of the world's most classically stylish retreats:

130 La Posada, Arizona, USA

+1 928 289 4366/www.laposada.org.
Until Zaha Hadid designs an entire hotel (instead of just a floor, as at Madrid's Hotel Puerta America), we have to make do with just one woman architect on our list. Mary Colter designed La Posada for the Santa Fe Railway in 1929 as one of the great railway hotels, filling the public spaces and private rooms with warm, local arts, crafts and materials. A sad 40-year closure came to an end a decade ago when it was rescued by Colter fans Allan Affeldt and his artist wife Tina Mion, who are restoring the hotel to its former glory. Arrive by plane into Winslow and you get to see the airport designed by US aviator and inventor Charles Lindbergh as an added bonus.

131 Atlanta Hotel, Bangkok, Thailand

+66 2 252 6069/www.theatlantahotelbangkok.com.
Something of an institution, this idiosyncratic hotel – 'a small resort for sleaze-free and wholesome tourism', proclaims the quirky website – contains Thailand's oldest swimming pool, constructed in 1954 and little changed, as well as a wondrous foyer that's often used for film sets. This detail would surely have pleased its designer, Berliner Dr Max Henn, whose influences included Central European theatre architecture and set designs of the 1920s and '30s.

132 Antumalal, Pucón, Chile

+56 45 441011/www.antumalal.com.
In 1945 Czech immigrants Guillermo and Catalina Pollack commissioned renowned Chilean architect Jorge Elton to build them a hotel between Lago Villarrica and the eponymous volcano. Elton was a fan of Bauhaus, and his creation, Antumalal – 'corral of the sun' in the native Mapuche tongue – is a perfect illustration of the harmony of form, natural environment and function. The 22-room hotel is in the heart of the Chilean lake district (and therefore popular with travellers looking to hike, undertake treks on horseback or ski) and behind the cool exterior are the essentials of a log cabin: each of the bedrooms is panelled in wood and stone and is made cosy by an open fire. Floor-to-ceiling windows overlook the lake and the hotel's well-kept lawns. Guests have included Queen Elizabeth II and Neil Armstrong.

133 Paxmontana, Obwalden, Switzerland

+41 41 660 22 33/www.paxmontana.ch.
If the functional simplicity of 20th-century modernism leaves you cold, warm up in a classic example of art nouveau. The six-storey wood-framed Paxmontana was built in 1896 and from the outside looks like a Swiss version of the terrifying Overlook Hotel from *The Shining*, all imposing grandeur plonked in the middle of central Switzerland's majestic scenery. But a 2008 refurbishment that followed the hotel's original designs has

resulted in an interior whose rich fittings and warm colours capture the spirit of the belle époque perfectly.

134 Barceló Formentor, Mallorca, Spain

ℛ ☋ ♡

+34 971 899 100/www.barceloformentor.com.
Going on for 80 but maintaining its effortless good looks and chic appeal, the Formentor's traditional Spanish style has attracted a number of stylish luminaries over the decades, among them Winston Churchill, Charles Chaplin and Laurence Olivier. They presumably came for the stunning beauty of the peninsula (near Pollença, on the northern coast), but the hotel itself is pretty impressive

too. A lovely, understated example of classic Iberian architecture, the hotel is in total harmony with the park surrounding it.

135 Parco dei Principi, Sorrento, Italy

ℛ ♡

+39 081 8784644/
www.grandhotelparcodeiprincipi.net.
Italian modernist Gio Ponti's stunning 1960s creation is set in a suitably dramatic location, overlooking the Neopolitan riviera cliffs in Sorrento. Making the most of the natural backdrop, Ponti set the hotel right on the cliff's edge, necessitating a sci-fi-style lift descent through cliffs to get to the hotel's tiny private beach. But it's the interiors

132: Antumalal, Pucón, Chile

that really stand out, from the lobbies with glass-and-tile mosaics through to the 170-odd rooms, all decorated with their own unique blue-and-white mosaic tiled floor, classic modernist furniture and a private balcony that gives you stirring sea views.

136 Hotel Le Corbusier, Marseilles, France

+33 4 91 16 78 00/www.hotellecorbusier.com.
Le Corbusier's grand paean to communal living, the Unité D'Habitations, or Cité Radieuse, is a glorious example of the way the architect's stark, sleek lines could work with colour. The building is out of bounds to tourists (though occasional free guided tours of the public areas and an apartment are organised by the tourist office), but staying in the third-floor hotel enables you to explore to your heart's content, from rooftop gym and crèche down through the bar and canteen to the colour-flooded foyer. Definitely the one to stay in when you head for Marseilles in 2013 for the Capital of Culture jamboree.

137: Biltmore, Florida

137 Biltmore, Coral Gables, Florida, USA

+1 305 445 8066/www.biltmorehotel.com.
A resort bearing classic Italian, Moorish and Spanish architectural influences in the middle of Florida? Amazingly, it works so well that the Biltmore, opened in 1926, has achieved National Historic Landmark status. Architect Leonard Schultze and contractor/developer S Fullerton Weaver had already collaborated on a number of prestigious projects – most notably Miami's Freedom Tower – but in this hotel they created a building that remains an extraordinary example of Mediterranean architecture, despite numerous refurbs.

138 SAS Royal Hotel, Copenhagen, Denmark

+45 38 15 65 00/www.radissonsas.com.
If it's Danish, it must be Jacobsen. The work of the great modernist designer lives on through countless classic furniture designs, but the SAS Royal is the only Jacobsen-designed hotel. He designed the hotel and everything in it in 1960, but refurbishments over the years buried much of his work. Room 606, however, has been restored to what Jacobsen's original would have looked like, down to custom-designed carpets and wenge-wood chairs reupholstered in an exact facsimile of Jacobsen's original fabrics. If you get to stay in it you receive a unique large-scale postcard of the room. If you don't, you can enjoy the soaring Jacobsen foyer and hopefully sneak a peak into the room when it's being cleaned.

139 Burgh Island Hotel, Devon, UK

01548 810514/www.burghisland.com.
Britain doesn't do adventurous architecture very well, so you need to head back to the 1930s for something special. Burgh Island is a fanciful but gorgeous example of art deco, located on its own tidal island (meaning you can't get off it once it's high tide, so choose who you want to spend a weekend here with carefully). It has maintained its quality and appeal by regularly refurbishing to keep standards in the 21st century, without compromising on any of the period detail. Simply sumptuous.

Ideas from the expert

140-149

Mark Crosby from HF Holidays rounds up ten great walks in the UK, Europe and beyond.

140 The walk around the Tarn and Malham Cove in the Yorkshire Dales (13 miles and 1,400 feet of ascent) takes in four classic features: Janet's Foss, Gordale Scar, Malham Tarn and the spectacular Malham Cove. Hike gently through magnificent limestone scenery and you may also spy peregrine falcons and owls.

141 Wainwright's Coast-to-Coast (www.thecoasttocoastwalk.info; complete trail 190 miles, with daily ascents of between 1,000 and 2,400 feet) is the most popular long-distance trail in the UK. It follows Alfred Wainwright's classic walk crossing England and taking in three of its National Parks, from the Irish Sea at St Bees to the North Sea at Robin Hood's Bay.

142 Striding Edge, Helvellyn and Swirral Edge (8 miles, 2,850 feet of ascent) is a classic 'horseshoe' walk around and to the top of Helvellyn – the Lakeland's most visited summit, with its cross-shaped shelter and memorial stones. Striding Edge is a well-known arête – or sharp rocky ridge – with views down to the Grisedale Valley and Red Tarn below; and the views are truly spectacular.

143 Europe's most popular long-distance trail is the Tour du Mont Blanc in the French Alps (112 miles, 4,692 feet of ascent), which goes around the majestic Mont Blanc massif, providing plenty of opportunities to look up at the mountain from great vantage points. This is a journey through France, Switzerland and Italy, with awe-inspiring panoramas of glaciers and snow-domed summits. The trail can be busy but there are enough interesting alternatives to avoid the crowds.

144 Turkey's Lycian Way (51 miles, 8-13 miles and up to 1,800 feet of ascent per day) is the country's first long-distance footpath. Opened in 1999, it's a classic coastal trail along the edge of the mountains of the Lycian peninsula, which drops steeply into the Mediterranean. You pass through remote but friendly villages and ancient Greco-Roman ruins, with a few stunning beaches to refresh you along the way.

145 Camino de Santiago, Galicia, Spain (www.caminodesantiago.me.uk; 73 miles, 9-15 miles and up to 2,100 feet of ascent per day): this is the final leg of the thousand-year-old pilgrimage to the Baroque cathedral at Santiago de Compostela, the final resting place of St James the apostle. Meandering through medieval villages, passing castles and stately fortresses, this trail evokes an extraordinary spirit among fellow walkers.

146 Corvara and the Sella Group, the Dolomites, Italy (7 miles and 1,550 feet of ascent, 3,900 feet of descent per day). This walk traverses the southern and eastern sides of the huge Sella mountain group in the stunning coral-hued Dolomites range. The terrain is rocky but the via ferrata views (or 'iron ways', a network of ladders and fixed cables that are a legacy of World War I) are worth the effort.

147 Amalfi Coast Path sections, Sorrento Peninsula, Italy (35 miles, 6.5-9 miles and 3,800 feet of ascent/descent per day). The highlights of this coastal walk are views of Naples and the beautiful journey up to the ridge of Mount Faito by cablecar where you get to look down on Vesuvius.

148 Routeburn Track, South Island, New Zealand (148; distance 24 miles, 6-9 miles and up to 1,000 feet of ascent per day). The Routeburn was first mooted in the 1860s as a route over the Southern Alps to New Zealand's west coast. Leading through the majestic Fiordland and Mount Aspiring National Parks, it traverses scenic mountain country, taking in waterfalls and lakes and staying in mountain lodges.

149 Contour Path via Mushroom Rock, Drakensberg, South Africa (ten miles and 2,200 feet of ascent per day). From the Cathedral Peak Hotel you follow a network of paths through a dramatic mountainscape. A steep start leads to a winding path that passes waterfalls, fields and grasslands, with views of the Cathedral range throughout.

■ **HF Holidays** 020 8732 1220/ www.hfholidays.co.uk.

139: Burgh Island Hotel

150-159 *Alternative camping in Britain*

Not satisfied with the canvas suburbia of organised campsites? Then forget the rows of neatly marshalled tents, chemical toilets and trappings of civilisation and try one of these quirky ways to sleep in the great British outdoors.

150 *Cosy up in a Romany caravan*

A traditional Romany caravan now has a permanent home, in a wildflower meadow near Llangrannog in West Wales. Built in 1924, the caravan has a wood-burning stove and is just big enough for two; best of all, you get exclusive use of the tranquil meadow in which it's located. As well as the caravan, there's a cabin with a shower room, kitchen and wooden veranda; sitting out on the veranda on a balmy summer evening is simply heavenly.
Under the Thatch *01239 851410/ www.underthethatch.co.uk.*

151 *Rent an Airstream*

A bottle of cold beer, the opening harmonies of 'Good Vibrations' wafting through the air, the sunlight glinting off the chrome curves of an Airstream caravan; this is about as close as you can get to starring in your own American road movie. OK, so you're stationary in the middle of a working dairy farm in a field on the Isle of Wight, but the same spirit of freedom is most certainly present. Vintage Vacations owns ten beautifully restored old caravans, most of them classic Airstreams from the 1950s and '60s, and they're available to hire for short breaks of up to a week. All amenities are included in the reasonable tariff, and the caravans boast shower facilities (though you are asked to use the farm's loo block; vintage caravan loos are a step too retro). Popular with both couples and families.
Vintage Vacations *07802 758113/ www.vintagevacations.co.uk.*

152 *Boutique camp at Bestival*

👪 ⏱

Camp Bestival (an offshoot of Bestival; www.
bestival.net) is, as the name suggests, not just for
music-lovers, but boutique campers too. And the
available options are great fun. Yurts and Squrts
offer fun, cosy and green accommodation in both
adult and child sizes; the Yurtel comes complete
with a king-size bed and miniature toiletries; the
solar-powered podpads are lovingly decorated
little wooden huts, with fitted carpet, shelving
and locks on the front door; while Eve's tipis are
set up for some serious luxury lounging on floor
cushions and sheepskin rugs. Campervans are
also available for hire.
Camp Bestival *www.campbestival.net.*

153 *Kip in a vintage caravan*

£ ⏱ ♡ 👪 ⏱

Deep in the woods of the North Yorkshire Moors,
La Rosa's 20-acre site is occupied by eight kitsch
and colourful caravans, each kitted out according
to a different retro theme – Vegas Vice pays
tribute to Elvis, while La Rosa's opulent, mirror-
bedecked interior is a homage to 1930s striptease
star Gypsy Rose Lee. The site is run on low-tech
lines so there's no electricity; three caravans are
cosily heated by wood-burning stoves, while
showers are candlelit affairs in a hay byre, and
toilet trips involve a compost loo in a converted
shepherd's hut. There's also a communal circus
tent, where children can delve into the dressing-
up box on rainy afternoons, and grown-ups take
afternoon tea from the charmingly mismatched
crockery. During the day, spot deer in the North
Yorkshire Moors National Park, ride the steam
railway from Grosmont Station, or drive to
nearby Whitby. Caravanning doesn't get cooler
than this – and all for just £26 a head.
La Rosa *07786 072866/www.larosa.co.uk.*

154 *Pitch your tent at Three Cliffs Bay*

🐾 ⏱

This clifftop campsite is justly famed for its
magnificent views over sandy Three Cliffs
Bay in Swansea, on Wales's Gower Peninsula.
The pitches on the field by the cliff's edge are
somewhat sloping – but with views like that,
who's complaining? (And if you really can't
handle it, there's a flatter back field for more
cautious campers.) The beach is a short but

**151: Vintage Vacations'
Airstream trailers**

slippery scramble down the cliff path; once you've made it safely down, you're rewarded by a picture-perfect, unspoilt stretch of sand: happily, limited car parking keeps the holidaymaking hordes away.
Three Cliffs Bay *01792 371218/ www.threecliffsbay.com.*

155 *Join the beach hut brigade*

Beach huts began life as mobile contraptions, wheeled to the water's edge to preserve the modesty of Victorian ladies with a horror of showing so much as an ankle in public. Once we got used to stripping off into swimsuits and cavorting merrily on the sands, someone had the bright idea of turning them into static huts offering a little piece of privacy on increasingly busy beaches.

These days, you'll be lucky to get your hands on one: price tags of £50,000 and upwards aren't unheard of, even though you're generally not allowed to stay in them overnight. A rare exception is Mudeford Spit in Dorset, where you can sleep in the huts between March and November. Prices to buy are eye-watering, but renting is more manageable, at around £400 a week (www.mudeford-beach-huts.co.uk).

Traditionalists, though, favour the jaunty row of beach huts at Southwold, a charmingly old-fashioned resort on the Suffolk coast. Waveney District Council recommends calling Durrants Estate Agents to find a hut to rent (01502 723292), or you can call the tourist information office in Southwold (01502 724729). Expect to pay around £200 a week in the school summer holidays.

155: Southwold

156 *Hit the road in a camper van*

Based in the surf mecca of Devon, O'Connors Campers (01837 659599, www.oconnors campers.co.uk) specialises in renovating authentic VWs – fitting them with new engines and interiors while retaining their classic boho look. There are 12 available for hire, from the 1960s splitscreen to '70s bay window models. Up in Oxfordshire, VW Camper Company (01295 812266, www.vwcamperco.com) has an eight-strong fleet of '70s Devon Moonraker conversions for hire – fitted with elevating roofs to accommodate full-size double beds. Last but

not least, Snail Trail in Bedfordshire (01767 600440, www.snailtrail.co.uk) ships in brand-new copies of original models from Brazil – so each of its fleet promises a smooth ride and gleaming good looks. Take your pick from the lovingly named Betty, Pearl, Flo, Elsie, Matilda, Nell, Pru, Dot, Sylvie and Ruby.

157 *Camp out on the Thames in a skiff*

The idea of navigating the Thames in an antiquated, round-bottomed rowing boat might sound alarming at first, but bear with us. For a start, it's the upper stretches of the Thames, where tranquillity reigns and the route is lined with idyllic waterside boozers.

And the boats in question are also things of beauty: a fleet of seven 100-year-old skiffs, stars of the annual Swan Upping swan census held on the river (not to mention *Shakespeare in Love* and *Harry Potter and the Goblet of Fire*). Everything you could possibly need is on board – sculls (oars), mooring spikes, a stove and cooking equipment, crockery, sleeping and rowing mats and, best of all, a wet-weather cover that enables your boat to double up as a three-berth tent. All in all, it's a Jerome K Jerome fan's dream come true.
Thames Skiff Hire *01932 232433/ www.skiffhire.com.*

158 *Sleep over on safari*

◇ ▥ ◔

Forget Kenya: a safari experience can be yours for a fraction of the price in Kent, at the Port Lympne Wild Animal Park. Home to some 650 animals, including the largest breeding herd of black rhino outside Africa, the park's latest offering is an overnight safari package. After dinner around the communal campfire and a surprisingly cosy night under canvas (in commodious tents with proper beds), you get to accompany the rangers on a magical dawn safari, getting up close and personal with the park's free-range zebra, giraffe, antelope and wildebeest.
Port Lympne Wild Animal Park *01303 264647/ www.totallywild.net.*

159 *Go wild camping*

£ ◇

In most parts of England and Wales, you have to ask the landowner's permission before pitching your tent. In practice, many turn a blind eye if you're only there for a night and are discreet; others don't even notice you're there (the golden rule being 'pitch late, leave early'). In Scotland, it's legal to camp wild, so long as you follow the rules: leave the flora and fauna as you found it (party animals and budding Ray Mears take note), avoid farmland, and camp well out of sight of any houses and roads. After that, it's simply a question of remembering to pack the essentials – an Ordnance Survey map, compass, torch, plenty of food and water, and a sturdy tent and sleeping bag. Dartmoor, England's last great wilderness, is a place where camping is encouraged. But beware:

according to folklore, the place is rife with strange apparitions – from a pair of disembodied throttling hands to the pack of demon hounds that inspired *The Hound of the Baskervilles*. It's also home to a notorious prison – a dour, forbidding cluster of grey stone buildings. For information on wild camping in Dartmoor, see www.dartmoor-npa.gov.uk. For more on wild camping in Scotland, visit www.mountaineering-scotland.org.uk.

160-169
Fabulous film locations

Love film? Fancy yourself as a Hollywood star? Then plan your holidays around classic films set in beautiful places. The USA is the obvious place to head, and **Monument Valley 160**, the location for classic Westerns, including John Ford's *Stagecoach* (1939) and *The Searchers* (1956) and Sergio Leone's masterpiece *Once Upon a Time in the West* (1968), is the ultimate cowboy fantasy setting. You can stay at the boutique-style View (www.monumentvalleyview.com), inside the park, or motel Goulding's Lodge (www.gouldings.com); both have jaw-dropping views of the buttes and spires of Monument Valley. Don't, though, expect saloon fights; the Monument Valley Navajo Tribal Park (www.navajonationparks.org/htm/monumentvalley.htm), to give it its full name, is in the dry Navajo Nation autonomous region.

If *Dances with Wolves* (1990) was more your cup of baked beans, then head to Sage Creek in the evocatively named **Badlands National Park** (www.nps.gov/badl) **161** in South Dakota. It's great hiking, camping and backpacking territory, so you can get in the Costner mode. Out on the prairies, you may see bison, bighorn sheep and black-footed ferrets, but you'll have to make do with prairie dogs and coyotes for the dancing.

Several of the flashback scenes for *The Godfather Part II* (1972) were filmed in the picturesque villages of Savoca and Forza d'Agro, near Taormina in eastern **Sicily 162**. The Bar Vitelli is still to be found in the former and pilgrims do stop by for a *granita*, while the surrounding countryside is still very charming. The actual town of Corleone is in western Sicily.

Offset your
flight with
Trees for Cities
and make your
trip mean
something for
years to come

www.treesforcities.org/offset

Trees for Cities
Charity registration number 1032154

Dublin 163 has also had its share of hard-man films. Head here to imagine yourself in *Michael Collins* (1996) and *In the Name of the Father* (1993), which was shot in Kilmainham Gaol (www.kilmainham-gaol.com), a notorious former prison that was closed by the new Irish Free State government in 1924, where fascinating guided tours are organised.

France is, of course, full of film sets. Paris vies with New York for the prize of location par excellence – but if you want rural romance, head to **Flavigny-sur-Ozerain** and other villages in the Cote D'Or **164**, where Lasse Hallström's *Chocolat* (2000) was filmed. The village is famous for a different sort of sweet: L'Anis de Flavigny, made here since the ninth century and sold in keepsake tins decorated with beautiful old-fashioned pictures. Visit www.bringmeburgundy.co.uk for information on wine-and-food tours of the region.

South America is coming up as a directors' favourite for ads as well as feature films. With its huge bay, gorgeous beaches and carnival buzz, **Rio de Janeiro 165** has long been a classic setting for movies. Some scenes in *Cidade de Deus* (City of God; 2002) were shot in the shanty town of that name; if you want to see a real favela up close, contact Favela Tour (www.favelatour.com.br). Alternatively, go for a walk round the cool but edgy Lapa neighbourhood and then go to Copacabana beach. Buy a yellow footie shirt, take off your shoes and kick a ball around to feel like a true brasileiro.

A far dreamier portrait of life in **Latin America 166** is that featured in *The Motorcycle Diaries* (2004), which sees Che Guevara and his best mate Alberto Granado biking through Argentina, Mexico, Chile and Peru – the latter's UNESCO World Heritage Site of Machu Picchu is the set for a critical scene in the film. Latin America holiday specialist Journey Latin America (www.journeylatinamerica.co.uk/Holiday-Types/Behind-the-scenes.aspx) can organise tailor-made film-themed tours to many countries in the region.

Harrison Ford must feel like he knows **Tunisia 167** rather well. The *Star Wars* (1977) scenes of Luke Skywalker's family home on the planet of Tatootine were filmed in Matmata, in the south, while *Raiders of the Lost Ark* (1981) was filmed in Sousse, on the north-eastern coast, which is more than 3,000

160: Monument Valley

161: Badlands National Park

years old and the site of a ninth-century mosque. Thomson (www.thomson.co.uk) does a range of Tunisia tours, and visits to film sets can be booked as part of your package.

New Zealand 168 has used the fact that the *Lord of the Rings* trilogy was shot there in all sorts of promotional campaigns. Kiwi Peter Jackson filmed all three movies in various locations around the country. To get a feel for Middle Earth go to hilly Matamata, which became Hobbiton. The setting for Mount Doom, meanwhile, was the volcanic region of Mount Ruapehu in New Zealand's 'adventure capital' of Queenstown – also the setting for the Eregion Hills and the Pillars of Argonath. Visit www.tourism.net.nz/lord-of-the-rings.html for further details.

For a classic movie location, go to a once classic resort – now out of the way for Western Europeans. *Battleship Potemkin* was shot in **Odessa, Ukraine 169** on the Black Sea. You can visit the steps where the famous scene of the massacre was filmed. Don't confuse fact and film, though – the actual 1905 massacre did not take place on the steps. You can combine a trip here with visits to Lviv and Kiev. Regent Holidays (www.regent-holidays.co.uk) is a tour operator with many years' experience in the region.

170-179
Foreign food: cookery schools

When you translate your sterling into euros – or, indeed, any other currency – you might find that you can't afford the wild-boar tagliatelle or lotus-leaf rice parcels you were dreaming of when planning that fortnight abroad. The choice: spend your holiday wad in Waitrose's foreign section or book a break that lets you get your hands dirty with oils, herbs, spices and exotic ingredients. There's no contest. You just have to choose when, where and how: you can squeeze an intensive session into an afternoon or indulge in a fortnight of taste-bud tantalising luxury at some of the world's best cookery schools. Here we provide a selection.

170 Tante Marie cheese workshop, San Francisco
+1 415 788 6699/www.tantemarie.com.
Baked camembert with dried fruit, gratins with fontina d'Aosta, and manchego tarts are among the mouth-watering dishes prepared during Tante Marie's one-day cheese workshop in San Francisco. If you have more time, you can spend a sinful three days in its pastry kitchen.

171 Cooking classes in a Moroccan medina
08708 998844/www.holidayonthemenu.com.
Venture off the Moroccan tourist trail to forgotten Kasbahs and old seaside medinas where village women teach you to prepare local dishes and bake traditional bread. Travel by mule between mountain routes and through valleys.

172 Elizabeth Andoh's cooking workshops, Tokyo
www.tasteofculture.com.
Learn the basics of Japanese home-cooking and washoku philosophy – based on the harmony of colour, preparation and flavour in its approach to food – at Elizabeth Andoh's cookery school in Tokyo.

173 Alpujarran cuisine with Sam Clark

020 8964 5333/www.tastingplaces.com.
For Spanish cuisine with an exotic stamp try a weekend in Mairena, a Moorish mountain village in southern Spain with chef Sam Clark, one half of the same-named pair who are behind London's renowned Moro restaurant. Local produce-picking and the dubious opportunity to milk a goat are included perks for adventurous guests.

174 Red Bridge Cooking School, Vietnam

+84 510 3933 222/www.visithoian.com.
Master four traditional Vietnamese dishes and go shopping for banana flowers at a local village market, on a one-day-tour with the Red Bridge Cooking School. The school is located on the banks of the Hoi An River in the city of the same name, on the south-central coast of Vietnam. Half-day tours and evening classes are also available.

175 Traditional Italian cookery classes, Etrusca

01273 600030/www.responsibletravel.com.
Flee to an Etruscan village where wild boar and wolves still roam the Tolfa Mountains north of Italy's capital. Locals teach traditional recipes and guide visitors through wine, grappa and olive oil tastings.

176 Goan cuisine, India

020 7371 1113/www.onthegotours.com.
Indian food-lovers bound for Goa, where the cuisine is flavoured by Portuguese colonisation – can sign up for one- to eight-day courses and trips to local spice plantations.

177 Langa Cookery School, South Africa

+27 21 461 2437/www.capefusion.co.za.
Luxury cooking tours in South Africa take you wine-, cheese- and chocolate-tasting between wildlife excursions and trips to beauty spots. Master the chakalaka at the Langa Cookery School, which trains poor locals at its restaurant built from shipping containers.

174: Red Bridge Cooking School

178 Jerk-meat classes, Jamaica

08000 223773/www.royalplantation.co.uk/
culinaryjourneys.cfm.
Learn traditional Caribbean recipes at a luxury resort in Jamaica. Discover how to curry goat meat and jerk pork between rosewater face-mistings on the beach and trips to the marbled, scented spa.

179 Ireland's Ballymaloe Cookery School

+353 21 464 6785/www.cookingisfun.ie.
The Ballymaloe Cookery School used to be an apple barn. Set in rolling hills on an organic farm by the sea, no-nonsense courses vary from producing butter and yoghurt to posh canapés. Run by Ireland's celebrity chef, Darina Allen, the centre also offers professional training.

180-189
Ultimate ski holidays

180 *St Anton, Austria*

Daredevils should head to St Anton in Austria, famed for table dancing, hardcore drinking and even harder off-piste action the morning after. Those still on their feet at midnight are rewarded with the chance to hit the slopes under the stars. There are 260 kilometres of pistes, best suited to intermediate to advanced skiers and, of course, boarders.
Go with *Iglu Ski (020 8542 6658/ www.igluski.com).*

181 *Banff, Canadian Rockies*

The spectacular views of the lakes from Banff in the Canadian Rockies alone would be worth the trip. There are 11 square miles of pistes popular with skiers and boarders of all levels. You can also try a dizzying range of adventures from dog sledding to heli-skiing. For more information, visit www.banff.ca.
Go with *Virgin Holidays (0844 557 5825/www.virginholidays.co.uk).*

182 *La Plagne, France*

There's a reason everyone goes skiing in France, and La Plagne is one of the country's most popular and emblematic resorts, being ideal for families and beginners, with over a hundred easy to intermediate runs spread over 220 kilometres. Thrill-seekers can head to Bellecôte Glacier's black pistes or brave the Olympic bobsleigh run.
Go with *Mark Warner (0871 703 3887/ www.markwarner.co.uk).*

183 *Bansko, Bulgaria*

Bulgarians may confuse the rest of Europe by nodding when they mean 'no' but their recently developed resorts have left budget-conscious skiers in no doubt. With 70 kilometres of marked pistes, modern lifts and cannons, Bansko is suited to skiers of all levels as well as boarders, who can build their own jumps at the fun park.
Go with *Crystal Ski (0871 231 5659/ www.crystalski.co.uk).*

184 *Slovenia*

Some of the best-value pistes in Europe are to be found in Slovenia, overlooking the Julian Alps. There are 65 kilometres of pistes in Kranjska Gora, and, with Ljubljana airport only 90 minutes away, they're accessible enough to make for an exciting weekend break. Alternatively, try a week's adventure cross-country skiing through the forests and rivers of Triglav National Park.
Go with *First Choice (0871 664 0130/ www.firstchoice-ski.co.uk).*

185 *Zermatt, Switzerland*

If you're going to do luxury, let the Swiss take care of it. In Zermatt, as well as 245 kilometres of pistes, there are gourmet restaurants, Europe's highest cable car and a frontier with Italy that you can ski through. Serious about après-ski, the clubs are packed with youngsters at night, while more refined visitors opt for the casino and glamorous hotels.
Go with *Oxford Ski (0870 787 1785/ www.oxfordski.com).*

186 *Japan*

Ice-sculpting festivals, bathing in hot springs with macaque monkeys and with over 700 resorts to choose from – Japan is an exotic and rewarding (if expensive) choice. The peaks may not be as high as you're used to, but there is plenty of snow and space. Still a novel destination for Westerners, you'll miss the lifestyle as much as the slopes when you get home. Find out more from Ski Japan (+81 136 22 4611/www.skijapan.com).
Go with *WeLoveSnow (www.welovesnow.com).*

187 *The Dolomites, Italy*

Film stars, adrenaline junkies and families after no-nonsense all-inclusive resorts will find their niche in the Dolomites, the Italian Alps. The superski pass includes well over a thousand kilometres of pistes under the dramatic skyline of jagged peaks up to three kilometres high.
Go with *Colletts Mountain Holidays (01763 289660/www.colletts.co.uk).*

188 *Lapland*

All-day pink twilights have long drawn romantics to Lapland, and now skiers have reason to go as well. Levi offers more than 40 crowd-free pistes, ice-fishing, husky safaris and snowmobiling. There is also a vibrant (and tasty) nightlife with open-fire reindeer feasts, cocktails and dancing. Santa visits can be arranged for children.
Go with *Inghams (020 8780 4433/ www.inghams.co.uk).*

189 *Brasov, Romania*

The generally gentle pistes of Romania will not give experienced skiers the shivers, though they are a respectable 12 kilometres long at the resort of Brasov. But beer is only 50p a bottle, and away from the slopes in the medieval town lies Dracula's castle, where you can bravely have lunch.
Go with *Balkan Holidays (0845 130 1114/ www.balkanholidays.co.uk).*

190-199 *Time Out's 21st-century European Grand Tour*

In the 19th century, toffs took their trunks (wooden ones, not briefs) and lackeys to Europe in order to see the most celebrated artworks and architectural sights and to party with their pals in the continental aristocracy. The route varied but almost always included Paris, then the Loire Valley (where the purest French accent was said to reside), Geneva and the Alps (in search of the Sublime and the 'picturesque', a recent coinage). From here, the culture vultures headed south towards the great Italian museum cities of Turin, Milan, Venice, Florence, Rome and perhaps Naples. The return journey might include the courts of Berlin, Dresden and Vienna, a few more university towns and also Amsterdam, already established as a fun town.

Times have changed. Most of the above remain popular stopovers for middle-aged coach tour passengers as well as young InterRailers, but it's debateable whether a classical education is the only or even best one, and also whether power and partying are still to be found in the same European hubs.

So here we go with an alternative 21st-century Grand Tour. Take the train as we suggest below, or use coaches. Whatever mode you opt for, you'll come back edified, energised and educated.

Start in **London 190** where you can see sculptures, ancient treasures, artworks and antiquarian books from all over Europe and the rest of the world. Here you can tick off your Greek marbles, your Italian busts and your French Impressionists and so leave all the fun bits for the Continent. Catch the Eurostar from grandiose St Pancras International to **Brussels 191** whether you love or hate the European Community project, its powerbase is here, as well as some great cuisine; expat residents say the restaurants in the Belgian capital beat those of Paris on quality and creativity, and they should know as they have hefty expense accounts thanks to us.

Catch a fast Thalys train to German train hub Cologne and change for **Berlin 192**. In the German capital you are – arguably – in Europe's most exciting cultural capital, as well as the powerhouse for the Continent's impressive economy. In 1989 the Berlin Wall came down; the following year, Berlin became the capital of a reunified Germany after a hiatus of 28 years. The city has been the setting for some of the 20th century's most affecting – and appalling – acts, but it's culturally thrilling, whether you want beer, Bauhaus buildings, Communist kitsch or cutting-edge art. What Florence was in the Renaissance and London was in Victorian times, Berlin is now.

After this headrush, **Vilnius 193** might seem pleasantly offbeat. But a Baltic nation that used to lie within the sphere of influence of the USSR is a must-see for any

199: Hagia Sofia, Istanbul

contemporary Grand Tourist who wants to dip his or her toe in history. Vilnius was a European Capital of Culture in 2009 and is also on the Euro stag circuit – the modern equivalent of the social whirligig of the aristo-fops of yore. Don't miss Grūtas Park, where the old Stalinist monuments are kept as a reminder of the Bad Old Days.

One of the cities that might have been included in a more daring 19th-century Grand Tour, **Prague 194** is now very mainstream and much loved by travellers. Its Gothic architecture, Pilsen beers, clubbing and gay scenes and romantic air appeal to all ages and budgets. From June to September, KI Bungee Jump (www.bungee.cz) does brisk business in pitching otherwise rational weekend visitors off Zvikovské podhradí, a bridge high over the Vltava valley. Just the sort of pointless fun the old GTers would have indulged in.

Another city that has been busy sloughing off its Soviet ghosts is **Budapest 195** where a boat trip along the Danube, a glass of Tokaj and a stroll along the boulevards evokes the golden era of the Habsburg Empire. Winter is high season for classical music – of excellent calibre and at reasonable prices – in venues like the Opera House, Franz Liszt Music Academy and the National Concert Hall at the Palace of Arts, built in 2005.

From here we'll veer to Central Europe and the Balkans, setting for the most recent major conflicts in the Old World. All of the cities involved in the 1991-2001 Yugoslav Wars are making progress, but **Sarajevo 196** stands out as a symbol of recent history: it was the setting for the assassination that kicked off World War I, and for the 1992-96 siege (the longest in modern times). A ten-minute stroll from focal Bascarsija reveals a mosque, a Catholic church, an Orthodox church and a synagogue. Divided by the narrow, fast-flowing Miljacka river, the city is a rich mix, with most of the action on the north side. A muezzin's call to prayer, traditional Ottoman coffeehouses, waves of foreign tourists

194: Prague's Astronomical Clock

arriving for skiing holidays, A-list names fraternising in the local bars during the Sarajevo Film Festival every August – these are the sights and sounds of today's Sarajevo.

From here it's only a short trip to **Tirana 197**, Albania's much-ignored capital. Still far poorer than its neighbours, Albania is friendly, intriguing and proud to carry on drinking and smoking while the rest of Europe is busy imposing draconian health measures.

Gradually, **Bucharest 198** is rising out of the long shadow left by Ceausescu to become a hot, edgy city for music, food and drink. New steel-and-glass structures stand beside Stalinist brutalist buildings and old churches, and at the centre of them all is the huge, infamous Parliament Palace, built in 1984. Head to the old city and university district after dark for dinner and dancing.

The legendary Orient Express railway used to link London to **Istanbul 199** and the Turkish capital – destined, surely, to join the EC in the next few decades – is a world-class city. Ottoman grandeur is much on show, and sights such as the Hagia Sofia and Blue Mosque are as impressive as anything in Italy and France. But the culture is also a melding of Christianity and Islam, east and west, European and Middle Eastern. This is the future of the Continent and a natural place to stop and take stock of 21st-century Europe – and you can fly home on a budget airline.

200-209

Ten natural wonders of the world

200 Uluru (Ayers Rock), Australia
🌳 ♡ 🏛

Central Australia's Uluru appears to rise out of nowhere, and is 450 kilometres from the closest town, Alice Springs. The large sandstone formation is 348 metres high with a circumference of 9.4 kilometres, and was sacred to the indigenous Pitjantjatjara and Yankunytjatjara peoples. Travellers linger here to see the changing colours as the sun strikes the rock at different times of the day; at sunset it glows deep crimson and is at its most photogenic and romantic. The area also features waterholes, springs and rock caves – ancient paintings found in the latter give the site special historical value.

A number of bus tours operate from Alice Springs to Uluru. Alternatively fly to Ayers Rock (Connellan) Airport from Alice Springs, Cairns, Sydney or Perth.

201 Victoria Falls, Zambia/ Zimbabwe, Africa

◊ 🏠

Getting there *Daily flights go from Johannesburg, South Africa to Livingstone, Zambia or Victoria Falls, Zimbabwe, for easy access to the falls.*

This infamous waterfall, located in southern Africa on the border between Zambia and Zimbabwe, is fed by the Zambezi River. Not the highest or widest falls in the world, their claim to fame is as the largest wall, or surface area, of falling water in the world. The falls are 1.7 kilometres wide and 108 metres high. They were named Victoria Falls by the Scottish explorer Dr David Livingstone, but are also called Mosi-oa-Tunya, meaning 'smoke that thunders'.

Note: avoid visiting during the rainy season between November and April, when the additional water makes it impossible to see the base of the falls.

202 Milford Sound, New Zealand

◊ 🏠

Getting there *Buses to Milford Sound depart from Queenstown. Once there, take one of the boat tours, which last between 1-2 hours, departing from the Milford Sound Visitors' Centre. Or take a scenic flight by light aircraft or helicopter from Milford Sound Airport.*

This fjord in the south west of New Zealand's South Island – within Fiordland National Park and the Te Wahipounamu UNESCO World Heritage Site – is named after Milford Haven in Wales. It runs 15 kilometres inland from the Tasman Sea, surrounded by sheer rock faces that rise 1,200 metres on either side. Among the most photogenic peaks are the Elephant, and Lion Mountain, both vaguely resembling those species. Rainforests cling to the cliffs, while seals, penguins and dolphins bob around in the waters below.

203 Lençóis Maranhenses National Park, Northern Brazil

◊

Getting there *There are regular bus routes between São Luís (Maranhão's capital) and nearby Barreirinhas. From here you can book day trips. Because of the park's protected status, entrance to the park for tourists is exclusively by 4-wheel drive truck.*

This vast area of large sand dunes is reminiscent of a desert, but receives regular rainfall that causes freshwater to collect between the dunes; the translucent pools are home to a variety of fish (their eggs are brought from the sea by birds). The park was created in 1981 and is in the state of Maranhão, south of the mouth of the Amazon River. It encompasses around 1,000 square kilometres, and, despite abundant rain, supports almost no vegetation. The water in the lagoons rises between July and September. Amazingly, this patch of desert dates from the period of the Gondwana supercontinent of 550-500 million years ago, when Brazil was connected to Africa.

204 Gunung Mulu National Park, Borneo

◊ 🏠

Getting there *The only practical way of getting to and from the national park is by air, mainly from Miri to Mulu; the flight takes about 45 minutes.*

This UNESCO World Heritage Site near Miri, Sarawak, in Malaysian Borneo, features incredible caves and karst formations in a mountainous rainforest setting. It's also home to the largest-known underground chamber in the world, the Sarawak Chamber: 700 metres long and 400 metres wide, it's big enough to accommodate St Peter's Basilica in Rome.

205 Great Barrier Reef, Australia

◊ 🏠

Getting there *Many cities along the coast of Queensland offer boating tours. To get the best diving and snorkelling, it's worth paying more for a boat trip away from the crowds.*

The world's largest coral reef encompasses over 2,900 separate reefs, and supports one of the most diverse ecosystems in the world. It spreads over almost 350,000 square kilometres, and includes more than 900 islands. Some two million visitors travel to the reef every year, but a large part of the reef is protected from this human impact and by factors such as overfishing. However, threats from pollution and climate change remain real.

206 Paricutin Volcano, Michoacán, Mexico

◊ 🏠

Getting there *The volcano is located 322km west of Mexico City; take a bus to Angahuan.*

Paricutin, 424 metres high and 3,170 metres above sea level, is an active cinder cone volcano in Michoacán, Mexico, often named one of the 'seven natural wonders of the world' because mankind witnessed its birth during the 1940s. It's been dormant since the last eruption in 1952.

207 Grand Canyon, Arizona, USA

Getting there *There are many ways to get there: you can fly over it by plane, take bus tours around it or go on horseback down into the canyon.*
Impressive for its scale, Arizona's Grand Canyon, carved by the Colorado River, is also set in beautiful landscape. The gorge is a massive 277 miles long and 18 miles wide, with a depth of over 1.14 miles. The best times to see it are early morning (before the coaches arrive) and at sunset.

208 Aurora Borealis (Northern Lights), Alaska

Getting there *Both Fairfax and Anchorage have international airports; you may have to fly via Seattle.*
Aurora Borealis are naturally occurring lights that create spectacular displays in the sky; the phenomenon is caused by the interaction between the earth's magnetic field and solar wind. The lights appear as a diffused glow, folded pages or waves of light above the horizon. Also known as polar auroras, the lights occur over northern Scandinavia too, as well as the southern tip of Greenland, Northern Canada and the northern coast of Siberia; Antarctica has Southern Lights.

The greatest chances of seeing them are from March to April and September to October; a late summer visit to Alaska (particularly the area around the city of Fairbanks) or Northern Canada presents a fair chance of experiencing this amazing phenomenon.

209 Mount Everest, Himalayas

Getting there *Your best bet is to book a hike to the Southern Base Camp on the Nepalese side. Expeditions usually entail flying to Lukla from Kathmandu and then heading to the town of Namche Bazaar, the starting point for the week-long trek to Base Camp.*
The highest peak on earth is located in the Himalayan mountain range, on the border between Nepal (where it's called Sagamartha) and Tibet, China (where it's called Chomolungma or Qomolangma). The summit lies at 8,948 metres above sea level. Everest is not technically the tallest mountain in the world, however: that honour goes to Mauna Kea in Hawaii – but most of it is under water.

See the website www.unesco.org for the full list of World Heritage Sites.

208: Northern Lights

214: West Wittering

210-224

Brilliant beaches in the British Isles

More than 100 British gems are detailed in the *Time Out Seaside* book (£16.99).

210 *Fistral Beach, Newquay, Cornwall*

The home of surfing in Britain; in fact, the British Surfing Association is based here and offers surfing lessons from its National Surfing Centre (www.nationalsurfingcentre.com), while various surfing competitions and tours are held throughout the year. The flat beach is backed by steep sand dunes, and can get pretty crowded with some visitors staying overnight in the stylish apartments right on the sand. For more information, visit www.fistralbeach.co.uk.
Getting there *Follow the A392 from the A30 or A39. Fistral Beach is signposted from Newquay's town centre.*

211 *Sandbanks Beach, Poole, Dorset*

The miles of fine sandy beach and clear waters here are said to have won more Blue Flag awards than any other beach in Britain. And the bay is so shallow that you can safely walk into the sea for nearly 656 feet, making it a good spot for children. It's also popular with windsurfers and other watersports enthusiasts. Check out www.sandbankspoole.com for more details.
Getting there *The main roads leading to Poole are the A35, A350 and A338.*

212 *Silver Beach, Isle of Wight*

This relatively small and sandy beach on the less-visited east coast of the Isle of Wight is ideal for learning watersports like windsurfing and, in particular, kitesurfing. The shallow water has very little shore-break, making it a relaxing environment in which to learn the ropes.
Getting there *Located just east of Bembridge harbour on the B3395.*

213 Holy Island, Northumberland

Holy Island is only accessible by the causeway at low tide, when a road is revealed from beneath the water, making it possible to drive or walk across from the mainland. If you walk across the dunes that run alongside the main access road, you'll discover a beautiful expanse of pristine sand, to be enjoyed in peace.
Getting there *Clearly signposted from the A1.*

214 West Wittering, West Sussex

Just an hour from London lies this mellow, gently shelving beach, sheltered by the Isle of Wight and the grassy swell of the South Downs. As well as drawing strollers in search of a hot chocolate at the café, it's beloved of kitesurfers and windsurfers, not least because its wind and swell suit just about all levels and there are surf-friendly conditions at almost every stage of the tide. On the beach is X-Train (01243 512552, 01243 513077, www.x-train.co.uk), the tuition arm of the West Wittering Windsurfing Club.
Getting there *From London or the M25, follow the A3 and then M3 and A27 and finally the A286.*

215 Woolacombe, Devon

A great beach for building sandcastles. This long, golden stretch of the North Devon coast has won a host of awards and has everything you expect of an English beach: fine sand, rock pools, easy access and decent facilities. The nearest town to Woolacombe is Ilfracombe. For more details, visit www.woolacombetourism.co.uk.
Getting there *Take the M25 and then the A361; from here, take the A3343.*

216 Wells-next-the-Sea, Norfolk

The unspoilt expanse of Wells beach, with its woodland backdrop separating the coast from the farmland behind, is perfect for anyone interested in wildlife. The beach is owned by the Holkham Estate and is in the middle of the Holkham National Nature Reserve. There are also some great scenic walks in the area, including the Norfolk Coast Path, a 47-mile hike from Hunstanton to Cromer, which passes along the beach.
Getting there *The village of Wells-next-the-Sea is located just off the A149.*

217 Charmouth, Dorset

One of the best places to find fossils along the 152-mile Jurassic Coast World Heritage Site (www.jurassiccoast.com). Charmouth Heritage Coast Centre organises guided walks led by experts throughout the year.
Getting there *East of Lyme Regis. Follow signs for Charmouth from the A35.*

222: Sinclair's Bay, Caithness

218 Dogs Bay, Roundstone, Galway

On the westernmost shores of Europe, this curving mile-long stretch of silvery-white Irish sand is imbued with the wildness of Connemara. Set below a grassy headland and lapped by clear turquoise Gulf Stream waters, it's a good place to spot dolphins.

Getting there *Take the N59 west out of Galway; the beach is off the R341 between Errisbeg and Murvey.*

219 South Beach, Tenby, Dyfed

Tenby is one of the finest resorts on the Welsh coast and its four expanses of sand – North, South, Castle and Harbour beaches – mean that there is always a sunny spot for swimming. The largest of these is South beach, fringed with attractive dunes. This draws large numbers of swimmers, although it is also a popular spot for other watersports, including windsurfing, canoeing and power-boating. For more details, visit Tenby Tourist Information (01834 842402, www.visitpembrokeshire.com).

Getting there *Take the M4 to get deep into South Wales, then the A40 and A477. Tenby is well signposted. There's also a railway station.*

220 Hell's Mouth, near Abersoch

Recognised as the most reliable surf spot in North Wales – facing the south-west and catching a serious swell – Hell's Mouth, or Porth Neigwl in Welsh, is mainly sand with a few rocks, and backs on to cliffs and dunes. Strong swimmers love the currents, and even non-surfers come along on late summer evenings for the parties.

Getting there *The A55 and A487 lead to the Llyn peninsula. Take the B4441 to Criccieth and then follow the A497, which becomes the A499, to Abersoch; from here head for Llanengan, following signs for Hell's Mouth.*

221 Sandwood Bay, Sutherland

Scotland's Sandwood Bay can lay claim to possessing some of the finest scenery in Europe, with magnificent sands and dune systems. The beach is a mile long, and a sea stack (Am Buachaille) and some ominously dramatic cliffs shouldn't detract from the peaceful bays that are found along this stretch of protected coast. The Sandwood Estate, which supports 54 crofts and ten working crofters, contains eight islands, a saltwater lagoon and the freshwater Sandwood Loch.

Getting there *Drive as far in a north-westerly direction as you can in Scotland and you're there. The A838 skirts the coast.*

222 Sinclair's Bay, Caithness

Once famous as the best spot in all Scotland for fresh, tasty lobsters and crabs, Sinclair's Bay is still much loved for its Caribbean-white sands. On a fair-weather day – which, to be honest, isn't that common on a coast that looks out fondly to Scandinavia for inspiration – it can be one of the prettiest beaches in the British Isles; when the storms roll in it is a scene from the closing stages of *Macbeth*. The village of John O' Groats is just a few miles further up the coast.

Getting there *Take the A9, then the A99 if coming from Inverness; follow signs for Wick Golf Course.*

223 Sanna Bay, Scottish Highlands

One of Britain's most secluded beaches, but it's worth the journey. The beach consists of an arc of soft, pristine white sand, which is as likely to be dotted with the footprints of the local wildlife as it is with those of humans. A short distance along the coast is the Point of Ardnamurchan, the most westerly point of the British mainland.

Getting there *Signposted from Kilchoan on the southern side of the Ardnamurchan peninsula, along mainly unclassified roads. Kilchoan is reached along the B8007 or by ferry from Tobermory on the island of Mull.*

224 Kynance Cove

Kynance Cove's white sand, turquoise water and multi-coloured islands are just four miles north of Cornwall's Lizard, the most southerly point of the British isles. One feature is the serpentine rock formations – the colours and markings resemble the patterned green or red skin of a serpent in places. For more information, call 01326 561407 or visit www.nationaltrust.org.uk.

Getting there *The A30, A39 and A294 get you all the way down England's western limb. From Helston, follow the A3083 to Lizard town.*

225-229 *Five hen-dos*

225 *Be pampered in Budapest, Hungary*

£ 🏛 🍸

Thermal baths and massages make Budapest one of the pampering capitals of Europe. Package-based activities available in the Hungarian capital include chocolate- or wine-tasting sessions and a cruise down the River Danube.

Book with *Stags & Hens (www.stagsandhens.com).*

226 *Learn pole-dancing in Prague, Czech Republic*

£ 🏛 🍸

Follow a cultural day at the city's historic sites with lessons in the not quite so ancient art of seduction involving a very long and shiny pole. At night, glam up for a classy cocktail tour of the coolest clubs in town.

Book with *Chillisauce (0845 450 8269/ www.chillisauce.co.uk).*

227 *Be stripped for in Brighton, UK*

£ 🍸

Warm up the hen with foreplay lessons and bubbly before taking her on a river-boat cruise with a sexy, stripping, midstream surprise. Or dish him up with dessert. Brighton's lively nightlife will allow the party to continue into the wee hours.

Book with *Last Night of Freedom (0845 260 2800/ www.lastnightoffreedom.co.uk).*

228 *Get sexy in Barcelona, Spain*

🏛 🍸

Learn to salsa with hot Latin dancers between swigs of sangria, then swing those hips all night long with free entry to a live music club. Recover on the beach the following day, in time for an evening tapas feast and fiery flamenco show.

Book with *Go Hen (0845 130 5225/ www.gohen.com).*

229 *Enjoy some shopping and the city in New York, USA*

🏛 🍸

Get super-chic at the shops Carrie swooned over and dine where the four friends sipped cocktails and winked at waiters on the 'Sex and the City' tour. Or just spend the weekend indulging in designer labels and stylish bars.

Book with *Hen Parties (0870 416 0280/ www.henparty.travel).*

228: Baja Beach Club, Barcelona

Bags packed, milk cancelled, house raised on stilts.

You've packed the suntan lotion, the snorkel set, the stay-pressed shirts. Just one more thing left to do – your bit for climate change. In some of the world's poorest countries, changing weather patterns are destroying lives.

You can help people to deal with the extreme effects of climate change. Raising houses in flood-prone regions is just one life-saving solution.

Climate change costs lives.
Give £5 and let's sort it *Here & Now*

www.oxfam.org.uk/climate-change

Be Humankind ⊗ Oxfam

230-239
Boutique Spain: inland

Away from the coast, Spain harbours some truly beautiful regions – and with so many gorgeous *casas rurales*, *paradores*, castles and mansions, as well as small boutique hotels to choose from, you can easily make a perfect base in one of the smaller towns and villages and explore by car or bicycle. For a quick look at some of the loveliest properties to be found inland, visit the website of Spanish specialist **Rusticae** (www.rusticae.es).

Here are ten top regions, with suggestions for somewhere to sleep and an itinerary for a fly-ride/drive holiday.

230 *Castile – La Mancha*

Head for sleepy Sigüenza, site of an impressive 12th-century cathedral. About 100 kilometres south of here is the historic city of Cuenca, another charming place to visit, with the dramatic gorges of the Huécar and Júcar rivers close by. Belmonte to Consuegra is the official Don Quijote route.

Villa Julia is a cosy, comfy five-room *casa rural* in Sigüenza.
Villa Julia *+34 949 391 965.*

231 *Extremadura*

Trujillo, a small, well-preserved town dating from the 15th century, is famous as the birthplace of Pizarro, the conqueror of Peru. From here you can drive to the Parque Nacional Monfrague to see birdlife, wilderness and classic oak-tree *dehesas* (groves) full of black-footed pigs eating acorns; a trip to Guadalupe to see its famous Virgin is also a must-do.

The 16th-century Renaissance-style NH Palacio de Santa Marta is situated a block away from Trujillo's main plaza, and provides suitably luxurious lodgings.
NH Palacio de Santa Marta *0800 0115 0116/www.nh-hotels.com.*

232 *Inland Mallorca*

Mallorca is an easy island to cover in a short space of time. Avoid the overdeveloped coastal resorts and head for Lluc, a small village spectacularly located in the Tramuntana Mountains – popular with hikers; its monastery (the Santuari de Lluc) still offers guest acccommodation for would-be pilgrims.

From here, drive (along winding, hairpin roads) to Pollença, for a popular but still smart beach. You'll doubtless pass through buzzing Palma on your way in and out of the island; the capital is full of stylish hotels, one of the

232: Dalt Murada, Palma, Mallorca

most characterful of which is the Dalt Murada. Be sure to also visit pretty Deia – which tumbles down a hill by the sea – to see how the other half holiday.
Santuari de Lluc *+34 971 871 525/www.lluc.net.* **Dalt Murada** *+34 971 425 300/ www.daltmurada.com.*

233 *Picos de Europa*

♦♡☼

Base yourself in Cangas de Onis, an old hamlet with a Romanesque bridge and eighth-century chapel that's a great gateway to the Picos de Europa National Park. You can drive to Potes, in the heart of the park, to go hiking and to dine; or to enchanting Ribadasella to dip your toe in the cold Cantabrian sea. Stay at the Aultre Naray, a converted 19th-century Astrurian house boasting great views of the Sierra de Escapa and the Picos.
Aultre Naray *+34 98 584 08 08/ www.aultrenaray.com.*

234 *Catalonia*

☙ ♦

Figueres, in the north-east corner of Catalonia, is famous as the birthplace, and final resting place, of painter Salvador Dalí (1904-89). Nearby is Sant Joan de les Abadesses, site of a monastery founded in 895. Puigcerda is worth a visit to see the Pyrenees, while the pretty little resort of Cadaqués, on the Costa Brava, is a good place to head to for its lovely little bay lined with fishing boats. The Hotel Durán was established in 1835, and is still owned by the same family; it has one of the best restaurants in town.
Hotel Durán *+34 972 501 250/ www.hotelduran.com.*

235 *Northern Andalucia*

♦☼

Grazalema, Spain's wettest town, may seem like an odd choice for a holiday base, but so much rainfall means that it's also one of the greenest spots in Andalucia – and a hub for hikers. Move on to Jerez, to explore sherry country, and then Ronda, to stroll around one of Andalucia's most beautiful small towns.

After all that walking, you'll want a comfy spot to recuperate. Hotel Fuerte, in Grazalema, has a nice pool with mountains on all sides.
Hotel Fuerte *+34 902 343 410/ www.hotelfuertegrazalema.com.*

236 *Castile countryside*

♦

Soria is an attractive but undiscovered (even for Spanish tourists) little town beside the banks of the Río Duero, famous for its wines. A reliable base here is the Solar de Tejeda. From here, drive to Numancia and the Sierra de Urbión just to the north, the former a Celtic-Iberian settlement and the latter a quiet mountain region with a beautiful lake, the Laguna Negrara, at its heart.
Solar de Tejeda *+34 975 310 054/ www.hosteriasolardetejada.com.*

237 *Rioja*

Haro is a handsome town, and the centre for winemaking in the Rioja Alta region – higher and cooler than the Rioja Baja. From here, drive on to (or, better, take a taxi to) any of the local vineyards and *bodegas* (Bilbainas, Muga and La Rioja Alta are open to the public) for a tasting; and to Nájera, to see the Gothic monastery.

Base yourself at Señorío de Briñas, a stone building three kilometres outside of Haro.
Señorío de Briñas *+34 941 304 224/ www.hotelesconencantodelarioja.com.*

238 *Basque Country*

Oñati is a historic town in the Udana Valley, in the province of Guipúzcoa. Dating back to the medieval period, it's also home to the University of the Basque Country. From here, you can drive north-west to Guernica, the cultural capital of the Basque Country, or north-east to San Sebastián, the culinary capital of Spain.

Stay at the recently renovated Santuario de Arantzazu, up a mountain road from Oñati.
Santuario de Arantzazu *+34 941 304 224/ www.hotelsantuariodearantzazu.com.*

239 *Old Castile*

▦

Salamanca, the most graceful city in Castilla y León, is a charming focus of any trip to this region. The old part of the city is a designated UNESCO World Heritage Site, and the place is famed as a centre of learning. Other highlights in the area are León, the region's other historic city, and Ciudad Rodrigo, on the road to Portugal.

The chic Petit Palace Las Torres on the Plaza Mayor in Salamanca makes a good base.
Petit Palace Las Torres *+34 923 212 100/ www.petitpalacelastorres.com.*

Ideas from the expert

240-249

Caroline Phillips, Product Manager at Explore, offers her top ten South-east Asia.

240 Sample the delicious street food in Hanoi, Vietnam, from crispy spring rolls known as *nem* to steaming bowls of *Pho*, the hugely popular fragrant beef noodle soup. The Old Quarter has a street café on virtually every corner and just a few pennies will ensure a good feed.

241 Catch a cocktail at Bangkok's Skybar (www.lebua.com/bangkok/dining.html) then dine at the Sirocco open-air restaurant; at 63 floors above the steamy city, it's reputed to be the world's highest alfresco eaterie. The views across Bangkok and the Chao Phraya River are awesome, especially at dusk when the city is lit up.

242 Take a slow boat down the Mekong in Laos to Luang Prabang. The former capital of Laos is now a UNESCO World Heritage Site, with hundreds of gilded wats (Buddhist temples). This is a beautiful and tranquil town. I love to get up at dawn to watch the orange-robed monks collecting alms.

243 Get your clothes made to measure for next to nothing in Hoi An – a small but popular backpacker city on the coast of south-central Vietnam. Select your materials from a dazzling array, including locally produced silks. These tailors can whip up a complete outfit overnight, from just a few dollars (USD is the preferred currency) for a simple shirt to as little as $30 for a full suit. Mrs Trang at Trang Tailors (47 Tran Hung Dao Street) is an old favourite.

244 Friends restaurant in Phnom Penh is the Cambodian precursor to Jamie Oliver's 15 concept. The Mith Samlanh project (meaning 'Friends' in Cambodian) takes street kids and trains them up to work in various ventures. The restaurant and Le Café du Centre are colourful eateries serving a mix of French- and Cambodian-influenced food. For more details, visit www.mithsamlanh.org.

245 Climb mighty Mount Kinabalu (4,095 metres) in Borneo to see the sun rise from the misty jungle lowlands below. It's South-east Asia's highest peak and well within the capability of most reasonably fit people. It's normally scaled over two days. Explore's Sabah Naturewatch ten-day tour includes the chance to climb Mount Kinabalu as well as enjoy Borneo's wildlife and culture. Or organise the trip locally through one of the travel agents in Kota Kinabalu. You'll need their help in organising necessary permits.

246 See Borneo's orang utans at the Sepilok Sanctuary (www.orangutan-appeal.org.uk/sepilok-rehabilitation-centre), where up to 80 primates live in the protected reserve and around 25 young orphans are looked after in the nurseries. Avoid the big hotels, and head for the numerous homestays available in the region to really get a feel for the area. Visit www.sabah-homestay.org for more information.

247 Sail by traditional Pinisi schooner around the isles of the old East Indies (from Bali to Flores), where you can climb volcanoes, hunt down komodo dragons and snorkel and dive. To me this is adventure and romance in all senses of the words. Explore's East Indies Seatrek tour features a ten-day schooner cruise with a couple of nights spent on beautiful Bali at either end.

248 Ride elephants through the jungle in Thailand's Khao Sok National Park, and make the most of the swaying, elevated viewpoint to enjoy the flowers, insects and other animals of the tropical forest. Stay in a treehouse for an enhanced taste of jungle life – really not as rugged as you might think. Visit www.krabidir.com/artsriverviewlodge for more details.

249 Once you've had mai tai cocktails on Khao San Road and done the Alex Garland thing on the islands, try to see a bit of rural Thailand. Trekking through the hill tribe villages in the north gives you a chance to stay in remote villages, overnighting in stilt houses and dining with locals. You can do part of the trek on elephants, and wrap up with a cruise on bamboo rafts along the Mae Ping River. Chiang Mai, the northern backpacker hub is good for post-trek RnR.

■ **Explore** 0845 013 1537/www.explore.com.

Madrid is mad about you.
Come and discover it.

about you

www.turismomadrid.es

250-254

Only here for the beer

Wine tourism is very well established, very enjoyable and, often, very romantic. But beer is surely at least as, if not more, important to our domestic culinary culture; so why not buy a round in these world-class hop havens?

250 *Pilsener, Czech Republic*

'Liquid bread', as the locals call it, has been brewed in the town of Pilsen for more than 1,000 years and the Czechs drink 157 litres of it each year.
Your round Pilsner Urquell, named after the famous town, is a classic but Gambrinus and Kozel's Medium are also worth a jar or two.

251 *Bruges, Belgium*

Belgians have some 600 beer types, most of which are served in their own glass, with its own shape, logo and beermat.
Your round Fine Trappist beers, brewed by monks, include Leffe, Gueuze, Duvel and De Koninck.

252 *Masham, Yorkshire, England*

Thomas Theakston built the famous brewery that stands at a spot known as Paradise Fields. Visit the Black Bull in the Paradise Visitor Centre to witness the ales being created (see www.theakstons. co.uk).
Your round Theakston Best Bitter, Old Peculier or Black Bull Bitter.

253 *Munich, Germany*

German Beer is older than Germany. Some historians say Bavarians have been getting wasted for 2,000 years. Munich's annual Oktoberfest beer festival witnesses the consumption of six million litres of beer over 16 days.
Your round Join in and sup Märzen, Altbier and Kölsch.

254 *Victoria, Australia*

Beer has played an iconic role in Australian culture since colonial times. Former Aussie Prime Minister Bob Hawke held a local record for the fastest consumption of beer, consuming 2.5 pints in 12 seconds. The most popular brew is lager and it's drunk in rounds – to be included in a shout is to be accepted by your beer peers.
Your round Forget Fosters, which Australians never drink, and go for Carlton Draught, Victoria Bitter and Melbourne Bitter.

255-262

Learn the lingo: foreign-language courses

255 *Learn German in Freiburg, Germany*

A fairytale town between the Black Forest and the Rhine, Freiburg is famed for its thermal baths, hikes and, of course, that world-renowned cake layered with cherries, cream and a dash of rum. The established Goethe-Institut (www.goethe.de) has been teaching German for more than 50 years, and also offers exam preparation and courses for children.
Book with *Learn4Good (www.learn4good.com).*

256 *Learn Chinese in Shanghai, China*

Try Chinese on tuition courses tailored to your stay; more dedicated students can opt for a full immersion and stay with a Chinese family. Work experience programmes and groups for teenagers are also available.
Book with *Mandarin House (+86 21 6137 1987/ www.mandarinhouse.cn).*

257 *Learn French on the Côte d'Azur, France*

Hang out on the chic French Riviera between Cannes and Nice, while brushing up on your

French, and wind down with celebrity-spotting, yacht-envying and excursions – and 'soft' language-themed activities in the centre. The Centre International d'Antibes will keep your children busy. A range of levels is available.
Book with *Centre International d'Antibes (+33 970 40 74 34/www.learn-french.fr).*

258 *Learn Arabic in Teutouan, Morocco*

The Mediterranean port of Teutouan, founded in 3 BC, was fought over by the Spanish and the Moors until 1956, and is now one of northern Morocco's most important centres. The old part of town is considered one of the finest medinas in the country and is a UNESCO World Heritage Site. A week-long course includes four hours' tuition per day, and two lessons in either traditional ceramics or cookery.
Book with *GoLearnTo (0844 502 0445/ www.golearnto.com).*

259 *Learn Italian in Capo Vaticano, Calabria, Italy*

Close to the tip of Italy's toes, dip yours into turquoise waters in peaceful bays between lessons. Spectacular views from the cliff tops led Greeks to consider this cape a holy spot. Popular with birdwatchers and scuba divers, it beats evening classes in the local tech.
Book with *Languages Abroad (www.languagesabroad.com).*

260 *Learn Japanese in Osaka, Japan*

Check the month for festivals before booking classes here. The Naked Festival in January boasts fighting men in loincloths, while almost every month there are traditional dances, geisha parades and ceremonies.
Book with *Languages in Action (www.languagesinaction.com).*

261 *Learn Portuguese in Salvador, Brazil*

Relax under palm trees on white-sand beaches. Learn to surf. Take a mask to snorkel among the beautiful reefs. They'll also teach you to samba… and if you have any energy left, there are 20 language classes a week.
Book with *GoLearnTo (0844 502 0445/ www.golearnto.com).*

262 *Learn Spanish in Cusco, Peru*

With classes in both the ancient Inca capital of Cusco and in a small town in the Sacred Valley, this course includes a four-day Inca Trail trek, three nights' camping, meals and entry to Machu Picchu.

Book with *responsibletravel.com (01273 600030/ www.responsibletravel.com).*

263-272

Ten inspiring island refuges

263 *Easter Island (Isla de Pascua)*

Where is it? *109 degrees 23' west in the middle of the South Pacific.*

The island that Polynesians call Te Pito O Te Henua ('The Navel of the World') and Rapa Nui ('The Great Rapa', after a mythical sailor) was christened with its present name by Dutch sailors who made landfall here in 1722. Gloriously isolated from the rest of the world, it's been a source of inspiration to poets and mystics for centuries. Though politically part of Chile, Easter Island is like nowhere else on earth thanks to its massive *moai* – 300 colossal statues carved from rock and dating from the 13th to 16th centuries – which stand sentinel all around the island. Grassland has replaced almost all of the island's original broadleaf forest, and while ecologists have expressed outrage at the centuries of devastation, the rather bald, barren look gives Easter Island a certain appeal.

Island home *Most accommodation is guesthouses; book with Explora (+56 2 206 6060/www.explora.com).*

264 *Curaçao*

Where is it? *69 degrees 00' west in the Dutch Antilles in the Caribbean, off the north coast of Venezuela.*

The name, derived from the Portuguese for heart, may be familiar for being home to the blue liquor found in many stag weekend cocktails. The largest of the six Dutch Antilles,

Curaçao is a long scrawny strip of arid land that tilts towards Venezuela, and is populated by a mix of Afro-Caribbeans, East Asians and Portuguese Jews. If that doesn't sound particularly idyllic, wait until you see the emerald-hued waters, which attract plenty of honeymooners. The prevailing trade winds make the coasts here ideal for windsurfing, and the island is also a diving mecca.

Island home *Aqualife Bungalow (+59 99 736 2030/www.curacao-villas.com).*

265 *Christmas Island*

Where is it? *105 degrees 40' east in the Indian Ocean, the territory of Australia.*

Discovered by East India Company navigator Captain William Mynors on 25 December 1643, Christmas Island looks like the best place on the planet to live, but nonetheless was never seriously settled. Only 1,400-odd people call it home and 65 per cent of the island territory remains untouched as a national park (www.environment.gov.au/parks/christmas). It's sometimes hailed by Australians as the 'Galapagos of the Indian Ocean' for its bird and marine life. From the end of October through to early December between 50-100 million red crabs march from their inland burrows to the shore and back in order to satisfy their mating and reproduction ritual – the migration is one of the planet's greatest natural wonders.

Island home *The Sunset (+61 8 9164 7500/ www.thesunset.cx).*

266 *Lampedusa*

Where is it? *12 degrees 36' east; one of the Pelagie islands in the Mediterranean and Italy's southernmost outpost.*

Desert-like thanks to its bleached white, stony soil, this tiny island hardly supports any agriculture, but white-sand beaches and guaranteed hot weather make it an ideal vacation spot. Each September, loggerhead turtles – endangered throughout the Mediterranean – bury their eggs in the dunes at Rabbit beach before heading back to sea. The babies hatch 60 days later, emerging from their eggs after dark.

Island home *Hotel Cupola Bianca (+39 0922 970126/www.hotelcupolabianca.it).*

267 *The Faroes*

Where are they? *6 degrees 47' west in the Norwegian Sea/North Atlantic, between the Shetlands and Iceland.*

Norwegian kings ruled over 18 Faroe Islands until 1380 when Denmark gained control. Removed from the movements, fads and fashions of mainland Europe, the islands are more rustic and somehow more Norse than the mainland: the Faroese maintain their own identity, language, music and cuisine. Fish, whale meat and even puffins have been known to grace their dinner tables and many of the houses have grass roofs. Note that hotels get booked up quickly on the island; see www.faroeislandshotels.com for further information.

Island home *Gjáargardur guesthouse (+298 42 31 71/www.gjaargardur.fo).*

268 *Santa Catarina*

Ὡ♡⩖

Where is it? *48 degrees 30' west on the Atlantic coast, off southern Brazil.*

First claimed by the Spanish in 1542 and later passed to the Portuguese along with the rest of Brazil, this island has long been popular with Argentinians and with Brazil's gauchos – those who dwell in the not very tropical southern ranching provinces. It ticks all the Brazilian boxes – sugar-sand beaches, summerhouses and beach volleyball with bikini-clad sun worshippers – and is safer and more chic than the beaches in the tropical zone.

Island home *The Costa Norte Ingleses hotel (+55 48 3261 3000/www.hoteiscostanorte.com.br).*

269 *Vanuatu*

Ὡ♡⩖

Where is it? *168 degrees 00' east in the South Pacific, north-east of Australia and next to New Caledonia.*

Vanuatu means 'the land that has always existed' in the local Melanesian tongue. A Y-shaped patchwork of 83 often-volcanic (with some volcanoes still active) islands – it boasts clichéd (in a good way) South Pacific beauty, with all the balmy breezes and diving opportunities you'd ever need, but is also home to intriguing indigenous ceremonies and dances. Adventure types can go waterfall abseiling, parasailing or make night trips to uninhabited islands. Come dusk, lounge beneath giant (as in absurdly humongous) banyan trees and catch the exotic, trancy music of the local string bands.

Island home *Le Lagon Resort Vanuatu (+678 22313/www.lelagonvanuatu.vu).*

269: Vanuatu

270 Cape Breton

◊♡

Where is it? *60 degrees 45' west in the North Atlantic off Canada.*
With its rugged coastline, rolling farmlands and eerie glacial valleys, this speck of deep green rock at the tip of Nova Scotia frequently makes the top five of the world's most beautiful islands. Thousands of Scots arrived here driven from their homeland by the scourge of the Highland Clearances in the 18th and 19th centuries, and the Gaelic influence can be seen in the fiddle music and low-stepping dances that still exist in the many pubs. Cape Breton is also home to one of the world's most beautiful drives: the Cabot Trail.
Island home *One of the four waterside retreats run by Cape Breton Resorts (www.capebretonresorts.com).*

271 Puerto Rico

♋ ♈

Where is it? *66 degrees 30' west in the Greater Antilles, Caribbean.*
Puerto Rico has historically had an on/off relationship with the USA; but despite that, there are now more Puerto Ricans in New York than on the island itself. Yes, there are baseball caps and burger bars, but there's more Latin attitude on this distinctive little island than in J-Lo's cola. Puerto Rico is the birthplace of salsa – well, one of them – and San Juan is arguably the world capital of reggaetón, but non-dancers and those looking for tranquillity will enjoy the rainforest, desert, beaches and caves.
Island home *Hix Island House (+76 5 787 741 2302/www.hixislandhouse.com).*

272 Chiloé Island

♋ ◊

Where is it? *73 degrees 50' west, on Chile's Pacific Coast.*
Shrouded in myth and mist, Chiloé is a lush little island just south of the Chilean lake district. Slower moving than the mainland, it has preserved many wood-tiled houses and churches, and the little taverns of the two main towns, Castro and Ancud, have a pre-modern ambience. For dinner, shellfish is the local speciality, and the iconic dish is *curanto* – shellfish wrapped in leaves and then cooked on a bonfire.
Island home *Espejo de Luna (+ 56 7431 3090/www.espejodeluna.cl).*

273-280
Wine cities & regions

273 Mendoza, Argentina

◊

In the bone-dry eastern foothills of the Andes, the stunning Mendoza region of central Argentina produces some 80 per cent of the country's wine. Best are the wines produced using the French red malbec grape in Luján de Cuyo, south of Mendoza city. Here, Nicolás Catena's family has been producing wine for more than a century in five vineyards that tumble southwards through the region. Angélica, Catena Zapata's 60-year-old malbec vineyard in Lunlunta, is one of the most impressive (www.catenawines.com).
Bring home a bottle of Angélica Zapata Malbec Alta 2003 – an elegant blend of malbec grapes featuring ripe plum flavours and a soft, supple mouth-feel. Drink it with grilled Argentine steak.
Book a tour with *Sunvil (020 8758 4774/ www.sunvil.co.uk).*

274 Bordeaux, France

◊⏱

Head for the northern part of the Graves region: the Graves Pessac-Léognan AC reds and whites are some of the best wines in Bordeaux. The vineyards here are awesome, stretching for miles to the surrounding woods and forests beyond.
The Domaine de Chevalier (www.domaine dechevalier.com) vineyard, south-west of the city, near Léognan, consistently comes up trumps for both reds and whites. Chevalier's 2008 red and whites were both lauded by the wine press. The red is smoky and offers a delicate rose fragrance; the oak-fermented

white is a fine pale yellow with hints of dried herbs. Both will improve over the years, so hold on to them for special occasions.

Book a tour with *Arblaster & Clarke (01730 263111/www.winetours.co.uk).*

275 *Porto, Portugal*

The Douro Valley is the famous home of port, but also the source of some of the country's top unfortified wines – and it's also the world's oldest demarcated wine region. The Quinta do Passadouro (www.quinta-do-passadouro.com) is a handsome port winery that also makes outstanding table wines.

If you're a Russian oligarch, bring back a Barca Velha, produced only in the finest years. For the rest of us, a dry, chocolatey Quinta de Leda red will do very nicely thank you.

Also be sure to take a side trip to discover the Alto Douro and the prehistoric rock art of the Coa Valley, a UNESCO World Heritage Site.

Book a tour with *Scott Dunn (020 8682 5080/ www.scottdunn.com).*

276 *Sonoma Valley, California, USA*

Caught between the Pacific to the west and the Mayacamas Mountains separating it from Napa

277: Chianti, Italy

Valley to the east, the Sonoma Valley has it all, from heavyweight chardonnays to macho merlots. The Arrowood winery produces a great range of reds and whites and is open daily for visits (www.arrowoodvineyards.com).

Buy a bottle of Amapola Creek 2005 Sonoma Valley Viña Antiguas, a complex and distinctive zinfandel with eucalyptus and citrus hues made from the 115-year-old vines of the Monte Rosso vineyard, adjacent to Arrowood's latest venture, Amapola Creek.

Book a tour with *Zephyr Adventures (+1 406 445 0802/www.SonomaVineyardWalks.com/ www.zephyradventures.com).*

277 *Chianti, Italy*

In the hills between Florence and Siena, the beautiful Chianti zone produces Italy's most famous wine. There are many variations, using different grapes and growing methods. One of the most beautiful and charming vineyards is the Castello di San Donato Estate, located in the hamlet of Castello di San Donato in Perano. The vineyard produces excellent Chianti Classico DOCG and Chianti Classico Riserva wines; bring home a bottle of Castello di San Donato in Perano Chianti Classico, Vendemmia 2005, as well as olive oil, limoncello, honey and spices. Dine or stock up on cured meats, great steaks and fancy fats at Dario Cecchini's butchers' shop and restaurant (+ 39 055 852727, www.dariocecchini.blogspot.com)

Book a tour with *Exodus (0845 863 9601/ www.exodus.co.uk).*

278 *Clare Valley, Australia*

South Australia has a wealth of great wine-producing areas, among them the Barossa, Eden Valley and Clare Valley, the upland region north of Adelaide known as the home of the riesling. Its cool climate and olde worlde villages, built by English and Irish settlers in the 19th century, make it a delightful place to explore.

Jeffrey Grosset's small but exceptional winery (www.grosset.com.au) specialises in just six premium wines each year. Grosset is a riesling specialist, but also produces some great reds, among them a lovely pinot noir.

Book a tour with *Bridge & Wickers (020 7483 6555/www.bridgeandwickers.co.uk).*

273: Mendoza, Argentina

279 *Jerez, Spain*

Located in the south-west of Spain, Jerez de la Frontera forms part of the romantic Sherry Triangle, along with the seaside towns of Sanlúcar de Barrameda and El Puerto de Santa Maria. It's home to the historic and aristocratic sherry *bodegas*, most of which are located right in the town centre. Stay for at least two days in this friendly city and, if you time it right, you can combine the wine tasting with the Cartujano horse festival or the annual *feria* (fair).

One of the most interesting estates to visit is Sandeman, which became a household name with the Orson Welles ads. This beautiful, mid-size historic cellar offers excellent daily tours and tastings in various languages as well as exclusive VIP tours for sherry and brandy connoisseurs, where you get the chance to taste rare vintages aged over 20 years and two fabulous brandies: Solera Reserva and Gran Reserva. Sandeman's Dry Don is an inexpensive, absolutely delicious Amontillado sherry that pairs magically with smoked cheeses, sautéed almonds and juicy olives.

For more information, visit www.wines fromspain.com.

Book a tour with *Cellar Tours (www.cellartours.com).*

280 *Champagne, France*

To the east of Paris lies Europe's most northerly premium wine region. From the chalk hills around Reims and Epernay comes the king of wine and the wine of kings. Ever since Dom Perignon uttered the words 'Come quickly, I'm tasting stars', this wine has become the must-have drink at every major celebration and sporting event.

The most prestigious champagne houses are generally located in Reims and Epernay and boast impressive cellars. Champagne Ruinart (www.ruinart.com) is the oldest, dating back to 1736, while its cellars pre-date this by over 1,300 years. Guides take visitors through the history of the House and the traditional method for producing sparkling wines. Dom Ruinart blanc de blancs 1996, made from 100 per cent chardonnay, is a wonderfully complex and elegant drink. It offers great balance and toasted notes typical of top-quality vintage bubbly. The famous light, powdery-pink Reims biscuits made by Fossier in Reims since 1690 are the perfect accompaniment to a rosé champagne, and are delicious in fruit charlottes and sorbets too.

Book a tour with *Grape Escapes (08456 430 860/ www.grapeescapes.net).*

281-290

Which Greek island?

Boasting white sand, blue water, winding cobbled streets, tear drop-shaped olives and temperatures reaching 27°C (80°F), the Greek islands are perfect for a European summer beach break.

If you're visiting Athens and feel like an island break but only have one or two days to spare, the **Argosaronic 281** offers the perfect opportunity for a rejuvenating getaway. Being just 40 minutes by hydrofoil from Piraeus means that it's close enough to pop over to for lunch and be back by evening. It's a world away from the fumes and angst of Athens, with horse-drawn carriages and pretty neo-classical buildings harking back to its days as Greece's first capital after the War of Independence (for just a year). The biggest island of the Argosaronic, measuring 85 square kilometres and with a population of 10,000, Aegina is centered around a pleasantly bustling town full of tavernas and cafés overlooking the main harbour.

Not to be missed, 12 kilometres east of Aegina Town, is the intricate and immaculately preserved fifth-century BC Temple of Aphaia, a local goddess, later identified with Athena. En route are the Monastery of St Nektarios and the island's abandoned, atmospheric medieval capital, Paleohora. The best spots for a swim are Marathona or Aeginitsa on the west coast, and Kleidi and Keri near the southern village of Perdika – an ideal place for a seaside lunch.

Picture-perfect (and car-free) **Hydra 282** is just 90 minutes by hydrofoil from the port of Piraeus. The distinctive neoclassical stone mansions of Hydra Town rise above the pretty port, where cafés teem with customers, and donkeys await their next expedition along cobbled lanes. Hydra is twice the size of neighbouring Spetses but has an even smaller population of around 3,000.

For spectacular sea views, follow Boundouri, a pebbly path winding upwards from the port to the fishing village of Kamini. Alternatively, climb the mountain from town to the Monastery of Profitis Ilias, the adjacent Convent of St Efpraxia and the nearby uninhabited Monastery of St Triada – views from the top make up for the one-hour trek.

Mandraki and Vlichos are the best beaches near the main harbour, but for more secluded spots, head to Bisti and Agios Nikolaos on the west of the island or Limioniza in the south.

The island of **Crete**'s **283** most beautiful and atmospheric city – the western port of Chania – is essentially Venetian. Most wanderings will be spent in the old town, but a visit to the bustling covered market, which marks the boundary between the Venetian-Ottoman districts and the modern city, is worthwhile.

A warren of alleys leads down to the waterfront, dominated on the east by massive Venetian arsenals and the mosque of the Janissaries, and on the west by row upon row of taverna and café tables, where locals and tourists congregate. This inner port is embraced by the Naval Museum/fortress on one side, the Venetian lighthouse on the other.

On the main street, Halidon, the basilica of San Francisco contains the only remnants of the Minoan palace and Greco-Roman Kydonia you're likely to see. Exploring the backstreets will reveal attractive and original restaurants, bars, galleries, shops and hotels. Look for the restored Itz Hayyim Synagogue among them and seek out the less frequented Splantzia quarter with its minaret.

287: Lesbos

Chania makes a fine base for day trips to Akrotiri's monasteries, beyond Souda Bay, drives into the White Mountains, and the trek down the Samaria Gorge, or to the 50,000-square-metre Water Park Anopolis, at Anopolis, for wavepools and racetracks.

The most well-known of the verdant Ionian islands is **Corfu 284**, lying just off Albania, and a large enough island to contain an attractive unspoilt hinterland behind the stretches of package resorts thrown up in the 1960s.

Corfu town is a bustling capital, close to the airport and ferries for the mainland and Italy. It comprises historic quarters squeezed between forts constructed by various invaders who have occupied the island over the last millennium – including the British, who came to Corfu in the 19th century.

The narrow alleyways of Campiello, Mandouki and a once-thriving Jewish neighbourhood jostle for space between a handful of churches and museums. Don't miss the icons in the cathedral or pre-Christian mosaics in the Byzantine Museum.

The island's Archaeological Museum is also impressive, with Neolithic and Ancient Greek finds. Evidence of British occupation includes the Palace of Saints Michael and George, where the High Commissioner lived, and a cemetery with ornate memorials.

If the southern Peloponnese appeals, then a good bet is the city of **Kalamata 285**, which stands between the Mediterranean and the endless silvery grove that produces Kalamata's famous tear drop olives.

For decades, it was chiefly known as the gateway to the western Mani, but since the mid 1990s there have been many reasons to linger. First is the annual International Dance Festival held in the third week of July. Most performances take place in the courtyard theatre of the medieval castle built by French Crusaders on Mycenaean foundations. The castle overlooks the old town with its elegant neoclassical buildings, lively main square and tempting, traditional food shops.

The Archaeological Museum conjures up a civilisation at perennial odds with its aggressive neighbour, Sparta, while the Folklore Museum depicts Kalamata's gentility two

centuries ago and its declaration of independence from the Ottomans in 1821, two days before the rest of Greece.

The town's long, clean beach lined with medium-sized hotels and good tavernas could delay your departure for the treks and towers of the Mani or a trip to explore Ancient Messene. The site, 31 kilometres north of Kalamata on Mount Ithomi, is one of the most impressive in the Peloponnese. On-going excavations have laid bare the major buildings of this fourth-century BC city and dozens of beautiful sculptures.

The book and film connection, courtesy of Louis de Bernières and *Captain Corelli's Mandolin*, has placed **Kefalonia 286** firmly on the holiday map, and there is lots to like here. This is a big, green island with the bluest water in the Ionian, lots of beaches and dramatic mountain scenery (some of the coastal drives, with steep drops and hairpin bends, are not for nervous passengers). Kefalonia is only 19 kilometres from the mainland, with several ferries daily from the east coast ports of Sami and Poros to Killini on the west coast of the Peloponnese.

Fiskardo, in the north, is a strong contender for the 'prettiest village' title, but some may find it just a bit too prettified. Those who like their fishing villages a bit more authentic may prefer Assos, on the west coast – it has the requisite tavernas under plane trees and there's an adequate beach with clean water right beside the quay. Motor boats can be rented in both villages.

The sights that most visitors remember longest are from the natural world. Deep within Kefalonia's limestone core, deep grottos have been carved out by aeons of winter rains. Many are off-limits to casual visitors, but the boat trip through the Melissani Cave, where a

deep turquoise pool some 200 metres long is lit by sunlight entering through the gap where the cavern's roof caved in during the 1953 earthquake, is unforgettable.

Boasting top brands of ouzo and olive oil alongside impressive antiquities and Europe's only petrified forest, **Lesbos 287** (Lesvos in Greek) has managed to achieve a good balance between a self-sufficient economy and a successful tourist industry. Mytilene, the capital, may be a bustling university town but it also accommodates a Hellenistic theatre, a Roman aqueduct and a massive Roman/Venetian castle. Go north to Molyvos and you'll find pure elegance: the town's red-tiled roofs spill down from the lofty Byzantine/Venetian castle to the harbour below; it's a stroller's paradise of cobbled streets with ancient fountains, a covered market and waterside cafés. Not far away, Orpheus's head and lyre are said to have washed up on the shore, giving Lesvians a special gift for music and poetry.

Of course, Lesbos's main claim to fame is the fact that the poetess Sappho came from the island – from the small west coast village of Eresos, now a popular lesbian venue. Close to Eresos is the petrified forest, created by volcanic action 20 million years ago, with fantastically colourful tree trunks up to 20 metres long. A drive around pine-covered Mount Olympus will land you in the faded grandeur of Plomari, olive oil hub and origin of the country's most famous ouzo brand.

Narrow, mountainous **Kos 288**, the second-largest island in the Dodecanese, is a heady mix of fascinating antiquity and mass tourism. Hippocrates, father of scientific medicine, was born here in the fifth century BC.

The remains of the Asklepion complex, built after his death as both treatment and research centre, is the island's premier ancient site. Kos town is full of Hellenistic and Roman remains and has its fair share of Italianate public buildings (they were in use from 1912 to 1943).

Still dominating the harbour is the castle of the Knights of St John, built in the 14th century as the crusaders' riposte to Ottoman aggression. Opposite its entrance is the so-called Hippocrates plane tree, under which the master was said to teach. Unlikely – it's old but not that old.

For the most picturesque inland villages drive up the forested slopes of Mount Dikeos in the area known as Asfendiou. A small winding road leads up as far as Zia (it's overrun by tour buses for sunset views). The best and least-developed beaches are on the little neck of land on the south coast near Antimahia. For a dramatic contrast, visit neighbouring Nisyros, a volcanic island where you can walk on lava.

Wildly off the beaten track, **Limnos 289** Greece's eighth largest island, opposite the entrance to the Dardanelles, offers a rare glimpse of Aegean life barely touched by tourism. The main town, Myrina, straddles a promontory of black volcanic rock encircled by the crenellated walls of a Byzantine Italian-Turkish fortress. From here, you have a good view of Myrina's two waterfronts: Romeikos Yialos or Greek Beach, with tavernas, neo-classical houses and the Archaeological Museum lined up along a strip of ochre shingle; and Tourkikos Yialos, where the buildings are humbler and the sand finer. The fishing port with its wall-to-wall taverna tables and the ferry landing are on this side.

The rest of the island is a peaceful blend of rolling wheat fields, vineyards, open bays, well-camouflaged air force bases, and shallow lakes. Moudros, at the back of the biggest bay, saw the launching of Churchill's disastrous Gallipoli campaign in 1915. East of it, at Poliochni, lie the ruins of what may be Europe's first city, dating back to the fifth millennium BC. There is little left of the sanctuary of the pre-Olympian Kabeiroi to the north, but don't miss Hephaistia and its elegant, newly restored Greco-Roman theatre. Limnos's beaches are not world-class but they're not mobbed either. From Limnos you can board a boat to Samothrace, Lesbos and Agios Efstratios.

Mykonos 290 has a lot of the things you expect from a small Cycladic island: sandy beaches, clean water, scuba diving, photogenic windmills, a pretty whitewashed *hora* (capital) – but the real magnet is its nightlife.

Mykonos may be busy and expensive but it does have style. Once considered an exclusively gay resort, this is no longer the case. Dress the part and wander down to Little Venice at sunset, stop for a drink in one of the evocative waterfront bars, drop into the nearby art galleries, fashion shops or jewellery stores. Maybe take dinner near the port and then head to the nearby clubs and discos or, for a bit more sophistication, try some of the bars around Enaplon Dinameon like Aroma or Celebrities.

By day, the hora is a delightful cluster of sparkling white houses and alleys, full of little churches and chapels, with colour provided by bushes of bougainvillea and hibiscus.

In the town's Archaeological Museum you'll find pottery from neighbouring Delos, a good reminder that you should take an excursion to the most important ancient site in the Cyclades, birthplace of the divine twins Apollo and Artemis.

291-299

Where the hell is it?

291 *Altai*

The Altai region isn't a nation at all, but a general name for an expansive mountainous region that straddles Russia's Altai Republic and Altai Krai, Western Mongolia, China and Kazakhstan. 'Altai' means 'Mountains of Gold' and the region is notable for its wildlife (bear, lynx, glutton, Siberian stag and even reindeer and snow leopard above the tree line) and ancient nomadic tribal traditions, including eagle hunting and playing horseback rugby with live sheep.

Can I go there? Altai is a popular destination for fans of yaks and yurts; several adventure tour operators go there for the annual Eagle Festival in Western Mongolia. Adventure tour firm Explore (0845 013 1539, www.explore.co.uk) offers trips that take in the festival.

292 *Nouakchott*

Nouakchott is the capital of Mauritania, one of the least-visited countries on the planet despite its proximity to Morocco and, indeed, Europe. On the fringes of the Sahara desert (and only a camel's spitting distance from the disputed region of Western Sahara), this forgotten city is often under a layer of sand.

Can I go there? Yes, there are flights from Casablanca, Morocco. Mountain Kingdoms (01453 844400, www.mountainkingdoms.com) offers trips to Mauritania that take in Nouakchott.

293 *Suriname*

Suriname is one of the Guyanas (the other two are French Guyane and Guyana, formerly British Guyana), situated on the north-eastern coast of South America. The British gave the country to the Dutch in the 1667 Treaty of Breda in exchange for New York. Though the capital, Paramaribo, is rough round the edges, most of the danger lies in the extensive jungles, with wild cats, Howler monkeys, tarantulas, termites, crocodiles, piranhas, anacondas and boa constrictors all calling it home.

Can I go there? Yes. KLM flies direct to Paramaribo from Schiphol in Amsterdam. And Latin American specialist tour operator Last Frontiers (01296 653000, www.last frontiers.com) can organise tailor-made holidays there.

294 *Nagorno-Karabakh*

Nagorno-Karabakh is in the South Caucasus, between Lower Karabakh and Zangezur (if you've heard of them). Though legally part of Azerbaijan, most of Nagorno-Karabakh is de facto governed by the internationally unrecognised Nagorno-Karabakh Republic. Since 1988 there has been a state of war between NK and Azerbaijan, with Chechens, Ukrainian and Russian mercenaries and Afghan mujahideen helping out. The population of NK detests that of Azerbaijan, and vice versa.

Can I go there? Mmm, no. At the time of going to print there was a ceasefire and flights planned between the Armenian capital, Yerevan, and the air base at Stepanakert, capital of NK. The FCO was advising against all travel to Nagorno-Karabakh and the military occupied area surrounding it, especially as some areas may be heavily landmined.

295 *Ouagadougou*

Ouagadougou is the capital of Burkina Faso in West Africa. Its name is often shortened to Ouaga – but not because it sounds funny; rather, because the name means 'where people get honour and respect'. It's a buzzing cultural and commercial hub, and hosts one of Africa's most important TV and film festivals (see www.fespaco.bf). It's a hot city – temperatures during the months of April and May can reach 45°C.

Can I go there? Yes. Ouagadougou has an international airport, rail links to Abidjan in Côte d'Ivoire and to Kaya in Burkina, and a highway to Niamey, Niger. Edgy travel firm Wild Frontiers (020 7736 3968, www.wild frontiers.co.uk) does holidays to Mali and Burkina Faso.

296 *Funafuti*

Turn right at the Marshall Islands and you'll reach Funafuti. Not much help, is it? Funafuti, the capital of Tuvalu, is one of the many small atolls that lie in the huge swathe of ocean between Australia and Polynesia. Like most of the others, Funafuti looks like a paradisiacal cliché, but Tuvalu has substance as well as sand and sun: in July 2009 the tiny South Pacific island nation announced it wanted to be the first zero-carbon country, vowing to abandon fossil fuels and generate all of its energy from renewable sources by 2020.

Can I go there? Easily-ish, if you've got 30 hours or so and don't suffer from DVT. See the country's official tourism website www.timelesstuvalu.com for flight information.

297 *Tristan da Cunha*

Located in the South Atlantic, 1,750 miles from South Africa and 2,088 miles from South America, the volcanic archipelago of Tristan da Cunha's greatest claim to fame is as the 'world's remotest island'. Despite its Portuguese name, the archipelago is a dependency of the British overseas territory of St Helena, another lonely lump of rock 1,510 miles to the north. The island has one TV channel, limited health care and no airport; on the upside, it's a beautifully bleak outpost and, depending on the time of the year, you may see Rockhopper penguins or albatrosses on the beaches.

Can I go there? Yes, but you need approval from the Island Council. As many as nine ships visit the island during the southern summer. See www.tristandc.com for shipping schedules.

298 *Sana'a*

Sana'a is the capital of Yemen, which is on the Arabian Gulf to the south of Saudi Arabia. Famous for its multistoreyed houses – some built more than 400 years ago – Sana'a's Old City is a UNESCO World Heritage Site.

Can I go there? Possibly, though Yemen yo-yos on and off the insurance map because of terrorism-related news – keep an eye on the Foreign & Commonwealth's travel advice website (www.fco.gov.uk/travel). Steppes Travel (01285 880980, www.steppes travel.co.uk) does tours to the region.

299 *Nauru*

The Republic of Nauru lies in the Pacific Ocean, some 40 kilometres south of the equator, and is the world's smallest island nation and its third smallest country (the Vatican City and Monaco take first and second place respectively). It's survived occupation by Germany, Australia, New Zealand, the UK and Japan, becoming independent in 1968. The tiny island (around 21 square kilometres) became one of the world's wealthiest countries in the 1960s and '70s, through exportation of phosphate; however, the industry dwindled from the 1980s, leading Nauru to resort to less wholesome measures, such as becoming a tax haven (and consequently a hotspot for money launderers).

Despite there being fewer than 10,000 (mostly Micronesian) residents, there is a university campus on the island.

Can I go there? Yes. However, the only airline to fly there is Our Airline (previously Air Nauru; www.ourairline.com.au), which operates flights from Brisbane, Australia. For information on the island's two hotels, see www.discovernauru.com.

298: Sana'a

300-309

Once-in-a-lifetime blowouts

300 *Heli-skiing in Kamchatka*
🌲 🏃

You don't need to be a banker to fly halfway round the world to be dropped on a volcano – but it helps. The Kamchatka peninsula in Russia's far east is the destination of choice for those in search of unexplored terrain and breathtaking descents of up to 4,000 metres, which take you through remote hot springs and right down to the beach. Stay at the four-star Hotel Antarius in the Hot Spring Valley, then catch a Russian M18 helicopter to the edge of the volcano rim from where you have access to tree skiing, long steep couloirs and wide open bowls. In short, anything your little daredevil skier's heart might desire. Elemental Adventure (020 7836 3547, www.eaheliskiing.com) can sort you out with a comprehensive all-inclusive package (from €4,150), although visas can be a little tricky.

301 Slow boat to Antarctica

Nature documentaries steal the thunder from most of our travel experiences – David Attenborough gets three months to hang around looking at cheetahs so of course he gets the best shots – but nothing can take anything away from Antarctica. Remote, inhospitable, wild and white, it is – paradoxically – a natural wonderland, home to 17 types of penguin, albatrosses, pretty fur seals and evil leopard seals, and several species of whale and dolphin. A lot of cruise ships are big and fast – they carry 2,000 to 3,000 people from Ushuaia in Argentine Tierra del Fuego, whiz them down to the peninsula and then back again. But if you're going to blow a few grand anyway, why not double it and double your time down here?

Approximate cost *From around £3,100 for a 10-day trip to £6,000 for a 3-week odyssey that takes in the Falkland Islands and South Georgia. Airfare is extra. Contact Imaginative Traveller (www.imaginative-traveller.com/0845 077 8802).*

302 Overland through Africa

Yeah, we thought *Long Way Down* was a load of rhino s**t too, but that doesn't mean driving through Africa need be about boys' egos and entourages. Foley Specialist Vehicles hires out sturdy Land Rover Defenders from £6,000 for three months – which is probably how long you'll need to do anything serious in the planet's slowest moving, least asphalted, most frontier-hasslesome continent. And allow time to familiarise yourself with the car's innards before your trip, because you can be certain you'll break down. The rest of the cost will be mainly on visas, border bribes, local agents 'facilitating' entry and exit, fuel, food and insurance. You can choose your route, but whether you opt for one of the two coasts or bang through the heart of darkness, you'll pass through some of the world's edgiest nations. Angola, Sierra Leone, Chad, Sudan… you choose. Avoid Somalia, though, where even ships are sometimes kidnapped.

Approximate cost *Around £8,500 for a group jaunt, not including any flights you need to make to escape. Plan your route with Tracks for Africa (www.tracks4africa.com) or Foley Specialist Vehicles (01279 793500/www.foleyspecialistvehicles.co.uk).*

303 Space tourism

Follow in the footsteps of director James Cameron – and the fat bloke from the Backstreet Boys – and blast off into space. Richard Branson is currently extending his empire into the only territory as yet untouched by the Virgin brand, and his company will soon be promising to take you on a suborbital flight to the zero gravity height of around 52,000 feet, after a mere three days of flight preparation at its Mojave Desert Spaceport. Space X is another private space company with a fleet of spacecrafts, and the Dragon capsule is capable of sending up to seven people to any space station they might care to visit.

Approximate cost *Wildwings (0117 9658 333/ www.wildwings.co.uk) already offers a range of cosmic kicks, from a suborbital flight for £60,000 to an orbital flight for £13 million. The company is also putting together moon packages – estimated to cost a mere £50 million (return; one-way flights are unlikely to be available). See also Virgin Galactic (www.virgingalactic.com) and Space X (+1310 363 6000/www.spacex.com).*

304 Take the South Pacific by storm in a chartered yacht

With names like *Major Wager* and *Maverick II*, the $200,000-a-week price tag to hire a yacht shouldn't come as a complete surprise. Feeling generous? Take your guests and crew around the Cook or Solomon Islands, or around the dive sites of the Great Barrier Reef, along with a team of on-board staff who are more than happy to serve your dinner out on deck, in one of the staterooms, or even on the beach under the stars. Diving is the ideal daytime occupation, or just soak up the rays for that perfect $4,000-a-day tan.

Approximate cost *Around $30,000 per week for a 6-berth boat. Contact International Yacht Charter Group (0800 011 2492/www.internationalyacht chartergroup.com).*

305 Drive a supercar through Italy

Forget the mid-life crisis accusations, and take a Ferrari Spider, a Lamborghini Gallardo or a snazzy little red Maserati out for a spin. Red Travel tutors drivers and rents out these fuel-guzzling, carbon-cacking beauties for anything from a four-hour drive

307: Rent an island

along the iconic Mille Miglia Gran Turismo route, to an all-out, five-day Rome–Florence–Monte Carlo extravaganza. It'll even throw in dining (Michelin starred, naturally) and a stay at the impossibly opulent Rome Cavalieri hotel.

Approximate cost *From €850 per person for a 4-hour session; longer tours are considerably more. Visit www.red-travel.com, or call +39 011 6165 219.*

306 *Incredibly expensive India – by luxury train*

If you're after the royal treatment, you can't do much better than the Palace on Wheels, a luxury train tour across India that takes in Delhi, Jaipur, Jodhpur and Agra, among others, with carriages that once played host to rulers of the princely states of Rajputana and the Viceroy of British India. Relaunched in 1982, the train now has 14 deluxe saloons with all mod-cons, and restaurants serving European as well as Indian cuisine. Imperial India is still very much in evidence, however, and not just in the opulent decor; a personal attendant or 'Khidmatgar' is always on hand to cater to your travel needs.

Approximate cost *$3,000-$4,000 for an 8-day ride. Contact Luxury Trains of India (020 3051 6851/www.luxurytrainsofindia.com).*

307 *Rent an island*

Despite the economic downturn, there's one area of the property market where business is booming: there are literally hundreds of private islands all over the world just waiting to be snapped up by anyone with a few thousand to spare. The modest little Ile de Patiras in the Gironde in France could be yours for just €620 per week, complete with 19th-century renovated vineyard estate and, of course, a private beach. Or choose a week on Musha Cay in the Bahamas, where up to 20 guests can enjoy exclusive access to tropical vegetation, white sandy beaches and the services of a live-on staff of 30 for a slightly awe-inspiring $325,000 per week.

Approximate cost *Surprisingly, renting an island doesn't have to break the bank, with prices starting at $84 per week for an admittedly slightly diminutive 50 acre-island. Contact Private Islands Online (+1 647 477 5581/ www.privateislandsonline.com).*

308 Live underwater

The Poseidon Resort in Fiji takes holidaying to the next level, with luxury suites at 40 feet under the sea. Futuristic-looking pods allow you to look out on the marine landscape, with a lagoon and reef teeming with underwater critters, while a button lets you release food to attract fish, James Bond villain-style. Interiors are all marble, leather and fine fabrics, and the largest suite – coming in at 1,000 square feet – is decked out to look like Jules Verne's fictional submarine. The resort itself is an underwater playground, and you can submerge yourself while watching a movie in the cinema, dining or drinking, or even getting hitched in the underwater chapel.
Approximate cost *A cool $15,000 per person for 7 days on Poseidon Mystery Island, including 2 days underwater. See www.poseidonresorts.com.*

309 Polar bear hunt, Spitsbergen

Snowmobile south through mountain passes to the fjord area of Van Mijenfjorden – during the 72-kilometre journey, you may encounter high-arctic reindeer, arctic fox and ptarmigan – to reach the remote east coast, where the land collides with pack ice and the sea. This is polar bear country, and with this fearsome predator in charge, you are now entirely dependent on your equipment, your guide's knowledge and experience – and your snow-chilled balls. Arrive at base camp in a location sheltered from the wind and the elements but still close to the polar bears. Depending on weather and distances, you'll trek, ski and/or snowmobile, staking out varied vantage points to observe the bears. During this season, females and cubs are emerging from hibernation, while lone males, thin from the long winter, hunt and track prey. Spitsbergen is the last protected natural polar bear habitat, and with a bear population of 4,500, sightings are highly likely.
Approximate cost *$13,995 per person. Departures in March and April. Contact Abercrombie & Kent (0845 618 2207/ www.akextremeadventures.co.uk).*

310-319
Mexico on the beach

310 Acapulco

Cancún may have the mass market and the miles of perfect white sand, but Acapulco has a certain retro-chic appeal. On the southwest Pacific coast and featured in countless films, songs, ads and Mexican soap operas, the resort oozes glamour, sex and fun, and remains popular with all generations. Check out the opulent Hotel Pierre Marques, built by Jean Paul Getty in the 1950s, the mask collection at Casa de la Máscara, the pretty town square (or Zócalo) and, above all, La Quebrada – the jagged cliffs where valiant cliff divers perform one of the world's most famous dive shows.

Stay at Boca Chica in the vibrant Caleta area, a walk away from a lovely beach cove. The exterior is 1950s, but the refurbished interior curated by Mexican artist Claudia Fernández is sophisticated and contemporary. The 30 rooms and six suites come with hammock, outdoor living room and private garden; amenities include Dr Bronner bath products, wireless internet and 24-hour room service.
Boca Chica *+52 744 483 6741/ www.bocachicahotel.com.*

311 Cancún

If you can summon the courage to face the beer-chugging spring-breakers and nearly four million sun-seeking visitors who arrive every year, you will discover a city that unabashedly revels in its party reputation and more than lives up to the hype. Spend days on the Laguna Nichupte, a protected area perfect for watersports, and nights indulging in the hedonistic mix of beach clubs and bars. The nearby Mayan settlement site El Rey provides a cultural retreat.

Resorts and cheap hotels abound but the Casa Turquesa, with 29 suites, is a boutique hotel with a sense of tranquillity you might not find elsewhere. Some rooms have private jacuzzis and terraces with ocean views.

Casa Turquesa *+52 998 193 2260/ www.casaturquesa.com.*

312 *Tulum, Riviera Maya*

Combine all the pleasures of a beach break with the opportunity to visit Tulum, a well-preserved Mayan walled city that sits atop 12-metre-high cliffs. The Riviera Maya – the stretch of Caribbean coast between Cancún and Tulum – has plenty of boutique hotels as well as all-inclusives. Esencia, 20 minutes south of Playa del Carme and 20 minutes north of Tulum, is a 50-acre private estate, with a gorgeous beachfront, two pools, spa and a great restaurant; once the beachside retreat of an Italian duchess, it still exudes heaps of class.

The area is also close to the Belize Barrier Reef, the world's second longest reef system.

Esencia *+52 984 873 4835/www.hotelesencia.com.*

313 *Bahia de San Carlos*

Lying in the Sonora Bay, and nestled between the Sonoran desert and mountains on one side and the dark blue Sea of Cortez on the other, this quiet harbour resort is home to only a few thousand people. The natural lagoon is ideal for snorkelling, fishing or sailing, or head up into the Bacochibampo Mountains for an unrivalled view of the town below.

The Paradiso Resort Mexico is supremely tranquil, despite being only a ten-minute drive from downtown San Carlos. Look out from your rustic room on to either a sea or lagoon vista.

Paradiso Resort Mexico *+52 622 225 2100/ www.paradisoresortmexico.com.*

314 *Punta Mita*

Just 40 minutes north of the popular Puerto Vallarta tourist resort, Punta Mita still remains what might be described as a picturesque fishing village. Real estate is selling fast, however, so don't wait too long to enjoy the pristine beaches and lush surrounding jungles. There are golf courses and spas on hand to remind you this is a luxury holiday rather than a rural retreat. A trip to the carefully preserved town of Viejo Vallerta provides a taste of nostalgia.

The Four Seasons hotel puts you right on the seafront, with an infinity pool that stretches out to the sea and a restaurant that cooks up the spanking fresh catch of the day on a *mesquite*

312: Esencia, Riviera Maya

grill. Tile-roofed Mexican-style *casitas*, all with an ocean view, complete the picture.
Four Seasons *+52 329 291 6000/ www.fourseasons.com/puntamita.*

315 *Punta Chivato*

Located between the coastal cities of Santa Rosalia and Mulege, Baja California's Punta Chivato attracts a large number of North American expats who come here for the unspoilt beaches and warm, crystal-clear waters of the Sea of Cortez. Nearby Santa Ines Bay is home to a wealth of ocean wildlife, including whales, and its calm conditions make it an ideal spot for diving, snorkelling and other watersports. Head inland for desert hikes and long walks into the surrounding untouched countryside.

A stay at the remote Posada de las Flores Resort – a beautiful adobe-coloured cluster of cosy villas with a desert garden of cacti and a lovely pool – offers total seclusion (the place can only be reached via an unpaved, 18-kilometre dirt track). Start the day with a breakfast of homemade bread before enjoying the beauty of the natural surroundings.
Posada de las Flores Resort *+52 55 8421 9606/ www.posadadelasflores.com.*

316 *Costalegre*

Jalisco's beautiful 'Happy Coast' stretches for more than 200 kilometres south from Puerto Vallerta to the border with Colima. However, the white sand backed by lush green mountain ranges, and the occasional banana plantation, is accessible only to guests at the luxury beach resorts, or those who fancy themselves strong enough swimmers to make it directly from the sea.

Las Alamandas – owned by Isabel Goldsmith, daughter of the late Sir James Goldsmith – is an intimate retreat, possessing no fewer than 1,200 acres of privately owned paradise, complete with exotic trees, palms, flowers, wild birds and a total of four beaches. There's a kids' club and a rooftop restaurant – one of two where organic, fresh produce is cooked up.
Las Alamandas *+52 322 285 5500/ www.alamandas.com.*

317 *San José del Cabo*

The Cabos (as in capes) on the southern tip of Baja California are dominated by American-style fun and games, and the resort town of

314: Punta Mita Four Seasons, Mexico

Cabo San Lucas is awash with burger joints, and party cruises that sail out into the bay at dusk. In contrast, San José del Cabo has a more laid-back atmosphere, in keeping with the pretty colonial architecture, leafy plazas and cobblestone streets. It's also a great base for deep-sea fishing and diving, or for setting out on the epic drive up Carreterra 1 towards Tijuan and San Diego.

Casa Natalia is a 'European-style' boutique hotel for those who prefer a more personal touch to the noise and activities of the chain hotels. Rooms are cool but cosy and the pool, though petite, is lovely to sit around during the siesta hour. The alfresco restaurant, Mi Cocina, serves 'Mexicarranean' fusions such as salmon marinated in tequila and lamb with charred *chile poblamo*.

Casa Natalia *+52 624 146 7100/ www.casanatalia.com.*

318 *Ensenada*

This busy and vibrant port destination is a popular spot for cruise ship passengers, who may find themselves wishing they didn't have to get back on the boat. The Bodegas de Santo Tomas is just south of the town, and offers tours and tasting of some of Baja's finest wines. The small but lively 'party district' clusters around the legendary Hussong's Cantina on the Avenida Lopez Mateos, while the giant gold sculptures of the heads of three national heroes – Juarez, Hidalgo and Carranza – in the main plaza are alone worth the stop-off.

It doesn't get much more exclusive than the Casa de los Siete Patios, with just seven villas (as the name makes clear), all overlooking a Mykonos blue pool and equally blue Pacific, and accompanied by a luxury spa. The decor incorporates antique Persian rugs and bronze sculptures, while unusual touches include a croquet lawn and an antique carrousel.

Casa de los Siete Patios *+52 858 414 4825/ www.casadelossietepatios.com*

319 *Puerto Escondido*

Puerto Escondido – 'the undiscovered port' – has managed to retain much of its fishing village character, despite being discovered

317: San José del Cabo

by the Western hippie community in the 1970s. Playa Marinero is the most popular beach, shaded by palm trees and lapped by gentle waves. Surfers head to the larger Playa Zicatela, however, which plays host to an international surfing festival at the end of November, when the town comes alive for a real Mexican fiesta. The Puerto is also a good base for expeditions to nearby freshwater lagoons such as Laguna Manialtpec.

Villas Carrizalillo is perched on the cliffs for maximum ocean-viewing opportunities, and right on the Playa Carrizalillo, another great beach for surfing, or simply lazing in the sun. There are 12 individually named villas to choose from, each with their own kitchen, which you can opt to ignore in favour of the competent rooftop restaurant.

Villas Carrizalillo *+52 954 582 1735/ www.villascarrizalillo.com.*

Ideas from the expert

320-329

Tom Barber, Director of Original Travel, suggests ten exciting short breaks.

Eight bank holidays, 52 weekends, occasional days off, and the odd sickie here and there; add up all those small days and you get a lot of mini holidays – if you know where to go and how to get there. Travel firm Original Travel coined the term 'Big Short Break' for those two-three day trips where we pack in as much as possible. Here Tom Barber shares his wisdom:

320 The UK's North East isn't necessarily top of most people's lists for a suitable short break destination, but the wealth of attractions in a relatively small space is a winner. Base yourself at Seaham Hall (+44 1915 161400, www.seaham-hall.co.uk), just south of Sunderland, and take time to wander the cobbled streets of Durham with its monumental cathedral. Next stop should be Lindisfarne or Holy Island up the coast in Northumberland. (Make sure to check the tide charts as the island is cut off at high tide.) On the way back check out Alnwick and Bamburgh Castles; the former has a starring role in the Harry Potter movies, while the latter looms over a beautiful white sand beach.

321 Britain's best city? Edinburgh is certainly in the running. With wonderful museums and galleries, shopping galore, elegant vistas and façades and the countryside never more than a short drive away, the Scottish capital is a perfect city break. Stay at the small but perfectly formed Ardmor House (0131 554 4944, www.ardmorhouse.com) on the road out towards Leith. There are only five bedrooms so it's necessary to book several months in advance, particularly in Festival and Fringe season.

322 North Norfolk has one of the most beautiful and unspoilt stretches of coastline anywhere in Britain, and – crucially – it's statistically less likely to be wet in summer than its west coast rivals. Highlights include the vast low tide expanses of Holkham Beach (which featured in Shakespeare in Love), bird sanctuaries, picture-perfect brick and flint villages and delicious seafood. The place to be seen is Burnham Market, full of boutiques and with an excellent coach house hotel, the Hoste Arms (01328 738777, www.hostearms.co.uk); or you can stay right by Holkham Beach at the Victoria Inn (01328 711008, www.holkham. co.uk/victoria), which is within walking distance of Holkham Hall itself, complete with staggering art collection.

323 If you can tear yourself away from Croatia's beautiful medieval city of Dubrovnik, the crystal clear waters around the nearby Elaphiti Islands are ripe for exploration by sea kayak. The islands, forming part of the Dalmatian Coast, run in a chain parallel to the mainland and boast an ideal sea kayaking environment, with inlets, caves and harbours, as well as restaurants serving delicious fresh seafood. Sea kayaking is a serene way to explore and, with the help of a guide, it's very easy to learn. Stay on the island of Lopud at the Villa Vilina (+385 20 759 333, www.villa-vilina.hr).

324 Leave the UK at the crack of dawn on a Friday morning, and that same afternoon experience the thrill of dog-sledding through the snow-covered forests of Swedish Lapland. Lead your team of eager huskies, staying two nights in comfortable woodland cabins each night and eating traditional Swedish delicacies such as reindeer stew with cloudberries. Then stay at the remarkable Ice Hotel (00 46 980 66 800, www.icehotel.com), where guests sleep on reindeer skin-covered mattresses on ice beds. Swedish Lapland is one of the best places in the world to see the Northern Lights.

325 Under four hours away, Marrakech is quite simply the most exotic destination in easy reach of the UK. Spend a day meandering through the colourful kasbah, medina and souqs, stay at the charming Riad de L'Orangerie (www.riadorangeraie. com) and then spend a night or two in the nearby High Atlas Mountains – particularly advisable in the hot summer months. I recommend a day's trekking with an experienced guide through walnut groves

and taking in the incredible valley views before spending the night at the wonderful Kasbah Toubkal (+33 5 4905 0135, www.kasbahdutoubkal.com).

326 Gozo is a tiny satellite island off the north-western corner of Malta. It at first seems a staunchly traditional island, and every summer weekend sees one village or other celebrating their patron saint's festival in traditions unchanged since the middle ages. But there's more to the island than nostalgia. It offers some of the finest snorkelling and diving opportunities in the Mediterranean, an excellent climate and, in the Kempinski San Lawrenz hotel (+356 2211 0000, www. kempinski-gozo.com), the tiny 25-square-mile island now has the biggest Ayurvedic spa hotel in Western Europe.

327 The south-westernmost tip of both Portugal and Europe has escaped over-development thanks to the protection of the Costa Vicentina Natural Park, which happens to contain some of the best surfing beaches in Europe. Just minutes from two of these beaches is the Monte Velho Nature Resort (+351 96 600 79 50, www.wonderfulland.com, montevelho). There's a great local surf school, while experienced surfers can rent equipment and take their pick of several reliable beach breaks. Once you've 'hung ten', you can just relax on the (often deserted) sandy beaches. Back at Monte Velho,

options include donkey-trekking, hiking and mountain biking in the peaceful surroundings, or simply chill out in a hammock and admire the view.

328 Away from the immaculate five-star hotels on the Muscat coast (we recommend the Chedi, +968 2452 4400, www.ghmhotels.com), Oman splits neatly into three categories: mountains, deserts and coastline – a mix of which makes for a memorable safari in a comfortable 4x4 with a driver/guide. Explore Wadi Bani Awf, the awesome mountain pass through the Hajar Mountains, to the city of Nizwa; visit the famous fort at Nakhl; and spend a night in the dunes of the Wahiba Sands. Finally, head to the coast, where you can spend days relaxing on the wide, shaded deck of a dhow, with dolphins swimming alongside.

329 Facing the ocean, and with Table Mountain as a towering backdrop, Cape Town enjoys arguably the most spectacular natural setting of any city in the world. Our favourite boutique hotel in town is Four Rosmead (+27 0 21 480 38 10, www.fourrosmead.com). Just an hour's drive inland from Cape Town, at the heart of the Cape winelands, is the historic town of Franschhoek, the gastronomic capital of South Africa. The nearby vineyards produce some of the finest New World wines, best sampled on a tour.
■ **Original Travel** (020 7978 7333/ www.originaltravel.co.uk).

328: Chedi hotel, Oman

330-337 *Christmas packages*

330 *Lapland's Northern Lights*

☼ 👪 🏠

If you've a yearning to see Father Christmas or the Northern Lights, then head for Luosto, an unspoilt national park in Finnish Lapland. Here, night-time snowmobile safaris are the order of the, er, night. Night kicks in rather early here, but if you zip off at 6pm for a two-hour circuit covering about 15 kilometres, there's a pretty good chance of seeing the Northern Lights. Organise your ride with Pyha Safaris (+358 40 778 9106, www.renthousepyha.com) or with the hotel listed below.
Stay at *Scandic Luosto (+358 16 3667 400/ www.scandichotels.com/luosto).*

331 *Manhattan malls and falls*

▦

A snow-covered Christmas in New York is always likely, allowing you to combine a merry atmosphere with some indulgent shopping and buzzing city vibe. Choose between Fifth Avenue glam and downtown chic, and hit Nolita and the Meatpacking District to explore the city's latest sartorial offerings. The shops at Columbus Circle and Trump Tower malls are great one-stop shops, especially if you're pressed for time and need that last-minute gift.

If you're looking for a grander vision of the wintry scene, then book yourself a place on the 14-hour Niagara Falls Day Trip By Air (+1 702 648 5873, www.viator.com).
Stay at *Hotel Pennsylvania (+1 212 736 5000/ www.hotelpenn.com).*

332 *London's seasonal South Bank*

Of the many exotic Christmas markets that set up shop each year in the capital, the South Bank's German Market (www.christmas markets.com) – in situ from late November onwards – is worth a *'prost'* or two, whether you're after a sausage butty and mulled wine, silver jewellery or unusual glass ornaments for the Christmas tree. Minutes away from the market is the London Eye (0870 5000 600, www.londoneye.com), great for seeing the whole of London from a different perspective, whether it's a blue, crisp and even winter's day or there's a blizzard to ride up into.
Stay at *Park Plaza County Hall hotel (020 7021 1810/www.parkplaza.com/countyhall_london).*

333 *Festive Fife, Scotland*

♡

Christmas in Fife, Scotland, can guarantee you romance and relaxation, as well as some festive, malt-sipping merriment. Choose between distillery tours, cycling, coastal walks, trips to St Andrews or – if you're well greased up – watersports in Fife Harbour.
Stay at *Balbirnie Hotel in Fife (01592 610066/ www.balbirnie.co.uk).*

334: Christmas market, Graz, Austria

334 Grand Christmas in Graz, Austria
♡♙

The Franciscan Quarter Christmas in Graz market is good for everything from regional farm goodies to hot punch, and is sure to get you in the Christmas spirit. For the kids there's a merry-go-round and toy stalls. **Stay at** *Grand Weisler hotel (+43 0 316 70 660/www.hotelwiesler.com).*

335 Bah humbug: a Jesus-free Christmas in Libya

Libya can cater extremely well to those who don't or won't celebrate Christmas. It's also warm and surrounded by desert, so instead of mumbling hymns about kings of orient, you can feel like one – and if you don't fancy a camel ride, then go on a 4x4 excursion into the Sahara. You will be shown ancient petroglyphs and a granary castle of Nalut in a spectacular position atop an escarpment. Specialist tour firm One Life Adventure (0161 265 5799, www.onelifeadventure.co.uk) offers a range of itineraries. **Stay at** *Corinthia Hotel (+218 21 335 1990/www.corinthiahotels.com).*

336 A proper winter, in Iceland
£ ۞♡♙

Britain in winter time is cold, wet and windy but just not very snowy, or even that cold. Iceland's steamy Blue Lagoon (+354 420 8800, www.bluelagoon.com), open to the general public, is fed by mineral-rich heated sea-water, and is a good place to mingle with the locals, smearing yourself with white mud while you chat about how cheap everything is, at last. **Stay at** *Hotel Keflavik (+354 420 7000/ www.hotelkeflavik.is/en).*

337 Holy Holiday in Palestine

It's so corny, it's original. How many of your friends have spent Christmas in the place where it all started: Bethlehem? Palestine's history is on show as soon as you arrive and you can book tours to holy sites – including Manger Square and the Church of the Nativity, in the heart of the town – and to refugee camps. **Stay at** *Everest Hotel, on the top of the mountain of Beit Jala (+972 2 2742604/ www.palestinehotels.ps).*

338-342
On the road: five unforgettable US drives

Many people dream of driving Route 66, perhaps in a Mustang or some other classic American car. On a historical level it's a key journey, but today quite a lot of it simply doesn't exist, having been usurped by the mighty Interstate network. However, if you still have the American dream of the open road and the wind in your hair, then try these five US drives instead.

338 The Pacific coast road
۞♙

Known as the 'Oregon Coast Highway' in Oregon and the 'Pacific Coast Highway' in California, US101 runs most of the 1,500-mile length of the USA's west coast, passing through the states of Washington, Oregon and California and the cities of Portland, San Francisco, Los Angeles and San Diego en route. In California, when it diverts inland, take Highway 1 instead for spectacular views – particularly at Big Sur – and miracles of road engineering. For a shorter trip, Monterey to Los Angeles is the honeypot two-day stretch.

339 Highway 61: The Blues Highway
۞

Highway 61 runs 1,400 miles from New Orleans in Louisiana north to the city of Wyoming in Minnesota. Give or take a few meanders, it follows the course of the Mississippi River and passes through eight states: Louisiana, Mississippi, Tennessee, Arkansas, Missouri, Iowa, Wisconsin and Minnesota. The landscape varies from cotton fields to humid lowlands to steamy swamps. Historically, southerners travelled from their rural homeland up Highway 61 to find work in Memphis, Chicago and St Louis; they took their music, the blues, with them. Muddy Waters, BB King and Bessie Smith all migrated up 61 to play the northern cities. Music fans should stop by the Stax Museum of American Soul Music in Memphis (870 East McLemore Avenue, +1 901 946 2535,

342: Highway-50

www.soulsvilleusa.com) and the more modest Delta Blues Museum (1 Blues Alley, Clarksdale, +1 662 627 6820). An album to take for the ride is Bob Dylan's *Highway 61 Revisited*; he was born in Duluth, Minnesota, formerly on the highway before the route was changed.

340 *Blue Ridge Parkway*

The Shenandoah National Park in Virginia and the Great Smoky Mountains National Park in North Carolina are the natural wonders at, respectively, the northern and southern extremes of this 469-mile drive through old-style America – expect split-rail fences, creaking farmsteads and wide open vistas of both wilderness and grazing land. The Parkway, which skirts the Appalachian mountains, was built in the 1930s as a Depression-era public works project, and was the US's first, and ultimately longest, rural parkway. The route is famous for its abundant wildflowers – including rhododendrons and dogwoods, and dramatically wind-shaped trees high on the ridge. For more information, visit www.blueridgeparkway.org.

341 *Miami to Key West*

It's easy to get carried way on the 150-mile, four-hour trip from Miami to Key West and suddenly find yourself at the western tip. But the drive should be done slowly and calmly, and with stops. Some sections, notably the Seven Mile Bridge between mile markers 40 and 47, are gloriously scenic: there is a wonderful illusion that you're driving on water. Key Largo isn't the prettiest stop, but detour to the John Pennekamp Coral Reef State Park to see dolphins. The islands of Islamorada make up a 'quaint little drinking town with a fishing problem', according to local T-shirts. Key West has all the Hemingway heritage as well as a kicking gay scene.

342 *The Big One: Highway 50 from Washington DC to Sacramento*

If you want an all-in-one cross-country road, this is a fine east–west mega-drive. You'll need two to three weeks to do it even cursorily. Make time to see Chesapeake Bay and the Atlantic Ocean: US 50 begins in Ocean City and that is where the drive starts. Head through the capital, catching all the famed monuments as you cruise, and then go to Northern Virginia and the northern edge of the Shenandoah Valley; south-eastern Ohio, for undulating hills; Indiana and the George Rogers Clark National Historic Park; Illinois and the crossing of the Mississippi River; and on into the American

West through Missouri. By Kansas you'll start seeing old-school cowboys, and follow the Arkansas River through the Great Plains into the Rockies of Colorado. The road climbs to 11,312 feet as Highway 50 crosses the Continental Divide over the Monarch Pass. More canyons and big rocks come in Utah, and the sky opens up in Nevada, preparing you for sunshine and the Pacific coast in California.

343-352

Easy Africa

Despite its proximity to Europe – just 8.5 miles separate Tarifa in Spain from the Moroccan coast – Africa is far less popular with British and European travellers than faraway lands in the US, Latin America and Australasia. The reasons are complex, from the heat of the Sahara to the grim news from Zimbabwe, to famines and droughts, civil wars and crime. But the continent is vast and there are many fabulous and thrilling countries where tourism is easy and as safe as in any of the more obvious, mass-tourism destinations.

In **North Africa 343**, choose between Fes in Morocco and Leptis Magna in Libya. The former has a wonderful, labyrinthine medieval souk and, being far less touristy than Marrakech, is sometimes described as the 'real Morocco'. The city is famous for its Arabesque architecture, and the city's medina of Old Fes (Fes el Bali), a UNESCO World Heritage Site, is thought to be the world's largest contiguous car-free urban area. You'll probably want to get behind those glorious Arabesque façades: the recent conversion of many of the smarter traditional houses (riads) into hotels means you can recharge your batteries in luxurious comfort before heading out into the whirl of people, goods and overburdened donkeys thronging the centre. Fleewinter (020 7112 0019, www.fleewinter.co.uk) can arrange trips to Fes.

A trip to **Libya 344** should definitely take in Tripoli, with its world-class Jamahiriya Museum – one of the finest collections of classical art in the Mediterranean – and impressive medina. Out of town, see the rock carvings of Wadi Methkandoush, and Akakus, a mountain range known for its gorgeous red sand and extraordinary rock formations. There are Roman archaeological sites all over Libya but Leptis Magna is the best preserved Roman city in North Africa, with a stunning location on the shores of the Mediterranean. Kuoni (01306 747002, www.kuoni.co.uk) and Explore (0845 013 1537, www.explore.co.uk) offer tours to Libya.

In the **Sahara 345**, world music fans are already flocking to Mali for the annual Festival au Desert, a three-day celebration of song and dance (www.festival-au-desert.org) that takes place in Essakane. If you're after a real out-there experience, travel along the Niger River to Timbuktu and visit Dogon villages that have remained unchanged for centuries.

In West Africa, the Anglophone **Gambia 346** and its French-speaking neighbour Senegal (which is wrapped around the border of the Gambia like a glove round a finger) are popular repeat destinations for many holidaymakers. The Gambia is a great destination for a winter-sun holiday, and is good value for money. The country's small size and the friendliness of its people are strong draws, and visitors can choose between a blissful do-nothing-at-all beach holiday and exploring the culture. There are many tribes – the main ones are Mandinka, Wolof, Fula and Jola – and it's common to receive an invitation to visit a Gambian settlement or 'compound'.

Senegal 347, between Guinea-Bissau and Mauritania, is Africa's most westerly point. It boasts three mighty rivers, which provide plenty of fertile land and some shimmering coastal lagoons, and support a variety of waders and birds of prey as well as hyenas, monkeys, baboons, manatees and dolphins. The Gambia Experience (0845 330 2060, www. gambia.co.uk) and sister company the Senegal Experience (0845 330 2080, www.senegal.co.uk) have a 20-year track record in the region.

Ghana 348 is another great option. US president Obama chose it in July 2009 as the first African country worthy of a presidential visit, praising its democratic traditions since independence in 1957. Accra, the capital, is vibrant, swinging to the music of Highlife and the more recent hip-hop fusion Hiplife; it's more modern than many people expect (Time Out even publishes a *Visitors Guide* there). The interior is varied and ideal for voluntourists and adventure travellers: visit Ho and its game park to see kobs, duikers and baboons, go mountain biking to the villages of Biakpa and Amedzofe, and hike through the Kulugu canyons to the Mountain Paradise ecolodge (www.mountainparadise-biakpa.com). Visit www.responsibletravel.com for a range of trips.

You can see gorillas in the mist, hippos surfing the waves and whales in the same day on a holiday to **Gabon 349**. This small West African country on the Gulf of Guinea is blessed with some of the most diverse tropical forest in the world – ancient jungles straddling the equator that are believed to contain more than 8,000 plant species, 600 different types of bird and 20 species of primate. Outsiders and locals hope Gabon will become the 'Costa Rica of Africa', attracting wildlife and adventure tourists to its 13 new national parks: some 85 per cent of the country is covered in tropical forest, and away from the few small population hubs are savannahs, mangroves, lagoons and beaches. There are thought to be about 20,000 western lowland gorillas and 60,000 forest elephants – the largest population in Africa. Gabon trips can be booked through Steppes Travel (01285 880980, www.steppestravel.co.uk).

The archipelago of **Cabo Verde 350** is the thinking traveller's Canaries. The bone-white, empty beaches, soaring volcanoes and lush tropical vegetation on these ten islands were kept a secret for years (although Cabo Verde always attracted a few Portuguese holidaymakers, thanks to the colonial connection), but now the year-round sun and unique blend of African, Portuguese and Brazilian cultures is even attracting package tourists.

The archipelago – ten islands and eight islets – is located 604 kilometres off the coast of West Africa. Visit Sal, famous for its 350 days of sunshine, one of the most popular resort hubs thanks to the lovely beaches of Santa Maria; on Boa Vista you can climb stunning dunes and dive to see marine turtles, and explore the 'tropical Lisbon' of Sal Rei, with its cobbled streets. Santo Antão is developing rural tourism, great if you want to meet locals and get away from the beaches. Santiago, in the leeward island chain to the south, is best known as the island where Darwin made landfall during his epic *Beagle* voyage. Thomson (0871 231 4691, www.thomson.co.uk) goes to Cabo Verde.

For wildlife, southern Africa reigns supreme. **Namibia 351** is wonderful for lion-, cheetah-,

351: Namibia

rhino- and leopard-spotting, and has the world's highest dunes and second deepest canyon.

It's a country with huge geographical variety, containing a large part of the Kalahari Desert in the east of the country. In the north is the Etosha Pan, a verdant, game-rich area with a huge range of species. The Namib Desert and Skeleton Coast lie along the western seaboard, while the Caprivi Strip is a dramatic, 280-mile-long sliver of Namibia between Botswana on the south and Angola and Zambia to the north that provides access to the Zambezi and the habitat of the endangered Wild African Dog.

South Africa 352 offers the opportunity to see the Big Five (lion, leopard, elephant, buffalo and rhino), as well as the chance to sample excellent wines in the Cape regions of Stellenbosch, Paarl and Constantia.

Southern Africa specialists include Expert Africa (020 8232 9777, www.expertafrica.com) and Wild about Africa (020 8758 4717, www.wildaboutafrica.com). And if you fancy a self-drive safari, contact Safari Africa (01488 71140, www.safaridrive.com).

353-359
Irish idylls

353 *Literary Dublin*

Dublin groans under the weight of its history and culture. Even a brief stroll can take in the sites of the 1916 Independence uprising, with museums, churches and bullet-pocked civic buildings along the way. As the city of WB Yeats, James Joyce, Oscar Wilde and the Abbey Theatre, it's the undisputed literary capital of Ireland. Stay at the Dylan Hotel, which combines style and comfort, and has a restaurant featuring locally sourced specialities like wild wicklow venison saddle and St Maure goat's cheese. Join a literary pub crawl (www.dublinpubcrawl.com) to get the best out of the city.
Dylan Hotel *+353 1 660 3000/www.dylan.ie.*

354 *Connemara*

Adventure beckons on Ireland's stunning west coast: activities such as climbing, surfing, kayaking and even archery can all be pursued under the looming gaze of the country's deep-green mountains, dripping with rivers and lakes.

After all of that strenuous activity, you'll want a space to recuperate. Book into the family-run Delphi Mountain Resort, where you can indulge in a full-body massage followed by a meal in the restaurant; freshly caught local lobster should do the trick.
Delphi Mountain Resort Spa *+353 954 2208/ www.delphimountainresort.com.*

355 *Wild West Cork*

The crash of a humpback's tail as it shatters the ocean is one of nature's most extraordinary and thrilling sights. Some 24 species of whale and dolphin have been recorded in the waters off Cork; some are residents, while others come and go. For the best chance of spotting humpbacks, visit in September to November. Book with Whale Watch West Cork (+353 86 120 0027, www.whalewatchwestcork.com). Back in the foodie heaven of Cork City, book into Hayfield Manor, set in two acres of gardens and with superb restaurants; then head for the lovely and unpretentious English Market (www.corkenglishmarket.ie).
Hayfield Manor *+353 21 484 5900/ www.hayfieldmanor.ie.*

356 *Artsy Galway*

Galway is internationally recognised for its annual July arts festival (www.galwayartsfestival.com), when 150,000 people descend on the city for a celebration of theatre, music, comedy, literature and street art. It offers all the festive delights of its more famous Scottish cousin – the Edinburgh Festival – without being too overwhelming. Book ahead for Petra House B&B – owners Frank and Joan have cemented their reputation as two of the best hosts in Ireland, and they serve up a fabulous breakfast. Outside the city, dramatic seascapes, expansive mountain ranges and wild Atlantic winds make the region an outdoors classic.
Petra House B&B *+353 91 566580/ www.galway.net/pages/petra-house.*

357 *Aran Islands*

Situated to the west of County Galway, the three rugged, iconic Aran Islands boast huge skies and craggy cliffs battered by the Atlantic Ocean. Come here to experience traditional Irish culture and hear Gaelic; there are also a number of Iron Age forts in varying states of disrepair.

Stay at Inis Meain Restaurant & Suites, run by a native chef and his wife; the unusual stone-and-glass building was created by celebrated Irish architects Blacam & Meagher, and designed to reflect the islands' limestone landscape. **Inis Meain Restaurant & Suites** *+353 86 826 6026/www.inismeain.com.*

358 *Torrhead*

£ 0

Carved from ancient volcanic rock, the Torr Head peninsula is a dramatic example of Northern Ireland's sometimes extraordinary coastline; the Torr Scenic Road, whether cycled or driven, is a superb way to take in spectacular views of the Mull of Kintyre across the water in Scotland.

The tiny village of Cushenden, which is almost entirely owned by the National Trust, makes for a great base. It has a population of just 138 and its beaches are often completely deserted. Self-catering guests are made welcome at the Barnhouse. **Barnhouse** *+353 28 2176 1554/ www.drumkeeringuesthouse.com.*

359 *Sperrin Mountains*

The relatively unexplored Sperrin Mountains are Northern Ireland's largest, and the nearby rivers and lakes teem with life, offering the region's very best freshwater fishing. Cycling and other outdoor pursuits can be enjoyed in this officially designated Area of Outstanding Natural Beauty.

Derry is a bustling base from which to explore the mountains, and one of the finest examples of a walled city in Europe. The city's Abbey B&B is known for its warm and welcoming service. **Abbey B&B** *+353 28 7127 9000/ www.abbeyaccommodation.com.*

360-369
Ten UK campsites

360 Syke Farm Camping Site, Lake District, England

£ 0 ⚡ ⊙

017687 70222/www.lakedistrictcamping.co.uk/ campsites/northwest/syke_farm.htm).
The lovely views between the slopes of Place Fell and the shores of Ullswater make this one of the most scenic campsites in Britain. There are lots of walking routes and the site can help you arrange boating or riding trips. The invigorating mountain air and tranquil, dreamy valleys make it a perfect escape for frazzled city-dwellers.

361 Camusdarach, West Highlands, Scotland

£ ⚡ 0 ⊙

01687 450221/www.road-to-the-isles.org.uk/ camusdarach.html.
Miles of sandy dunes along the north-western coast of Scotland are the perfect escape from stuffy offices – and only a three-minute walk from this campsite. Set on a Victorian estate, the fields and dunes surrounding the site are home to a small flock of Hebridean sheep and chickens and a wealth of wildlife, including buzzards, rabbits and many interesting plants. The dramatic islands of Skye, Rhum, Eigg, Canna and Muck are all within easy reach, but book in advance to bag a berth at this popular spot.

362 Graig Wen, Snowdonia, Wales

£ 0 ⚡ ⊙

01341 250482/www.graigwen.co.uk.
Fish away the hours at Cregennan Lake in this wild location of lush green hills falling into the Mawddach Estuary. Inside Snowdonia National Park, this quiet site is sheltered by oak, birch and rowan trees and fringed by hillsides covered in heather and moss. For adventure, horseride along the beaches, sail the underground caverns or climb to the Arhog waterfalls of Cadair Idris.

363 North Morte Farm, Woolacombe, North Devon

£ ⚡ 0 🏕 ⊙

01271 870381/www.northmortefarm.co.uk.

If you fancy a cream tea and some country walks by the coast, this family-run farm is the ideal location. It's just 500 yards from Rockham Beach where you can explore rock pools on over two miles of golden sands, or take walks along the South West Coast Path; the picturesque village of Mortehoe is five minutes away, surrounded by an Area of Outstanding Natural Beauty.

364 Westermill Farm, Somerset

£ ۞ ۞

01643 831238/www.westermill.com.
For fresh, free-range produce, head to this secluded valley site in the centre of Exmoor National Park and camp next to a working farm in smoothly mown meadows beside the River Exe. Try the free-range lamb, pork and Aberdeen Angus beef from the local farm shop for lunch and then head off to do some fishing.

365 Roundhill, New Forest, Hampshire

£ ۞ ۩ ⌂ ۞

01590 624344/www.forestholidays.co.uk.
Head to the New Forest and get close to horses, donkeys, cattle and squirrels; you can even camp in the middle of the forest, where horses roam freely. The best way to explore is on foot or by bike (with several bike hire shops in close range); and if you want to head out of the forest, Beaulieu Car Museum is nearby.

366 Yurtcamp, Liverton, South Devon

£ ۞ ۞

01626 824666/www.yurtcamp.co.uk.
For something a bit wacky, stay in a yurt… in Wales. Set in 40 acres of Devonshire woodland, between Exeter and Plymouth, are 15 yurts, offering accommodation for up to six people. This site is minutes from Dartmoor and close to the beautiful English Riviera, with Blue Flag beaches in Dawlish, Teignmouth, Torquay and Paignton.

367 Braceland, Gloucestershire

£ ۞ ۩ ⌂ ۞

01594 833376/www.forestholidays.co.uk.
Set in the heart of the Forest of Dean, on the upper slopes of the Wye Valley, is this peaceful retreat surrounded by woodland. Forest walks such as the Sculpture Trail – trees interspersed with sculptures and works of art – can be enjoyed, as well as cycle routes, picnic sites and play areas for kids. If you're there around the May Bank Holiday, go to the annual cheese-rolling event on Coopers Hill.

368 St Ives Farm, St Ives, East Sussex

£ ۞ ۩ ⌂ ۞

01892 770213.

362: Graig Wen, Snowdonia, Wales

Hartfield village is where AA Milne penned his famous stories about Winnie the Pooh. The site, just five minutes' drive north of the village, is beside a picturesque fishing lake surrounded by farmland. Visit Hartfield to stock up on Pooh-related paraphernalia and buy a map that directs you to all the famous Pooh haunts such as 100-Acre Wood and Poohstick Bridge. But if this is all a bit too much, go for an amble into the Ashdown Forest and fish for carp and perch.

369 Hooks House Farm, North Yorkshire

£ ♋ ⚲ ☀

01947 880283/www.hookshousefarm.co.uk.
Enjoy the views of Robin Hood's Bay near Whitby from this friendly farm location. The dark, rocky beach with its sweeping bay calls out for bracing walks and exploration. The Yorkshire Moors are also within walking distance and you can cycle along the disused railway line from Scarborough to Whitby to see the busy fishing harbour.

370-379

From St Pancras International train terminal to...

Eurostar began operating fast trains from London Waterloo to Paris and Brussels in November 1994. In November 2007 the UK terminus moved to the capital's St Pancras station, and a fast new line through north Kent called High Speed One reduced journey times by an average of 23-25 minutes. St Pancras, served by trains from Paris, Brussels and Lille (as well as Luton, Derby and Sheffield), is only a short walk from Euston and King's Cross stations. At the time of writing there were reports of bids by German rail operator Deutsche Bahn and Dutch operator NedRail to offer routes from St Pancras to the Continent, which could open up even more routes. Belgium-bound readers should also note that a Eurostar ticket to Brussels covers onward national train travel to elsewhere in the country (including Bruges, Ghent and Antwerp), for no extra charge.

On a more general point, use the Deutsche Bahn website (www.bahn.co.uk) for searching European timetables; to make bookings on trains visit www.eurostar.com or www.raileurope.co.uk.

370 *Paris*

📱 ♡ ☺ ☕

It's almost unbelievable anyone still flies or ferries to France, when you can go by Eurostar for less than 60 quid. For that quick romantic getaway, a weekend in the city of love, especially in spring or autumn, still delivers in terms of candlelit bistros, afternoons in cafés and boulevardiering in the Marais. Get yourself in the mood by having some bubbly on board the train.
Route *London St Pancras–Paris Gare du Nord.*
Journey time *from 2hrs 15mins.*

371 *Cologne*

📱 ☺ ☕

Getting to Germany's liveliest city requires just a quick platform change in Brussels. Once there you can enjoy a cruise down the Rhine, see some modern art at the Museum Ludwig or simply take in the city's Romanesque architecture and towering cathedral, Germany's largest. The other advantage of taking the train? Cologne is known for being Europe's party city, so you need all the rest you can get on the way.
Route *London St Pancras–Bruxelles-Midi–Koln Hauptbahnhof (Cologne Central Station).*
Journey time *from 4hrs 41mins.*

372 *Ostend*

☺ 👫 ☀

From Britain to the Belgian beach with minimum hassle. Natives call Ostend the 'Queen of the Belgian seaside resorts', which is a rather long-winded way of saying that the Flemish town has some lovely sandy shores, a sweet old fishing harbour and pleasant coastal promenades.
Route *London St Pancras–Bruxelles-Midi–Ostend.*
Journey time *from 3hrs 41mins.*

373 *Avignon*

📱 ⚘

See the bridge that inspired the song, as well as the many other treasures of Avignon and the wider South of France area. Enjoy the changing scenery of France as you head south to lavender

370: Paris

country. A direct Eurostar service runs on Saturdays between July and September, but the rest of the year you need to change at Paris on to the high-speed TGV service, adding maybe half an hour more on to your travel. Go in July for the annual performing arts festival (www.festival-avignon.com).
Route *London St Pancras–Paris Gare du Nord–Avignon TGV.*
Journey time *from 5hrs 49mins.*

374 *Strasbourg*

Although not yet a direct route, this may still be one of the easiest flight-free journeys you'll encounter. At Paris (Gare du Nord) it's a mere 800-metre-switchover to the Gare de l'Est station, where you hop on to a TGV train. In Strasbourg, the city centre is minutes from the station, meaning all the more time to peruse the city's historic streets and Gothic spires, or even to stop for a bite at La Cloche à Fromage, the only all-cheese restaurant on the planet.
Route *London St Pancras–Paris Gare du Nord–Strasbourg.*
Journey time *from 5hrs 15mins.*

375 *Lille*

Got a day to spare, but feel like you've done Paris to death? Underappreciated Lille can be reached in less time than a football match. So you can easily make it for lunch in a brasserie, followed by an afternoon wandering La Piscine Museum of Art, and still have time to browse one of the many stores at the Euralille mega-mall.
Route *London St Pancras–Lille.*
Journey time *from 1hr 20mins.*

376 *Bordeaux*

Pack light for this one; the necessary change between north and south Paris is a good 30-minute metro ride, although if you book through Eurostar it will allow you plenty of transit time. Once en route to Bordeaux, relax with the knowledge that you'll soon have a good glass of local wine in your hand, to be drunk overlooking some magnificent Atlantic coastline, possibly while staying in one of Bordeaux's many châteaux.
Route *London St Pancras–Paris Gare du Nord–Bordeaux St-Jean.*
Journey time *from 6hrs 40mins.*

377 *Rheims*

Unless you're a teetotaler, it's hard not to find something to do in Rheims. The town is at the heart of champagne country, and visitors can tour *les grandes marques* – the headquarters of the famed champagne houses. You should also visit the famous cathedral of Notre-Dame de Rheims, former coronation spot of the French monarchy. The return journey is just long enough for the hangover to wear off.
Route *London St Pancras–Paris Gare du Nords–Rheims.*
Journey time *from 3hrs 43mins.*

378 *Brussels*

Gaze out of the train window as the nondescript French countryside morphs into Jacques Brel's mythically flat Flemish landscape as you near Brussels. The city has something for everyone: a well-established night scene for the party animal; Magritte's artwork for the creative;

and, for the power hungry, Europe's political centre. Quicker than a trip to Paris, and with much friendlier locals.

Route *London St Pancras–Bruxelles-Midi.*
Journey time *1hr 51mins.*

379 *Alps*

Eurostar's Ski Train service runs every winter between December and April, giving you more than enough time to hop on a train and hit the slopes. With three direct Alpine destinations to choose from, plus easy connections to a host of other ski resorts, this is an easy way to travel. Maximise your time on the piste by booking evening trains both ways.

Route *London St Pancras–Moûtiers/Aime-la-Plagne/Bourg-St-Maurice.*
Journey time *5hrs 30mins.*

380-389
Fabulous food festivals

380 *Galway International Oyster Festival, Ireland*

Shucking marvellous. Emerald hills, black-velvet Guinness and pale-grey oysters: Galway looks good even when it's raining, which is a good job since the foodie capital of Ireland isn't known for its dry spells. This four-day mollusc fiesta in September features food, drink, live music and the Guinness Irish Oyster Opening Championships – an assemblage of words evocative enough to get you salting and slurping.
www.galwayoysterfest.com.

381 *La Tomatina tomato festival, Bunyol, Valencia, Spain*

Chucking perfectly good food at your neighbour is the kind of thing you're only going to do with a glut, but that's OK – the Valencians have tomatoes to spare. On the last Wednesday of August, in the middle of a week of fiestas, almost 140 tons of tomatoes are trucked in for locals and visitors to throw at each other. The fight lasts an hour. Its origins are obscure, but if you've been picking soft red fruit all summer, the temptation to lob a few at a *compañero* must be pretty strong, and Valencia is a major tomato-growing region. You didn't know tomatoes were a fruit? One in the face for you then.
www.latomatina.org.

382 *Chianti classico festival, Greve, Italy*

Once the grapes have all been harvested, it's party time, and Italy's best-known wine region knows how to do that: this festival in September is just one of several post-picking wine festivals in Tuscany. There are wine tastings, local food product tastings, fireworks, concerts… and more wine tastings. But then, we Brits have the sour taste of years of wicker-wrapped rotgut in substandard pasta gaffs to wipe from our taste buds. And anyway, there's no such thing as too much good Chianti. Cin cin!
www.greve-in-chianti.com.

381: La Tomatina

383 Vegas Uncork'd, Las Vegas, USA

Gamblers need to eat; drag them away from the tables (not something Las Vegas generally likes to encourage) and they might even spend their ill-gotten gains on quality fuel for the next all-nighter. Which explains why so many high-end chefs – Joël Robuchon, Guy Savoy, Alain Ducasse, Daniel Boulud – have opened outlets in this high-rolling slab of the Nevada desert, and why this annual festival in May is as outré and extravagant as only a city-size gambling den could make it. There are workshops, discussions, tastings and dinners, and when you're sated there is always the option of trying your luck.
www.vegasuncorked.com.

384 Isle of Wight Garlic Festival

You wouldn't think this little island could provide enough garlic to keep 300 stalls and 20,000 people happy, but it turns out that garlic enhances everything else the island produces, from bread to ice-cream – as this August festival aims to prove. There's beer too, although they probably don't stick garlic in that. And there is also lots of live entertainment, from puppets to classic cars and live music. Bestival, however, it ain't: the 2009 headliner was Alvin Stardust.
www.garlic-festival.co.uk.

385 La Sagra del Cappero, Sicily

If you don't know your tondina from your nonpareille, this one-day festival on the Sicilian island of Salina (where *Il Postino* was shot) is an idyllic way to learn; the latter are the capers that come in a jar in Waitrose; the former are the organic kind that Sicilians grow, eat and, on the first Sunday of June, celebrate with folk music, street games and stalls serving everything you ever knew you could combine with capers and a fair few things you probably didn't: caper-stuffed cheeses, caper pâté, spaghetti with capers and tomato and caper salad. The festival may be short but there are also degustation dinners and wine tastings for several days leading up to it, so even the most fanatical caper-lover will

get their fix. It's like the Monty Python spam skit, only far, far more tasteful.

386 West Dean Chilli Fiesta, West Sussex, UK

This August festival boasts Latin music and Latin dance classes, but it's a safe bet that a fair number of the participants – and over 5,000 people generally attend – are just trying to distract themselves from the pain in their mouths. Sure, we all know that eating chillis produces endorphins, but when that natural high has to compete with the tongue-busting properties of, say, the Dorset naga, a home-grown version of a Bangladeshi chilli that's probably the world's hottest, then a bit of help is likely to be in order. Salsa, perhaps. Or morphine. Not that anyone's forced to snack on nagas: there are 300 types of chilli here, and some even come with food on the side.
www.westdean.org.uk.

387 Limassol (Lemesos) Wine Festival, Limassol, Cyprus

Commandaria may or may not be the world's oldest plonk, but the Cypriot dessert wine is certainly pretty venerable: it's been around for at least 4,000 years (Homer mentions it). Not that the much-disputed island rests on its laurels: Cyprus's wines may not crowd UK supermarket shelves, but that says more about our narrow drinking habits than about the wines. This fortnight-long festival in August/September, a-slosh with free drink, is a great place to try wines red and white, sweet and savoury, made from local grapes or blends with international varietals by artisans or big producers. There are also fireworks, songs and music from the local philharmonic orchestra, folk dances, comedy and magic shows.
www.limassolmunicipal.com.cy/wine.

388 Foire au Boudin, Mortagne-au-Perche, France

Every March, in the pulsing heart of *boudin noir* country, this world-famous dried-blood sausage gets its own celebration, complete with stalls for traders and artisan pudding-makers, tastings, and competitions to find the best black pudding – and the biggest black pudding eater. More than five kilometres of pudding are sold, which no doubt adds zest to the pig-squealing competition. Still, with over 100 stalls, every attendee has the opportunity to access their inner pig. And if the resemblance starts to bother you, there are other local products to try too. *www.foireauboudin.free.fr.*

389 *Maine Lobster Festival, USA*

America gets its claws into lobster season (July-August) in typically boisterous fashion, with piles of fresh-cooked seafood plus a crate race (how many can you run across before you fall into the freezing Atlantic?), cookery competition, arts and crafts, a parade and various gigs, mainly jazz, folk and blues. There are carnival rides and a Sea Princess competition, but if any of this feels over the top, bear in mind that the festival has been going for over 60 years, so they must be doing something right. Like serving lots and lots of freshly caught, just-boiled lobster. *www.mainelobsterfestival.com.*

390-399
New Zealand wonders

It's a long, long flight, but New Zealand is well worth it. Find yourself on a vast, deserted beach, 'lose' yourself in ancient rainforests, and reinvent yourself as an explorer scaling a snowy peak. Maori legends will add a layer of mystery to your visit to Aotearoa – the 'land of the long white cloud' – and after all the anticipation and adrenaline, you can kick back with giant green-lipped mussels harvested off the local rocks, and a bottle of classy sauvignon blanc from one of the country's vineyards.

390 *Fiords*

Milford Sound, Doubtful Sound, Manapouri… the evocative names for wild regions where snow-capped peaks plunge deep into fiords, mirrored perfectly in the clear blue water. The tranquillity is disturbed only by waterfalls raging over rocks from dizzying heights, exotic birds calling in the dense rainforest and dolphins breaking the surface. This is a walkers' wonderland and you'll want to spend as much of your time as

possible high up and in the open air, but do visit the underwater observatory to get a 360-degree view of life beneath the fiords. *www.fiordland.org.nz.*

391 *Beach*

Make the vibrant coastal town of Whitianga your base. First stop is Cathedral Cove (aka Te Whanganui-A-Hei) on the Coromandel pensinsula, unique for the giant, jagged arches of rock that interrupt the expanse of white sand. Pristine reefs and underwater caves make for some great diving. Decompress on Hot Water Beach, where you can dig into the sand to reveal hot spring water. *www.cathedralcove.co.nz or www.whitianga.co.nz.*

392 *Exploration*

The best way to visit the Bay of Islands is to rent a car and explore the quiet fishing villages, first settled by whalers in the 18th century. If the views are beautiful by day, they are magical at dusk, and the diving opportunities are rated among the best in the world. Rent a boat and venture out into the ocean, learn to sail or try a hair-raising skydive. *www.bay-of-islands.co.nz.*

393 *Surf*

Thousands of surfers test their skills at Piha, 40 kilometres from Auckland, every year. Iron-sand beaches and rugged parkland frame this break, famous for treacherous rips and currents that have snapped canoes in two. Experienced surfers will raise their game, while novices can take up the sport at one of the many surf schools. *www.pihabeach.co.nz.*

394 *Soak*

A bonanza of geothermal pools and sulphurous springs, Rotorua has been a prime pampering spot for more than 160 years. Maori legend says it was created by two spirit sisters carrying fire to their frozen brother at the Pink and White Terraces, destroyed by a volcanic eruption in 1886. Now the native residents welcome visitors with spellbinding dances and feasts. *www.rotoruanz.com.*

395 *Walk*

Abel Tasman National Park, named after the Dutch explorer who 'discovered' New Zealand, is in the Nelson region, known for its fine dining, art scene and busy port. The two famous walks, along the golden coast or in the forested headlands, take you for several days across clear blue estuaries, hidden bays and natural wonders. *www.doc.govt.nz/parks-and-recreation/national-parks.*

396 *Train*

Cross the gorges and glistening white peaks of the Southern Alps on a spectacular train journey from one coast of the island to the other in four and a half hours. To the east, historic Christchurch is the largest town on the South Island, while in Greymouth the Greenstone Trail (Te Ara Pounamu; call +64 3 768 9292) follows the routes of Maori traders hunting for jade.
Book with *Tranz Scenic (+64 4 495 07750/ www.tranzscenic.co.nz).*

397 *Wine*

Sheep are passé and rugby prowess is no longer all black. Global fame is shifting to the excellent wines produced in the Marlborough region, best known for its unrivalled sauvignon blanc. Tasting tours with small groups let you choose the vineyard and itinerary.
Book with *Marlborough Wine Tours (+64 3 578 9515/www.marlboroughwinetours.co.nz).*

398 *Adrenaline*

Queenstown on Lake Wakatipu – locked in the Southern Alps – is a year-round party town where après-ski is taken as seriously as the sport itself. Get your adrenaline fix with heli-skiing, sky-diving, daredevil jumps and slopes, which can be incorporated into snow safaris. There are also plenty of pistes perfect for beginners.
Book with *Haka Tours (+64 3 980 4252/ www.hakatours.com).*

399 *Wildlife*

From the fluffy kiwi to the mighty sperm whale, the slinky skink to the cute fur seal, New Zealand's wildlife is as varied as its landscape. Forests resemble their Jurassic-era ancestors, dreamy bays seem almost otherworldly, and wildflowers and endemic herbs and shrubs spread out like multicoloured, perfumed carpets across uninhabited valleys. Ensure you don't miss anything by joining a nature-themed tour of the most beautiful and exciting spots.
Book with *Naturetrek (01962 733051/ www.naturetrek.co.uk)*

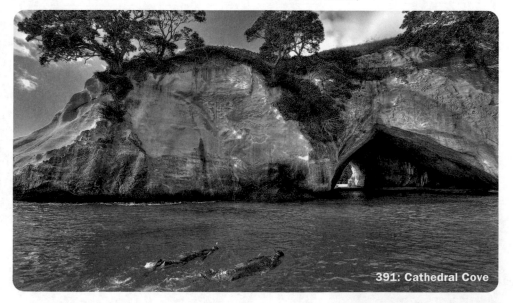

391: Cathedral Cove

400-409

A room (and table) with a view

400 Tokyo Park Hyatt, Japan

Look down on the full Tokyo cityscape from a height of more than 200 metres in the luxury Tokyo Park Hyatt hotel (+81 3 5322 1234, www.tokyo.park.hyatt.com) in Shinjuku, and picture Scarlett Johansson in Lost in Translation, which was filmed here. The hotel crams in four restaurants, two bars, a bakery, deli, spa, gym and pool, most complete with spectacular view.

To experience hearty, home-style Japanese cooking, head over to the hotel's Kozue restaurant, which uses the freshest seasonal ingredients, beautifully presented, and which boasts an extensive saké list.

401 Hilton Embassy Suites, Canada

+905 356 3600/www.embassysuitesniagara.com.
Jaw-droppingly close views of the Niagara
Falls are part of the deal at this high-rise hotel.
The natural drama is so close you may not
even feel the need to step outside; but the
hotel offers tours that'll take you right up
to, and even behind, the thundering waters.

Tuck into king-size slabs of meat at the Keg
Steakhouse & Bar on the ninth floor, with
tables right next to the king-size view of the
Falls. Check the year-round firework schedule
for maximum viewing pleasure.

402 Amazing View Hotel, Greece

+30 22890 22053/www.amazingviewhotel.com.
The name says it all; make sure you get a
room with a balcony at this Naxos Island
hotel, and soak up amazing views of the
Aegean Sea.

The views continue at the beachside Sergiani
Naxos (+30 22850 24206, www.sergiani-
naxos.gr), with a traditional Greek menu
featuring some good vegetarian soups.

403 Millennium Hilton Bangkok, Thailand

*+66 2 651 9501/www.bangkok.com/
millenniumhilton.*
Bangkok is a city of temporal and spiritual
contrasts; skyscrapers shoulder shrines and
temples, and you can see them all from the
Millennium Hilton, which towers imposingly
above the Chao Praya River. Take the Skytrain,
the city's mass transit system, for equally
impressive cityscape panoramas.

If you're looking for culinary delights,
take to the streets. But for decent food with
an unsurpassable 360-degree skyline to boot,
head to Zense (+66 2 100 9898, www.zense
bangkok.com) at the top of the Central World
mall, where you can choose from four types
of world cuisine.

404 Copacabana Palace, Brazil

+55 21 2548 7070/www.copacabanapalace.com.
Nothing to do with Mr Manilow, this luxurious
hotel provides a perfect view of Copacabana's
classic horseshoe beach; dusk is dreamy,
while sunsets can be magical. Set yourself
up with a sunlounger and caipirinha and gaze
out on to white sands, blue seas and brown
Brazilian beach bodies. With overcrowding
a feature, Rio de Janeiro's most popular
beach is almost better now as a view than
as a sunbathing experience.

Choose from *feijoada* (a traditional stew of
black beans and pork) or more international
fare at the poolside hotel restaurant Pérgula.
Fresh seafood is a speciality.

405 Hilton Istanbul, Turkey

+90 212 3156000/www.hilton.co.uk/istanbul.
All rooms here come with a balcony and a
breathtaking view of the Bosphorus sea that
divides Europe and Asia (as well as Istanbul)
and runs alongside the hotel.

Dine next to the water at the hotel's Roof
Restaurant & Bar, where meals are accompanied
by live music; or, for a quieter option, the Terrace
Restaurant, where Turkish and Mediterranean
dishes are served up with aplomb.

406 Blancaneaux Lodge, Belize

+ 50 1 824 4912/www.blancaneaux.com.
Part of Francis Ford Coppola's burgeoning
hotel empire, Blancaneaux Lodge's individual
cabañas and villas seem to merge seamlessly
with the lush Belize landscape, providing
views of the Privassion River, beautiful
creeks and waterfalls and manicured gardens.
The riverside spa, horse stables and organic
garden are carefully integrated into, rather
than imposed on, the flourishing forest.

The hotel's treehouse-like Montagna
restaurant serves up the best (OK, the only)
Italian in the Belizian jungle, while at the
poolside Guatemaltecqua you're more likely
to savour authentic Mayan dishes. The
ceiling fans in the Jaguar Bar are souvenirs
from *Apocalypse Now.*

407 Jade Mountain Resort, St Lucia

020 8339 6888/www.jademountain.com.
Individual bridges lead to private infinity pools
and each 'sanctuary' has, in place of a fourth
wall, a vista of the Caribbean Sea and the St
Lucia Piton, two volcanic plugs that are listed

as a World Heritage Site. The 'organic architecture' of this mountain-top resort, along with the banning of telephones or any connective technology, pulls you irresistibly into what must be some of the world's most stunning natural surroundings.

Breakfast on guavas, tangerines and breadfruit picked from the surrounding trees. Dine on fresh fish and Caribbean recipes, finishing off with a glass of St Lucian rum, while overlooking the mountains and sea.

408 Lomas de Tzununá, Guatemala

+502 5 201 82 72/www.lomasdetzununa.com.
It takes some initiative and a small hike to get there, but once you've reached your (extremely reasonably priced) balcony room at Lomas de Tzununá, the view is unrivalled. Two huge

mountains sit like islands on a lake that stretches away for miles in front of the hotel, an occasional fair-weather cumulus cloud in a blue sky the only thing to obscure your vision.

A restaurant and poolside bar offer perfect viewing spots, especially after sunset.

409 Hotel Arenal Springs, Costa Rica

+506 2479 1212/www.hotelarenalsprings.com.
The Arenal volcano, which overlooks this resort, is one of the most active in the world, and while you sit in the terrace bar, drink in hand, watching one of its frequent eruptions, you're just a kilometre away but perfectly safe. We hope.

The Ti-Cain restaurant has one of the prime views of the volcano, and serves up food from the on-resort farm (a popular attraction for kids).

407: Jade Mountain Resort, St Lucia

Ideas from the expert

410-419

Paul Burston, Time Out magazine's Gay & Lesbian editor, suggests ten glorious gaycations.

410 Not overwhelmingly gay in the way Gran Canaria can be, Sitges has gay bars aplenty and even a gay beach, but also boasts some great restaurants and a pretty coastline with a real Spanish fishing town flavour. And with Barcelona only a short train ride away, you can enjoy the best of both worlds – a bustling city and a quieter seaside resort. Sitges offers a number of gay and gay-friendly hotels, but for location and price, the first choice has to be the Hotel Liberty (+34 93 811 08 72, www.libertyhotelsitges.com)

411 Despite being pricey compared to the neighbouring Cyclades islands, Mykonos is still a firm favourite with the gay crowd. The town itself is stunningly beautiful, and with beaches like Super Paradise packed with gay sun worshippers, there's always plenty of eye candy. The Elysium Hotel (+30 22890 23952, www.elysiumhotel.com) is one of the best on the island. You can stay here, or simply join friends for drinks by the pool and watch the sun go down. July is best avoided, when the island is at its busiest.

412 Not an obvious choice for the gay traveller, Gozo has no gay scene to speak of, though there is some nightlife and the locals are friendly. Growing numbers of gay tourists are discovering the island, though, and with good reason. Only a short ferry ride from Malta, Gozo is far quieter and unspoilt – rather as one imagines Greece might have been 40 years ago. Masalforn is the place to stay if you're keen on diving. Or if a bunch of you club together, stunning converted farmhouses can be booked very reasonably at Gozo Farmhouses (+356 2156 1280, http://gozofarmhouses.com).

413 It's hard to imagine, but there are still some gay men left living in Rio – they haven't all moved to London. Despite the dominance of the Catholic Church, the power of the almighty pink pound means that Rio is a gay-friendly city. There's even a gay beach at Ipanema now, so it's not only the girls from Ipanema who go walking. In fact, at Ipanema everyone power-walks or runs. Beach culture rules, as does the body beautiful. One of the best-located and cheapest places to stay is the Arpoador Inn (+55 21 2274 6995, www.arpoadorinn.com.br), between Ipanema and Copacabana. Make time for a trip to nearby Buzios – the quiet peninsula where Bardot used to hide out is now a thriving party town.

414 Madrid is the place Pedro Almodóvar calls home, and it isn't hard to imagine the director prowling the city streets in search of inspiration for his next film. Madrid's gay nightlife is far quirkier than Barcelona's, and every bit as raunchy. The gay area, Chueca, is situated in the old quarter at the centre of the city, and has more than its fair share of backrooms. The Spanish also love their foam parties, so bring your swimming trunks and be prepared to ditch your clothes. Stay at the Hotel Lusso Infantas (+34 91 521 28 28, www.hotelinfantas.com).

415 Love its shameless hedonism, or loathe its shallow attachment to all things buff and beautiful, but there's no denying the impact Miami's gay district has had on gay culture at large. South Beach is the spiritual home of the circuit party, the clubbing phenomenon that began in the early 1990s and spread across North America and Europe. Each year in March, South Beach hosts the original White Party, so-called because of the dress code not the various powders the party boys shove up their noses as they show off the results of all those hours at the gym. Sleep, if you get round to it, at Hotel Victor (+1 305 428 1234, ww.hotelvictorsouthbeach.com).

416 No list of great gay holiday destinations would be complete without Sydney, but make sure you go for Mardi Gras or just before – the city is dead afterwards. Surprisingly for such a famous gay city, the scene is rather small. But what Sydney lacks in size it makes up for in other departments. The Opera House is a wonder to behold, proving there's no truth in the old cliché about there being less culture in Oz than in a pot of yoghurt. Stay at Morgans Boutique Apartment hotel (+61 2 9318 2361, www.parklodgesydney.com).

417 Still hugely popular and finally recovering from the onslaught of AIDS that wiped out so many in the 1980s and early '90s, San Francisco benefits from its legendary gay history, immortalised in Armistead Maupin's *Tales of the City* and the recent film *Milk*. It also boasts the iconic Golden Gate Bridge, and has plenty in the way of gay culture. The LGBT Film Festival is amust. Smart rooms are offered at the boutique-style Galleria Park (+1 415 781 3060, www.jdvhotels.com/hotels/galleria_park).

418 In the straight, often homophobic world of big game and bush camps, British-born William Gibbon and his South African partner Ravin Maharaj have stuck their necks out and set up a gay-friendly resort called Iganu (+27 78 383 9182, www.iganu.com) in the lush Limpopo region of South Africa, north of Johannesburg. The farm provides protection for more than 30 species, including giraffe, eland, oryx, warthog, impala and wildebeest. Accommodation is in stylish straw-roofed chalets, and all the food is home-cooked and served as communal meals.

419 For bars, clubs and even saunas, gay Paris isn't nearly as well served as gay London. But there's still a lot going on, whether it's the latest gay circuit party or the older piano bars where drag queens still mime to Edith Piaf. The gay scene is mainly concentrated around the Marais. And if it's a romantic weekend you're after, you'd go a long way to beat gay Paree. I like the charming Hotel de la Bretonnerie (+33 1 48 87 77 63, www.bretonnerie.com).

416: Sydney

420-429
Ski-free snow fun

420 *Ice golf*

Austria's Lake Weissensee, located high up in the Gailtal Alps (at 930 metres), freezes in November to become the largest natural ice surface in Europe. Golfers can compete in the International Ice Golf Tournament held every February and, when thrashed by ice-hardened Greenland golfers, retreat to the fairytale hills. Watch out too for dazzling speed skating contests and horse-drawn sleighs.

Contact *Weissensee's tourism website (+43 0 4713 22200/www.weissensee.naturarena.com).*

421 *Glacier walking*

If you're feeling brave – or cool and hard – hike across the glaciers of southern Norway. The largest mainland ice-sheet lies in Jostedalsbreen National Park, its arms stretching into smaller glaciers hanging above the rivers that wind through the valleys beneath. Don't try this alone – gorges dozens of metres wide, and deep enough to look very dark indeed, open up into the moving glaciers and may be thinly disguised by fallen snow.

Contact *Visit Norway (+47 22 00 25 00/ www.visitnorway.com).*

422 *Dog sledding*

In Finland's remote wilderness, along its border with Russia, lies an expanse of ancient, silent forest and frozen lakes. From your base at the Border Inn (+358 400 202 270, www.theborderinn.com), a team of dogs and a wooden sled will lead you to the heart of the landscape, covering up to 100 kilometres in a day and racing after wild reindeer and elk. Back at the lodge, saunas and Lappish stone fireplaces will keep you warm and cosy.

Contact *Visit Finland (www.visitfinland.com).*

422: Border Inn, Finland

423 Horseriding on ice

Icelandic horses were brought to the country by Vikings in the ninth century and have remained pure-bred ever since. Icelanders have a special affection for horses – they say the ratio of horses to people here is the highest in the world – and there are strict rules relating to the animals. One is that no horse leaving the island can ever return. One recommended ride is up to the Mrdalsjökull glacier; you may want to avoid hoof-skating but Icelanders love performing tricks on horseback on the ice. Catch a show if the opportunity arises.
Contact *Icelandic Mountain Guides (+354 587 9999/www.mountainguides.is).*

424 Ice skating

Go ice skating in Central Park's Woollman Rink, where the crisp winter sky and illuminated skyscrapers are a perfect backdrop to a romantic evening. If you get carried away, you can book to arrange a proposal at the rink: you'll get dinner in a private tent, a customised soundtrack and lots of champagne all for just, erm, $1,500.
Contact *+1 212 439 6900/ www.wollmanskatingrink.com.*

425 Wolf watching

From terrifying children's bedtime stories to the wonderful world of Jack London novels, few creatures have inspired as much awe and mystery as the wolf. Penetrate the fir- and pine-tree forests of Canada's Prince Alberta National Park on dog sleds, and venture deep inside the wolves' realm. Chill – or freeze your crampons off, more like – by spending a night under the stars beside a bonfire, listening to howls blown in from the darkness.
Contact *Windows on the Wild (020 8742 1556/www.windowsonthewild.com).*

426 Icy adventure park

If the closest you've come to ice art is pretty shaped cubes in a fancy bar, the ice festival of Harbin in China will blow your mind. Soft pinks, blues, yellows and more illuminate a vast adventure park built from blocks of ice, with precipitous slides and steps and soaring turrets. Endlessly intricate sculptures rise up in the park during the festival, held in February.
Contact *Travel China Guide (0800 666 88666/ www.travelchinaguide.com).*

427 Snowmobiling

Between the old villages of Jukkasjärvi and Kaupinnen, the Arctic Circle becomes a playground for adventurous travellers. Day excursions on snowmobiles pierce deep into the Swedish wilderness, but you can also learn to build an igloo and drive your own dog sled. A night at the ice hotel made from 40,000 tonnes of snow and ice that melts into the river every year is included on this tour.

Contact *why don't you… (0845 838 6262/ www.whydontyou.com).*

428 Rock climbing

If you're feeling slightly suicidal, scale the icy peaks in the Alps on a rock climbing tour that will lead you up the daunting ascents of Mont Blanc, the Matterhorn and the Eiger. Seasoned climbers take on the vertical drops and hair-raising views of the North Face. Entry-level courses designed for complete beginners are available for first-time alpinists.

Contact *Alpine Guides (07940 407533/ www.alpine-guides.com).*

420: Ice golf

429 Wilderness trekking

A 20-mile mountain trail – or, rather more probably, a boat ride – leads to Knoydart, a Scottish wilderness where quiet mountains roll into peaceful lochs and overlook the sea. On the peninsula, the Old Forge serves scallops, hake or 'whatever makes it from the lochs and hills' with wholemeal bread. Relax in the evening after exploring the icy trails with a whisky before a roaring fire.

Contact *Wilderness Scotland (0131 625 6635/ www.wildernessscotland.com).*

430-439
Modern travelogues to inspire

There are thousands of travel books, but many are either old and dusty or new and tediously self-regarding. Here are ten travelogues to get you thinking about routes to follow, pilgrimages to make and, if you can't get away just now, armchairs to sink into…

430 *A Year in Provence* by Peter Mayle

Inspiration for *trips to rural France.*
There have been many inferior copies, but this is the original relocation text. During their first year in rural Provence, Mayle and his wife had to cope with fierce weather, blackmarket truffle dealers and inflexible French workers. The story is told with flair and humour.

431 *The Great Railway Bazaar* by Paul Theroux

Inspiration for *travel to Central Asia, or any long train trip.*
Published in 1975, Theroux's train odyssey through Cold War Europe and Central Asia, and the return journey on the Trans-Siberian Railway, is a model of intelligent – but unpretentious – free-spirited overland travel.

432 *Notes from a Small Island* by Bill Bryson

Inspiration for *a weekend break in Blackpool.*
Pseuds like to judge Bryson as a lowbrow travel writer, but in this extended goodbye

to his adopted home he made a final trip around the island, stopping over in villages such as Farleigh Wallop, Titsey and Shellow Bowells and celebrating British eccentricities such as Marmite-philia.

433 Journey Without Maps by Graham Greene

Inspiration for *being a more daring traveller.*
Between writing novels and lighter 'entertainments', Greene was an untiring traveller and wrote several memoirs and travelogues. This story of a 350-mile, four-week walk through the interior of Liberia in 1935, taken with his female cousin, Barbara Greene, is a genuine search for a heart of darkness in a country still rarely visited by Europeans.

434 In Siberia by Colin Thubron

Inspiration for *trips to Eastern Russia, reached by the Trans-Siberian Railway.*
Most of us can't or don't want to to visit the Gulags of frozen Siberia, but this book is rich in the details of political history and cultural context that gave rise to the place as well as the myth.

435 Coasting by Jonathan Raban

Inspiration for *UK breaks, especially coastal ones.*
In 1982 Jonathan Raban sailed single-handedly around Britain in an old 32-foot seagoing ketch, the *Gosfield Maid*. This travelogue charts his travels on board, and his existential state – coasting as a man adrift on life's sea.

436 The Beach by Alex Garland

Inspiration for *a gap-year odyssey.*
Occupying an imaginative space somewhere between William Golding's *Lord of the Flies* and a travel guidebook, Garland's bestselling novel about a utopian community on an island

in Thailand captures the deceptive delights and dangers of open-ended travel.

437 Terra Incognita by Sara Wheeler

Inspiration for *an Antarctic cruise.*
South Pole bores love to tell you how they've read all of Shackleton's journals or all the books about Scott and Amundsen, but Wheeler gives us a very accessible, human, contemporary and above-all engaging account of a winter on the Big Ice.

438 In Patagonia by Bruce Chatwin

Inspiration for *travel to the Patagonian regions of Southern Chile and Southern Argentina.*
Described as a 'minor classic' shortly after its publication in 1977, this thin book of slim chapters introduced novelistic techniques and invention, effectively modernising the travelogue for a new generation of world travellers.

439 On the Road by Jack Kerouac

Inspiration for *an east–west cross-country road trip in the United States.*
A fiction based on travels Kerouac shared with his friend and spiritual mentor, Neil Cassady, this classic of Beat literature has the rolling energy and easy rhythm of a long drive.

440-449
I want to ride my bicycle

440 Land's End to John O'Groat's

See Britain by bike, and brave the weather, as you cover the country from the bottom up. Over ten to 14 days, and around a thousand miles (it's longer than the motorway route, which is around 830 miles), you'll see the landscape change from green to brown, flat to hilly, man-made to natural. Routes vary but it's easy to take in some of the UK's finest sights. For an excellent guide to the East of Pennines route, accommodation along the way, and other

442: Transamerica Trail

443: The Danube

need-to-know information, visit www.users. waitrose.com/~ianclare/links.html. Go to www.sustrans.org for general information.

441 *Across Cuba*

Cuba may not be known as the easiest place to travel around, but it's actually a cyclist's dream. Being one of the last bastions of communism has kept car ownership archaically low, so outside of Havana cyclists need not fight for space. If you have a fortnight to spare, ride from the capital to the colonial town of Trinidad via the looming Escambray Mountains; alternatively, go west towards the lush valleys of Viñales. Even if you only take the bike out for a day, it's a great way to find the Cuba that lies off the tour-bus track.
Book with *Explore (0845 013 1539/ www.explore.co.uk)*.

442 *Transamerica Trail*

It's the American dream, just you and the open road; but rather than crossing the country by car, do it on your bike. One tried-and-tested route goes from Virginia to Oregon, passing through ten states on the way. This being America, food and accommodation, or at least a good camping

spot, should be no trouble, but keep to the summer season (May to October) to avoid the Colorado snow. If you haven't got three months to spare, try cycling down the Pacific or Atlantic coasts, or follow in the tracks of the Underground Railroad – a secret route used by escaped slaves in the 19th century to reach 'free states'.

The website www.adventurecycling.org has detailed route information for several American routes. For inspiration read Donna Lynn Ikenberry's book *Bicycling Coast to Coast: A Complete Route Guide Virginia to Oregon*.

443 *The Danube*

Rising in Germany's Black Forest, and extending to Romania and the Ukraine at its delta with the Black Sea, Europe's second longest river crosses nine countries. Once an important trading route, its modern incarnation seems to be as a much-loved cruising river, but if you fancy seeing the romantic cities and towns of Central Europe in a more active fashion, the banks of the Danube also make for a great cycling route. Tackling the whole length is unwise unless you're writing a travelogue; the best bet is a week to cycle the relatively undemanding terrain along the

German and Austrian sections of the river. Start in Passau, move through the Wachau vineyards and end up in the beautiful city of Vienna.
Book with *Discovery Travel (01904 632226/ www.discoverytravel.co.uk).*

444 *Round the world*

At the time of writing, Mark Beaumont holds the record for circumnavigating the globe (with James Bowthorpe hot on his trail). The Scot took 195 days to complete the exhausting tour, but whether or not you're trying to match his feat, follow his route. Start and end in Paris, going through the wilds of Pakistan, the Australian outback, then back round via America.

Read *The Man Who Cycled the World*, by Mark Beaumont, for inspiration.

445 *Luxury cycling*

Who says a cycling trip needs to mean slumming it? Ride around the French countryside by day, and by night, rest your weary legs in luxury hotels. Cycling for Softies offers a range of indulgent cycling holiday ideas, from the challenging Tarn to Provence route to a more peaceful ride round the châteaux of the Loire valley or a trip that goes via Cognac distilleries. Bags are carried for you and a number of the trips are child-friendly, with options to go by car for non-cycling companions. Ideal if you want to leave the tent behind.
Cycling for Softies *0161 248 8282/ www.cycling-for-softies.co.uk.*

446 *The Netherlands*

Some say there are more bikes than people in the Netherlands. Whether or not that's true, the largely flat terrain makes for a relaxing cycling holiday and is particularly well suited to first-timers. Planning your own trip is relatively easy as English is widely spoken and routes are expertly signed across the country – so getting lost is unlikely. Take a week to explore Arnhem and the lower Rhine region, or choose a route that takes you from the tulip fields of Schagen to the bustling port of Amsterdam, via the market town Edam, famed for its eponymous cheese. For help planning your trip visit www.holland.com/uk/discoverholland/active/cycling.

447 *Canal du Midi*

The historic thread of water that links France's Atlantic coast to the Mediterranean makes an unforgettable cycle route. Its plane-tree shaded 430 kilometres lead you from Bordeaux to Sète, near Montpellier, passing through Toulouse, Carcassonne and Béziers en route, as well as a host of medieval villages and pretty, untouristed towns. Go just a little off-piste to explore the wine country of Bordeaux or the Languedoc, Roman Narbonne and its beaches or the Cap d'Agde. You'll need a mountain bike or hybrid for the occasional rough or rocky stretch, but for much of its length the towpath is smooth-surfaced. Count on ten days for a leisurely ride. For more information, see www.canal-du-midi.org.

448 *Wales*

There is certainly more to Wales than rolling countryside and epic scenery, but it does have those in plentiful supply, making the small country to the left of England an attractive prospect for a shorter, lower-budget cycling holiday. Choose from valleys, beaches and mountains depending on how strenuous you want your trip to be. Cross Wales at its widest point by cycling the 225-mile Celtic trail between Fishguard and Chepstow or take a day trip and ride along the north coast from Llandudno to Conwy. For information about cycle routes in Wales, visit www.routes2ride.org.uk/wales.

449 *L'Etape du Tour*

If you can't compete in the Tour de France itself, at least you can tackle a part of it. Every summer, after the professionals have passed through, organisers open up one of the toughest mountain sections of the race to the public. This is one for those in great shape who are confident with vertiginous heights; the 2009 route followed the 170-kilometre penultimate stage from Montelimar to the 2,000-metre summit of Mount Ventoux. Budding Lance Armstrongs should sign up on www.letapedutour.com; places fill up fast, so register when it opens, usually around October or November. The site links to packages for accommodation and transfers, but save money by booking independently. Just be sure your bed for the night is near tomorrow's starting point because many roads in the area will be closed for the Tour. Extend your stay by plotting an Alpine cycle with www.mapmyride.com.

450-459
Self-indulgent wellness breaks

From ancient hammams to stem cell facials… here's a selection of restorative retreats and spas in exotic locations around the world.

450 Ritz Carlton Istanbul, Turkey
📟 ⏱

+90 212 334 44 44/www.ritzcarlton.com.
Among the oldest water therapies is the Turkish hammam or steam bath. Experience it in luxury, at a spa overlooking the azure waters

of the Bosphorus strait. For pure indulgence, try a chocolate body treatment before heading to the rooftop terrace for a refreshing cocktail.

451 Hotel Kalevala, Kuhmo, Finland
🔥

+58 086 554 100/www.hotellikalevala.fi.
With its traditional remedies that range from 'bone-setting' to jumping into ice-holes, Finland may not seem an obvious choice for those whose idea of wellness involves oil and maybe a candle or two. On Lake Lammasjärvi, near the Russian border, you can stick to peat body wraps, saunas and jacuzzis while wolves howl in the snowy forest outside.

452 Terme Di Saturnia, Italy
🏠

+39 0564 600111/www.termedisaturnia.it.
These hot bubbling springs in Tuscany were created by a lightning bolt hurled from the heavens by Roman god Saturn, who was fed up with fighting on the Maremma, according to local folklore. Overlooking Etruscan ruins, water from ancient springs and state-of-the-art remedies mesh centuries of tradition with modern techniques.

457: Gleneagles, Scotland

456: Royal Crescent Hotel

453 Daintree Ecolodge, Queensland, Australia

+61 07 4098 6100/www.daintree-ecolodge.com.au.
Take your body and soul on a sensory journey
in the place the Aborigines named 'Wawu-
karrba', meaning healing of the spirit.
Rainforest retreat Daintree offers a range of
natural therapies, and many treatments draw
on Aboriginal rituals. Try Kambarr rain
therapy or a Walu BalBal facial, and detox
your innards with local rainforest snacks.

454 Hotel U Sládka, Chodová Planá, Czech Republic

+420 374 617 100/www.chodovar.cz.
This unconventional wellness holiday should
appeal to the less hardcore detoxers out there.
The 'beer wellness land' of Chodová Planá is
the first beer spa (apparently, the brew can
have remedial effects – although this won't
be news to many people), where you spend
all day bathing in beer, and yes, drinking
the stuff as part of the treatment. Lava stone
massages and tours of the family brewery
are also available.

455 Spa Cavas Wine Lodge, Mendoza, Argentina

+54 261 410 6927/www.cavaswinelodge.com.
Wine-lovers looking for a hands-on experience
in Argentina's wine country should consider the
Wine Body Glow, a beauty and cleansing
treatment based on the region's delicious
produce. Take refuge in an expanse of
vineyards at the Cavas Wine Lodge.

456 Royal Crescent Hotel, Bath, UK

01225 823333/www.royalcrescent.co.uk.
Fine dining and long walks in the secluded
gardens of the Royal Crescent Hotel will take
you back to the times of Jane Austen. From full
body algae wraps to a special space for men,
the hotel's spa – converted from the property's
stables – has all the amenities you'd expect.

457 Gleneagles, Scotland

01764 662231/www.gleneagles.com.
Known for its world-class golf courses and
posh country pursuits, Gleneagles is one of
Scotland's grandest properties. While you

unwind at the spa, your children can occupy themselves learning the forgotten art of falconry. From heated limestone floors to Arctic mist showers, the range of treatments should suit all tastes.

458 Two Bunch Palms, Palm Springs, California

+1 760 329 8791/www.twobunchpalms.com.
The place to spot celebrities, although be warned they might be lurking under several feet of mud in the healing baths of the Two Bunch Palms resort. The grotto and steaming waters were a sanctuary for Native Americans and, later, for Al Capone; his cottage, which still bears a bullet hole and his initials on a desktop, is now Suite 14.

459 Spa Ein Gedi Country Hotel, Israel

+972 8659 4221/www.ein-gedi.co.il.
Head to the palm-tree lined Ein Gedi kibbutz in the south of Israel and cover yourself from head to toe in the therapeutic black mud found on the shores of the Dead Sea. The unique mineral properties of the saline waters, which lie 400 metres below sea level at the lowest point on

earth, will refresh and revitalise tired skin. Just don't shave too soon before entering the water – it will sting.

460-469

Boutique Spain: coast

Notorious for their tower blocks, mock-English pubs and blighted beach resorts, the Spanish Costas are waking up to the understated allure of the boutique hotel. Away from the skyscrapers and crowds, small, smart premises are opening up to offer a stylish alternative to the brash brutality of the big tourist complexes.

460 *Tarifa, Cádiz*

Windy and wild Tarifa forms the most southern point of Spain, just before the Costa de la Luz joins its more notorious neighbour, the Costa del Sol. This stretch of coast boasts expansive beaches empty of sunbeds and the shadows cast by high-rise hotels. Strong winds from

461: Cudillero, Asturias

east and west have made Tarifa the region's kite- and windsurfing capital, bringing with it a surfer-hippie vibe that is laid-back by day and buzzing by night. Head here if you're into watersports. Naturism is also big on some stretches.

The Posada La Sacristia is an oasis of calm offering some time out from the sometimes too lively town. A charming touch here is the inner courtyard-cum-restaurant, with its ancient well and Andalucian arches. Rooms are chic yet simple, with four-poster beds, Moorish architecture and ethnic-inspired decor.
Posada La Sacristia *+34 956 68 1759/www.lasacristia.net.*

461 *Ballota, Cudillero, Asturias*

This is a great place from which to explore both the green countryside inland – the whole north coast is known as España Verde – and the wild, unspoilt beaches such as Playa del Silencio, Ballota, Concha de Artedo, Otur and Barayo. Also worth a visit is Cudillero, one of Asturia's most scenic fishing villages, where houses hang from steep rock walls and the cider and fresh sardines are top notch.

Head to this area if you're into arts and crafts and outdoorsy breaks. Local activities include fishing, scuba diving, horseriding, mountain biking and quad biking. One of the best places to stay is Artehotel, a minimalist-style hotel with spectacular views, which lies in the heart of a protected landscape featuring deep green forests and the dark blue Cantabrian Sea. The place exhibits sculptures and paintings and also provides materials for visitors to create their own.
Artehotel *+34 985 59 8111/www.artehotel.net.*

462 *Sant Pere de Ribes, Garraf*

The village of Sant Pere de Ribes does not quite touch the Catalonian coast, but it's a stone's throw from Sitges, Barcelona's gay-glam party town. Around Garraf and Sitges are plenty of pretty little beaches, some of which require you to wear appropriate clothes, and some which don't. Sitges itself is a throbbing party hotspot that plays host, every February, to Spain's campest carnival.

Tucked away between the coast and the mountains is the Ostería Ibai, a farmhouse that's been converted into a stylish hotel.
Ostería Ibai *+34 938 96 5490/www.ibaiosteria.com.*

469: Alicante

463 *Aigua Blava, Girona*

On the picturesque northern side of Spain's wildest coast, the Costa Brava, rocky cliffs hide some intimate coves. The bay of Aigua Blava, popular with sailors and small cruisers, is small but well served by seafood restaurants. Head up to the top of the rocky promontory for panoramic views. Head here if you're into cliff walks.

The Parador de Aiguablava, though relatively large, retains an intimate feel due to its secluded location in the Punta D'Es Muts enclave, surrounded by pine trees and overlooking the stunning Aigua Blava bay. Ask for a room with a panoramic sea view, or enjoy the wonderful vista from the swimming pool.
Parador de Aiguablava *+34 902 54 7979/ www.parador.es.*

464 *San Sebastián*

Widely regarded as Spain's gastronomic capital, the elegant Basque city of San Sebastián (aka Donostia) surprises and enchants visitors perhaps more than any other place on Spain's northern coast. The sea can be breathtakingly cold in the Bay of Biscay, but the city boasts three fine beaches – diminutive Zurriola, sweeping La Concha and tranquil Ondarreta – and a beautiful promenade. Eat San Sebastián's equivalent of tapas – the pintxo – in the vibrant Parte Vieja (old town); or, if you want to try *alta cocina*, head for Arzak (+34 943 278 465, www.arzak.ies) or out of town to Mugaritz (+34 943 518 343). This area is great for foodies, whether you long for the best Basque cuisine or delicious fresh tapas.

Villa Soro is a handsomely renovated 19th-century townhouse, which offers all the comfort and services of a top hotel while retaining a homely warmth.

Villa Soro *+34 943 29 7971/www.villasoro.com.*

465 *Agua Amarga, Cabo de Gata*

At the southern end of sun-scorched Almería is Cabo de Gata, Andalucía's largest coastal nature park, now protected for its flora, fauna and underwater wildlife. Agua Amarga is the nicest village in the region, and hotel El Tío Kiko is right at its heart, offering elegant rooms with four-poster beds, jacuzzis and private terraces. The bay itself is sheltered by two cliffs and fringed by 800 metres of fine sand and turquoise waters, which can be seen from the hotel's sea-facing rooms.

Head here if you're a couple in search of romance, or a recluse in need of a beach break.

El Tío Kiko *+34 950 10 6201/www.eltiokiko.com.*

466 *Mijas Costa, Marbella*

On the outskirts of the village of La Cala, the Beach House is located in a pocket of tranquillity, about halfway between the bustling port city of Málaga and Southern Spain's most upscale resort, Marbella. This small, tastefully understated hotel has a clean, modern design and just ten bedrooms, giving it the ambience of a private villa. A private doorway leads right on to a beach used solely by a few locals, while La Cala resort and its amenities and beaches are only a short walk away.

Beach House *+34 952 49 4550/ www.beachhouse.nu.*

467 *Garachico, Tenerife*

Garachico is a pretty cobbled village and harbour on Tenerife's lush north-west coast. On this more remote side of the island, swells of the Atlantic Ocean form natural volcanic pools. If you're feeling energetic, hike up Teide, the highest mountain in the Canaries (and in all Spain) and the third largest volcano in the world.

At the Hotel San Roque, pastel walls and a terracotta façade give this peaceful hideaway a Mediterranean feel, while gleaming floorboards and arched stone doorways add more than a touch of elegance. The 20 rooms are strikingly simple and each boasts its own jacuzzi. There's also a lovely courtyard pool.

Hotel San Roque *+34 922 12 3435/ www.hotelsanroque.com.*

468 *Sant Josep de sa Talaia, Ibiza*

On the west side of the island, near to but worlds apart from the carnage of San Antonio (aka Sant Antoni), the village of Sant Josep de sa Talaia boasts a privileged natural setting surrounded by swathes of green vegetation. The beach lies just 200 metres away, and a regular bus service takes sun-lovers to the coves of Cala Comte, Cala Tarida and Cala Bassa – all great for ogling the famous Ibizan sunset. For those who fancy something more lively once the sun goes down, the island's nightlife options are only a taxi ride away.

Hotel Ses Pitreras is located in a 1970s building that combines traditional Ibizan architecture with a trendy Modernist style. With just seven rooms, decorated by respected texture-obsessed interior designer Joan Lao, and individual terraces, the hotel retains an intimate feel, and is the perfect respite from some of the more intense aspects of the Ibizan experience.

Ses Pitreras *+34 971 34 5000/www.sespitreras.com.*

469 *Alicante*

Best known as the airport of entry for package tourists heading for Benidorm and the other hellholes of the Costa Blanca, Alicante is an unexplored secret. The Greeks called it Akra Leuka (White Summit) and the Romans named it

Lucentum (City of Light), in reference to the resplendent light on the coast here. Looming over the city is the Castillo de Santa Bárbara and, below, the grand Explanada, lined with date palms and a pretty harbour – a joy at night when the paella and fideuà restaurants and bars open.

Once a Dominican convent, the assertively modern Hospes Amerigo had its first facelift in 1858 when the railway arrived, sparking the city's modernisation. The hotel retains the original stone floors and arched windows, but the ecclesiastical starkness has been mellowed with warm beige, vibrant red and rust.
Hospes Amerigo *+34 932 38 8314/ www.hospes.com/amerigo.*

470-479
Clubbing destinations

470 Berghain, Berlin
🏢 ☾ 🍸

www.berghain.de.
Berlin has long been recognised as Techno-Mecca and Berghain/Panorama Bar is Berlin's – and thus the world's – premier techno club. Both the main club Berghain, with its 18-metre-high dance space, and the upstairs bar pump out intense techno in tune with the power generation this massive building was once used for.

With large comfortable rooms and good transport links, Hotel-Pension Bregenz (+49 0 30 88 14 307, www.hotelbregenz-berlin.de) is probably the best value hotel in Berlin, leaving you with more money to spend on partying through the night.

471 APT, New York
🏢 🍸

+1 212 414 4245/www.aptnyc.com.
New York is primarily a bar city, but the cultural capital of the USA has thousands of clubs beneath its skyscrapers. Apartment-themed club APT, with its sleek basement bar and cosier street-level room, is one of the best places in the city for hearing the sound of the underground. From the techno of Carl Craig to Zulu Nation-founder Afrika Bambaataa, an eclectic mix of DJs and sounds can be heard here. The place is rammed on weekends.

For kipping down, head to the Bryant Park (+1 877 640 9300, www.bryantparkhotel.com), at a fantastic location on West 40th Street. Many rooms have terrific views of the park and all are modern and spotlessly clean.

471: APT, New York

477: Space, Ibiza

island of Hvar to dance with Croatia's beautiful people. The beach bar doubles as a lovely restaurant – and don't miss the fantastic full-moon parties. Carpe Noctem!

It's worth having your own apartment on Hvar, and it's not too expensive; Ana Dujmovic is endlessly helpful and has a number of lovely well-furnished apartments to let. Contact her on +385 21 742 010, or visit www.hvar-croatia.com/dujmovic/index.htm.

474 Razzmatazz, Barcelona

+34 93 320 8200/www.salarazzmatazz.com.
The impossibly happening Catalan capital has a dazzling array of clubs and scenes, all of which are melded together at Razzmatazz. Across several floors, music ranges from indie and pop to techno and trance. And when you need to escape the dancefloor, just head for the beautiful roof-terrace.

The Raval is effortlessly edgy and the coolest area for Barcelona's many bars; Hostal Gat Raval (+ 36 93 481 66 70, www. gataccommodation.com) is smart, clean and funky, with each room displaying work by a local artist.

475 Mass, London

www.mass-club.com.
London has many overpriced and oversubscribed fashionista clubs, but to get away from the hipster hype, head to Mass. This converted church is Brixton's house of rave-worship, with room for 1,500 people. Mass offers a variety of clubbing experiences, with none of the posers. Don't miss DMZ – the world's most important dubstep night.

Stay local, avoiding the silly central London prices and an even sillier taxi fare. Boutique-style Pasha Hotel (020 7277 2228, www.hotel pasha.com), with its Turkish hammam and Kazakh cuisine, is putting south-east London on the cool tourist map.

472 Trouw, Amsterdam

+31 20 463 7788/www.trouwamsterdam.nl.
The Amsterdam New School, pioneered by techno DJs Dylan and Shinedoe, is gaining worldwide recognition, and this is the best place to experience it. From the people who brought Amsterdam the legendary Club 11, Trouw is an industrial space – a former newspaper building – where the line-up always makes headlines.

Stumble in at 9am to the award-winning Fusion Suites (+31 20 618 4642, www. fusionsuites.com), a pretty mansion next to Vondelpark; and make sure you stay up for the incredible home-cooked breakfast.

473 Carpe Diem, Croatia

www.carpe-diem-hvar.com.
With one of the best festivals in Europe – Garden Festival – Croatia is building up a reputation as Eastern Europe's clubbing capital. Head for Carpe Diem on the stunning

476 Tocqueville 13, Milan

+39 335 681 96 31/www.tokvill.com.
The clubbing in Milan isn't exclusively about footballers and models, though they certainly frequent Tocqueville 13. The music here is

as varied as the drinks list, and the venue less aggressively pretentious than the close-by Hollywood – but just as glamorous.

The absurdly modern STRAF (+39 028 909 52 94, www.straf.it) is right in the centre of the city, with every room on the fifth floor boasting a mini-spa; the ultra-hip hotel bar is a must-visit.

477 Space, Ibiza

ℛ ⏱ ℽ

www.space-ibiza.es.

Ibiza is arguably the clubbing capital of the universe, and a huge part of that universe is Space – considered by many, and with a truckful of awards to show it, to be the very best club in the world. You'll need to take out a second mortgage just to get a sip of water here, but it'll (hopefully) be worth it.

After all that dancing, you'll need a comfortable bed to recuperate in: Es Mitjorn (+34 971 340 902, www.esmitjorn.com) is the hidden gem of Ibiza. Fantastic value for the island, it's in a great location, with a lovely pool and clean rooms.

478 Gianpula, Malta

ℛ ℽ

+356 9947 2133/www.gianpula.com.

Malta is loudly making its case as the great-value alternative to Ibiza. Gianpula, housed in a converted farm, is the country's biggest open-air club: its 4,000-clubber capacity means it can in theory accommodate one per cent of the island's population. The music menu features everything from posh trance to R&B.

The Fortina (+356 2346 0000, www.hotel fortina.com) in Sliema is a classy four-star hotel with five restaurants and two salt-water swimming pools; the company also has a spa resort on the same beach. Enjoy spending the money you saved from avoiding Ibiza.

479 Manga Rosa, São Paulo

▦ ℽ

+55 11 5507 3938/
www.obaoba.com.br/manga-rosa.

One of the biggest cities on the planet, Brazil's business capital has a vast number of clubs to choose from, with the best music probably at Manga Rosa. A world away from the derivative pop, rock and R&B of São Paulo's more commercial clubs, the DJs here play progressive house, techno and other electronic music to a young, beautiful crowd who are always up for a good time.

Considered one of South America's best hotels, the Emiliano (+55 11 3068 4399, www. emiliano.com.br) is the only accommodation option if you're not on a budget; from the elegant spa to the delicious food, this excellently located boutique hotel is the best that Brazil's biggest city has to offer. If you're on a budget… go to Rio.

480-489
Volunteering projects

480 *Tracking lynx and wolves in Slovakia*

£ ⏱ ☀

Romanticised and demonised over time, no animal has stalked through the darker recesses of the human imagination more than the wolf. Join scientists in the highest peaks of the West Carpathian Mountains, where carnivore populations – not only the wolf but also the lynx and the bear – are stirring old fears among the locals. You will spend the week tracking wolves and lynx and carry out research into their populations, habits and predatory impact.
Contact *Biosphere Expeditions (0870 446 0801/ www.biosphere-expeditions.org).*

481 *Repairing castle walls or cleaning up coasts around the UK*

£ ☀

It's easier than you think to break from the grind, be good, and even enjoy a holiday while you're at it. Across the UK, conservation projects offer the chance to escape to the countryside, meet new people and relax – at minimum expense. Choose from a range of projects, from rebuilding Scottish castle grounds to conserving the beautiful beaches of Devon.
Contact *British Trust for Conservation Volunteers (01302 388883/www.btcv.org).*

482: Orphanage, Kenya

482 Orphanage volunteer work in Kenya

In Mombasa, where the greatest obstacle to schooling for many is hunger, a children's centre depends on volunteers to support education, care and fundraising. Based in Bombolulu, the city's largest slum that sits right beside the wealthy district of Nyali, you can help give kids another chance – while you also absorb the vibrancy of Swahili culture and find peace among the palm trees of its beaches.
Contact *Global Vision International (01727 250250/www.gvi.co.uk).*

483 Helping favela communities in Rio de Janeiro, Brazil

Brazilian *favelas* (hillside slums) are about more than machine guns and drug factories. In Rio de Janeiro's Mangueira favela, children look forward to carnival, games on the beach and day trips to the jungle like any other kids.

Join them to explore the colourful land, cuisine and culture while you pick up Portuguese and learn to samba like a carioca.
Contact *Quest Overseas (01273 777206/ www.questoverseas.com).*

484 Rescuing seals and other wildlife in Ireland

At this sanctuary on the east coast of Ireland you can learn to rescue and rehabilitate seals, either working onsite or as a driver. The fluffy, whiskered pups are extremely vulnerable in the summer – starvation, predation by gulls and crows, infection and abandonment are just some of the causes. Around 75 seals are rescued every year, together with seabirds and other wild animals. Room and board is self-funded.
Contact *Irish Seal Sanctuary (+353 1 835 4370/ www.irishsealsanctuary.ie).*

485 Building homes for local communities in Kathmandu

Travel to a remote village in Nepal and live and work alongside local people to build

much-needed family homes for a community of ex-bonded workers. It's a great opportunity to experience Nepalese rural culture first-hand, and to help those living in poverty. Volunteers also get to explore the city of Kathmandu.
Contact *Action Aid (01460 238000/ www.actionaid.org.uk).*

486 *Working holidays in the UK*
£ ⚒

Herding goats might not be everyone's idea of a holiday, but it's just one of the many invigorating breaks across Britain offered by the National Trust to reconnect people with their island's agricultural roots and history. Choose from a range of trips from two to seven days starting at £60, many of which are suitable for families. Projects involve everything from restoring ancient monuments to dirtying your hands in the wet grasslands.
Contact *National Trust (0844 800 1895/www.nationaltrust.org.uk).*

487 *Teaching English abroad*

Get certified to teach English as a second language and you can help children and adults in developing countries learn one of the world's most widely spoken languages, giving them a valuable skill. Several organisations manage placements in vulnerable communities, such as shantytowns in South America; contact Real Gap Experience for information on voluntary teaching in Argentinian *villas miserias*, and the Children at Risk Foundation for the equivalent in Brazilian *favelas*.
Contact *Real Gap Experience (01892 516164/ www.realgap.co.uk/Argentina-Teaching-English); Children at Risk Foundation (www.carfweb.net).*

488 *French farming holidays*
£ 👪

French cuisine and wines taste good in the UK but nothing beats sampling them on the soil they grew from – especially when you've picked the produce yourself. On a farming holiday, you learn the ancient harvesting, preserving and cooking techniques that gave rise to one of the world's finest cuisines, all the time savouring country air and organic, healthy food. Join a family and help them work on the farm, practise your French and learn the local style of cooking.
Contact *WWOOF France (www.wwoof.fr).*

489 *Cruising for nothing*
£

Getting paid to sail the world on a luxury cruise may sound like a dream, but land a job on a boat and you can do just that. Set sail for the Caribbean and when you arrive you'll find a pay cheque helps make the most of time on land; though with palm-fringed beaches and white sand, the best stuff really is free. From sweaty jobs on deck to bowing a violin, there's work for everyone.
Contact *Work on Cruiseships (www.workoncruiseships.com).*

490-499
Beyond the Eurozone

During 2009-10, the travel media went into hysterical mode, reporting that the UK 'staycation' had replaced the European holiday. It was all about exchange rates: from mid 2003 to mid 2007, the pound/euro rate remained around €1.45 (give or take five per cent), but after this period decline set in, and the pound fell to below €1.25 against the euro in April 2008. In December 2008 and in April and September 2009, the pound dipped again, and while it's since rallied, the dye is cast: Brits abroad are broke. Of course, this isn't entirely true, especially for those Britons who live or holiday in expensive cities like London and Bristol; and British hotels and B&Bs are generally more expensive than their equivalents in, say, Spain or Greece. But as long as the euro remains strong, the old reliable beach holidays in Mallorca, Corfu and Malta will seem relatively pricey, while already expensive places like Paris and Dublin will seem astronomical. So, here's how to keep life simple: head out of the Eurozone, where countries with their own currencies make for a cheaper and refreshing alternative.

490 *The Nile is the new Med*
£ ♡ 🏠

Instead of dishing out euros on a Greek island cruise, why not spend Egyptian pounds on a

Nile tour? The flight may cost more and take a bit longer, but once in the historic land of pyramids and pharaohs, you can get your money's worth by bartering in the many bazaars.

Book with *Thomas Cook (08444 125969/ www.thomascook.com), for a seven-day Cruise down the Nile.*

491 *Turkey is the new Spain*

£ ⚘ ✿ ⛹

Spain is 'so last summer', so instead head to Turkey. Still not accepted into the EU, the country's currency is the Turkish lira. Enjoy spending it on freshly baked pitta bread, nutty houmous and apple tea instead of seafood-bereft paellas and Full Englishes. In summer 2009 Turkey replaced Spain as the No.1 destination for UK visitors.

Book with *The Co-op (0844 335 6439/ www.co-operativetravelholidays.co.uk).*

492 *Tunisia is the new Italy*

£ ⚘

Spend your Tunisian dinar on one of the many sunloungers lining the sandy beaches of the east coast. At the height of their empire, the Romans had at least 200 cities in Tunisia: the legacy of some 26,000 sites. Take a break from the beach with trips to Dougga, Thuburbo Majus and El Jem.

Book with *First Choice, which goes to Sousse (08712 004455/www.firstchoice.co.uk/tunisia), and Aspects of Tunisia, which organises history and archaeology tours (020 8994 1011/ www.aspectsoftunisia.co.uk).*

493 *Croatia is the new Greece*

£ ⚘ ✿ ♡ ⛹ ♈

This country has it all: beaches, sun, islands and the Croatian kuna currency. Keep costs under control by dining where the locals dine, and even if you normally travel independently, consider an off-peak package and just use the flight and perhaps the hotel as a base for a few days before you go off to explore.

Book with *Simply Travel (020 8541 2214/ www.simplytravel.com).*

494 *Lithuania is the new Poland*

£ ▦

Cheap as chips Lithuania – the largest of the Baltic States – still has the litas currency, which has been pegged to the euro at the rate

496: Iceland

of 1:3.5 since 2002. The country enjoyed an economic boom following the collapse of the Soviet Union, and its proud citizens will wax lyrical about the country's beautiful, forest-filled countryside. Vilnius, the tiny capital, was European Capital of Culture in 2009, and has art galleries and baroque architecture aplenty, while eating out in cafés and restaurants is extremely kind on the wallet. Lithuania is planning to join the eurozone in January 2013, so get in there while the goings good.

Book with *Baltic Holidays (0845 070 5711/ www.balticholidays.com).*

495 *Bulgaria is the new Romania*
£ ☕

Bulgaria is so hot right now, and not just because of the reliable Black Sea sunshine. The up-and-coming holiday destination is overtaking Spain and Greece with its 200 kilometres of golden sands, gentle (and so child-friendly) tides and food and drink at much cheaper prices. Enjoy spending your Bulgarian lev on excursions to Roman ruins, ancient castles and monasteries, and vineyards.

Book with *Monarch/Cosmos (0871 423 8549/ http://holidays.monarch.co.uk).*

496 *Iceland is the new Scandinavia*
£ ☼ ♟

In Iceland the currency is the krona. For many years it was a currency viewed with the sort of disdain reserved for Scandinavian beer, but since the Icelandic economy imploded in late 2008, this remote island has become a viable option even for budget travellers. Prices for the Blue Lagoon, accommodation, Northern Lights excursions and, yes, even beer in the teeming bars of Reykjavik have gone down significantly. See the Iceland tourist board website (www.visiticeland.com) for general information.

Book with *Iceland Express (0118 321 8384/ www.icelandexpress.com) or Iceland2go (0845 277 3390/www.iceland2go.com).*

497 *The Turkish Republic of Northern Cyprus is the new, er, Cyprus*
£ ☕

Want reliable sun, tasty food, Brit-free beaches and something to tell the neighbours? Then head to Northern Cyprus, owned by Turkey. Here you can indulge in a Cypriot welcome while spending Turkish lira, rather than the Cypriot euro. One hassle: you can't fly direct from the UK, but to make the trip via Turkey less painful, why not combine it with a break in Istanbul?

Book with *Lemon Tree Holidays (020 8133 8350/www.lemontreeholidays.com).*

498 *The Isle of Man is the new Ireland*
£ ♟♟

As Ken Dodd once pointed out, 'No man is an island, apart from the Isle of Man.' His remark encapsulated a society set aside from the mainland (it's right in the middle of the Irish Sea) and determined to maintain its own identity, whether through the running of a perilous motorcycle race – the famous Tourist Trophy (TT) held every year – to managing its own political affairs. But now the island is looking to reinvent itself as a weekend break destination, on the basis of its fantastic scenery, great seafood and unique and important history.

Book with *The website www.iselofman.com lists hundreds of accommodation options. To get to the island, take the ferry from Liverpool or Lancashire (2-3hrs).*

499 *Moldova is the new France*
£ ☼

OK, so there are some obvious differences between the two countries (not least the cuisine), but the Republic of Moldova, situated between Romania and the Ukraine, has been raising its stakes in the international wine market of late – giving France a run for its money. A mild climate and plenty of green hills explain why viticulture and winemaking have been principal occupations here for centuries, with recent varieties including some excellent pinot noirs and sauvignons. Get there while the Moldovan leu is still the currency – the possibility of a change of currency over the next few years is fairly strong, as the country has its sights on EU membership.

Book with *Regent Holidays (0845 277 3317/ www.regent-holidays.co.uk) or Responsible Travel (www.responsibletravel.com).*

500-509

Man-made wonders

500 *The Great Pyramid of Giza, Egypt*

⌂

The last remaining intact monument of the Seven Wonders of the Ancient World, the pyramid remains an incomprehensible feat of engineering and sheer manpower.

It was built around 2560 BC as a tomb for King Khufu, and took 20 years and probably cost thousands of slaves' lives in the making. It's estimated that 2.3 million blocks of stone, at 2.5 tonnes per block, were dragged from quarry to desert to complete the landmark. The accuracy of the pyramid's design dimensions still confounds modern-day mathematicians.

501 Empire State Building, New York

www.esbnyc.com.
A landmark New York skyline landmark for more than 80 years and still going strong, this beautiful building was designed by Gregory Johnson from the top down, and took 410 days to complete. Beaten by the World Trade Center for a 30-year spell, 9/11 restored the Empire State to its position as the tallest building in the city and the fifth tallest in the world. A trip to the top means a breathtaking view of the metropolis below, and over three million visitors scale the vertigo-inducing heights every year to step out on to one of the world's most popular outdoor observatories.

502 London Eye, London

www.londoneye.com.
Opened in 1999 by then Prime Minister Tony Blair as part of London's millennial celebrations, the Eye was not actually in use until March 2000 due to numerous 'technical problems'. Despite this stumbling start, the Eye now looks set to be a permanent fixture, and since it opened over 30 million visitors have hopped into one of its 32 sealed capsules to make the half-hour journey round Europe's largest Ferris wheel.

503 Eiffel Tower, Paris

www.tour-eiffel.fr.
Originally planned for Barcelona, but dismissed by the city's authorities as bizarre and too expensive, Gustave Eiffel's iconic structure finally landed in Paris in 1889, in time to mark the centennial of the French Revolution at the Exposition Universelle. At 324 metres, it's the tallest building in the city, and weighs in at a hefty 10,000 tonnes of puddle iron, all held in place by over 2.5 million rivets. Despite this, on a windy day the tower can sway up to seven centimetres, so watch out!

504 Taj Mahal, Agra, India

http://agra-india.com/tajmahalhistoryand legends.htm.
Built in 1648 by Mughal Emperor Shah Jahan as a memorial to mourn the death

502: Eiffel Tower

of his favourite wife, Mumtaz Mahal, the building is an epic architectural icon in its own right. It combines Persian, Indian and Islamic styles and 28 types of precious stones to create one of the most easily recognisable palaces on the planet. Thanks to the benign Agra weather, the classic sight is of its 14 purely decorative white marble minarets standing against a background of pure sky and again in the placid waters of the reflecting pool that lies on a north–south axis.

505 Great Wall of China, near Beijing, China

Built in stages and under various dynasties from the fifth century BC onwards to protect the northern borders of the Chinese Empire, the wall stretches 6,400 kilometres from Shanhaiguan in the east to Lop Nur in the west, is up to nine metres wide, and was at one point guarded by more than one million men. It quickly became less a defence bastion and more of an elevated highway and trade route, part of the all-important Silk Road. Today, the wall still functions as a money-spinner, and Beijing-based tourists are herded towards Badaling and Jinshanling where the wall has been kitted out with souvenir shops, restaurants and amusement-park rides. Hiking the wall is best done with an organised tour. Can it be seen from space? Well, yes, if you have military-standard observational gear.

506 Berlin Wall remains, Germany

Built at the height of Cold War-induced paranoia in 1961 to separate East Germany from West, the wall was finally brought down on 9 November 1989 in a historic night of spontaneous riots and, um, singing by David Hasselhoff. Once reinforced by 116 watchtowers, barbed wire and vicious dogs, an estimated 200 people were killed trying to cross the wall into West Germany. The location of the wall is now marked by a row of cobblestones in the street, and the memorial remains an important part of German history.

507 Angkor Wat, Cambodia

This vast temple is a national symbol – appearing on Cambodia's flag – and has been appropriated by both Hindus and Buddhists as a centre for worship since it was built in the early 12th century as a tomb for King Suryavarman II in the high classical Khmer style, using more than five million tonnes of sandstone. To avoid the crowds, visit smaller, lesser-known temples such as the Bayon, with its numerous enigmatic faces; or indulge your sense of adventure with a helicopter ride over the temples (www.helicopterscambodia.com).

508 Mayan Pyramids of Palenque, Mexico

www.mesoweb.com/palenque
Smaller than the better-known Mayan archaeological sites Tikal (in Guatemala) or Copán (in Honduras), Palenque nonetheless contains some of the finest architecture, sculpture and carvings the Maya produced. It's estimated that only five per cent of the total city has been uncovered, and its misty isolation near the Usumacinta River in the heart of the Mexican rainforest can really make you feel like an explorer who's just stumbled on an undiscovered ancient settlement. But this is not just archaeology; visit nearby Indian villages and you'll find the language and culture are very much alive.

509 Machu Picchu, Sacred Valley, Peru

Official web: www.peru.info; see also www.peru-machu-picchu.com and www.machupicchu.org.
The most famous of the Inca citadels, this 15th-century archaeological site – set on a mountain ridge 2,438 metres above sea level in the Urubamba Valley – remained virtually undiscovered until the early part of the 20th century. Despite now attracting its maximum tourist allowance of 2,500 visitors daily, the 'Lost City of the Incas' still retains its air of grandeur and mystery. Often shrouded in mist, the space is composed of 140 structures including temples, sanctuaries, parks and an impressive system of water fountains designed for irrigation.

For more information on these, and to see the entire list of UNESCO World Heritage Sites, visit www.unesco.org.

510-519

Ten things to do in London for under a tenner

510 Get around town on a clipper
£ ▦

The waterboatmen of Elizabethan times have been replaced by something a little more modern. The speedy and sleek catamaran service Thames Clippers was launched in 1999 and is designed for commuters who aren't going to pay tourist prices. The service is still going strong and is one of the best ways to see the city.
Thames Clippers *020 7001 2222/www.thamesclippers.com.*

511 Get shown the money
£ ▦ ᴪ

Attached to the bank itself, the Bank of England Museum is housed in a replica of the original 18th-century bank's interior designed by John Soane. Here, you can discover how *Wind in the Willows* creator Kenneth Grahame, who worked at the bank for 30 years, foiled an armed bank robbery. You can even test the weight of a real-life gold bar (28lbs). Well, we can all dream.
Bank of England Museum *020 7601 5545/www.bankofengland.co.uk/education/museum.*

512 Have a taste
£ ▦

Borough Market in Southwark and other markets may have raised the bar for quality and reminded many supermarket-goers of the social pleasures of market shopping, but a lot of the food on offer comes with a pretty hefty price tag alongside its Soil Association sticker. Lucky, then, that most of the stalls offer free tasters, and you can line your stomach quite adequately with stilton and spicy sausage before finishing off with a £2 brownie.
Borough Market *www.boroughmarket.org.uk.*

513 See a performance at the Scoop
£ ▦

The Scoop at More London, to use its full name, is a sunken open-air amphitheatre with seating for 800 people on the South Bank (in front of City Hall). It runs a programme of free concerts, plays and films from May to October each year, and one evening each Christmas it's turned into a magical setting for carols and storytelling. *www.morelondon.com/scoop.html.*

514 Go to the Proms
£ ▦

True to its original democratic principals, you can still attend Promenade concerts at the Royal Albert Hall for under a fiver, with a programme that covers the full range of classical music in around 70 performances (www.bbc.co.uk/proms, from mid July to early September). You have a choice of standing in the Arena pit in the middle or standing in the gallery that runs around the top of the hall. Queues start early and snake around the block for the popular shows, but for many you will rarely have to wait more than half an hour to see world-class classical music performances.

515 Tuck into something sweet at an iconic ice-cream parlour
£ ▦ ᴪ

Chalk Farm's Marine Ices has been on this site since 1931 but the ice-cream (or rather sorbet) production began back in Gaetano Mansi's original Euston grocery store – because he didn't like to waste fruit. The family hails from Italy's Amalfi Coast so expect classic Italian faves like *stracciatella* – and competitive prices. You can have a full meal here too (Italian of course). It's popular with both families and groups of friends. *020 7482 9003/www.marineices.co.uk.*

516 Wander, cycle or float along Regent's Canal
£ ▦ ♡

Opened in 1820 to provide a transport link between east and west London, Regent's Canal was developed as a scenic public foot and cycle path in the 1960s. Any stretch of it is worth a stroll, but the most popular patch is from Camden Lock west to Little Venice, passing Regent's Park and London Zoo. Narrowboat cruises also depart from the Lock, and are around £8 for a return (Jason's Canal Trips, 020 7286 3428, www.jasons.co.uk).

517 Inspect (but don't lie on) Freud's couch

£ ▥

Preserved as it was when he died, Sigmund Freud's family home was in turn modelled on the house he had in Vienna before fleeing in 1938 (he had written down the position of everything in his study, so it could be recreated in London). The centrepiece of the museum is Freud's library and study; check out his collection of Greek, Roman and oriental antiquities, along with the infamous couch.

Freud Museum *020 7435 2002/www.freud.org.uk.*

518 Eat at one of Brick Lane's oldest curry houses

£ ▥

Successive waves of immigration have shaped Brick Lane, and any walk from north to south is pungent with the fragrance of different cuisines – most famously the curries. The restaurants can be hit and miss, but because pretty much all are BYOB, and most will offer you decent discounts to get you through the door, it's easy to keep the bill low. The Aladdin (No.132; 7247 8210) has been around for a while, and even got a look in from Prince Charles when he toured the East End.

Aladdin *020 247 8210.*

519 Chill in St Pancras Crypt Gallery

£ ▥

Under the watchful gaze of the caryatids of St Pancras Parish Church, young, emerging artists exhibit their work in what used to be the final resting place for the Bloomsbury gentry back in the 1800s. The echoing corridors, low ceilings and uneven cobbled floor are constant reminders of the building's past, but the year-round programme of (free) group shows that has been going strong since 2002 is decidedly modern, often curated by the artists themselves and inspired by their setting.

020 7388 1461/www.cryptgallery.org.uk.

513: The Scoop

Ideas from the expert

520-524

Bob Greig of Only Dads suggests five great holidays for single parents.

Bob Greig, a single dad with two young daughters, runs Only Dads (www.onlydads.org) and Only Mums (www.onlymums.org), dedicated websites for lone parents. Having suffered the slings and arrows of holidays designed for traditional families and the gleefully childless, he has found a handful of top options for parents with limited resources and only one pair of hands.

520 Family-owned Longmynd Hotel (01694 722244, www.longmynd.co.uk) in Shropshire is set in woodland just outside the quaint market town of Church Stretton. As well as a 50-room hotel, the estate has a range of self-catering lodges within the grounds, great for single-parent families, where children (and dogs) are welcome. You get use of the hotel's heated outdoor swimming pool and it's also nice to potter around the town and explore the Capability Brown-landscaped woodlands. For those nights when self-catering seems like a chore, there's a handful of decent takeaways in Church Stretton.

521 As thousands of single parents already know, a Butlins holiday means reliable fun for children and a break for mum or dad. The classic recipe is still in force: round-the-clock entertainment, clean but basic accommodation, plentiful supplies of traditional English food, and very energetic redcoats. Children love it and the staff know how to look after them. At Butlins Minehead (0845 070 4734, www.butlins.com) in Somerset you also get a beautiful coastline and easy access to Exmoor. Nursery facilities are available for very young children.

522 For single parents, camping provides a cheap and fun way of entertaining children during the holiday season. If you're after a campsite that offers a degree of tranquillity, but which still has some facilities, Watergate Bay Touring Park (01637 860387, www.watergatebaytouringpark.co.uk) in Tregurrian, Cornwall, is a good choice. A level campsite, entertainment facilities for when it's raining, and golden sands a ten-minute walk away make it a near perfect location. If you've got older kids, surfer beaches like Newquay are easily reachable.

523 La Pignade, in France's Charente Martitime (book with Siblu: 0871 911 2288, www.siblu.com), offers a range of static caravans with superb facilities, one mile inland from the beautiful coastline just north of Bordeaux. Despite its relatively small scale, the holiday park boasts a well-stocked shop, bar and restaurant, and a gleamingly clean swimming pool with slides. The children's clubs are imaginatively run and well staffed, the park is surrounded by woodland rich in birdlife and the local beaches are worth a visit – as are the nearby towns of La Rochelle and Royan.

524 For those who want to holiday in an organised group with other single parents, Mango (01902 373410, www.mangoholidays.co.uk) organises an eight-day trip to Morocco that features a couple of nights in Marrakech before heading to the foothills of the Atlas Mountains to experience life with local Berber families. Flights, hotels, board and meals are all fixed up for you, and living in the gite with a Berber family will allow you to have meals prepared for you in the traditional way.

524: Morocco with Mango holidays

525-532
Wilderness lodges

525 Iniakuk Lake Wilderness Lodge, Alaska's Arctic Circle

£ ◊

+1 907 479 6354/www.goranorth.com.
Some 85 miles above the Arctic Circle, and nestled alongside the Atlanta River, the Arrigetch Wilderness Cabin certainly comes with a view. It also comes with black and grizzly bears, wolves, caribou and moose, so keep your eyes and ears peeled. Canoe in the frosty river, or make use of your guide to explore the surrounding mountains and dense forests. The cabin fits four and is heated by a wood stove. There is no indoor plumbing but an outdoor privy suffices. And if things are getting too rustic for your tastes, dinner from the Iniakuk Lake Wilderness Lodge is prepared and served nightly.

526 Rincón del Socorro, Argentina's wetlands

◊ ⌖

+54 3782 497172/www.rincondelsocorro.com.
Not exactly wilderness, but the 12,000 uninhabited hectares of former cattle ranch and wetlands in which the Rincón del Socorro is situated certainly won't leave you feeling overcrowded. The effortlessly welcoming ranch is dedicated to preserving the natural landscape, so boat trips to see alligator and water birds on the laguna and nature trails and horserides that take in jaguars and maned wolves are careful not to disturb the area's rich ecosystem. The bungalows are all in the classic Spanish *estancia* style, as is the barbecue hut, where you can enjoy Argentine wine, locally farmed meat and vegetables on the grill for a full *asado* lunch.

527 Manda Wilderness Lodge, Lake Niassa, Mozambique

◊

www.mandawilderness.org.
Last year's winner of a Responsible Tourism Award, Manda Wilderness Lodge, on the shores of Lake Niassa, prides itself on benefiting the local community and not disturbing the local environment, with only 14 visitors to the lodge allowed at any one time. Niassa is one of the world's largest freshwater lakes, perfect for snorkelling in crystal-clear waters, and boasts pristine white sands backed by lush green forest. Head inland – camping equipment and guides are provided – to the Manda Wilderness Reserve, to spot elephant, reedbuck and leopard in 600 square kilometres of woodland, grassy plains and deep, rocky gorges. Local produce is used to combine traditional African food with Western recipes, and you can choose to dine under the stars on the beach, or in the shade of a 2,000-year-old baobab tree.

528 Spirituality and self-catering at Samakanda, Sri Lanka

⛺ ⌖

+94 0 777 424 770/www.samakanda.org.
Set your own holiday pace in one of Sri Lanka's lovingly restored tea planter's bungalows and cottages high in the hills of Nakiyadeniya, 45 minutes from Galle. There are views over the Bowl, an area shaped like a natural amphitheatre, and an orchard with over 1,500 fruit trees – where you can pick wood apple, limes, oranges and avocado – along with spices like clove and pepper vines, and herbs and vegetables. If kitchen gardening doesn't suffice, take a mountain bike ride down to the coast, or hike up to the river or nearby Galle Fort. Or try a spot of spirituality at the banyan tree shrine. Accommodation is fully equipped for a self-catering family, so you can do as much or as little as you'd like.

529 Daintree Lodge: Attenborough's magical Australia

◊

+61 7 4098 9105/www.daintreewilderness lodge.com.au.
Some 14 kilometres north of the Daintree River, and half an hour away from Cape Tribulation, is Daintree Lodge, in the heart of the rainforest that David Attenborough called 'one of the most magical experiences of my life'. Although on-site facilities include a pool, more-than-passable restaurant, and a bar featuring 'rainforest cocktails', you're nevertheless constantly aware that you're right in the centre of the rainforest canopy ecosystem, with striped possums, sunbirds and tree frogs visible from your balcony and a deep creek a few steps down a palm-fringed walkway from your cabin door. Pristine white sand is a short drive away.

527: Manda Wilderness Lodge, Mozambique

November to April visits are most likely to be rain-drenched in the rainforest wet season, but the seven cabins on high stilts that make up the lodge are open year-round.

530 Uakari Floating Lodge, Brazilian Amazonia

◊ ⚐

+55 97 3343 4160/www.uakarilodge.com.br.
The ten-bedroom Uakari Floating Lodge is, quite literally, on the Amazon River, in the Mamiraua Sustainable Development Reserve. Paddle through the flooded forest and see sloths, Red Howler monkeys and the scarlet-faced White Uakari monkey, and pink river dolphins, manatees and caiman swimming among the submerged trees. In the dry season, when the waters have receded, fish and predators concentrate around the remaining water courses and it's wise not to stray too close to the alligator-inhabited waters around the lodge. The local communities are active in the management of the lodge, with its focus on sustainable ecotourism, and fresh fish and local fruits and juices make up the menu. The lodge is a one-hour flight from Manaus to the town of Tefe, followed by a boat ride.

531 Luangwa Wilderness Lodge, Zambia

◊

+49 221 971 207/www.luangwawilderness.com.
Africa has plenty of luxury safari experiences on offer, but you can sometimes feel as if you're trampling over the environment. The Luangwa Wilderness Lodge in the Luambe National Park in Eastern Zambia was established by professional animal conservationists with the local community in mind, and the five safari-style tents, built on platforms overlooking the Luangwa River, take you to the heart of a landscape otherwise inaccessible. The park plays host to an endless list of wildlife, including elephants, zebras, lions and hippos, and a game drive can take you from the riverbank to hidden inland lagoons, across plains and through miombo woodland.

532 Northern Comfort Lodge, Sweden

◊ ♡

01929 463774/www.naturetravels.co.uk.
For a snowy winter getaway, you can't get much more picture-postcard than the Northern Comfort Lodge on the shore of Lake Revsund in Jämtland. Look out for reindeer for bonus magical winter-wonderland points. Everything is built in traditional Swedish timber, from the log cabin itself, to the outdoor wood-heated sauna and hot-tub 'bathing barrel'. With a lake on one side and dense pine forest on the other, there's snowshoed hiking or ice fishing up for grabs; or just curl up in front of a roaring log fire. The cabin accommodates eight and the large kitchen and living area are all decorated – unsurprisingly – in traditional Swedish style.

533-537
The Gulf: Dubai and beyond

533 *Dizzy in Dubai*

▤ ⚐

What was merely a windswept desert outpost 40 years ago has become a sprawling orgy of luxury hotels, absurdly ambitious architectural projects and opportunities to spend your hard-earned millions. There are the 300 man-made islands that make up the World, the globe's tallest tower in Burj Dubai, and the Atlantis Palm Resort, with its sunken city and a bay thoughtfully stocked with friendly dolphins. For full immersion in the 21st-century *Arabian Nights* fantasy, stay in one of the luxury Bedouin-style, tent-roofed suites of the Al Maha Desert Resort & Spa (+971 4 303 4222, www.al-maha.com), located in a vast conservation reserve in the desert just outside the city. Many companies run 4x4 expeditions into the surrounding terrain. There's also camel racing, alongside the world's richest annual horserace. The city is part Disneyland, part genuine doorway to the mysterious East.

534 *Artistic Abu Dhabi*

▤

Abu Dhabi may have the seven-star hotel, the Emirates Palace (www.emiratespalace.com), which cost over £2 billion to build, but as Frank Gehry, the architect responsible for the city's new Guggenheim museum, has stated, 'What they don't want is a repeat of Dubai.' His

537: Grand Mosque, Muscat

537: Grand Hyatt Rooftop Grill House

Guggenheim is being built on Saadiyat Island, a vast project encompassing a Performing Arts Centre by Zaha Hadid and Tadao Ando's Zen concrete Maritime Museum. Saadiyat Island's other big arts project is an outpost of the Louvre, and there's talk of the British Museum getting involved too. Cementing its title as the cultural heart of the Emirates is the Cultural Foundation (www.adach.ae), which hosts art exhibitions and lectures, as well as concerts and operas; it also organised the first Middle Eastern WOMAD festival in 2009. More classic holiday pursuits are also on offer, from the large, public Corniche beach to the Sir Bani Yas nature reserve island.

535 *Skiing in Iran*

Unexpected, yes, but the Alborz mountain range, within which Iran's capital is nestled, is home to no fewer than 16 pistes, and skiing has long been popular with Iran's elite. The sport was briefly banned after the revolution, but is back in vogue again, and the remote mountain resorts provide a welcome escape from Islamic state control for many young Iranians. The

largest resort is less than an hour's drive from Tehran at Dizin, where you can ski for under a fiver a day. Equipment and clothes are also available to hire incredibly cheaply. Lifts are still segregated and bars cannot sell booze, but the locals make up for this by entertaining in large rented chalets where you can top off a day's hard skiing down the 3,658-metre pistes with a widely available homebrew.

536 *Mini-break in Musandam*

Just a two-hour drive away from Dubai, Musandam has become a favourite for Emirates-based holidaymakers in need of a quiet weekend retreat. Instead of glass-walled skyscrapers, you get to look up at the medieval castle in the centre of regional capital Khasab, surrounded by stunning plateaux of grey mountains. The Golden Tulip Resort (just outside town; +96 82 673 0777, www.goldentulipkhasab.com) offers beautiful coastal views, a terrace shisha bar and more than passable local fare. Or take a boat trip through the fjords, which have earned Musandam the nickname 'the Norway of Arabia', and from which you'll be able to spot Telegraph Island, the now deserted site of the British Empire's attempt to lay a telegraph cable from Bombay to Basra.

537 *Muscat*

The name originally comes from the word for 'safe anchorage', and the mountains that encircle this small but perfectly formed port town make it just that. Strict architectural regulations and features such as the impossibly elegant Grand Mosque make this arguably the most beautiful city in the Gulf. In 2006 it was named as Arab Cultural Capital, and its recently opened Bait al-Baranda Museum is home to a wealth of Omani artefacts. History is everywhere, from the carefully preserved port itself, to the opportunity to partake in the time-honoured tradition of bartering in the city's ancient Mutrah Souk. For a great view of the city, head up to the Grand Hyatt hotel's Rooftop Grill House (www.muscat.grand.hyatt.com) for dinner.

538-547
Rural refuges in the UK

538 *Be bowled over by the Forest of Bowland*

Lancashire's Forest of Bowland is dominated by its wild uplands – huge hump-backed fells covered with heather and gorse moor. To the south, the Forest is bisected by the pretty Ribble Valley, home to beautiful Clitheroe.

Stay at the Inn at Whitewell, set on the River Hodder, with matchless views across the fells. The country inn seduces with its effortlessly hospitable attitude, cosy rug-strewn rooms, and antiques and hunting and fishing paraphernalia. It's also a dining destination in its own right.
Inn at Whitewell *01200 448222/ www.innatwhitewell.com.*

539 *Keswick – the loveliest part of the Lake District*

With landscapes ranging from picturesque waterscapes and sublime ranges of rolling fells to bleak scrub-covered crags, the area around Keswick is seldom short of awe-inspiring.

Stay at Lyzzick Hall, Underskiddaw, which manages to combine the majestic visual splendour of a traditional country hotel with a fun and informal air. Rooms range from simple to strikingly modern; there's also an indoor swimming pool, sauna and jacuzzi, plus a delightful terrace overlooking the gardens.
Lyzzick Hall *017687 72277/www.lyzzickhall.co.uk.*

540 *See heart-stopping views from the Herefordshire Beacon*

Deep in the Malverns lies the British Camp, the Iron Age fort where Caractacus allegedly surrendered to the Romans. The breathtaking views from the 1,109-foot peak, deemed one of 'the goodliest vistas' in England by 17th-century diarist John Evelyn, stretch across the Welsh border. Eastnor Castle and the picturesque town of Ledbury are nearby.

Stay at the Malvern Hills Hotel, an intimate 19th-century building that offers simple but well-equipped rooms, from four-poster to family sized. The romantic natural surroundings are enhanced by a candlelit bar and restaurant.
Malvern Hill Hotel *01684 540690.*

541 *Quaint and classy Cookham*

Cookham belongs in a different time – specifically that of Stanley Spencer. The artist described his birthplace as a 'village in heaven', and visitors can enjoy the sleepy Thameside destination's gorgeous river views and gentle woodland walks, not forgetting Spencer's masterpieces.

Big spenders should head to Cliveden House for accommodation, a short drive away. The stately home has a history as decorous as its furnishings; it was the home of Lady Astor, and Winston Churchill, George Bernard Shaw and Charlie Chaplin have all spent the night.
Cliveden House *01628 668561/ www.clivedenhouse.co.uk.*

542 *Gorgeous Glencoe*

With scenery as intimidating as it is impressive, the Highlands showcase nature at its rawest and wildest. From the towering peak of the Bauchaille to the vast waters of Loch Leven, Glencoe is bleak, brilliant and breathtaking all at once. A hotspot for climbing, hiking and fly-fishing, this is perfect for outdoorsy types, but also for those looking for a spot of existential contemplation.

Stay and eat at the three-centuries-old Clachaig Inn, which has a selection of pleasant but no-nonsense en suite rooms, and is the perfect place for weary walkers to lay their heads.
Clachaig Inn *01855 811252/www.clachaig.com.*

543 *Little Llanbedr*

Tucked between snow-capped peaks and Wales's north-western coast lies the tiny village of Llanbedr. The surrounding area is awash with sights, from prehistoric roads to the medieval Harlech Castle, with a stunningly diverse landscape home to waterfalls, beaches and hidden caverns. For the intrepid climber, Snowdonia is just 40 minutes away.

Stay at the Bryn Artro Country Residence, which was once a Victorian gentleman's house. The rooms are charmingly old-fashioned but not ill equipped. The beautiful landscaped gardens are perfect for a summer stroll.
Bryn Artro Country Residence *01341 241619.*

544 *Lakeside serenity at Lough Neagh*

Britain's largest freshwater lake is one of the country's most tranquil spots. Easily accessible from Belfast, but far enough away that you can leave urban life behind, it's ideal for watersports, fishing and cycling.

Lough-side accommodation is lacking, but Newforge House is near the south-eastern shore. A family-run Georgian mansion with just six rooms, it feels more like visiting friends than staying in a hotel. Rooms are classic and luxurious, and the hotel is set in 40 acres of scenic grassland.
Newforge House *028 9261 1255.*

545 *Woodstock: well-chosen wining and dining*

Not the festival but the historic market town, Woodstock is the perfect place from which to discover the South Cotswolds. Day trips abound, to Oxford or to the Roman remains at Cirencester, and there's plenty to see nearer the town, whether it's Churchill's birthplace, Blenheim Palace, or the thatched cottages at the tiny unspoilt village of Minster Lovell. It's worth the trip to the neighbouring town of Witney for excellent cuisine (try Fleece: www.fleecewitney.co.uk).

Stay at the Macdonald Bear, minutes from Blenheim. It's part of a chain, but don't be put off: it has the unusual comforts of a 13th-century coaching inn adjoined to a former glove factory.
Macdonald Bear *0844 879 9143/ www.macdonaldhotels.co.uk/bear.*

544: Newforge House, Lough Neagh

546 *Wharfedale – Queen of the Yorkshire Dales*

◐ ◔

Wharfedale isn't called the Queen of the Dales for nothing, there is no shortage of natural, and indeed man-made, phenomena in the vicinity. Vast, angry waterfalls, and a dramatic Ice Age sheer cliff and quaint dry-stone walls are some of the treats, and the less intrepid will find plenty of places to wander off the beaten track in this walkers' paradise. For food, head for the Angel Inn (01756 730263, www.angelhetton.co.uk), recognised as the original gastropub.

Stay at the George Inn, set in the blink-and-you'll-miss-it hamlet of Hubberholme, amid endless green countryside and with stone walls, antiques and roaring fires.
George Inn *01756 760223/ www.thegeorge-inn.co.uk*

547 *Sustainable style at Swaffham*

◐ ◔

A quaint market town in the Norfolk Brecks, Swaffham is a pastoral wonderland that could certainly be counted among England's most beautiful lowland areas. Wildlife watchers will be spoilt for choice, from deer roaming freely in the forest to the coastal bird reserves.

Stay and eat at Strattons, a boutique hotel with a difference. It has perhaps the lowest carbon footprint of any British hotel, but ecologically sound doesn't mean shabby.
Strattons *01760 723845/www.strattons-hotel.co.uk.*

548-554
Cute Alpine villages linked to vast ski areas

548 *Champagny-en-Vanoise, France (linked to La Plagne)*

◐ ♡ ⛷ ◔

Champagny-en-Vanoise, linked by a seven-minute gondola ride to La Plagne's vast 225-kilometre ski area, is charm itself, far removed from the brutal 1960s architecture of its high-altitude concrete cousins. Champagny is about as attractive a ski resort as you're ever likely to find, and it also sits at the bottom of the wild, back-country Mont de la Guerre run; when it's open, this is one of the loveliest pistes in the Alps. For an even slower pace of life, the nearby hamlet of Champagny-le-Haut plays host to 30 kilometres of peaceful cross-country trails and little else, save the blissful sound of silence. *www.champagny.com.*

549 *Samnaun, Switzerland (linked to Ischgl, Austria)*

◐ ⛷ ◔

Ischgl is Austria's party resort par excellence, with long runs and late nights throughout the season. For a change of scene, take the lift up to Palinkopf, at 2,900 metres, and head down piste no.10 – about 1,000 metres further down you'll cross the border into Switzerland as you glide through the trees into the duty-free village of Samnaun. At lunchtime the hills are alive with the sound of… tills, as cross-border cruisers stash bargain bottles into their rucksacks before ordering a plate of *rösti*. But linger a little longer and you'll discover that this lost corner of Switzerland is also a great place to stay, with comfy hotels, a civilised village centre and a queue-free double-decker cable car straight into the heart of Ischgl's 240-kilometre network of pistes. *www.samnaun.ch.*

550 *Stüben, Austria (linked to St Anton)*

◐ ⛷ ◔

Austria's St Anton is renowned both for its tough skiing and relentless party atmosphere. If you want to share the impressive skiing but skip the intense socialising, then Stüben is a compact and friendly village clustered around a handsome church at the foot of the Albona lift system – the access point for the most reliable north-facing slopes in the area. Be warned, though, that this is one of the coldest spots in the Alps, as the quilts supplied at the bottom of the chairlifts suggest. The village is also the finishing line for one of the Alps' longest runs – a massive ten kilometres of sweeping piste from the top of the Valluga Grat cable car, via the Ulmerhütte ice bar. At the end of that, you'll be so knackered that partying will be the last thing on your mind. *www.stuben.com.*

548: Champagny-en-Vanoise, France

551 *Samoëns, France*
(linked to Flaine)

☼ ⚡ ☺

The Grand Massif ski area sits in the lee of Mont Blanc, a passport to decent snow conditions, even though the area only tops out at 2,500 metres. However, the main town of Flaine is famously ugly, its Marcel Breuer-designed Bauhaus apartment blocks more akin to an urban council estate than a ski resort. If you want to get away from the brutalist blocks but still be part of this great area, book into Samoëns instead. Situated in the beautiful Giffre Valley, it's the only French ski resort classified by the National Register of Historic Monuments. But the town isn't stuck in the dark ages – an eight-seater gondola whisks skiers up to 1,600 metres in just eight minutes, giving a direct link to the Grand Massif.
www.samoens.com.

552 *Champéry, Switzerland*
(linked to the Portes du Soleil)

☼ ♡ ⚡ ☺

The Portes du Soleil, which straddles the border between France and Switzerland, is the largest linked ski area in the world, with a whopping 650 kilometres of pistes to choose from each morning. Many visitors stay in high-altitude Avoriaz, a futuristic 1960s resort designed by Squaw Valley gold medallist and future sunglasses tycoon Jean Vuarnet, but the area is littered with charming valley villages, none more so than Swiss Champéry – a chocolate-box collection of hotels and chalets on a sun-soaked shelf overlooking a magnificent cliffscape. If that all sounds too civilised, the local ski area is also home to the infamous Swiss Wall, one of the longest and steepest mogul fields in Europe.
www.champery.com.

553 *Venosc, France*
(linked to Les Deux Alpes)

☼ ⚡ ☺

The sprawling resort of Les Deux Alpes is a full-on party destination. At night the town's 40-plus hotels release an avalanche of young, thirsty, often British après-skiers into the arms of the waiting bartenders, and with everything from toffee vodkas to bucking broncos on offer, there's every opportunity for things to get very messy. If you prefer it quiet and quaint, but don't want to miss out on Les Deux Alpes' seriously snowsure slopes – skiing here tops out at a breathless 3,550 metres – then the ancient hamlet of Venosc, a 700-metre gondola ride below the main resort, makes a great alternative, with après-ski attractions more along the lines of donkey sleigh rides than bucking broncos.
www.venosc.com.

554 Leogang, Austria (linked to Saalbach-Hinterglemm)

The twin ski towns of Saalbach and Hinterglemm are attractive, but they also have a seedy edge with plenty of rowdy, beer-fuelled pubs, neon signs and a go-go bar quota that Heidi would never have approved of. Which is a shame, as the resorts form part of Austria's largest ski circus, with some 200 kilometres of pistes. If the thought of high-altitude girlie bars doesn't turn you on, help is at hand in the shape of infinitely more well-behaved Leogang, a tiny village linked to the ski area via the Asitz gondola. On the way down to Leogang, don't miss out on a pit stop at the wonderful Alte Schmiede (old smithy) – a beautiful old 'museum' restaurant at the top of the gondola, with character galore and not a dancing pole in sight.
www.leogang-saalfelden.at.

554: Leogang, Austria

555-564
Wicked winter sun

555 Tenerife, Canary Islands

Tenerife, the island of the eternal spring and to some the eternal party, is the largest of the Canary Islands and only a 4-5-hour flight from the UK (often included in outrageously cheap package deals). Its golden beaches may be as busy as its bars, but you can leave the resorts for a dramatic hike up Pico del Teide, the tallest peak in the Atlantic, or head north for quieter spots of cheap-rate paradise.
Book with *Holiday Hypermarket (0800 916 5100/ www.holidayhypermarket.co.uk/tenerife).*

556 Fes, Morocco

If you're travelling through seasons, you might as well travel through time. Fes was Morocco's capital in medieval times, and little has changed since then. Stay at one of the restored palaces – Dar Roumana is a delight (www.darroumana.com) – and prepare for sensory overload. Artisans labour in colourful shopping streets as they have for hundreds of years, and the donkey is still the chosen means of transport.
Book with *Atlas Blue (020 7307 5803/ www.atlas-blue.com).*

557 Sinai, Egypt

There are two ways of visiting Sinai. You can opt for a luxury resort in the spectacular diving and pampering capital Sharm El Sheikh, or join a camel safari on a rustic desert adventure to Mount Sinai, where Moses is believed to have received the Ten Commandments. Either way, you'll have plenty of sunshine to enjoy, as even in winter the temperature peaks at 26 degrees.
Book with *Co-op Travel (for a budget beach break; 01922 700007/www.cooptravel.co.uk/Egypt); Baobab Travel (for a camel safari; 0121 314 6011/ www.baobabtravel.com).*

558 *Dominican Republic, Caribbean*

The Caribbean is for serious summery sunshine all year round. For vast stretches of deserted white-sand beaches, head to Punta Cana in the Dominican Republic. Dotted with palm trees, it is surprisingly easy to walk the coast for miles without seeing anyone but the odd local sitting in the shade with a machete and mound of fresh coconuts. Inland, the mountainous rainforest offers respite from the heat.

Book with *Thomas Cook (0871 895 0055/ www.thomascook.com).*

559 *The Gambia, Africa*

There may be no time difference between the UK and the Gambia, but the six-hour flight will take you from the middle of the European winter to the height of the African summer. Palm-fringed beaches and chic hotels are found in Kololi and Kotu, but it would be a pity not to take advantage of a stay in this exotic land to discover the wildlife in its parks, mangroves and islands.

Book with *Gambia Experience (0845 330 2060/ www.gambia.co.uk).*

560 *Azores, Atlantic Ocean*

A thousand miles west of Portugal, warmed by the Gulf Stream, the nine temperate islands of the Azores are warm all year round, although you may need a jumper in January. The ravines and rocks contrast with the lush green meadows, bursts of flowers and stone settlements dating back to the archipelago's first visitors in the 1400s. Local specialities include fine liqueurs, cheeses and cakes.

Book with *Sunvil (020 8758 4722/http://azores-holidays.sunvil.co.uk).*

561 *Beirut, Lebanon*

After 5,000 years of civilisation, Beirut still trembles with political conflict; but be a bit daring, and you'll get to discover Lebanon's capital before the crowds do. The 'Paris of the East', its museums and bars match those of many European cities, and Beirut's restaurants are said to serve the best houmous in the Middle East. Visit in April or October, when the heat is in the moderate 20s.

Book with *bmi (0870 6070 555/www.flybmi.com).*

562 *Cape Town, South Africa*

Cape Town combines a sultry Mediterranean climate with African culture and a dramatic natural setting. Refugees from the grey northern winter come here frequently for the white sand beaches and the internationally famed wine valleys. Those with a taste for adventure can go diving with great white

558: Punta Cana, Dominican Republic

sharks, or hike to the peak of Table Mountain, where its spectacular national park stretches into the sky for over a kilometre.

Book with *Virgin Holidays (0844 557 5825/ www.virginholidays.co.uk).*

563 *Salvador da Bahia, Brazil*

Founded in 1549, Salvador was Brazil's most important city for the next three centuries. Even then, it was renowned for its decadence and sensuality, and colonial buildings – some peeling and evocative, some prettified – remain the backdrop to wild street festivals, beating drum music and capoeira circles. Cool off in the tropical waters along the coast and follow your nose from the plazas to refuel with the city's delicious African cuisine.

Book with *Steppes Travel (01285 880980/ www.steppestravel.co.uk).*

564 *Cancún, Mexico*

The Miami of Mexico, Cancún is a more exotic version of its Floridian cousin; white-sand beach stretches around the vast lagoon of Nichupte for 22 kilometres. If you can bear to lose sight of the Caribbean, try a jungle tour in the mangrove near Puerto Morelos, and visit one of the many ancient Maya ruins; the Yucatán peninsula where Cancún is found is home to the sites of Uxmal, Kabah, Labna, Sayil, Dzibilchaltun and the impressive ceremonial grounds of Chichen Itza.

Book with *Asda Travel (www.asda-travel.co.uk).*

565-571

Classic America

565 *Chicago – the last Great American City*

It may not have won its 2016 Olympic bid, but Chicago remains a city out to impress, from its towering skyscrapers to its ambitious Millennium Park, which arrived four years behind schedule and $300 million over budget – a symptom of the political scandals that have

never been absent from the city's history for long. Street names are no more content to remain anonymous, with the world-famous shopping promenade of N Michigan Avenue re-titled the Magnificent Mile. Joining the urban highlights are a number of sandy beaches on the shores of the vast Lake Michigan. The best place to enjoy a scenic view of both lake and skyline is outside the excellent Adler Planetarium; or you might want to opt for local colour inland, in the hipster areas of Wicker Park and Bucktown. Chicago citizens are proud of what's on offer in their city, and aren't quiet about showing it, so make like a native and join the crowd at a baseball game (local teams are the White Sox and the Cubs), a local bar (this is a great drinking town) or one of the myriad theatres and comedy clubs.

566 *Disneyland – happiest place on earth?*

Disneyworld Florida may be the biggest and Tokyo's DisneySea might be the most bizarre, but Disneyland California is the original and, arguably, still the best. Approached with an appropriately sunny outlook, it might just fulfil its promise to be 'the happiest place on earth'. The park is imbued with 60-plus years of history – from the names of its 'streets', taken from various Disney stars and collaborators, to a petrified tree in 'Adventureland' that Walt actually gave to his wife as an anniversary present. There are eight different 'lands' to explore, from the historical mock-ups of Main Street and New Orleans Square, to the thrill-rides and cowboys-and-indians escapades of Frontierland. Every land is, of course, full of opportunities to spend Disney dollars (exchange rate one real dollar to a Mickey-endorsed one), but you can save money by staying in one of the nearby hotels as opposed to one of several operations within the park.

www.disneyland.disney.go.com.

567 *Las Vegas – escapist entertainment and then some*

The gambling capital of the world, Las Vegas is a town with a chequered history, rescued from ruin in the 1930s by Mob money, and again more recently by the founding of the Steve Wynn hotel empire. Wynn and his imitators returned the city

571: Fenway Park, Boston

to its former role as the American epicentre of excess and decadence. The city as a whole provides escapism enough, but you can also choose to travel back in time at the Arthurian-themed Excalibur Hotel, or witness Vegas's attempt at European sophistication at Paris Las Vegas or the Venetian. Or suspend your disbelief at the still-extraordinary Cirque de Soleil. Save money by booking midweek rather than weekends, and by staying a little distance from the Strip. But beware: the further you travel from the centre, the closer you come to encountering the reality of full-time gamblers holding on to faded Vegas dreams.
www.visitlasvegas.com.

568 *Los Angeles – film-set fantasies*

The city is one of the world's largest metropolitan areas, and despite expanding metro and bus systems, it's likely that without a car you'll feel slightly stranded. However, with constant sunshine, perfectly manicured areas like Beverly Hills, and the chance that you may wander past the former residence of Elvis Presley or John Travolta, you may be quite content to walk. Star-spotting opportunities abound, from shopping trips on Rodeo Drive to hotels like the Chateau Marmont, where John Belushi died. If you've reached Hollywood saturation point, and the wannabes on Venice Beach really aren't doing it for you, the Getty Center up in the hills offers cultural relief and spectacular views.

569 *Big Bend National Park – north of the border, just*

The Big Bend is named for the vast stretch of the Rio Grande river that forms the border between south-west Texas and Mexico, 244 square miles of which is contained within the national park – which remains one of the least-visited in the US. Big Bend covers over 1,000 miles of public land, and includes vast desert expanses and the entire Chisos mountain range. Hiking, driving and riding are all catered for, and a canoe or raft is the ideal transport down the Santa Elena Canyon. Wander around the eerie ruins of the once-thriving mining community in the Terelingua 'ghost town', or visit the specially constructed viewing area

and try to see the mysterious Marfa Lights. The Big Bend Resort provides facilities, but the smaller hotels and restaurants in Marfa, Alpine and Marathon are more charming.

570 *Yellowstone National Park – the real wild west*

From the endangered lynx to the rare grey wolf, Yogi Bear-style grizzlies and herds of free-ranging bisons, Yellowstone Park has it all, holding on to its status as the largest intact ecosystem in the northern hemisphere. There are lakes, canyons, rivers and mountain ranges, as well as an impressive half of the world's geysers, the most popular of which is affectionately named Old Faithful. It was established in 1872 as the USA's first national park, and it gets Wyoming's top billing, with more than 30,000 people a day making the pilgrimage in summer. In winter, visitors can make use of snowmobiles and coaches. Rangers are on hand to co-ordinate camping, hiking and riding expeditions, and to minister to the nine types of accommodation available, ranging from winter snow cabins to the rustic Roosevelt Cabins.
www.travelyellowstone.com.

567: Las Vegas

570: Yellowstone National Park

571 *Boston – tea party town*

'The Athens of America' is relatively small in size, but a heavyweight in history and culture. Follow the self-guided tour – the Freedom Trail – and find yourself on top of Bunker Hill Monument, the site of the first major conflict of the American Revolution, and provider of a perfect view of the city's quaint, leafy streets. It's worth struggling through the crowds at the 250-year-old Faneuil Hall marketplace to sample the famous New England oysters at one of America's oldest restaurants, Union Oyster House. Followed, naturally, by a Sam Adams beer – the brewery named after the famous Abolitionist is just around the corner. The Museum of Fine Art is packed with masterpieces, but the smaller Isabella Stewart Museum is imbued with the spirit of John Singer Sargeant and Henry James. Literary types abound in the beautiful Harvard campus in nearby Cambridge. And if you can get tickets, visit Fenway Park for the ultimate patriotic experience: a Red Sox baseball game.

572-576
Coach holidays

Anyone who has seen the Channel 4 reality show *Coach Trip*, in which a raggle-taggle bunch of British tourists experience the delights and downsides of Europe's top attractions – all the while trading snappy putdowns and cringe-inducing innuendos – might think twice before booking themselves on a four-wheeled holiday. But while the classic coach trip is still a force across Britain – freighting pensioners to Eastbourne, stags to Blackpool and rugby fans to Twickenham – there is another way to tour the UK and beyond en masse.

In fact, there are literally hundreds of options without even stepping outside the the borders of our own **green and pleasant land 572**, from the sun (here's hoping) and sand of Newquay, St Ives or the wistfully nicknamed 'English Riviera' at Torquay, to more niche options such as a tour of the Great Northern Railways or along Hadrian's Wall. Shearings Holidays (0844 824 6350, www.shearings.com) runs very reasonably priced, well-organised package coach tours to all these places and further afield – Scotland, Wales and Ireland – with accommodation and expeditions to surrounding attractions all planned for you. And its most popular trip? Blackpool is still up there, donkey rides included.

Come December, a coach tour can let you create your very own picture-postcard Christmas, complete with reindeer, crisp white snow and enough twinkly lit European Christmas markets to satisfy the most enthusiastic shopper. Newmarket Holidays (0845 226 7756, www.newmarketholidays.co.uk) runs **yuletide trips to the Continent 573** that take in Europe's biggest nativity scene in Ruedesheimer,

Germany, offer carriage rides through the snowy cobbled streets of Bruges, or a chance to taste Black Forest gâteau in its native land. Scrooges need not apply.

The classic American road trip doesn't have to be made in a vintage Cadillac. The **Greyhound coach company 574** (+1 800 231 2222, www. greyhound.com) is almost as iconic as the sign for Route 66, and with 2,300 destinations across the States, it can take you pretty much anywhere you want to go. You can get all the way from New York to New Mexico for less than 150 bucks, or use it to hug the West coastline, hopping off at LA, San Francisco and San Diego, as well as gems like Berkeley and Anaheim.

If you've always wanted to travel through **India or South America 575** but the prospect of finding your way in a big bad continent by yourself was too daunting, then the rigours of a coach tour itinerary might be just the right way to make sure you don't miss anything off the list. Archers Direct (0844 573 4806, www.archersdirect.co.uk) can take you to Chile and show you the sea, volcanoes and glaciers, all in under two weeks. Or try a whistle-stop tour of India, taking in Delhi, Mumbai and innumerable Mughal palaces, with your very own learned professor as tour guide on hand to help you keep up.

InterRail trips can all too often become costly nightmares of intricate timetabling and restrictive train tracks. With **Eurolines coaches 576** (www.eurolines.com) to almost every destination in Europe leaving direct from London Victoria, and a trip across the Channel starting at 19 quid, it's the ultimate way to start a trip if you're not quite sure where you want to end up. Under-25s can get an unlimited access pass for two weeks for about £160. Go from Amsterdam to Berlin in less than a day, then head over to the incredibly cheap delights of Eastern Europe and Croatia. You can head back through Classical Italy and stop off in Paris before you head home on the ferry.

577-583

Best stopovers

So you're flying long-haul to Australia or New Zealand, a former Spanish colony in the New World, an out-of-the-way American town, or the outliers of South-east Asia. Chances are you'll have to get off one plane and on to another, maybe even spend the night somewhere. Don't grumble – think of it as an opportunity for another mini-holiday. Here's what to do between flights at seven of the big hubs.

577 Dubai International Airport

Dubai's airport (www.dubaiairport.com) has never been better for shoppers. If pressed for time, make a trip to the airport's expansive – but not always expensive – duty-free area; for a real retail adventure, though, pay a visit to the Burjuman Centre on Trade Centre Road. It's great for major fashion chains. To refuel, pop into the Exchange Grill at the Fairmont hotel (www.fairmont.com/dubai) or, if you're homesick, the Dubliners bar at Le Méridien, which serves a pint and decent pub grub.
One night stand *Millennium hotel (+971 429 50500, www.millenniumhotels.com/ae/ copthornehoteldubai).*

578 Changi Airport, Singapore

There are plenty of activities to enjoy at Singapore's Changi Airport (www.changiairport. com). If your thighs are stiff and flight-weary, head for the roof-top pool. For something more hardcore, there's in-line skating at East Coast Park and you can rent equipment from one of the numerous kiosks for a small fee. Should you fancy a ride on the water, go down to the Ski 360 Cableski Park (www.ski360degree.com) to experience the new water-ski track.
One night stand *Crown Plaza, Changi (0871 423 4896/www.ichotelsgroup.com/h/d/cp/1/en/hotel/sincp).*

579 Barajas Airport, Madrid

The gobsmacking, Richard Rogers-designed Barajas terminal (www.aena.es) in Madrid is only half an hour away from the city by taxi, or you can catch the Metro from Terminal 2 to the city centre. Foodies (even Catalan foodies) admit the Spanish capital has the best restaurants and bars. Head for the Sol Metro and take your pick of classic bar-restaurants for a quick glass of vermouth or sherry accompanied by tapas.
One night stand *Hotel de las Letras (+34 915 237 980/www.hoteldelasletras.com).*

582: Hotel Unique, São Paulo

580 Los Angeles International Airport (LAX)

Los Angeles is best known for its film culture, so why not spend an evening in one of the city's many picturehouses? Catch the bus from LAX (www.lawa.org/welcomelax.aspx) and get off at Fairfax Avenue North; the art deco Silent Movie Theatre (www.silentmovietheatre.com), built in 1945 and lovingly restored, is one of the oldest cinemas around. Or take your pick of the multiplexes, the most popular being the Landmark in Westwood (www.fandango.com).
One night stand *The Palomar in Westwood (+1 310 475 8711/www.hotelpalomar-lawestwood.com).*

581 Hong Kong International Airport

Stopping off in Hong Kong (www.hongkong airport.com) is an opportunity to make some money: the difference between the price of having a suit tailored in the UK and getting it made in Hong Kong can help you recover the cost of your flight ticket. Make the 45-minute taxi journey to Raja Fashions in Tsim Sha Tsui (www.raja-fashions.com) for a range of suits, coats and jackets. If you're with the kids, Disneyland (www.park.hongkongdisneyland. com) is near the airport, and you can get there using the Lantau link between the airport and HK island. It also has accommodation.
One night stand *Regal Airport Hotel (+852 2286 8888/www.regalhotel.com).*

582 Guarulhos International Airport, São Paulo

São Paulo's airport is almost as ugly as its URL (www.infraero.gov.br/usa/aero_prev_home.php? ai=217), but cosmopolitan, super-cool São Paulo is home to several of Brazil's best restaurants. Brasil a Gosto (www.brasilagosto.com.br), in the leafy Jardins district, serves up great local cuisine and home-made liqueurs. Burn it off clubbing: the nightlife in Brazil's biggest city is heady and hectic. Go to the Bela Vista neighbourhood for a choice of bars and clubs. Transfer back by helicopter using a sky-taxi: it doesn't come cheap, but it's an hourly service and is popular with city slickers wanting to circumvent the city's endless traffic jams.
One night stand *Hotel Unique (+55 11 3055 4710/www.hotelunique.com.br).*

583 Dallas/Fort Worth International Airport

Stopping off at Dallas/Fort Worth (www. dfwairport.com) overnight could mean a chance to experience, should you choose, the world's largest bull-riding event. Billy Bob's Texas rodeo (www.billybobstexas.com) has shows daily and is genuinely unlike anything else you'll have seen before. Hop in a taxi for front seats at 2520 Rodeo Plaza, Fort Worth.
One night stand *Adolphus Hotel (+1 214 742 8200/www.hoteladolphus.com).*

584-593
Brilliant budgeting ideas

584 *Go online*

Yes, there's a mind-boggling maelstrom of data out there, but if you're savvy, a bit of searching of virtual resources can save you real money. As well as budget flight search portals and price comparison sites, you can sign up for email and Twitter alerts that put you at the front of the line for price slashes and up-to-the-minute deals. And don't forget Teletext (also online at www.teletextholidays.co.uk).

585 *Go off-peak*

For UK residents, peak seasons for European travel are between school terms, especially July to September, meaning that the so-called 'shoulder seasons' – spring and late autumn in the UK – are good for European holidays as you get the sunshine but not the crowds, and competitive prices. For the southern hemisphere, the peak period is the UK winter, so aim for holidays in October and November, or April and May if heading to places like South Africa or Argentina. For the Western world and much of the Eastern, Christmas and Easter are peak. Airlines with their main hubs in non-Christian countries – such as the Gulf – don't experience quite the same rush in late December.

586 *The early bird...*

It's definitely a drag getting up before you go to bed, and taking a night bus to Luton hardly feels like the start of a memorable holiday. But if you can brave pre-dawn departures, you can save a sizeable wad of money.

587 *Haggle with your travel agent*

In the current economic climate, and with online competitors muscling in on their territory, your local travel agent may well be prepared to offer you some impressive discounts if you're prepared to push for them.

588 *Say no to the euro?*

Well, yes and no. The weak pound in the Eurozone and politicians' lobbying for the 'staycation' might tempt you into thinking that your wallet would be better off if you planned a holiday in the UK – but that's not always the case. Taking into account food, drink, board and other costs, as well as the airfare deals available, means that a weekend in sunny Seville could cost less than one in rather less sunny Scotland; just make sure you do your research and include all extras in your final cost calculation.

589 *Prepay your way*

You can lose a lot in little ways by withdrawing money or using a credit card abroad, so why not look after the pennies by getting a prepaid debit card before you go? These combine the principle of traveller's cheques with the convenience of a debit card that you can use in most places. It can be loaded up with dollars or euros, doesn't charge for ATM withdrawal, and there's the advantage of security; if you lose your card, for a fee of around £10 most providers will replace it, with all the funds intact.

590 *Stay and save*

Don't rely on the hotel star system – it's based on facilities not quality, and isn't a true indicator of a hotel's standards, so always do a bit of research to get full value for your money. In big-name holiday destinations, you can save hundreds of pounds if you book midweek as opposed to weekends.

591 *Beware hidden charges!*

With proposals under way to charge passengers for using the loo, it's worth figuring out how you can dodge those 'extras' airlines use to snare unsuspecting flyers. Make sure you check the baggage restrictions – travelling light can save you up to £15 per kilo of excess luggage weight. And always, always print out your travel documents; Ryanair, for instance, whacks on a £40 fine for those who forget them.

592 *Ditch the motor*

If you can face lugging your luggage, public transport and buses can be miles cheaper than a taxi or airport parking. If you're in London, take the tube to Heathrow for just £4, or an Easybus to Luton, Gatwick or Stansted from central London for less than £13 return. Stagecoach operates 24 hours in Manchester,

Leeds and Sheffield, and National Express runs airport services in Glasgow and Edinburgh.

593 *Canny car parking*

Book it well in advance – most airports offer discounts to fill up spaces 30 days ahead of time. Also see www.airportparkingsite.co.uk, which offers unofficial but cheaper parking for most national airports; and you can save even more if you pick up your car slightly further away. Visit www.myvouchercodes.co.uk for discount parking.

594-599
Far Eastern journeys

594 *Taiwan*
◊

Route *Taipei–Chihpen–Kenting–Alishan–Sun Moon Lake.*
When the Portuguese chanced upon it, they called it Formosa – the beautiful island – and Taiwan lives up to its name. As a legacy of the Cultural Revolution, it's the best place to view Chinese artefacts, being home to a collection of treasures dating back 3,000 years. Yet this perhaps takes second place to marvelling at the unusual landscape around the country's jagged coastline, Yehliu's curious candle rock formations, the marble-walled Taroko Gorge or the fabulously titled Sun Moon Lake. Taiwan is relatively small, so it's possible to explore the postcard-perfect beaches of Chihpen, the lush tropical woodland of Kentang and the vibrant metropolis of Taipei.
Book with *Cox & Kings (020 7873 5000/ www.coxandkings.co.uk).*

595 *Japan*
▤ ◊

Route
Tokyo–Hakone–Kyoto–Miyajima–Hiroshima.
Japan fascinates the West, and it's easy to see why. Quite apart from its enviable culinary customs, fascinating history and quirky dress sense, Japan's frenetic pace and – paradoxically – its timeless traditions make for an enthralling encounter. You can get caught up in all this in the major cities, whether you opt for the bright lights and subway trains of Tokyo, or the geisha girls and ornate shrines of Kyoto. But preconceptions won't prepare you fully for the imaginative overload of the interior. Head north to the Shinto and Buddhist mountain shrine at Nikko, and the fishing villages off the Hokkaido coast, or travel south through Japan's scattered islands. There, take in Okinawa's subtropical jungle and breathtakingly clear waters. Japan's tragic past is visible at Hiroshima's evocative Peace Park, but, as evidenced by Nagasaki's lovely port, the country has moved far beyond this to become a delight for tourists.
Book with *Inside Japan (01173 144620/ www.insidejapantours.com).*

596 *South Korea*
▤ ⌂

Route *Seoul–Chungju–Haeinsa–Gyeongju.*
Far friendlier than its northern neighbour, there's more to South Korea than meets the eye. In half a century it has shaken off its war-torn past and been transformed into a dynamic, energetic place. Only the dubiously monikered Demilitarised Zone (DMZ) provides whispers of the tragedies of yesteryear. Seoul may be a buzzing and very contemporary place, but it's been the capital for six centuries; push past the skyscrapers to see four UNESCO World Heritage Sites: Changdeokgung, Hwaseong Fortress, Jongmyo Shrine and the Royal Tombs of the Joseon Dynasty. Raft down the roaring rivers and dramatic gorges of Seorak National Park, and take in the 'museum without walls', as the ancient cultural centre of Gyeongju is

599: Mongolia

sometimes referred to. Off the typical trail at the country's southern tip lies Jeju Island, a secluded pocket with unique traditions, architecture and even dialect, as well as the resplendent volcanic scenery surrounding Korea's highest peak, Mount Hallasan.
Book with *CTS Horizons (020 7836 9911/ www.ctshorizons.com).*

597 *Philippines*

Route *Manila–Banaue–El Nido–Tagbilaran.*
An archipelago of more than 7,000 islands, it's hardly surprising that there's plenty for the discerning tourist to enjoy in the Philippines. The country's complex history manifests itself most in the cities. Go from the Conquistador-built Fort Santiago in Manila to the Taoist temple in Cebu, then take a ride on one of the marvellously flamboyant Jeepney buses, fashioned out of World War II-era American trucks. Elsewhere, the Philippines has remained stubbornly local in character. The 2,000-year-old rice terraces at Banaue are still farmed today by members of the Ifugao tribe, one of the many ethnic groups of a heavily traditional people. Of course, with gorgeous seas never far away, the country is a hotspot for nautical activity, whether boating, diving or more adventurous watersports.
Book with *Audley Travel (01993 838100/ www.audleytravel.com).*

598 *China*

Route *Beijing–Xian–Yangtze River –Shanghai–Hangzhou–Guilin.*
Covering almost ten million square kilometres and spanning several civilisations, China is a place where East meets West and historical meets modern. Belying its closeted political environment, China offers the traveller a glimpse of some of the planet's richest cultural treasures, most spellbinding landscapes and most cosmopolitan cities. Devour the delicious, and unexpectedly diverse, food; marvel at the magnitude of the terracotta army; and walk in the footsteps of the Qin Dynasty along the Great Wall. Most of all, as you explore the lonely fishing villages of Guilin, the startling vistas of the Yangtze River and the bustling streets of Beijing, experience the diversity and dizzying pace of a country steeped in ancient

595: Tokyo, Japan

lore but hurtling towards the future.
Book with *Trailfinders (0845 050 5890/ www.trailfinders.com).*

599 *Mongolia*

Route *Ulaanbaatar–Gobi Desert–Kharkorin –Oghi Lake–Khognokhan Mountain.*
Flown over often but routinely ignored by tourists, the country made famous by Genghis Khan is a vast expanse that moves gracefully between desert and mountain. Mongolians are traditionally a nomadic people, and even large cities like capital Ulaanbaatar have the air of places untainted by time. The country boasts breathtaking scenery and colourful culture: independent-minded travellers can revel in the magnificent Erdene Zuu Monastery, the wonders of the Khongor Sand Dunes and the astonishing ice sheet at Eagle Valley. Mongolia is one for those in search of a unique adventure; where else can you ride a yak, spend the night in a traditional 'ger' camp (yurt resort) or visit a family of reindeer herders? July's Naadam Festival, a three-day-long mêlée of food, artistry and sport, is best experienced in Ulaanbaatar.
Book with *Transindus (020 8566 2729/ www.transindus.com).*

600-609

Ten best worldwide road trips

600 *Ireland*

For the Disneyfied version of Ireland, choose the tourist-clogged drive around the Ring of Kerry. But for something with a little less blarney and a real dip into the majestic Irish countryside, choose the drive along the south coast road from Cork to Dingle, County Kerry. Stop at Kinsale, where breakfast at the White House guesthouse (+353 21 4772125, www.whitehouse-kinsale.ie) includes fish straight from the harbour your window seat overlooks; don't miss out smaller towns like Rosscarbery – where you can stop for a cosy pint of Guinness. Then wind your way down to the Dingle Peninsula, which sits happily alongside miles of untouched sandy beaches.

601 Land's End to John O'Groats

The suggestion that you could drive from one end of this country to the other and actively enjoy the experience may seem an absurd one. However, a five-day trip gives you the time to get off the M5 and M6 motorways, cruise along quieter A and B roads and explore some of the breathtaking majesty and magical variety of the British landscape, including rugged coastal stretches, gentle pasturelands, photogenic fells and the bleakly beautiful Scottish Highlands. Use the A30, A386, A39 and then the M5 through to the xxxx; then take the A53 and do a long, winding drive through the Peak District, then the A6 and A624; from Glossop, drive up the tangle of A roads towards Todmorden and Clitheroe and then take the B roads and lovely lanes into the Forest of Bowland, to take the M6 and A591 into the Lake District. Use the A5092, A595 and A5086 to explore the Western Lakes and then head into Scotland on the M6, using the A82.

602 Amalfi Coast, Italy

This stretch of road – the star of numerous TV car adverts – between Sorrento and Salerno looks directly over the Bay of Naples, and is a treasure trail of sandy beaches, medieval towers, terraced orchards and exquisite restaurants. You can stop for a lunch of the finest Southern Italian fare at Michelin-starred Don Alfonso (+39 081 878 00 26, www.don alfonso.com), for a sensual delight, and spend a day and night in pastel-coloured beach town Positano (perhaps at 18th-century palazzo-hotel Le Sirenuse: +39 089 87 50 66, www.sirenuse.it). From there, head down to Amalfi itself, where the grand cathedral is an impressive remnant of the town's history as Southern Italy's largest port town.

603 Cuba

Instead of spending two weeks sucking on the ubiquitous Cuban cigar and falling into tourist traps in Havana, why not rent a car (visit www.rex-rentacar.com) and take the A1 highway out of the city along the coast, ending your trip at the Playa Ancon, often described as Cuba's most beautiful stretch of beach. First stop should be Cinefuegos, where a painstakingly restored theatre and museum will transport you right back to the 1950s. An ice-cold Cuba Libre on the terrace of the neo-classical La Union hotel should complete the picture (www.hotellaunion-cuba.com). About four hours down the road is the stunning colonial town of Trinidad, a riot of banana yellows, verdant greens and blinding turquoise, where you can eat like a king alongside the locals in one of the many *paladares* (restaurants operated out of family homes).

604 Australia – the savannah way

Not for the faint-hearted, this classic road trip from Cairns in Queensland to Broome in Western Australia covers an epic 3,500 kilometres of road, and will require about 30 days and most definitely a sense of adventure. The place names are also suitably epic, and the road out of town will take you across the vast Atherton Tablelands right to Hell's Gate, where the Undara Lava Tubes constitute the world's longest molten rock tunnels. Be further intimidated by the towering sandstone formations of the 'Lost City' on Cape Crawford, or awed by the mystically serene Roper River and thermal pools of the Maratanka region. For more earthly pleasures, a stop-off at Boroloola and the Sir Edmund Pellew islands offers you the best fishing in the country. A four-wheel-drive is, understandably, recommended (and available for hire at www.cairnsdirect.com.au).

605 Argentina

The Motorcycle Diaries is a fairly good model for a free-spirited road trip, and the trip from north to south down Ruta 40 follows the example of Che Guevara, taking in over 5,000 kilometres of tarmac and dirt, and giving you a keen sense of the country's bewildering scale. Head south from Salta, following the snow-capped spine of the Andes, and you'll soon find yourself pretty much alone on the road in the vast steppes and pampas of Patagonia, the world's third largest desert. Highlights of 'La Ruta Cuarenta' include the huge, monster-filled deep blue Lago Nahuel Hapi, 'Argentina's Grand Canyon' in Talampaya National Park, and the dinosaur-fossil strewn wastes of Mendoza. The latter region is also the heart of Argentina's thriving wine industry. Stop off at pretty much any roadside *estaneria* on your journey to enjoy a cheap meal of delicious Patagonian lamb or grass-fed beef.

606 *Scotland*
£ ۞☺

'The Road to the Isles', from Fort William to the port town of Mallaig, has long since achieved mythical status as the route through the majestic Scottish Highlands, which Bonnie Prince Charlie once chose in order to evade his captors. The views of craggy mountains, highland wildlife and spectacular sunsets over the islands of Rum, Eigg and Skye do not disappoint. You can book boat trips to the smaller islands, coo at seal colonies from the Arisaig Marina, and sample organic peat-smoked salmon and freshly caught mussels in the Rick Stein-recommended Andy Race Fish Merchants (01687 462626). Lodges like the Prince's House in Glenfinnan (01397 722246, www.glenfinnan.co.uk) are nestled in the forest scenery and are no less cosy and comfortable for playing on their historic location.

607 *France*
☜

A trip along the French coast in summer delivers exactly what it says on the tin: miles and miles of white, sandy beaches, countless cafés and delicious seafood restaurants, and hundreds and hundreds of beach umbrellas. If the crowds don't put you off, why not take the road down the western coast from Vannes in Brittany to Arcachon, the quintessential French beach town and the oyster capital of Europe. You'll pass through La Rochelle, one of France's best-preserved port towns, with its sun-bleached 18th-century architecture and impressive fortified harbour. And while in Bordeaux, you can complete the French experience by making the rounds of the vineyards – Medoc, Margaux and Saint-Emilion are all a short drive away.

608 *India*
£

Delhi in a car is not unlike hell reimagined as a traffic jam, but if you make it out along the Jaipur Highway towards Rajasthan, it won't be long before you find yourself one of the few cars on the road, and surrounded by

602: Le Sirenuse, Amalfi Coast

spectacular views of Sahara-style sand dunes and stark desert landscape. The Castle Mandawa Resort in Shekawati (01592 223124, www.castlemandawa.com), recreated in the style of a typical Rajasthani village, offers an oasis. Jaisalmer is home to a giant sandcastle fort, and further palatial majesty is in store at the unbelievably opulent Umaid Bhavan Palace Hotel (+91 141 2316184, www.umaidbhawan.com) in Jodhpur. The drive back to Delhi on the NH8 takes in Ajmer and Jaipur, the Pink City, whose carefully reconstructed Old City is crammed with bazaars.

609 *Pyrenees*

£ ⚘ ☺

For the price of a budget flight to Bordeaux, Toulouse, Perpignan, Barcelona or Girona, plus car hire, you can find yourself with unlimited access to the mountain range that's been described as the rooftop of Europe, with unbelievable views, as well as the freedom to drive back and forth over the ridge that divides France and Spain. There's excellent low-cost skiing at Andorra, while the Refuge Baysellance (+33 5 62 92 40 25, www.refuge.bayssellance.free.fr) is the highest hostel in the French Pyrenees at 2,651 metres, providing views in every direction. There are rivers, waterfalls and lakes in hidden valleys, and eagles whiz over the lonely peaks on the high stretch of road from Mollo to Navarre. You might even want to choose a convertible (try www.europcar.co.uk), as the summer months mean 14-hour days of steady sunshine.

610-619
Gourmet Britain

610 Fairyhill, Gower Peninsula, South Wales

01792 390139/www.fairyhill.net.
One of Britain's finest restaurants with rooms, Fairy Hill, at the Swansea end of the Gower, is sublime in all its details. The 18th-century house is understated but grand, with 24 acres of parkland. But the restaurant,

612: Manoir aux Quat'Saisons, Oxford

cheffed by James Hamilton, is the main draw. Andrew Hetherington, front-of-house, and his partner Paul Davies, who have run the place since 1993, pride themselves on using local produce; the Gower peninsula is a wonderful source for foodstuffs, from sea bass and cockles to salt marsh lamb and Welsh Black beef. From neighbouring Carmarthenshire come delicious cheeses. The wine list competes with any in London.

611 Three Chimneys, Skye

♤

01470 511258/www.threechimneys.co.uk.
It takes some doing to make a name for yourself when your restaurant is as far north as you can get before falling into the Atlantic, but Eddie and Shirley Spear have managed it. Their little restaurant on the edge of Skye (pretty much everything in Skye is on the edge, but this is a particularly scenic section) is tucked into three tiny stone-lined rooms of a former crofters' cottage. The food is fresh, inventive and as local as possible. The Spears have turned the cottage next door into a luxurious B&B (the House Over-By) for those who can't stagger any further after dinner, but be warned: it has only six rooms, and they're deservedly popular.

612 Manoir aux Quat'Saisons, Oxford

♡

01844 278881/www.manoir.com.
Raymond Blanc may be a quintessential Frenchman, complete with culinary skills and comedy accent, but his gaff is a gorgeous Oxfordshire manor house with 32 individualised bedrooms and a garden that provides a remarkable amount of the ingredients that end up on your plate in the superb, Michelin-starred glass-walled dining room. Oh, and the wine cellar is fit for a Frenchman too. Not cheap by any means, but a good bet for a special celebration.

613 Calcot Manor, Cotswolds

👪

01666 890391/www.calcotmanor.co.uk.
Famous winemakers on lightning tours of Britain often hold events at Calcot Manor, a gracious Cotswolds manor house. There are two restaurants, both very good but pitched differently: the Gumstool is gastropub-style,

the elegant glass-roofed Conservatory more ambitious. There are 35 exquisite bedrooms and a spa and pool to work off the unavoidable gastronomic excesses, and foodie parents will be particularly happy as Calcot is famously child-friendly.

614 Hotel TerraVina, New Forest

♤♡

023 8029 3784/www.hotelterravina.co.uk.
Gerard Basset is one of the best sommeliers this side of the Channel (yes, OK, he's French, but we own him now). He co-founded the Hotel du Vin chain but has since downsized to this gorgeous boutique hotel near Southampton, where each of 11 bedrooms boasts that vital foodie accoutrement, an espresso machine. The restaurant's wine list is all you'd expect from a Master of Wine with an international reputation to uphold, and the food does it justice. You're well placed to explore the New Forest outside the front door… but you may not make it outside the front door.

615 The Pheasant at Harome, Yorkshire

01439 771241/www.thepheasanthotel.com.
The Harome blacksmith wouldn't recognise his smithy now: 14 rooms, of which two are suites, an indoor heated pool and a lovely restaurant, all run by the same people – Andrew and Jacquie Pern – who own the Michelin-starred Star Inn down the road, plus a couple of local delis. Despite the pool and the village prettiness, the Pheasant (which reopened in 2009) is cheaper than its big sister – and naturally the staff can still book you dinner at the posher venue – assuming there's availability, of course.

616 Polrode Mill Cottage, Allen Valley, nr St Tudy, Cornwall

01208 850203/www.polrodemillcottage.co.uk.
This gorgeous Cornish cottage, with its acres of grounds and salmon stream, was apparently mentioned in the Domesday Book, but it's moved on considerably since then: the current building is 17th century, and no restaurant with rooms survives this close to Padstow (or Padstein, as those unfavourably disposed to Rick Stein call it) if the food is still at the mead and trencher stage of evolution. There's an open fire and an ambitious menu featuring Cornish boar and lots of fish.

617 Three Horseshoes Inn, High Wycombe, Buckinghamshire

01494 483273/www.thethreehorseshoes.net.
The Chilterns are designated an Area of Outstanding Natural Beauty, which is all well and good: one must do something between lunch and dinner, after all. The Three Horseshoes isn't bad-looking itself: an 18th-century red-brick building with six comfy attic rooms, a titchy front bar serving real ale, and a restaurant good enough, in gastronomic and economic terms, to have won the place a Bib Gourmand from those finicky Michelin types. Puddings in particular are beauteous enough to offer a serious challenge to the landscape.

618 Langar Hall, Nottinghamshire

01949 860559/www.langarhall.com.
Once the home of Admiral Lord Howe, Nelson's 'great master in tactics and bravery' (although the present hall postdates him, thanks to a 19th-century fire), Langar is a 12-bedroom country house at the end of a lime-tree avenue in the Vale of Belvoir. Imogen Skirving is the current incumbent (her family has been here since 1860, although letting the hoi polloi in was her idea) and she oversees a kitchen full of locally sourced produce – always a good move when the ancestral home is in stilton country.

619 Fawsley Hall, near Daventry, Northamptonshire

01327 892000/www.fawsleyhall.com.
Fawsley Hall is steeped in history. A former royal manor, it dates to the 15th century and boasts royal connections. Inside, muted tones, luxurious armchairs, grand staircases and the wood-panelled Great Hall contribute to an air of sophisticated decadence. Chef Nigel Godwin's Modern British restaurant, Equilibrium, proves you don't have to go to Barcelona (or Bray) to indulge in the multisensory delights of designer cuisine. Between starters of Cornish crab with avocado mousse or rich slow-cooked pork and mains of local partridge and lamb noisettes come palate-cleansing buccal bombs of fresh mint and camomile frozen in liquid nitrogen, and aromatic wafts of delicate parfait. A wine list that would grace the finest city restaurant is taken for granted, as is an artisan cheese board that contains the very best from the UK.

620-634
Festivals, parties, carnivals

620 *Sónar, Barcelona, Spain*

For three nights (from the third Thursday in June), a site just outside Barcelona (there are coaches to take you there) plays host to the cream of the dance music scene; while in the daytime, events take place at the Centre of Contemporary Culture (CCCB) and the Museum of Contemporary Art (MACBA), in the city's Rambla neighbourhood. Sónar attracts a slightly older crowd than its local cousin Benicassim, with none of the indie headliners or their screaming fans. There's a varied electronic line-up; Bjork has played, as well as Laurent Garnier, Hot Chip and 2005's legendary and groundbreaking set from Skream.
www.sonar.es.

621 *Hay Festival, Wales, UK*

For ten days at the end of May, the Welsh idyll of Hay-on-Wye attracts a stack of international writers and thinkers. At one location just outside of town, there are talks and discussions with everyone from Armatya Sen to Stephen Fry and David Simon. In recent years, the literature festival has expanded to include live music and film previews, adding further variation to the festival Bill Clinton once called 'the Woodstock of the mind'.
0870 990 1299/www.hayfestival.com.

622 *Garden Festival, Petracane, Croatia*

Started in 2006, the Garden Festival is the last word in boutique intimacy. Set over nine days and two weekends in the first half of July, and with a capacity of only 2,000 people, the focus here is on quality rather than headliners. The location, on a tiny peninsula in the waters of the Adriatic, must be one of the prettiest places in the world to have a festival. Don't miss the parties; a big wooden boat sets sail twice daily for hours of music, dancing and nautical naughtiness. *+385 23 364 739/www.thegardenfestival.eu.*

623 *Burning Man, Nevada, USA*

Not so much a festival as a way of life, the focus of Burning Man is on creation and participation. On the last Monday of August, some 50,000 people make their way to Nevada's Black Rock Desert to construct colossal art installations and indulge in neo-hippie revelry (public nudity is a common feature) for this week-long festival. No commerce is permitted (instead, a gift economy is in place) as Burning Man is all about untainted self-expression. The festival was originally free, but a ticketing system has been in place since 1995. The ritual burning of a wooden effigy takes place on the Saturday evening. *+1 415 86 35263/www.burningman.com.*

624 *Carnaval, Rio de Janeiro, Brazil*

The world's greatest party, Rio de Janiero's *carnaval* (Brazil's biggest) attracts millions of tourists each year for four days of dancing and shameless fun on the Saturday to Tuesday preceding Lent (so normally in February). The giant Sambadrome, where the city's samba schools compete, attracts most of the visitors, and the costumes on display are awe-inspiring. But the real fun to be had is in the smaller *blocos* – street parties organised by each neighbourhood. The atmosphere is like nowhere else in the world, and it's a perfect escape from the dreary UK winter. *www.rio-carnival.net.*

625 *Les Recontres d'Arles, France*

The quiet town of Arles has long been associated with art: for one thing, it's the spot where Van Gogh removed his ear. The Arles photography festival – from mid July to mid September – has been running since the 1970s (it celebrated its 40th anniversary in 2009); and while it's inevitably been a date on the professional photographer's calendar for decades, it now attracts some 55,000 visitors, many of whom are amateur enthusiasts. View scores of exhibitions by the world's leading photographers, and attend debates, prize-giving ceremonies and photography workshops. *+33 4 90 96 76 06/www.rencontres-arles.com.*

622: Garden Festival, Croatia

629: Edinburgh Festival

626 *WOMAD, Charlton Park, UK*

When Peter Gabriel set up WOMAD in 1986, he got little support from major labels or any investors. Now the festival, held over the last weekend of July at Wiltshire's Charlton Park (near Malmesbury), is as popular as ever, with various different incarnations across the world. The focus is on world music, although there's also jazz, hip hop and rock. What marks this festival out is the inclusive atmosphere, with tents full of people of all ages.
http://womad.org/festivals/charlton-park.

627 *Fuji Rocks, Naeba, Japan*

Fuji Rocks (so named because it was originally held in the foothills of Mount Fiji) has become one of the world's best rock festivals, with over 100,000 visitors attending the event, held over the last weekend of July in Naeba (a ski resort during the winter months). The sound systems are volcanic, blasting out headliners such as My

Bloody Valentine, as well as smaller acts. International but quintessentially Japanese, the festival achieves its stated aim to be 'the cleanest festival in the world'.
www.smash-uk.com.

628 *La Biennale di Venezia, Italy*

For over a century the Venice Biennale has been showcasing cutting-edge art from all corners of the globe, from June to November every other (odd-numbered) year. With 30 permanent national pavilions, ambitious fringe, theatre, music and dance events, as well as one of the most prestigious film festivals in the world, this festival of culture is exceptionally high profile.
www.labiennale.org.

629 *Edinburgh Festival, Scotland*

Every August, the Scottish capital's amalgamation of festivals almost triples the city's population. There's film and music,

but the real attraction is the Fringe, where comedians and actors from the amateur to the internationally famous can be seen. The whole city fizzes with atmosphere, and even the street performers are astounding. Book very early for accommodation.
www.edinburghfestivals.co.uk.

630 *Shambhala Music Festival, British Columbia, Canada*
Y

Set in the heart of Canada's Kootenay Mountains, at the Salmo River Ranch, is this rave festival like no other; stages are nestled in trees, placed by rivers and even surrounded by twisting wooden walkways and glowing tunnels of light. An electric mix of dance music is blasted out of colossal speakers to 10,000 hippies and ravers, who travel here on the second weekend in August annually. North America's best dance festival.
www.shambhalamusicfestival.com.

631 *Los Angeles Film Festival, USA*
The home of Hollywood naturally plays host to a diverse and successful film festival, for ten days every June at the city's Westwood Village. Yet, unlike the plethora of fashionista film festivals out there, LA is set up as much for industry types as for the film-going public. Yet with 85,000 visitors, over 200 feature, documentary and short North American films – as well as music videos – there's something for everyone.
www.lafilmfest.com.

632 *Glastonbury, Somerset, UK*
👪 ☾ Y

The UK's most famous music festival. The toilets are grim and a stagnant quagmire is guaranteed, but Glasto still pulls a crowd like no other . 'It's shit when it's muddy,' says Deborah Armstrong, one of the original producers of Lost Vagueness, 'But – and sorry for sounding like an old hippie – magical things happen at Glastonbury. Things that just don't happen anywhere else.' Preregistration (essential to even be in with a chance of buying a ticket) starts in October.
www.glastonburyfestivals.co.uk.

633 *San Fermín Festival, Pamplona, Spain*
☾ Y

The festivities in honour of St Fermín, patron saint of Navarra, attract over a million people to the town of Pamplona in the north of Spain, from 6 to 14 July. Various traditional and folkloric events are held, the most famous – and by far the most dangerous – being the *encierro*, the running of the bull.
www.sanfermin.com.

634 *Mardi Gras, New Orleans, USA*
Y

A category five hurricane couldn't (quite) knock the party spirit out of the inhabitants of New Orleans, who still celebrate Mardi Gras every year here, during the two weeks before Ash Wednesday. Giant floats, costumes and music attract national and international visitors to a city full of people who take their partying seriously. Leave any inhibitions at home.
www.mardisgrasneworleans.com.

628: La Biennale di Venezia

Ideas from the expert

635-644

Arvind Malhotra of GapGuru offers ten ideas for a worthwhile gap year.

635 Work as a surf instructor in Australia. Become a qualified instructor on a gap-year project, and share your passion with others as you teach surfing while enjoying the Australian sunshine. For more information, visit www.flyingfish online. com/sports/surfing or www.walkinonwater.com.

636 If you have a passion for writing and travelling, you could spend time as a reporter for an Indian newspaper. Discover the country from the inside, chasing your own stories and writing your own articles. What a great feeling to see your name in print with a newspaper that reaches out to millions! There are opportunities in Chennai (South India), working for the local office of a national newspaper.

637 In parts of Northern Tanzania, Africa, 50 per cent of the adult population is HIV positive. Working through a registered charity, an HIV grants programme helps widows to set up small sustainable businesses to maintain their livelihood. Volunteers will provide guidance, advisory support and business training to women working alongside the local team. For more details, see www.mondochallenge.co.uk/grants-for-hiv-affected-families.html.

638 The Maasai are a semi-nomadic ethnic group settled in Kenya and northern Tanzania. They speak Maa, as well as Swahili and English, which are the official languages of Tanzania, but volunteers are needed to raise the level of English in schools as there is a lack of good teachers in the area. This is a great opportunity to discover more about this fascinating culture while teaching English to Maasai women and children. Visit www.mondo challenge.co.uk/teaching-in-a-traditional-maasai-village.html.

639 Football is very popular in Africa, and sports lovers who can teach techniques or simply play games with the children are always welcome. Volunteers work with enthusiastic children organising games and competitions in schools. Even though the infrastructures are quite basic, there's a lot to keep you busy, and most volunteers quickly form close bonds with the children.

640 The six-month Global Xchange programme (www.globalxchange.org.uk) gathers together young people from different countries so they can make a contribution where help is needed. UK students can live and work with a foreign student, volunteer with him or her for three months in the UK before heading to your partner's home country for another three months. This is a great opportunity for cross-cultural understanding, and a chance to discover a different side to your own country.

641 Spend your summer working with 6-16 year olds on a summer camp in the USA, with BUNAC

37: Tanzania, Africa

(www.bunac.org/uk/summercampus). You'll be involved in an international cultural exchange programme, and participate in instructing and teaching sporting activities, such as canoeing, swimming, climbing and horse riding.

642 The lost city of Machu Picchu is nestled in Peru's magnificent Andes. Discover this pre-Inca site and experience trekking in the unspoiled mountains while volunteering in a school near Cuzco, the historic capital of the Inca Empire. You can also use this trip to raise funds for a charity of your choice, while having an experience of a lifetime! For more information, visit www.different-travel. com/destinations/package-peru.php.

643 The movie *Slumdog Millionaire* highlighted the conditions in which Indian street children live, and emphasised how much these communities desperately need help. Work with a local NGO dedicated to helping and bringing joy to children in the slums of Bangalore, through a range of fun and educational activities.

644 Plan your round the world trip and visit every continent of the world! Fly from the UK to Africa, and then discover Asia, Australia and South America before ending up in the USA. Enjoy the breathtaking landscapes of Kenya and South Africa, visit Nepal, trek through the Himalayas, discover many cities, explore the Andean mountains and finally experience life in New York City. This truly is the trip of a lifetime. See www.statravel.co.uk for more details and routes.

■ **GapGuru** 08000 32 33 50/www.gapguru.com.

645-649
Thailand for all budgets

645 *Ko Phangan*
£ ♀ ♈
Grade *Cheap.*
If you're doing Thailand on the cheap, and have the benefit of youth, chances are the infamous full moon party is on your itinerary. Fuelled by legal and not-so-legal substances, ravers still come from afar every month to party all night on the country's south-eastern shores. Most budget accommodation enforces a five-night minimum stay over the party week, but there's plenty to fill the time, like a boat ride to the extraordinary Bottle Beach, a cookery course, or watching the rather brutal national sport of Muay Tai. Book into the Coral Bungalow, a short walk from central Had Rin, and with basic but, crucially, air-conditioned rooms. Its prices are backpacker friendly, and its pre-full moon pool parties are a must.
Coral Bungalow *www.coralhaadrin.com.*

646 *Chiang Mai*
£ ♈ ♒
Grade *Cheap*
The Thailand of the imagination starts in Chiang Mai. The country's northern hub is the entrance to its jungle wilderness; here you'll find diverse tribal societies, exotic wildlife and countless trekking opportunities. It's also the place to organise elephant rides, bamboo rafting and snake shows. The night market makes for a great shopping trip, while the phenomenal mountainside temple of Wat Phra That Doi Suthep and the Umbrella Village of Bor Sang are worth a visit. What's more, prices are cheaper and locals friendlier and less tourist-savvy here than down south, so there's plenty of pleasant budget accommodation to choose from. And sign up to one of the cheap overnight hikes, and you could have the unmatchable experience of sleeping in a remote bamboo hut with the Long Neck people.
Book a tour with *Greenhouse BKK (www.greenhousebkk.com).*

646: Chiang Mai

649: Bangkok

647 *Pai*

Grade *Affordable.*

For off-the-beaten-track Thailand, the often-overlooked northern town of Pai is the place to go. Set so high up in the mountains you'll be looking down through the clouds, its slower pace of life, ambling streets and tranquil vistas are a world apart from the bustle of the rest of the country. Perfectly positioned for a trip to see the Golden Triangle, Thailand's window into Burma, Laos and Vietnam, there are also hot springs and endless jungle scenery nearby, and the town itself is lovely to wander through. This is the place to have a Thai massage, head out for a cocktail or opt for some slightly nicer beds for the night (try Lilu Hotel). The lower prices and cooler air will mean the relaxed feeling won't disappear as soon as you leave the salon.
Lilu Hotel *+66 53 064 351/www.liluhotel.com.*

648 *Ko Samui*

Grade *Expensive.*

Although Phuket is often the first place that comes to mind when choosing from Thailand's upmarket coastal destinations, Ko Samui has everything a holidayer could want, and the beaches are as paradise-perfect as they come – all golden sands, turquoise seas and sunsets an artist couldn't imagine up. There are endless market stalls to peruse, fabulous restaurants and a thriving nightlife, with some unforgettable ladyboy cabarets. There aren't many official 'sights', but trips to Ko Tao island are de rigueur for divers, or at least take the time to snorkel through the colourful waters of the gulf. With much of the island dedicated to tourism, luxury hotels abound. Built in 2007, and with a magnificent pool and private beach, the palatial Dara Samui is extremely well equipped, and each room comes with its own water feature.
Dara Samui *+66 77 231 3227/ www.darasamui.com.*

649 *Bangkok*

Grade *Expensive.*

Thailand's capital is not for the faint-hearted. Like New York, it never sleeps and can be oppressively humid, mind-numbingly noisy and is always a seething mass of people. On the other hand, the city's kaleidoscopic temples and palaces and its astonishingly large Buddhist shrines are the best in the country. Equally unmissable are the floating markets, great for buying fresh fruit and knick-knacks, and where being pursued by an overeager stall owner takes on new meaning. To bag designer knock-offs and pirate DVDs, acclimatise yourself to the inevitable cries of 'same same but different' and head to the Patpong market. Escape to nearby Kanchanaburi, where you can see the bridge at Kwai, laid by prisoners of war, then relish the unusual opportunity to stroke a live tiger at the Buddhist monk-run Tiger Temple. After mere hours in such a crazy city, you'll be glad of a nice place to go back to, so for utter splendour, book in at the Mandarin Oriental.

Mandarin Oriental *+66 2 659 9000/ www.mandarinoriental.com/bangkok.*

650-654
Five alfresco dining spots

650 *Richmond Park, London, UK*
£☺

Assuming the weather holds, England's green and pleasant land has some great places to eat outdoors. For alfresco dining within easy reach of the M25, grab the picnic box and the bottle of Pimms and head to Richmond Park. You shouldn't have any trouble finding a peaceful spot in London's largest (deer-filled) park, whether your tastes run to dining amid the exotic beauty of the Isabella Plantation gardens or on higher ground for magnificent views of St Paul's Cathedral. If the rain clouds loom, Petersham Nurseries (020 8605 3627, www. petershamnurseries.com) is minutes away, offering shelter and a splendid sheltered café. *www.royalparks.org.uk/parks/richmond_park.*

651 *Bryant Park, New York, USA*
People scouting out a picnic place in the Big Apple will invariably choose Central Park. While that is a great spot, it's always seething with people. For a more intimate but equally accessible space, head to midtown's Bryant Park. A green island surrounded by skyscrapers, the ambience is escapist and

summer evenings see outdoor movies and concerts aplenty; but surely the best time to come is at twilight, with a blanket and a takeaway from one of the city's signature delis. *www.bryantpark.org.*

652 *Hotel Poseidon, Positano, Italy*
♡

Alfresco dining will always be synonymous with romance. For that under the stars, just you two and the world sort of evening, look no further than Italy's mountainside town of Positano. In this poetic place, there's no better spot to whisper sweet nothings than the luxury Hotel Poseidon, whose crown jewel is its restaurant (which accepts reservations from non-guests). The terrace eaterie overlooks much of the town, as well as the sparkling turquoise waters of the Amalfi Coast. Charming staff, a storybook setting and lovely sunsets, not to mention delectable food, all add up to a night to remember. *+39 089 811 111/www.hotelposeidonpositano.it.*

653 *Cascades d'Ouzoud, Morocco*
☺♡🏠

Anyone can eat outside, but chowing down on what seems like the edge of the world is no mean feat. The Cascades d'Ouzoud in Morocco,

650: Petersham Nurseries, Richmond

a few hours out of Marrakech, might just meet the challenge. The 100-metre waterfalls lie in the Middle Atlas Mountains and are a photographer's dream. Best of all, the area isn't swamped by tourists. Drink orange juice freshly squeezed by the locals, pick a pomegranate from the ground, or set up camp overnight to have a romantic dinner under the stars or breakfast as the sun rises. You should be free from much human disturbance, but watch out for the Barbary apes.

654 *Segovia, Spain*
♡

According to legend, Walt Disney based his eponymous castle on the Alcazar de Segovia, the silver-turreted palace that completes the skyline of this picturesque and well-hidden little village. In fact, the whole moutainside area, a few hours from Madrid, looks like it comes straight out of a fairytale. And Segovia's many authentic and unashamedly simple outdoor cafés are the just the place for low-key alfresco dining – for that lunch that ebbs slowly into dinner type of experience, or for a starry evening away from the craziness of contemporary life.

655-659
Edgy escapes

We'd never recommend you go to a war zone or a region where famine and drought would make a 'holiday' of any kind inappropriate or impossible. Nor would we advocate travelling in a region where tourist dollars directly prop up tyrannical dictators or slavery. Then again, Cuba is a dictatorship, and the US and UK are warmongers, and we'd hardly boycott travelling to/in these – so personal opinion is a major element in deciding what edgy – but ethical – tourism means. The following are countries or regions that are firmly on the responsible tourist radar, but where recent events – or just reputation – make a trip there exciting and sure to impress.

655 *Colombia*

Until the mid 1990s, Colombia was best known as the planet's chief source of cocaine and the setting for bloody civil conflicts. But in the last few years, some factions have been bought off and former Farc-controlled areas are now accessible. In fact, the central strip of this vibrant country is as safe as anywhere else in Latin America. With Pacific and Caribbean beaches at its edges and snow-capped Andes at its heart – as well as romantic colonial towns, archaeological ruins and coffee haciendas – it's diverse and dramatically beautiful, and you'll find the locals warm and welcoming – not least because tourists have kept away for decades. A few words of Spanish go a long way.

Head to Bogotá, Popayán, the 'Lost City' (Ciudad Perdida) and Parque Nacional Tayrona. Avoid areas along the border with Ecuador and Peru.
Book with *Responsible Travel (01273 600030/ www.responsibletravel.com).*

656 *Yemen*

Yemen's capital, Sana'a, is a magical layering of icing-cake houses, temples and a desert backdrop; founded by one of Noah's sons (they say), it's also the world's oldest city. The four-island archipelago of Socotra (or Soqotra) was isolated for much of history due to its

656: Yemen

reputation as a refuge for dragons. It does indeed harbour extraordinary flora and fauna and is also said to hold the secret to eternal life. The romantic myths end when it comes to local sayings, like 'Everyone in the West carries a mobile phone, almost everyone in Yemen carries a gun.'

Avoid travelling here when the country is blacklisted, for insurance purposes as well as for survival; read up on the news as kidnappings are sometimes a risk in the Sana'a province and elsewhere.

Book with *Wild Frontiers (020 7736 3968/ www.wildfrontiers.co.uk).*

657 *Mexico*

Swine flu, gunfights between cops and arms- and drug-traffickers along the US border, plus regular meteorological 'challenges' (hurricanes every year, floods from time to time) make Mexico a dead cert for lovers of out-there tourism. Tijuana has the edginess of a lawless cowboy town, Mexico City can seem dark and dodgy, and too many tequilas can make for lively fistful *fiestas* in the provinces – but this is still one of the most visited countries in the world with a huge range of resorts and types of experiences.

For safe(ish) bets, head to the Mayan Riviera, Oaxaca and Baja California. Avoid Ciudad Juárez on the US–Mexico border.

Book with *020 8747 8315/ www.journeylatinamerica.co.uk.*

658 *Burma aka Myanmar*

Edgy or just wrong? Severed from the world by one of its toughest military regimes, Burma is South-east Asia's forgotten wonderland. Nobel Peace Prize Laureate Aung San Suu Kyi and many human rights groups have frequently stated that travelling to Burma effectively sponsors the government and should therefore be avoided. Others say its long-suffering people crave contact with the outside world and visitors can bring them hope. Whichever camp you join, Burma's natural beauty inspired Rudyard Kipling, and those who do visit are blown away by its Buddhist temples, unspoilt landscapes and the warmth of its people.

If you decide to make the trip, don't miss the Buddhist temples of Bagan, the mystical scenery of Inle Lake and the ancient cities near Mandalay.

Book with *TransIndus (020 8566 3739/ www.transindus.co.uk).*

659 *Kurdistan, Iraq*

For 8,000 years, civilisations and states have risen and fallen on this extraordinary land. You may prefer not to tell your parents, but for an exhilarating voyage through time, you can tread the remains of the biblical city of Babylon, tour ancient Sumerian cities and even see Saddam's presidential palaces. Visits to Basra, notorious for British soldiers' battles for hearts and minds, and Baghdad, can also be arranged. Make sure you read the FCO travel advice before planning your trip, and bear in mind that operators may change the itinerary without warning.

Babylon, Dohuk and surrounding areas, Ur and Eridu are the country's highlights. Avoid insurgent strongholds by reading up on the news, and be especially vigilant on Fridays after weekly prayers and during religious holidays.

Book with *Hinterland Travel (01484 719549/ www.hinterlandtravel.com).*

660-669
Failsafe honeymoons

660 *The Seychelles*

After months of wedding planning and weeks juggling florists, fittings and photographers, your honeymoon should offer escapism of the highest measure. A speck on the map off the southern African coast, the Seychelles are an escapist fantasy, with all the luscious coastline and classic paradise features you could want, and then some. You could spend a day exploring one of the globe's smallest capital cities, Victoria, try some deep-sea fishing or go mountain biking, but you'll probably be more tempted to relax on the beach, in front of some astonishing cliff faces, in the mostly brilliant sunshine. However you spend your time, you'll have one of the world's most romantic destinations as your backdrop.

Book with *Beachcomber (01483 445621/ www.beachcombertours.co.uk).*

661 *The Maldives*

♀♡

If you're looking for a honeymoon where it's just you, your new husband or wife, and the great outdoors, the secluded islands of the Maldives is it. With fabulous weather almost the whole year round and all the palm trees you could wish for, the tiny coral reef islands are a magical place to kick back and relax with your loved one. There's little to see and do, beyond snorkelling to see the exotic underworld of the Indian Ocean, or a trip to one of the many spa resorts, but with evocative sunsets, dazzling waters and sparkling golden sands in such ample supply, you'll likely never want to leave. For that undisturbed romantic stay, head to one of the thatched roof bungalows of Makunudu. *+44 1548 831550/www.makunudu.com.*

662 *Greek Island hopping*

♀♢♡🏠

If you don't fancy a long haul flight on the back of all that champagne, Greece might just be the answer. The weather is nice all year round but not normally stifling, the coastline is as delightful as any more exotic destination, and there are plenty of sumptuous hotels and idyllic self-catering villas to choose from. Your best bet is an island stay, but why stop at just the one? Short distances and easy interchanges make an island-hopping honeymoon an attractive and, of course, romantic prospect. Move from the mountains of Crete to the clear seas of Paxos, or go on the trail of Odysseus on Ithaca then wander the wooded greenery of Zakynthos. There are destinations to suit every type of couple, a rich cultural heritage and fantastic scenery to see, not forgetting all the lively tavernas serving copious amounts of Ouzo.

Book with *Islands of Greece (0845 675 2600/ www.islands-of-greece.co.uk).*

663 *Riviera Maya, Mexico*

♀♡🏠

Mexico's Riviera Maya is home to the country's most paradisiacal beaches. For boutique pleasures by the sand just a short drive from Playa del Carmen – and light years away from brash Cancún in terms of ambience – is Esencia, probably Mexico's best hotel. Originally the coastal retreat of an Italian duchess, the 50-acre estate comprises two swimming pools, an organic spa with Mayan-style domed steam rooms and a gourmet restaurant, and looks out on to an empty, two-mile-long beach. Both guest rooms and cottages are plain and elegant, with native hardwood furnishings, high ceilings, mahogany doors and tall windows with views of tropical vegetation and the sea. The romantic Sal Y Fuego Restaurant serves superlative seafood dishes in a relaxed, but refined, setting.

Hotel Esencia *+52 984 873 4835/ www.hotelesencia.com.*

664 *The UK's Lake District*

£♢♡♤

Honeymoons don't have to mean going abroad. Staycations are the new byword for holiday cool, so ditch the phrasebook, avoid the airport and instead head to one of the sleepy villages of the Lake District. Check into the Swinside Lodge Hotel, a sweet and stylish lakeside resort in the Newlands Valley. You'll be staying amid some of England's richest natural terrain; moody lakes and lush greenery. While they might not be as exotic as the Caribbean or the Seychelles, British sunsets are no less magical, and you'll find it much easier to secure a private viewing spot. Of course, the weather on our fair isle is tenacious, but nestled away in a picturesque country inn with your loved one, there'll be no need to go outside.

Swinside Lodge Hotel *017687 72948/ www.swinsidelodge-hotel.co.uk.*

665 *Eden Rock, St Barths, Caribbean*

♀♡

Of all the Caribbean islands, St Barths has accrued a name for itself as the showiest, starriest and sexiest. Like the rest of the region, the island is heavy on the romance, all tropical landscapes and achingly perfect panoramas. With a small local population and visits from only the most exclusive of tourists, honeymooners can appreciate the place undisturbed, while at the same time enjoying food that pays homage to the island's French heritage. Originally the home of a Dutch adventurer, the exquisite Eden Rock resort was once frequented by celebrities like Greta Garbo, and remains to this day a top glitterati haunt. It's certainly opulent, but falls just the right side of gaudy, and is made more impressive by snatches of the owner's well-cultivated art collection around the place. Of course, you'll be too busy staring into each other's eyes to notice. **Eden Rock Hotel** + *590 590 29 79 99/ www.edenrockhotel.com.*

666 *Bali*

The beaches of Bali are well trodden by all kinds of tourists, from backpackers to the well-heeled, and they also make for a sensational honeymoon destination. In the balmy waters of southern Asia, the Indonesian island, complete with verdant landscape, volcanic lakes and cultural gems, is as close to paradise as they come. Head to the Karma Kandara resort on Bali's secluded southernmost tip, a stunning architectural feat merging classic Balinese design with pure luxury. Honeymoon undisturbed in one of the beautifully furnished individual villas, which come with their own tropical courtyard, private pool and personal access to the beach. Enjoy candlelit cuisine at the cliff-face restaurant and sip champagne under the stars at the hotel's rooftop bar. One tip to note: it's wise to avoid monsoon season between December and March. **Karma Kandara** + *62 361 848 2200/ www.karmakandara.com.*

667 *Paris, France*

Well known as one of the most romantic places on earth, a trip to Paris with your loved one is ideal if you're pressed for time. Wander the charming streets and meet the quirky locals, indulge in the delicious culinary delights and take in all the sights of the French capital. Take a moonlit cruise down the Seine, head to the Museé Rodin to see the sculptor's famous work *The Kiss*, and choose from the many lavish hotels the city lays claim to. The honeymoon suite, with resplendent four-poster bed, at the intimate Hôtel Duc de Saint Simon is one winner. It's a gem of a place with adorably classic decor and fabulous antique furnishings. For more modern tastes, head to the edgily designed Five Hotel in the Latin Quarter, where your bed will lie under a starry ceiling. If the city of love doesn't put you in the mood, the wine certainly will.

666: Karma Kandara, Bali

Hôtel Duc de Saint Simon *+33 1 44 49 20 20/*
www.hotelducdesaintsimon.com.
Five Hotel *+33 1 43 31 74 21/*
www.thefivehotel.com.

668 *Seville, Spain*

▣♡◔

Follow up your fairytale wedding with a trip
to a castle; specifically, the Royal Palace of
Seville – just one of the many historic treasures
in the Andalucian capital. Spain hardly seems
a honeymooners' paradise, but this quiet city an
hour or so from Spain's southern Atlantic coast
should not be dismissed. The Moorish history of
the region is visible in the stunning architecture
of the town, while restaurants offer delectable
tapas from a variety of culinary influences.
Within easy reach is the Costa de la Luz, with
golden sands, trendy but relaxed resorts and,
for the more confident couple, various naturist
beaches. Of course, that's assuming you want to
leave your hotel, and if you stay at the gorgeous
Hacienda Belaluza, that's even less likely.
Converted from an old Moorish household,
and located in a dreamy little village just
outside Seville, it also has a lavish terrace and
pool and a Michelin-starred eaterie on site.
Hacienda Belaluza *+34 955 703 344/*
www.elbullihotel.com.

669 *Fernando de Noronha, Brazil*

♁♡

When all you want to do is be left alone with
a loved one, it pays to head to a group of
pristine islands with almost no local population
and a limit of 400-odd tourists at any one
time. The secluded archipelago of Fernando
de Noronha, a former penal colony, is about
as far away from any city lights as you can
ask. Located a few hundred miles off the north-
eastern Brazilian coast, expect all the typical
paradise trimmings of ravaged rock faces,
stupendous sunsets and sensational coastline.
In addition, look forward to some great
diving and some astonishing flora and fauna,
including dolphins and sea tortoises. A
favourite of Naomi Campbell and Mario
Testino, in recent years it has also become
known as a gay and lesbian honeymoon
hotspot. The stunning beach-facing villas of
the Pousada Maravilha resort are a good bet.
Pousada Maravilha *+55 81 3619 0028/*
www.pousadamaravilha.com.br.

670-679
Animal magic
....

670 *Birdwatching in Camargue and Provence, France*

◔◔

Some 150-170 bird species place this national
park among Europe's best, with its colony of
15,000 Greater Flamingos and rare breeding
birds, including the Little Bustard, Lesser Kestrel
and the Pin-tailed Sandgrouse. Its array of
wetland birds is most dazzling in May, when
they stopover after winter in Africa as they head
north. Nearby Arles was once home to Van Gogh,
and inspired some of his best-known paintings.
Contact *Limosa Holidays (01263 578143/*
www.limosaholidays.co.uk).

671 *Whale watching from Vancouver Island, Canada*

◔

Vancouver Island's northern strait is famous for
spotting orcas, but other species include minke
and humpback whales, white-sided dolphins
and porpoises. Visit the Orcalab research centre,
which tunes in to orcas' core habitats all day
from its remote base on Hudson Island. Then
catch the grizzly bears as they snack on shellfish
on the river lowlands and take a hike through
the wilderness along the new North Coast Trail.
The best months to visit are July and August.
Contact *Out of the Blue (0845 290 3218/*
www.oceansworldwide.co.uk).

672 *Swimming with dolphins in Kaikoura, New Zealand*

◔

Head to Kaikoura, on the east coast of New
Zealand's South Island, between October and
April to see back-flipping, somersaulting Wild
Dusky dolphins in their natural habitat. Pod
sizes number up to a thousand in winter and
while you're encouraged to jump in and get close,
don't expect to touch them. This is not a Flipper-
type experience! Refuel on local rock lobster,
scallops and delicious green-lipped mussels.
Contact *Dolphin Encounter (+ 64 3 319 6777/*
www.dolphin.co.nz).

673 'The big five' safari in Kenya, Africa

◊

The lion, elephant, buffalo, leopard and rhinoceros were called the 'big five' by hunters because they were the hardest to hunt on foot. In Kenya, you can track down these beasts and a vast array of others, including cheetahs, giraffes and zebras, on a safari tailor-made to your needs and budget. Thousands of flamingos, hippo-filled rivers and the wildebeest migration are all part of the fun. What's more, trips can be organised all year round.

Contact *Somak Holidays (020 8423 3000/ www.somak.co.uk).*

674 Butterflies everywhere, in St Albans, UK

There are 54 species of butterfly in the UK, but you can discover another 250 tropical varieties at the newly opened Butterfly World. When complete (completion is scheduled for May-June 2011), the biome will count 10,000 specimens and the walkway will lead visitors through waterfalls, reproductions of ancient Mayan ruins, and underground caverns filled with artefacts, birds and spiders. For more information, visit www.futuregardens.org.index.php.

Contact *01727 869203/www.butterfly-world.org.*

675 Orang-utans in Borneo, South-east Asia

◊

Meet the so-called 'wild men' of Borneo – the orang-utans – at the conservation centres in the Malay states of Sabah and Sarawak on the island's north coast. You can also visit Lankayan Island to see turtles, or take a cruise down the Kinabatangan River to spot proboscis monkeys. The ancient rainforest way of life survives with the Iban tribes, whose villages deep in the jungle can be reached by longtail boat. The best months to visit are March to October.

Contact *Audley Travel (01993 838100/01993 838118/www.audleytravel.com/Destinations/Southeast-Asia/Countries/Borneo/Introduction.aspx).*

676 Big cats in Nagpur, India

◊

Head to the city of Nagpur in India for the chance to join treks to spot tigers and leopards, who also share the forest with devilish langur monkeys, striped hyenas and a great many other mammals, such as Chousingha (the Four-horned Antelope). The success of Project Tiger reserves is partly due to the surge in ecotourism, which has added an economical incentive to set aside land for wildlife. Lodging may not be luxurious, but it's worth the peaceful retreat off the beaten track.

Contact *Naturetrek (01962 733051/ www.naturetrek.co.uk).*

677 Polar bears in Spitsbergen, Norway

◊

The Norwegian island of Spitsbergen is the best/most accessible place in the northern hemisphere to spot polar bears in their natural habitat; the surrounding archipelago is home to several hundred of these beguiling and sadly endangered creatures. But it's not all about the bears: Arctic foxes, seals and walruses are also common spots on expeditions deep into the Arctic Ocean. Only a few hundred miles from the North Pole, a purpose-built ice-breaker and its dinghies can take you to the feet of immense

677: Spitsbergen

679: Galapagos Islands

glaciers, round vast icebergs and through spectacular fjords (between June and August). **Contact** *Specialised Tours (01342 712785/ www.specialisedtours.com).*

678 *Alligators in Florida, USA*
♀

A trip to Florida's Everglades Alligator Farm in the state's national park doesn't have to just stop at *seeing* these reptiles; if you really want to get involved, then, er, snap up the chance to give one of them a cuddle – a baby one at least, as there are always plenty of little nippers among the 2,000 specimens here. You can also watch their larger, scarier parents get fed, see exotic snakes and take an airboat trip down the green canals, home to soft-shell turtles, birds and fish. The farm has featured on BBC TV programmes and been used to train the Miami Fire and Rescue team to catch wild alligators. **Contact** +1 305 247 2628/www.everglades.com.

679 *Everything, in the Galapagos Islands*
♀

Retracing the steps of Charles Darwin as he made history, meet Giant Galapagos Turtles at their breeding grounds and snorkel with rays, penguins and sealions. Humans are not feared here; you'd do well to outstare the iguanas on Isla Fernandina. Be prepared, however, for landscapes more reminiscent of the moon than a tropical paradise, and rules introduced since Darwin's time that bar riding or indeed eating the wildlife. It's best to avoid travelling here from July to September, when the sea gets rough. **Contact** *Tribes Travel (01728 685971/ www.tribes.co.uk).*

680-689

Ten cheap or free things to do in New York

680 *Jazz things up, at Minton's*
£ ☕

Few clubs in the city can boast as rich a history as Minton's Playhouse (208 W 118th Street, between St Nicholas Avenue & Adam Clayton Powell Jr Boulevard), which Miles Davis dubbed 'the black jazz capital of the world'. During the 1940s, when Thelonious Monk was the resident pianist here, late-night jams brought in such luminaries as Dizzy Gillespie and Charlie Parker, giving birth to bebop. Today, the long wooden bar offers a good vantage point for the nightly shows, which cost $5 on weeknights. *+1 212 864 8346/www.uptownatmintons.com.*

681 *Go rowing in Central Park*
£ ▥ ♡

The Loeb Boathouse (Midpark, at 75th Street) is open daily from April to October, weather permitting. Boat rental is $10 per hour plus $30 deposit. Head out on to the lake and admire the Bow Bridge; picnic and poetry optional. *+1 212 864 8346/www.uptownatmintons.com.*

682 *Ride the Cyclone at Coney Island, Brooklyn*
£ 👪

Although its legendary Astroland amusement park closed in 2008 following a slump in fortunes, Coney Island's Cyclone wooden rollercoaster ride – which was made an official New York City landmark in the 1980s – remains in action, having been bought up by the recently opened Dreamland Amusement Park. The vintage ride first opened in 1927, and costs $8 a ride. *www.coneyislandcyclone.com.*

683 *Browse 18 miles of books*
£ ▥

Boasting an extraordinary 18 miles of books, the Strand Bookstore (828 Broadway, at 12th Street) offers a collection of more than two million discount and used titles, starting at 50 cents, and made all the more daunting by its towering, chaotic bookshelves and surly staff. Find anything from an out-of-print tome on Victorian manners to the kitschest of sci-fi novelettes. *+1 212 473 1452/www.strandbooks.com.*

684 *Shop at Union Square Greenmarket*
£ ▥

You might want to avoid the latte-sipping owners of little yippy dogs that make up a large portion of the regulars at this weekly foodfest

(Monday, Wednesday, Friday and Saturday), but the supreme visual appeal of edible flora, fauna and baked deliciousness is undeniable, and make this the cheapest of eats. *www.cenyc.org/greenmarket.*

685 *Visit the Folk Art Museum*
£ ▦

The stunning eight-floor American Folk Art Museum celebrates traditional craft-based work. One of the best ways to explore the collection of unusual pottery, trade signs, delicately stitched log-cabin quilts and wind-up toys is on one of the Free Music Fridays (5.30-7.30pm), when the exhibitions are free, accompanied by music in the magnificent atrium. *+1 212 265 1040/www.folkartmuseum.org.*

686 *Rummage for a bargain at Century 21*
£ ▦

A white Gucci suit for $300? A Marc Jacobs cashmere sweater for less than $200? No, you're not dreaming – you're shopping at Century 21. The prized score is admittedly rare, but the place is still intoxicating: savings range from 25 per cent to 75 per cent off regular prices. *+1 212-227-9092/www.c21stores.com.*

682: Coney Island

687 *Feed your TV addiction at the Paley Center*
£ ▦

Formerly the Museum of TV & Radio, the Paley Center (25 West 52nd Street, between 5th & 6th Avenues) is nirvana for couch potatoes and pop-culture junkies. You can search through a computerised archive system of more than a million radio and television programmes, and enjoy your favourite *I Love Lucy* or *Star Trek* episode at your own personal console. Admission is $5-$10. *+1 212 621 6600/www.paleycenter.org.*

688 *Drink and dance at Water Taxi Beach*
£ ▦ ▼

When Water Taxi Beach (north side of Pier 17, Fulton Street, at South Street) opened, NYC became the land of sand, parties, ping-pong and electric palm trees. Sip beers or mixed drinks while playing one of the many available games. The Fish Shack dispenses beachy grub, including burgers and Baja-style fish tacos. Admission is free before 8pm. *+1 877 974 6998/www.watertaxibeach.com.*

689 *Go to Brooklyn Flea*
£ ▦

You'll be spared the sight of dodgy, overpriced tourist wares at this Fort Greene bazaar (Lafayette Avenue between Vanderbilt & Clermont Avenues; also at Front Street, at Washington Street): the space outside Bishop Loughlin Memorial High School hosts a quirky roster of cut-price items, including antiques, vintage clothes, records, art and jewellery.

690-699
Original (or quirky) UK weekend breaks

Fancy staying somewhere a bit different? As you'd expect, Britain has plenty of extra special, even eccentric, hotels and holiday lets to lay your head down in. We've chosen ten of the best, which are remote, romantic, historic and a little bit bonkers.

685: American Folk Art Museum

690 *Head for a lighthouse*

♀♡☾

Holidaying in a lighthouse keeper's cottage is about as remote and romantic as you'll get. Views of the open sea, the sound of waves as a bedtime lullaby – there's no better place to unwind and relax those stiff city shoulders. Trinity House, the UK's Lighthouse Authority, has converted over 30 former keepers' cottages into holiday lets, dotted all around the coast. Just be aware that some of the lighthouses are still operational, which means a powerful foghorn is liable to sound on misty nights; earplugs are thoughtfully provided.
Contact *Rural Retreats (01386 701177/ www.ruralretreats.co.uk).*

691 *Escape to Burgh Island*

♀☾♡

Although easily reached from shore, ten-acre Burgh Island feels wonderfully remote. Pilchard fishermen and pirates once made a lonely living here, but for most of the 20th century the island was the preserve of socialites, who holed up in the Burgh Island Hotel. Noël Coward came for three days and stayed three weeks. After a period of post-war decline, painstaking restoration has returned the hotel to its art deco

glory. Nowadays, Burgh offers a distinctly old-fashioned luxury. Televisions are out, and ballgowns and billiards are definitely in. (As are weekly arrivals by helicopter, greeted with champagne.)
Contact *01548 810514/www.burghisland.com.*

692 *Wind down in a windmill*

♡♔☾

Is this tranquil 18th-century windmill-turned-guesthouse in Cley-next-the-Sea, Norfolk, the perfect romantic hideaway? It has the requisite four-posters, an atmospheric circular sitting room with roaring fire, and spectacular sea views. If you're weekending with friends, it's like being on a Famous Five adventure, with odd-shaped rooms, crannies and ladders that lead to lookouts – but crucial grown-ups' stuff such as quality linen on comfortable beds isn't sacrificed. Go for ambles on the shingle beach, birdwatch, and wander around the charming village. The mill has six bedrooms; there are three more in the courtyard cottages.
Contact *01263 740209/www.cleymill.co.uk.*

693 *Get fruity in a pineapple*

☾

There's no need to venture abroad for a taste of the tropics, when you can stay in your very own prickly pear – albeit one made of stone. The 75-foot pineapple folly at Dunmore Park, near Stirling, is one of the oldest examples of the fashion for architectural flights of fancy. Built as a garden retreat for the earl and his wife, the fruit was chosen as it represented the height of gourmet luxury in the 1760s. These days, the peculiar pavilion can be rented out through the Landmark Trust, which specialises in rescuing quirky old buildings and turning them into holiday homes with a difference (check the website for other unusual options).
Landmark Trust *01628 825925/ www.landmarktrust.org.uk.*

694 *Stay in a train station*

♀☾

Set on the gloriously scenic Settle to Carlisle line, high above the Yorkshire Dales, Grade II-listed Dent Station is now an unusual holiday let. This is a true rural retreat, and no mistake: the nearest village is four miles away. You can roam the countryside in splendid isolation –

693: Dunmore Park

although with regular train services passing through, you're not completely alone.
Contact *07824 665266/www.dentstation.co.uk.*

695 *Get rustic on Bardsey Island*

◊♨

In the Middle Ages, the abbey on Bardsey Island was a magnet for pilgrims. Today, the abbey is in ruins and the visitors to this tiny island off the Llyn peninsula in North Wales are more likely to be in search of peace and quiet than spiritual sustenance. That and the wildlife, which is abundant: Bardsey is a great place for spotting seals, dolphins and porpoises. The trust that looks after the island rents out a handful of charmingly rustic cottages to visitors. Be warned: they don't have running water or electricity.
Contact *0845 811 2233/www.bardsey.org.*

696 *Perch on the cliff's edge on Rhossili Bay*

♜ ◊♨

There are beaches for walking and talking. There are beaches for swimming and surfing. And then there are beaches for sitting and staring. Rhossili Bay is made for the latter: this is the landscape of the sublime. The Gower peninsula, in the south-west corner of Wales, was the first area in Britain to be designated an Area of Outstanding Natural Beauty, and it's not difficult to see why. The beach gives new meaning to the word sweeping; the dunes are mountainous; the downs behind are majestic; and the thundering surf is relentless. On a breezy day, the wind might whip you raw, but you can always seek shelter in the Worm's Head Hotel, perched on the edge of the cliff.
Worm's Head Hotel *01792 390512/ www.thewormshead.co.uk.*

697 *Kip in a castle*

♡⛺♨

English Heritage offers 13 holiday cottages and apartments on its properties, from castles and ruined abbeys to rambling grand estates. Each is unique, and all boast stylish, contemporary interiors; there's history enough when you step outside. If you opt for a stay in Carisbrooke Castle on the Isle of Wight, banish any images of a cold, dank dungeon: you'll be kipping in a swish second-floor apartment (sleeping a family

of four), within the castle's walls. Couples might prefer to cosy up in the snug Custodian's House at Henry VIII's Pendennis Castle in Cornwall.
English Heritage *www.english-heritage.org.uk.*

698 *Be grand on a budget*

£

Forget your preconceptions about dank dorms and basic huts: there are some seriously stylish joints on the Youth Hostel Association's books. Planning a trip to London? You can stay in the middle of Holland Park in a Jacobean mansion for around £20. Equally impressive surrounds can be found at Bath's Youth Hostel.
YHA *01629 592700/www.yha.org.uk.*

699 *Sleep with your head in the clouds*

This famed folly in Uplands, Suffolk, was erected in 1923 as the new water tower for nearby Thorpeness. The water tank was cunningly 'disguised' as a quaint little cottage – now a highly unusual holiday let.
Contact *020 7224 3615/ www.houseintheclouds.co.uk.*

699: House in the Clouds

New boutique hotels

700 **El Silencio, Costa Rica** ♻

In the heart of the Costa Rican rainforest, El Silencio Lodge & Spa's 16 cottages (+506 2761 0301, www.elsilenciolodge.com) are made from the environment's friendliest materials, while the food is sourced from the lodge's own organic garden and prepared by renowned Chef Marco Gonzalez. The outdoor yoga platform gazes out across the rainforest; and with no internet or mobile reception, this silent hideaway is a genuine escape.

701 Riad Noir d'Ivoire, Marrakech

+212 24 38 09 75/www.noir-d-ivoire.com.
A sanctuary in the heart of the city, each room of this small riad was individually decorated by the owner Jill, an interior designer. The inner courtyard boasts an ancient and supremely tranquil swimming pool and the fabulous breakfast is served on the riad's roof terrace.

702 Michel Berger, Berlin

+49 30 2977 8590/www.michelbergerhotel.com.
Opened in August 2009, Michel Berger caters for the trendy crowd that frequents Berlin's arts festivals and nightlife. Draws include a spa and a beer garden, as well as handmade wooden furniture in each room. The old factory building (natch) exemplifies Berlin's affordably edgy chic.

703 Sanctum Soho, London

020 7292 6100/www.sanctumsoho.com.
Sanctum Soho offers proof that sometimes money can buy style, with an underground cinema, a 24-hour rooftop bar and exquisitely modern interior design from Lesley Purcell.

Located in the heart of London's West End, this is an ideal base from which to explore the city.

704 Commune by the Great Wall, China

+86 10 8118 1888/
www.communebythegreatwall.com/en.
For a truly wild experience, head to the Kempinski-managed Commune, where a cluster of unique, cutting-edge villas designed by 12 leading Asian architects enjoys unbelievable views of the Great Wall. With three restaurants serving Western and Chinese fare, as well as a gym and a superb spa, it's a wonderful getaway.

705 Awasi, San Pedro de Atacama

+56 55 851460/0808 101 6778/www.awasi.cl.
In the tiny town of San Pedro de Atacama in Chile, this small hotel of just eight cottages offers secluded and spacious luxury, with outstanding cuisine and home-baked bread. The real attraction here is the Atacama Desert, thus each cottage has its own Jeep and endlessly helpful private guide to take guests on various exciting excursions.

706: Xudum Okavango Delta Lodge

703: Sanctum Soho

706 Xudum Okavango Delta Lodge, Botswana

♦

*+27 11 809 4300/www.andbeyondafrica.com/
luxury_safari/botswana/okavango_delta/
and_beyond_xudum.*

The Okavango Delta is a unique region of countless waterways and impossibly abundant wildlife. This new lodge is built on an island in the middle of a 250-square-kilometre private reserve. Each of the nine suites includes a plunge pool and a hideout from which the region's unparalleled birdlife can be viewed. Even in this remote corner of paradise, Priscilla the chef conjures up outstanding modern cuisine.

707 The Blue Moon Hotel, New York

This 22-room hotel has a classic style that reflects the history of New York's Lower East Side. Abandoned since 1935, it was recently completely refurbished, with every salvageable ornamental detail in place. It's a unique tribute to the character of the area.
+1 212 533 9080/www.bluemoon-nyc.com.

708 Titilaka Inkaterra Hotel Puno, Peru

0808 234 2368/www.andean-experience.com/titilaka.
In the heart of the Andes, looking out over Lake Titicaca, the 12 suites of this secluded

hideaway offer modern design and luxury as an ideal base for exploring this unique place. A local guide can take you to visit the lake's islands and local colonial churches, as well as on hikes up the Andean mountains.

709 Emporium Hotel, Brisbane

+61 7 3253 6999/www.emporiumhotel.com.au.
The first luxury boutique hotel in Brisbane has set the standard impossibly high; the award-winning splendour is apparent in the spacious and classically modern design, the lavish attention and effortlessly stylish Emporium Cocktail Bar.

710-716
Cool cruises

710 *Chilean fjords*

♦

Navimag runs what it uninspiringly calls a 'ferry' from the city of Puerto Montt to Puerto Natales in Patagonia – but what is really a stunning excursion through a wild landscape of glowering mountains, evergreen forested islands and vast glaciers. Seal colonies and cormorants populate the waters, as do clutches of colourful waterside palafitte houses, providing a taste of local culture and food. The Villarrica volcano offers wannabe explorers a challenge, with 2,800 metres of hiking material. Dining and entertainment are basic, but the impressive scenery more than makes up for it.

Navimag *+56 65 432 300/www.navimag.com.*

711 *Norway's Hurtigruten*

Travel with the Hurtigruten line from Kirkenes in the north to the Arctic landscape of Bergen in the south and you'll find yourself squeezing through some of the most breathtaking fjord scenery available. There are stop-offs at Hammerfest – the world's most northerly town – the medieval city of Trondheim, and Tromsø, nestled between the Arctic Ocean and towering mountains and the perfect base for Northern Lights viewing and dog-sledding excursions. Go in summer, and you're in for lush Norwegian coastal scenery, unbeatable birdwatching at Varangerfjord and a glimpse of Hitra, island of deer.

0845 225 6640/www.hurtigruten.co.uk.

712 *Up the Amazon in Peru*

The Amazon Basin is beyond vast, making up 65 per cent of Peru, so prepare yourself to feel like a dot on the ocean when you pick a cruise up this mammoth river. Head off the tourist trail and you'll find a few ramshackle but comfortable boats ready to take you on a trip through the Pacaya-Samiria National Reserve, exploring creeks and lagoons inhabited by Howler monkeys, pink river dolphins and blue morpho butterflies the size of your hand. Fortify yourself with a pisco sour at the bar and go fishing for piranhas off the side of the boat. During the rainy season, your feet won't touch land for several days at a time.

Book with *Cox & Kings (020 7873 5000/ www.coxandkings.co.uk).*

713 *Mekong voyage*

For a sense of the spectacular diversity of South-east Asia, take a colonial-style river steamer along the Mekong for an eight-day trip from Saigon to Angkor. Visit the colourful floating markets and quiet Catholic monasteries of Cai Be

and Sa Dec, a Cham tribal village and a catfish farm at Chau Doc, and the remnants of Khmer Rouge culture in the Cambodian capital Phnom Penh. Private pedicabs can be arranged for those in need of a little independence. The journey ends with a visit to the landmark Angkor Wat temple.

Book with *Pandaw (0131 514 1035/ www.pandaw.com).*

714 *Transatlantic crossing*

Book yourself in as a 'grill' passenger (a discreet way of saying 'first class') on the legendary *Queen Mary II* to New York, and prepare yourself for six days of what can only be described as royal treatment, with traditional afternoon tea in the Queens Room, lavish balls where dressing up is de rigueur, and your own personal butler. Aside from the old-school service, haute cuisine and ballroom-dancing extravaganzas, there are lectures from leading authorities on just about everything, classes on anything from acting to salsa, and on-board spas, theatres and cinemas. And all in the most opulent surroundings imaginable.

Book with *Cunard (0845 678 0013/ www.cunard.co.uk).*

716: A dahabiyya along the Nile

715 *Round the British Isles*

If fantastic scenery, fresh air and a sense of a fading heritage are further up your holiday agenda than cheesy nightlife and suntans, then consider a cruise around the British Isles. Learn about Scottish clans and knock back home-made whisky on the Isle of Skye, hike through rocks and wild heather in the Hebrides and along the Antrim coast in Northern Island, and enjoy a few nights of craic in Dublin and Edinburgh. There's even a white sandy beach or two in the Inner Hebrides, all the better for the lack of tourists and beach umbrellas. Be prepared for slightly older companions, but also for a sophisticated cruise experience, with plush boats, lectures from botanists and historians, and silver-service meals with polite conversation.
Book with *Noble Caledonia (020 7752 0000/ www.noble-caledonia.co.uk).*

716 *A dahabiyya along the Nile*

🏠

Ignore the big tourist cruises, and opt for the intimate group atmosphere of one of these comfortably grand houseboats for the 120-kilometre trip south along the Nile from Esna to Aswan. The Temple of Horus at Edfu is one of Egypt's most perfectly preserved specimens and the area oozes mystery. Once you reach Aswan there is a chance to visit the majestic rock-cut temples of Abu Simbel. The traditional 1920s style of boat means your trip is more Agatha Christie than P&O, and the smaller size gives you access to archaeological sites like Gebel Silsela that larger boats can't reach.
Book with *Explore (0845 013 1537/ www.explore.co.uk).*

717-724
Holiday camps in the UK and Europe

717 Norton Grange Resort, Isle of Wight

☝ ❦ ☺

01983 760323/www.isleofwight.com/nortongrange.
'Adults-only' might be the operative words in what attracts you to this Warner Break resort, but the location is faultless, within walking distance of picturesquely twee Yarmouth and sandy beaches, and with its own grounds dotted with tropical palms and a year-round heated swimming pool. Entertainment comes in the forms of nightly shows of all varieties and 'experience breaks', which include digital photography and wildlife watching.

718 Butlins Skegness, Lincolnshire
£ ❦ ☺ ❦

0845 070 4750/www.butlins.com/resorts/skegness.
The original 'a week's stay for a week's pay' resort, Billy Butlin's first venture is still going strong after 70 years. Kids are key, with a funfair, Splash Wonderland and innumerable sports and outdoor activities all on offer, but the surprisingly stylish Front Room Bar and luxury spa make it a getaway for the adults too.

719 Potters Leisure Resort, Great Yarmouth, Norfolk
☝ ❦ ☺

01502 730345/www.pottersholidays.com.
Proudly advertising itself as 'the UK's only five-star holiday village', Potters does not disappoint. Its 65 acres of land include a private sandy beach, golf course and a clay pigeon shooting range, and accommodation ranges from self-catering bungalows to luxury hotel suites. There are also 'special breaks' designed just for adults.

720 Manjushri Kadampa Meditation Centre, Ulverston, Cumbria
❦ ☺

01229 584029/www.nkt-kmc-manjushri.org.
Every year, hordes of holidaymakers head to the Lake District in search of a retreat from city life. If you're looking to escape the crowds, along with a foray into Buddhist teaching and meditation, try the Manjushri Kadampa Meditation Centre. Based at Conishead Priory, a historic house set in 70 acres on the shores of Morecambe Bay, it couldn't be situated in a more beautiful location, perfect for doing a bit of soul-searching.

721 Camping Piani di Clodia, Lake Garda, Italy
☝ ❦

+39 045 759 0456/www.gardalake.it/pianidiclodia.
If the clear blue water at the private beach on the shores of the stunning Lake Garda doesn't suffice, the resort is attached to a guest-only

720: Manjushri Kadampa
Meditation Centre

water park, made up of five areas with something for pretty much everyone. There's also the usual array of children's activities, entertainment (Italian-style – you have been warned), and a full range of accommodation types, from large caravans to cosy bungalows.

722 L'Hippocampe, Languedoc-Roussillon, France

0871 911 7777/www.siblu.com/hippocampe.
European holiday camps tend to be overcrowded and overrun by the kind of boozy teenagers you'd rather do without. Most of them choose the larger La Sirène, close by L'Hippocampe, and whose extensive facilities you are free to use before returning to this, more tranquil, resort. Situated within walking distance of long, sandy beaches and the busy holiday village of Argelès-sur-Mer, and with adrenaline-fuelled watersports and tamer kids' activities on offer, this really could strike the perfect balance.

723 Sunparks Eifel Gunderath, Germany

0904 0110 011/www.sunparks.co.uk.
Germany is no Mediterranean island, but luckily the nearby (perhaps providentially named) Freisen beach is not the only thing on offer here, with an indoor water park and lush surrounding countryside boasting a network of over 250 kilometres of cycle lanes. The Wattenmeer National Park is also worth a look, and you can take a guided tour over the mudflats, which have been declared a World Natural Heritage Site. The carefully styled picturesque 'holiday village' provides self-catering villas and hotel rooms.

724 Club Med Bodrum Palmiye, Turkey

+90 252 368 91 52/www.clubmed.co.uk.
The charm of Club Med is that it's well and truly a package deal, with bed, board and even booze all paid for before you go. So you can spend your time concentrating on the picture-perfect Mediterranean beach, beautiful gardens and unexpectedly delicious restaurants that serve everything from steak to sushi, as well as limitless opportunities for watersports.

725-732
Eight things to do in Croatia

725 Sleep in a lighthouse
♀♡

Holidaying in a lighthouse is about as far away from the hustle and bustle as you can get. Adriagate offers a variety of waterside abodes dotted around the coast and islands; some are more remote than others but all are great for ocean views, sea sounds and wildlife spotting. **Adriagate** *+385 21 340 880/020 7043 1875/ www.adriagate.com.*

726 Sail away
♀ 🏊

Croatia has more than 1,000 islands, many of them unblemished by man, industry or motorboat. Transport options vary from sleep-on-board package deal tours to short-hop catamaran services and a state-run ferry. For a more hands-on experience, choose a tailormade trip with a sailing charter company where a private yacht will become your temporary floating home and a qualified skipper will be able to show you the ropes if you fancy getting your hands on deck. Sail Croatia has bases in Kastela, Split, Pula and Dubrovnik. **Sail Croatia** *www.sailcroatia.net.*

727 Tour the wine and olive routes of Istria
♀

Bursting with produce and inventive chefs, Istria is the culinary heart of Croatia and the No.1 choice for gastronomes. Although rarely exported, wine is a speciality of the region, along with olive oil and truffles. Explore the wine and olive roads, a maze of trails that wind their way through 15,200 acres of vineyards and olive groves to take you to your oil- or wine-tasting destination. Maps helpfully differentiate between larger plants and cellars and those using more traditional techniques, and can be picked up from any tourist office. See www.istra.hr for more details.

728 Visit a car-free island
♀♡

Prvic is a quiet island in the north dotted with olive groves, pine forests and vineyards and home to one of the most stunning hotels in the Adriatic region, the Hotel Maestral (+385 22 448 300, www.hotelmaestral.com). Kolocep is another car-free spot on the southernmost side of Croatia, and although Dubrovnik lies just a 25-minute boat ride away, this densely forested isle feels wonderfully remote; perfect for couples.

729 Get active in Croatia's national parks
♀ 🏊

More than just a pretty place, Croatia's mountainous landscape and unspoilt terrain make it a godsend for active types. Kornati National Park, a protected area of 89 islands fringed by reefs and bays, is perfect for kayaking. Between navigating the maze of shorelines and snorkelling in the reefs, binocular-clad kayakers

729: Explore Croatia's national parks

728: Prvic

can check out some of the birdlife on the islands themselves. For on-land adventures, Velebit Nature Park, stretching from the Vratnik Saddle to the Zrmanje Valley, has endless hiking routes, one of the biggest cave complexes in Croatia and 18 lodging sites from which to choose (note that camping is not permitted).

730 *Take a regal retreat at the Lesic Dimitri hotel on Korcula*
♡

Next door to Marco Polo's house and only a stone's throw from the Adriatic Sea, the Lesic Demitri hotel is a stunningly restored bishop's palace in the medieval town of Korcula. With original 18th-century features, handcrafted furniture, private yachts and six luxurious residences, it offers a Dalmatian experience fit for a king. From here, take a sunset cruise around the island, wander through the winding alleyways of this charming 14th-century town or, if you're feeling lethargic, simply lay back for a pampering at the palace's luxury spa.
+385 91 2626218/www.lesic-dimitri.com.

731 *Soak up some culture in the 'city of museums'*

With no beaches for distraction and over 80 museums and art venues, the pocket-sized metropolis of Zagreb is the perfect place for taking in some culture. In this self-proclaimed city of museums, art-lovers can choose between Manets and Rembrandts at the Mimara Museum or Breughels and El Grecos at Strossmayer's Gallery of Old Masters. The Museum of Contemporary Art (www.msu.hr) – made over, expanded and relocated to the Novi Zagreb area – was due to reopen in late 2009 (after a long delay). The glittering new building, whose front façade forms a 90-metre LED display for films and media art, harbours some 6,000 works from home and abroad.

732 *Volunteer with vultures*
£ ♻ ♲

The Caput Insulae ecology centre on the island of Cres dedicates its expertise and energies to caring for 140 griffon vultures – one of the world's most majestic birds but also one whose future is hanging in the balance. Poisoning, habitat destruction and the encroachment of tourism all threaten its home. Cres is a largely unspoilt island of rock and forest, a natural habitat for the birds. Its tiny hilltop village, Beli, is the headquarters for ornithological research (+385 51 840 55, www.caput-insulae.com).

733-737
Diving and snorkelling

733 *Belize*

The Red Sea and Great Barrier Reef are better known but Belize is the world's 'other' top diving area, and benefits from some 298 kilometres of coral reef – the largest in the northern hemisphere. All levels are catered for, from virgin snorkellers to pro divers. The former will relish watching myriad colourful reef fish as well as (hopefully) stingrays, dolphins and nurse sharks. Scuba divers – whether beginners or seasoned pros –

might expect to see barracuda, turtles, hammerhead sharks and eagle rays. Scuba divers can also go to Glover's Reef Atoll, a UNESCO World Heritage Site 56 kilometres from Belize.
Stay at *Hamanasi Adventure & Dive Resort (+501 520 7073/www.hamanasi.com).*

734 *Red Sea, Egypt*

Staying on a 'liveaboard' will give you the opportunity to enjoy the best diving – living on a boat for a week or so means you'll be able to reach remote parts of the ocean that you can't get to in a day – though it's possible to base yourself on the Egyptian mainland and make daily trips out to the reef. The popular and well-developed resort of Sharm el Sheikh is within easy reach of the Ras Mohammed Marine National Park, which has some 40 superb dive sites and caters for divers of all abilities, as well as snorkellers. The terraced coral reefs are stunning and are home to hundreds of species of marine animals, such as stingrays, moray eels and barracuda.
Book with *Blue O Two (01752 480 808/ www.blueotwo.com).*

735: Thailand

735 *Thailand*

♀ ⅍

With its calm, clear waters, beautiful beaches, tasty food and friendly hospitality, it's no wonder Thailand is popular with divers and snorkellers. It's also particularly good for underwater photography enthusiasts, with excellent visibility. Noted diving resorts are at Phuket on the south-west coast; Pattaya, a beach resort a few hours' drive from Bangkok; and the rocky, jungle island of Koh Tao ('Turtle Island') in the Gulf of Thailand. The latter is particularly good if you're new to scuba diving. For more information, see the impartial website www.scubatravel.com.

Book with *DiveWorldWide (0845 130 6980/ www.diveworldwide.com).*

736 *Providencia, Colombia*

♀ ◑ ⅍

Providencia is an undeveloped island with no pretensions whatsoever. It's old-school Caribbean: somewhat shabby and rustic, with no-frills hotels, laid-back locals and not much to do but take a dip in the clean, warm waters. Rent a boat or join one of the daily group trips (you'll find you get chatting to locals if you so much as walk down the road) and enjoy a snorkelling excursion to one of the reefs. Cajo Cangrego (or 'Crab Key') is a tiny island off Providencia's north-west coast that's easy to circumnavigate on a half-hour snorkelling expedition; spot turtles and numerous fish and spy on the frigate birds soaring overhead. The crab migration takes place in May – a great time to visit as it's off-season for Colombians.

Book with *Journey Latin America (020 8747 8315/www.journeylatinamerica.co.uk).*

737 *Wreck dives, Indonesia*

◑ ⅍

The thousands of islands that make up Indonesia have been attracting treasure hunters in search of buried riches for years. Most recently, the wreck of buccaneering 19th-century English ship *The Forbes*, which had King George III's approval to plunder foreign vessels until it ran aground in 1806, was explored by German divers, who found a £6 million booty of gold and silver. If you fancy scouting for your own treasure,

Regaldive offers trips to the Indonesian island of Bali, where scuba divers can scour the seabeds. Though wreck diving is for experienced divers only, novices can delight in the bountiful aquatic life (manta rays, pristine corals and sponges, and, if you're lucky, juvenile whale sharks).

Regaldive *01353 659999/www.regaldive.co.uk.*

738-747
Family-friendly holidays worldwide

738 *A classic holiday in the Lake District*

£ ◑ ⋒ ⅍ ◔

Get them thinking green right from the start by holidaying at home. The Lake District is both peaceful and exciting, offering plenty of opportunities for Arthur Ransome-inspired adventure based on fishing and sailing (think *Swallows and Amazons*). Accommodation at 17th-century High Wray Farm is especially child-friendly, with a childcare service, animals on the farm for petting, and locally sourced food deliveries. And if your tots are papoose sized, you can take them out on nearby lakeside walks in a baby carrier.

High Wray Farm *01539 432 280/ www.highwrayfarm.co.uk.*

739 *Temples in tot-friendly Thailand*

♀ ◑ ⋒

On a two-week family-oriented tour of Thailand with ethical travel agent responsibletravel.com, you'll get to see the key sights in Bangkok (where the trip begins), explore the wildlife-filled jungles of Khao Soke National Park, and finally wind down on picture-perfect beaches. And accommodation in local homestays means that the kids will gain a fascinating insight into the local culture and cuisine. *www.responsibletravel.com.*

740 *Serious fun in the Isles of Scilly*

♀ ⋒

If you live in London, a fun way to start off a Scilly trip is to first travel by sleeper train to

Cornwall's Penzance. From there, travel in style – by boat, plane or helicopter, depending on your budget – to Tresco. The island has sandy beaches to rival those in the Caribbean (yet without the un-family-friendly long-haul flight) and a ruined castle, and is great for rambles or thrill-seeking in the form of kayaking, cycling or boating. Self-catering cottages are available for hire. For more details, visit www.tresco.co.uk/holidays.

741 Kids go cruising with Royal Caribbean

A cruise… really? Well yes, as grey nomads and old salts make room for the new generation of sailors. Whether travelling around the icy edges of Alaska or anchoring off Hawaii, cruise ship staff will divide kids into age-based clubs, starting from three years, and indulge them in everything from drawing to on-board rock climbing and ice-skating.
Royal Caribbean *0844 493 4005/ www.royalcaribbean.co.uk.*

742 Go wild in Canada

Grizzly bear sightings are among the many highlights on a family escapade to the pristine wildernesses of Canada. Active kids will love scrambling through national parklands in search of rare wildlife, spying glaciers through the trees and getting wet from the spray of icy waterfalls. This is definitely one to shake off the apathy created by a world of computer games, text messaging and the like; you'll all come back with glowing skin and lots of stories.
Book with *Holidays2Canada (0800 988 4611/www.holidays2canada.co.uk).*

743 Child-friendly camping with Feather Down Farms

The hugely successful Feather Down Farms concept – posh camping for those who want a taste of the simple life without the hassle and discomfort – has spawned a whole trend for

743: Feather Down Farms

boutique camping. Located on farms on nature reserves and country estates, Feather Down holidays provide all the ingredients of a classic family camping break (fresh air, outdoor activity, farm animals, and cooking food bought from the farm shop together), yet with comfy beds, running (cold) water, oil lamps and a wood-burning stove in each spacious tent – as well as that classic middle-class staple, a coffee grinder. There are more than 20 sites available throughout the UK. *01420 80804/www.featherdownfarms.co.uk.*

744 *Egypt 101*

🔍 £ 👪 🏛

Bring all those lessons about mummies and pharaohs to life with an ancient history class disguised as a holiday. See the pyramids and great sphinx at Giza and Valley of the Kings on the west bank of the Nile opposite Luxor (Thebes). As a reward, swim in the Red Sea and teach 'em how to snorkel. Sharm

743: Feather Down Farms

el Sheihk, sought after for its beaches and Brit-friendly food options, is a popular spot for families and regular charter flights make it friendly on family budgets.
Book with *Red Sea Holidays (0845 026 5980/ www.redseaholidays.co.uk).*

745 *Disneyland Paris by rail*

👪 ☺

As rapaciously commercial as family holidays come, Disneyland is nevertheless a must before the kids grow up into cynical teenagers; but if your offspring can't hack the long flight to Florida, then head for Paris. Sip champagne on the Eurostar to celebrate the money you've saved by not flying, and tell the kids how green this all is, and then stumble upon much-adored characters, movie-themed shows and an abundance of rides fit for both parent and child, spread over two different parks.
www.disneylandparisdirect.com.

746 *Venezuelan 'Lost World' adventure*

🌳 👪 ⛷ 🏠

Thrill-seeking families in search of tropical delights will be taken aback by Venezuela. Its jungle interior and towering Angel Falls are the perfect backdrop for an Indiana Jones-style camping and exploring holiday. Whitewater rafting and mountain biking are also available in the region, and we suggest joining a prearranged tour with a reputable operator to get expert guides who speak good English.
Book with *Explore (0845 013 1537/ www.explore.co.uk).*

747 *Swiss slopes for all ages*

🌳 👪 ⛷

Ride the slopes of Arosa, Switzerland, with your family in tow. Located in the Alps, this ski resort has soft runs for children and beginners, as well as options for more experienced skiers. And if you want to opt for a luxury pad to recuperate in at the end of a day's activity, there are five-star hotel options complete with monorail from the lobby, spas and childcare.
Book with *Powder Byrne (020 8246 5300/ www.powderbyrne.com).*

Ideas from the expert

748-757

*Amanda Wills,
of Virgin Holidays,
suggests ten exotic spots
in which to tie the knot.*

748 Nestled on the northern tip of Mauritius, the Paul & Virginie is a small hotel with heaps of local character. It got its name from a 1700s tragic love story, and doesn't disappoint – the word is that many a love story (sans heartache) has blossomed in its pared-down, chic guest rooms. Weddings take place on the beach overlooking the craggy cliffs to the north of the hotel. Perfect for low-key brides.

749 The capital of all things bling, Miami is great for brides unabashed in their intention to have all eyes on them. Ceremonies often take place on the beach and the place is popular for same-sex unions. A post-wedding walk along Ocean Drive, followed by a reception in one of the cool hotels (try the Shore Club or the Tides) creates a great art deco backdrop for photos.

750 MIckey certainly knows how to put on a wedding, and Disney World's 'Deluxe Escape' would be my pick. It includes a reception at your choice of hotel – the Polynesia is a g ood bet – a photographer and limo service, a personal wedding co-ordinator, and lots more. New brides, princesses for the day, start married life in the Magic Kingdom, hitting the rides or just waving regally at the crowds in the park.

751 The sheer natural drama of Niagara Falls makes it a stunning place to get hitched. My top tip is to get married after dusk when the falls are lit up. We arrange weddings in a gazebo overlooking the Falls, and guests can then take a walk along the top; the more adventurous have been known to hop on the 'Maid of the Mist' boat in full wedding attire, to get up close and personal with the Falls as well as each other.

752 The Hard Rock Hotel in Las Vegas has lots of wedding options. My tip for Beatles enthusiasts would be its John Lennon Room – a replica of the singer's Manhattan apartment, complete with original artwork and a white baby grand piano (to serenade the bride with *Love Me Do*?), with keys autographed by popular Vegas performers like Elton John. Alternatively, tie the knot overlooking the strip in a private jet-copter – a clergyman will conduct an inflight ceremony for the ultimate mile-high wedding.

753 The Almond Morgan Bay is a beautiful traditional St Lucian hotel nestled in the rainforest of this Caribbean island. Suites have recently been added to the complex for the extra luxury required for wedding parties; many guests get hitched here then stay on for an extra week of sunshine. Nothing beats the famous Pitons volcanic plugs as a backdrop for a wedding picture.

754 Turtle Beach Barbados is one of our most popular wedding destinations. It's great value for money, and the wedding pictures are sure to cause bride envy back home. The hotel has its own wedding co-ordinator, who sorts all arrangements, including top-notch meals in Barbados's finest eateries.

755 For those wanting to engage all their senses while saying 'I do', a wedding at the Sydney Botanical gardens is hard to beat, with panoramic views of the Opera House and the Harbour Bridge as well as tantalising scents from the surrounding gardens. Guests can reserve one of the lush lawns, a feature garden or one of the historic lodges and pavilions for their ceremony.

756 An Empire State Wedding offers romantic nuptials with plenty of old-school charm, not to mention the wow factor of getting married in the tallest building in New York. The ceremony takes place 55 floors above the city streets, with breathtaking views of the Chrysler Building and the East River. If it's good enough for Carrie...

757 The emphasis at La Source, on the Caribbean island of Grenada, is on rejuvenating mind and body; whether by meditation, tai chi, spa treatments, scuba diving or just lying by the pool, it's all included to make sure there are no bridezilla moments. The resort borders Pink Gin beach and ticks all the boxes for luxury and sea views. It's perfect for those who have an idyllic Caribbean wedding in mind.

■ **Virgin Holidays** 0844 557 5825/
www.virginholidays.co.uk

758-764
Creative breaks

758 Painting and printmaking at Atelier Montmiral, France

○

+33 563 405 155 (07980 165993 in winter)/ www.ateliermontmiral.com.
Established artists Bunny and Mick Newth have been running seven- and ten-day art courses covering drawing, painting and printmaking from the village of Castelnau de Montmiral in south-west France since 2005. Held between early spring and late autumn, the flexible structure of the courses means that a wide range of levels are accommodated, from complete beginners to experienced artists and art graduates. Excellent studio facilities (which include an etching press), a magnificent rural location, and inspiring and affable hosts explain the high number of repeat bookings. Prices include tuition, some art supplies, rustic accommodation and delicious food and drink.

760: African drumming courses

759 Frui photography holidays

▦ ○

020 7241 5006/www.frui.co.uk.
Frui offers five- to eight-day photography holidays for beginners and more experienced snappers in Istanbul, Marrakech, Croatian Istria, the unspoilt Italian region of Abruzzo, and Syria. Tuition by a team of youthful and experienced art graduates covers technical basics as well as more creative techniques, in a lively and sociable environment, with group meals every evening an integral part of the experience. See the website for the full range of courses, which cover painting and cookery.

760 African drumming in the Gambia

07809 456490/www.african-drumming.co.uk/ drumming-holiday.html.
Inspired by Damon Albarn's promotion of African music? Now you can take the first steps in learning to play the djembe yourself at this friendly and relaxed drumming school in the Gambia, West Africa. Courses, taught by local expert musicians, are fairly intensive, at around four hours' tuition each day for one or two weeks (or longer, if you wish), and prices are very reasonable.

761 Sculpture in the Brecon Beacons

☾

01873 830410/www.studysculpture.com.
Simon and Anna Cooley's three- to five-day sculpture breaks take place at the grounds of their beautifully situated family home, three miles from Abergavenny in the Brecon Beacons, Wales. Courses, which cover metalwork, stone carving, clay sculpture and casting, are taught by Simon – an established sculptor – in an atmospheric stone barn, while Anna is in charge of the delicious food. Accommodation is booked separately, but details of local options are available.

762 Creative writing in Greece

www.responsibletravel.com/Trip/Trip902199.htm.
Open to novices as well as established novelists, these creative writing courses on the green and idyllic Sporades Islands aim to free the imagination, overcome fear and help students to develop a personal style through exercises and feedback sessions – with the chance to learn from writers as

distinguished as Steven Berkoff, Margaret Drabble and Julia Bell. The holidays include morning yoga sessions, and opportunities to sample local wine, learn about Greek cuisine and join in sociable events.

763 Traditional crafts in Ireland

☺

www.responsibletravel.com/Trip/Trip902260.htm.
If applied arts are more your focus, then these residential courses – run by responsible travel.com, and taught by local craftsmen in East Clare on Ireland's west coast – might fit the bill. Courses are offered in basket weaving, copper- and silversmithing and wood- and stone-carving, and you can also learn eco-building skills (like dry-stone walling) and traditional herb lore. County Clare has a strong musical heritage, and pub outings and folk music festivals are par for the, er, course.

764 Landscape painting in Andalucia

◊

01453 834137/www.andalucian-adventures.co.uk.
Andalucia Adventures specialises in painting holidays as a way of seeing and appreciating the landscapes and culture of Southern Spain and beyond. Groups are of mixed ability and led by a range of experienced tutors, while media tends to be fairly traditional, with a focus on watercolours, pastel, oils and acrylic paints. Courses are run over five days, with one day aligned for independent sightseeing.

765-769
UK heritage trains

765 West Highland line

◊☺

Soon after pulling out of Glasgow, you leave the urban sprawl behind and reach the tree-filled countryside that announces the southern boundary of the Scottish Highlands. There are three trains a day to Fort William, taking approximately three-and-a-half hours, on a journey that's unhurried – giving time to gaze out the window and daydream. The most striking vistas are along the banks of Loch

Lomond, on the right as the train heads north. If inclement weather thwarts a clamber to the Ben Nevis summit, take the Jacobite Steam Train (between May and October) – the route of the Hogwarts Express in the Harry Potter movies – through the wild Highlands across the 21-arch Glenfinnan viaduct to Mallaig, and indulge in fish and chips for lunch before the return trip to Fort William, where the Lime Tree (www.lime treefortwilliam.co.uk) makes for a good spot to rest your head. Visit www.scotrail.co.uk or www.steamtrain.info for further details.

766 East Lancashire Railway

👫

The East Lancs Railway is a charming heritage route that runs steam and diesel trains throughout the year and is staffed by enthusiastic volunteers. At 12 miles, it's only a shortie, but the journey between termini – Heywood and Rawtenstall – takes one hour each way. It's most easily accessed at Bolton Street Station in the market town of Bury (a short tram ride from Manchester); get on board for a sedate journey through the western slopes of the Pennines to Ramsbottom, a quiet village nestling in unspoilt countryside. Here, indulge in a sumptuous ten-course tasting lunch at Ramsons (www.ramsons-restaurant.com) before hopping back on the train for the journey back. The platforms are all about nostalgia; each one is filled with travel paraphernalia such as vintage leather suitcases, metal fire buckets and original signage.
www.east-lancs-rly.co.uk.

767 Heart of Wales line

This mini-odyssey through the centre of Wales – from the medieval town of Shrewsbury in England's Shropshire to Swansea, Wales's vibrant second city on the south-west coast – takes around four hours and is a treat even if you're not a train buff. The train winds its way along 121 miles, passing through the rolling Shropshire hills and over Offa's Dyke, the huge ditch marking the boundary between Wales and England, then over the impressive Knucklas viaduct, through pretty Welsh spa towns and the Sugar Loaf tunnel before arriving in Swansea. There are four trains per day from Monday to Saturday, and two services on Sundays.
01554 820586/www.heart-of-wales.co.uk.

768: Steam Dreams

768 *Steam Dreams*

An evocative steam train trip serves to remind us that it's the journey, not the destination, that can be the most important part of travelling. Steam Dreams runs various day trips to locations across England from London. Its fleet of beautifully maintained locomotives include a stunning green A160163 Tornado, which was in regular service in post-World War II Britain until steam trains were phased out in the mid 1960s. For a memorable day out, board the vintage carriages of the Cathedrals Express to Bath, where you can wander round the Roman Baths and the Pump Room, admire the Royal Crescent and gaze up at Bath Abbey. Special services run at Christmas for carol services and shopping, and during the summer months to the coast.
01483 209888/www.steamdreams.com.

769 *Settle–Carlisle Railway*

The 72-mile route takes just over an hour and a half to travel south-eastwards across the Yorkshire Dales, passing through some of the most scenic countryside in the UK. The route was built from 1869 to 1875 and passes over the Ribblehead Viaduct and through the Blea Moor tunnel. The route forms part of Network Rail, which operates modern diesel trains, but steam services and charters run occasionally for train enthusiasts. Passes that allow you to break your journey and explore the market towns en route are available. And once you reach Carlisle, Willowbeck Lodge (01228 513607/ www.willowbeck-lodge.com) is a lovely place to stay the night.
0800 980 0766 (answerphone)/ www.settle-carlisle.co.uk.

770-779
Ten singles holidays

So you're single – but that doesn't mean you want to enter a forced shagathon. Here we list ten ideas for ways to meet members of the opposite sex, make new friends or simply enjoy a holiday alone.

Single travellers can get stung by the singles supplement – a charge levied on solo travellers who use a room that tour and hotel operators want to fit two people in. The levy is justified on the basis that the room costs just as much for them to provide, and it can be quite pricey. Thankfully, however, more and more operators are choosing to lift this levy.

770 African safaris

Wild about Africa has an array of trips suitable for singles in Botswana, Namibia and Zambia, offering the chance to get to know other like-minded wildlife enthusiasts. In Botswana, see the Kalahari game reserve's black-maned lions, before beholding the astounding number and diversity of the Okovango Delta's birdlife.
Wild about Africa *020 8758 4717/ www.wildaboutafrica.com.*

771 Conservation volunteering in the UK

Have yourself an active, sociable break helping out the National Trust in its restorative and agricultural efforts. Join a group of volunteers to herd goats, build dry-stone walls, garden and more. All activities take place in stunning countryside, and banter with your fellow team members is part of the fun.
National Trust *0844 800 3099/ www.nationaltrust.org.uk/volunteering.*

772 Kiwi bus tours

Special bonds are often formed on buses. Kiwi Experience bus tours offer the chance to meet scores of travelling companions as you explore the awesome country of New Zealand. Visit the otherworldly Franz Josef glacier and the Tolkien-esque Mount Aspiring National Park. The unlimited pass means you have the flexibility to hop on and off whenever you feel like it at no extra cost.
Kiwi Experience *+64 9 369 9410/ www.kiwiexperience.com.*

773 French cycling holidays

Join a group of fellow two-wheelers on a Tour de France, passing ancient castles, beautiful town squares and expertly tended gardens – there are few better ways to see so much. Explore offers a range of different itineraries, covering most levels of fitness;

check the website for a whole host of options for solo travellers.
Explore *0844 499 0901/www.explore.co.uk.*

774 Boot Camp Spain

If the focus is more about toning up to improve your confidence to meet someone on home turf – or simply about meeting fellow women – then consider this one-week women-only boot camp in Spain. The company promises to take a dress size off you (if that's desired), as well as teach you to incorporate nutrition and exercise into your daily life. The luxury break includes boxing, yoga, circuit training and an hour a day of time alone.
Boot Camp Spain *0800 334 5077/ www.bootcampspain.com.*

775 Trekking across the American West

The epic landscapes of the American West offer superb trekking opportunities. Traverse the instantly recognisable Monument Valley and fail to comprehend the sheer size of the Grand Canyon with a knowledgeable Navajo guide, courtesy of the Adventure Company, which offers a range of 'Solo Adventures'.
Adventure Company *0845 450 5312/www.adventurecompany.co.uk.*

776 Eastern Europe's capitals, by train

Eastern Europe's cities teem with breathtaking architecture, museums and cafés; from Warsaw to Prague via Vienna and Budapest, the view from a rail carriage is the perfect perspective for the verdant and mountainous countryside, with plenty of opportunity to enjoy some personal space, cultural nourishment and time for contemplation. The trip can be organised by Just You, specialist in singles holidays.
Just You *0800 915 8000/www.justyou.co.uk.*

777 Windsurfing holidays

Whether pursuing your passion or learning a new skill, there are few more exhilarating feelings than your board cutting through the

crystal-clear waters of the Mediterranean or Red Sea. Instructors at Club Vass, experts in active watersports holidays, are the most highly qualified in the world, and used to encouraging lone travellers to engage in social activities.
Club Vass *0870 145 1387/www.clubvass.com.*

778 *Independently adventurous*

Travel to the frozen north for the adventure of a lifetime that has a tragic best-before date; or speed across the frozen tundra on a dog sled to see first-hand the majesty of polar bears. These are just two options offered by Independent Traveller – specialist in adventure travel.
Independent Traveller *01628 522772/ www.independenttraveller.com.*

779 *Hostelling around the world*
£

Hostels are ideal for single travellers, with dorm rooms at no extra cost and endless new people to engage with and get tips from. South-east Asia is the No.1 destination for backpackers, who often land with no definitive plan – which is part of the fun of it.

780-784
The best of Portugal

780 *Lisbon*

Portugal's capital city is spread across the hillsides that overlook the Rio Tejo, and offers Gothic cathedrals, majestic Moorish castles and quaint museums. Although it has all the cultural offerings you'd expect, Lisbon remains scandalously cheap; you can book a room in a hotel like the beautifully restored ex-convent York House at a fraction of the price you'd expect. Or stay at one of the many *pensoes* in downtown Baixa, a grid-like network of lovely backstreets. Start the day with a *pastel de nata* (custard-filled pastry) and espresso in Belem, and end it in the hilltop district of Bairro Alto, where the streets are lined with restaurants and bars packed with friendly locals. The eastern waterfront has been revamped in recent years, and now boasts an Oceanarium and great seafood restaurants.
York House *+351 21 396 24 35/ www.yorkhouselisboa.com.*

781 *Madeira*

This little island has long been a retreat for tourists and Portuguese alike. Rustic villages set along a coastline of sandy beaches or nestled in clifftops and valleys, and beautiful parks and gardens, draw thousands each year. Visit Funchal for one of the most vibrant fish markets you'll ever see. One of the nicest ways to experience the scenery is to stay at a *quinta*, an old Portuguese homestead. The Quinta das Vinhas in Calheta is one of the oldest manor houses on the island, and the 17th-century flagstone floors, wooden ceilings and hand-painted tiles exude tradition – as does the very fine home-brewed Madeira served with delicious food. The house is flanked by mountains with views that sweep over its vineyards to the sea.
Quinta das Vinhas *+351 291 824086/ www.qdvmadeira.com.*

782 *The Algarve*

The Algarve is well known as a massive tourist draw, and with good reason. You can book a package trip for an extremely affordable price and end up with exactly what you expected. The town of Albufeira is a good option, offering little secluded coves as well as long stretches of sandy beaches, plenty of watersports and golfing opportunities, walks into lush Portuguese countryside, and a year-round sunny climate. The Bayside Salgados Apartments (www.bayside-salgados.com) are an affordable option, with terraces overlooking the sea. If you want to avoid the tourist resort-packed Litoral area, then venture into the *serra* (hills) to experience traditional Algarve folklore, song and dance, especially popular on feast and saints' days during summer. The Barlavento region to the west has a rockier coastline and beautiful hidden bays, while the Sotavento area to the east is mile after mile of sandy beaches and warm(ish) seas.

783 *The Azores*

This group of nine volcanic islands scattered across the Atlantic are all uniquely stunning, but all share a similarly lush, green landscape and relaxed island attitude. São Miguel is the biggest, and boasts a village of thermal springs and fertile vegetation inside its central crater. A speciality here is *cozido do Portugal* (salted cod) cooked up inside the springs. Santa Maria is the most southerly of the islands and provides good surfing off the Praia do Formosa, and similar ribbons of white sandy beaches are to be found on Terceira – the most densely populated of the group – along with historic cathedrals and palaces. The central cluster of islands – Graciosa, Faial and Pico – do a great line in geological wonders, meanwhile, with sulphur caverns, tunnels to gashes in the earth's crust, and Portugal's highest mountain, Ponta de Pico. During the summer, boats operated by Atlantico Line (+351 296 288 933, www.atlanticoline.pt) connect all the islands, or book a Biosphere Expeditions package (0870 446 0801, www.biosphere-expeditions.org) to travel by boat tracking whales, dolphins and rare sea turtles.

784 *Alentejo*

Alentejo is a rural landscape unlike anywhere else in Portugal, with rolling grass plains and

780: Lisbon

undulating corn fields interspersed with sprawling forests of cork oaks and pine. Down along the coast, the long, sandy beaches are brisker and breezier than the Algarve, and crowd-free. The pace of life here is southern and slow, so linger in the little villages that appear like tiny nests of whitewashed houses, while enjoying local wines and scoffing traditional sweets from local monasteries. Take time to explore the hills, which conceal regal Roman temples at Evora, and crumbling medieval ruins at Monsaraz. Dine underneath 18th-century frescoes at the Hotel Convento de São Paulo, a beautiful 12th-century convent converted into a comfortable hotel.

Hotel Convento de São Paulo *+351 266 989 160/www.hotelconventospaulo.com.*

785-791
Argentina and Chile

785 *Ride... Mountain biking in Argentina's Lake District*
◊ ⚡

The lakeside town of San Martín de los Andes may not be as pretty as Argentinians would have you believe, but it's a great base for cycling and horse-riding adventures, with stunning surrounding scenery. A native Mapuche myth tells how God tripped over here – perhaps stumbling into the Andes – and dropped all the best bits of Creation he just happened to be carrying. There are good mountain biking circuits around the base of the Lanín volcano, at the north end of the Nahuel Huapi National Park and around Cerro Chapelco (the region's main ski mountain). Routes and maps are available at the bilingual portal ww.sanmartindelosandes.gov.ar. If you're spending a while in the region, consider a road trip along the Ruta de los Siete Lagos too.

786 *Dance... Tango in Buenos Aires*
▦ ♡ ⚡ ⅄

Dance it, watch it, think it, see it – you can choose whichever approach suits you, but at some stage of your trip to the Argentinian capital, you'll have to confront tango – quite possibly in the form of a dandruff-shouldered old gent inviting you to dance. The handsome face of legendary crooner Carlos Gardel is painted on all the walls of the neighbourhood of Abasto, his former home; while over in San Telmo, which claims (not altogether dubiously) to be the 'birthplace of tango', there are clubs, bars and *milongas* (dancehalls) on many backstreets. In La Boca, the touristy street El Caminito is named after an old tango song, and there are academies, museums, tango record shops and clothes stores galore across the city. But for a night of intelligent pleasure, head to San Telmo's Centro Cultural Torcuato Tasso (+54 11 4307 6506, www.tangotasso.com), where you can eat well, catch a show and – if you feel up to it – try out some steps on the dancefloor.

787 *Stargaze... Atacama Desert, Chile*
◊

The driest place on earth, Chile's Atacama is a sight to behold: dramatic dunes, Martian mountainscapes, geyser fields, thermal lakes, salt flats populated by pink flamingos and, when it rains (as it occasionally does), flowers bursting through the arid crust creating fiery colour. The skies are so clear that the coastal strip is the site of the European Southern Observatory Very Large Telescope, while the Atacama Large Millimeter/submillimeter Array (ALMA) telescope is currently being built in the interior of the desert. When night falls, the sky glows with the Milky Way and Magellanic Clouds. The oasis town, San Pedro de Atacama, is a lively backpacker hub, and also a great base for setting off on a four-wheeled drive journey to Bolivia across the vast Salar de Uyuni.

788 *Drive... Route 40 in Argentina's North-west*

One of the most popular stretches of the iconic Ruta Nacional 40 lies between Tucumán and Salta, where the road winds high up through the Valles Calchaquies. While the tourist coaches hurtle down the fast, sleek RN68, through the Cafayate Canyon, the RN40 slows everything down, taking endless turns through a wilderness of candelabra cactuses. There are still vestiges of pre-Columbian life away from the main towns, with Quechua-speaking families living in adobe houses, raising llama and planting quinoa on the slopes. More enticingly, this is also a wine region, and torrontes and other grapes are nurtured around

Colomé and Cafayate. Break your journey at out-of-the-way Cachi, one of the prettiest little hamlets in North-west Argentina.

789 *Gawp... Iguazú Falls, Argentina*

The name comes from two native Guarani words meaning 'big' and 'water'. With 275 separate falls along 2.7 kilometres of river, and a maximum height of about 82 metres, these are some of the most impressive falls in the world. You can see them panoramically from Brazil, but to get up close to the brown girders of plummeting chocolate-brown water, stay in Argentina and follow the boardwalks along the top and down below the dozens of individual cataracts. For some adrenaline-releasing action, take a boat and Jeep trip with an operator such as Iguazú Jungle Explorer (www.iguazujungleexplorer.com). Avoid the crowds around Easter and July.

790 *Gawp some more...*
Glaciers of Patagonia

Patagonia, which spans Argentina and Chile, is a bleakly beautiful region. Only a few animals are attuned to such an environment – on drives down the dead straight roads you'll see armadillos and skunks on the roadside, troops of lesser rhea (the South American ostrich) hurtling across the plain and, up above, condors wheeling and watching for roadkill. El Calafate is the main hub, and while it's no beauty, it has all the smart hotels, outdoorsy shops, grill restaurants (lamb is the big meat in the south) and cosy bars you'll need between active excursions to the surrounding mountains, lakes and deserts. The highlight of a trip to southern Patagonia is the Perito Moreno glacier – a huge tongue of the southern ice field that comes down from the Andes to lap up turquoise Lago Argentino. You can catch boats to get up close to the glacier or put on crampons and go hiking on the top of it.
Parque Nacional Los Glaciares
+ 54 2902 491 005/www.losglaciares.com.

791 *Photograph... Chilean*
Tierra del Fuego

In the rush to see the wastes of Patagonia or the lush forests of the lakes, travellers sometimes overlook Tierra del Fuego, the large island at the tip of South America. Wetter than the steppes to the north but less windy, 'Fireland' – in fact an archipelago and the place where the Andes chain finally plunges into the sea – is rich in history and full of photogenic landscapes. From Punta Arenas – once an important port city – you can take trips out to see penguin colonies, glaciers and national parks and explore the channels and bays sounded and mapped by FitzRoy during the Beagle voyage. A trip to Tierra del Fuego is also a great opportunity to see both Chile and Argentina, either by taking the ferry from Porvenir in Chile across the Strait of Magellan or doing one of Cruceros Australis' wonderful four-night cruises through the fjords that run between Punta Arenas and Ushuaia, so you get to see the two southernmost cities of the world.

789: Iguazú Falls, Argentina

792-799

Cities for foodies

792 Buenos Aires, Argentina

Food speciality *Steak.*
With flat, fertile grasslands spreading south, west and north for hundreds of miles, it's little wonder the Argentinian capital has some of the best steakhouses in the world. Knife-wielding, blood-splattered cooks at the grills are a key part of the raucous scene at El Desnivel (Defensa 855, San Telmo, +54 11 4300 9081), which seduces in locals and visitors alike with the whiff of charred cow.
Also try The local, very cheesy pizzas, *locro* (thick Andean stew) and great ice-cream – and of course the malbec wine; for home-made empanadas and *guiso de lentejas con chocolate* (lentil stew with chocolate), try La Cupertina (José Antonio Cabrera 5099, +54 11 4777 3711).

793 Bologna, Italy

Food speciality *Pasta.*
Known as 'la grassa' (the fat one) due to its love of food, Bologna is as good a place as any to

794: Beijing, China

explore the range of Italian pastas – in particular the tortellini (the official food of Italian Christmas) and tagliatelle (supposedly created to honour Lucretia Borgia's hair). Situated in the fertile Po River valley, Bologna's larder is ample and the local delis and restaurants are great for cheeses, meat dishes and broths. The city is, of course, also the home of the global classic Bolognese sauce – known locally simply as *ragù*. Standards are high, but the central Rosteria Luciano (via Nazario Sauro 19, +39 051 231 249, www.rosterialuciano.it) has been around since the 1940s and changed little since then.
Also try Cured pork meats such as mortadella and salame, and the Bologna sausage.

794 Beijing, China

Food speciality *Penis. And testicles.*
If you're going to eat a penis (or many) then you might as well visit Beijing's experts – at least where cooking them is concerned. If pressed, the cock-chefs at Guo Li Zhuang (+84 11 6405 5966), in the Xicheng district, will get you a Canadian seal's penis. Size matters when it comes to all-night feasting, so if you're feeling frisky, order the huge buffalo member, which will arrive skinned and shaved into bite-sized morsels.
Also try Other extreme Cantonese dishes – bear paws, snake and live baby mice.

795 Mexico City, Mexico

Food speciality *Hot stuff.*
From fragrant to flaming, there are hundreds of types of chilli in Mexico. Mexican food isn't quite as hot as Tex-Mex, but many starters (*antojitos*) and most of the delicious street food has a fiery kick. One of the city's most famous restaurants, Café Tacuba (Calle Tacuba 28, +55 5512 8482), dates from 1912 and boasts handsome colonial-era decor. (It also inspired the eponymous Grammy Award-winning rock group.) Guests are welcomed into one of two long dining rooms, with brass lamps, dark oil paintings and a large mural of nuns working in a kitchen. The menu is authentic Mexican with traditional dishes, including tamales, enchiladas, *chiles rellenos* and pozole.
Also try Mole, a sauce that contains bitter chocolate, and ceviche – raw fish marinated in lemon juice.

796 New York, USA

Food speciality

Lots, but we like the fast food.

Fast doesn't always mean fatty and it certainly doesn't have to mean bland. The States has great diners and fast-food outlets for thin-based pizzas, barbecued ribs and the fullest breakfasts imaginable – as well as the ubiquitous burgers and donuts. For an all-American breakfast in New York, Sarabeth's (+1 212 410 7335, www.sarabethseast.com) has to be among the best, so book ahead or bring a takeaway coffee to keep you going while you wait. Later on, stop by at Burger Joint at Le Parker Meridien (+1 212 708 7414, www.parker meridien.com), an old-style emporium that won't break the bank and which serves thick, sinful milkshakes with its picture-perfect burgers.

Also try Regional cuisine, if you're exploring the States – from LA's extreme fusions (kosher Scottish cuisine, anyone?) to spicy Cajun food in Louisiana.

797 Mumbai, India

£ ▦

Food speciality *Vegetarian food.*

Because Hinduism – practised by over three quarters of Indians – regards the cow as sacred, Indian cities are heaven for vegetarians, with fresh produce baked, boiled, fried and spiced up in curries of every variety. Mumbai may not boast the best vegetarian cuisine in the country (for that you should probably head to Kerala), but, being a city of economic immigrants, its culinary offerings are incredibly diverse. Kailash Parbat (+91 22 2287 4823, www.kailashparbat.in) in Colaba is the aloo and paneer dish master, although it became famous for its Sindhi snacks – some of which, like the samosa, you'll recognise. If you need a protein fix, try the Mangalorean seafood at the Mahesh Lunch Home (+91 22 2287 0938, www.maheshlunchhome.com).

Also try Chana bhatura (chickpeas with deep-fried bread), dosas (thin filled pancakes), dum aloo and sweet fried gulab jamun.

798 Madrid, Spain

▦ ◔

Food speciality

Cured ham (jamón ibérico).

In the past decade, the famously traditional (when it comes to food) madrileños have been embracing *cocina creativa*. But whether you opt for classic or forward-looking eateries, *jamón ibérico* is still likely to feature on the menu. Ham from black-footed pigs that feed on acorns is produced in many parts of Spain – in particular in Extremadura; but Spain's best restaurants and tapas bar are still to be found in the capital. Restaurante Extremadura (+34 915 318 222, www.restauranteextremadura.com) is a good bet for authenticity, or head to the newly refurbished Mercado de San Miguel, south of Plaza Mayor, for tapas or produce to take away. Madrid is even home to a museum-shop dedicated to *jamón*.

Also try *Cocido madrileño* (a hearty stew of chickpeas, veg, meat and potatoes), wild boar and other game, and *migas extremeñas* (chunks of bread fried up with peppers and cured sausage).

799 Tokyo, Japan

▦

Food speciality *Sushi and sashimi*

With more Michelin stars than any other city, Tokyo is the world's new dining capital. From *kaiseki ryori* haute cuisine to the tiny eateries of ramshackle Omoide Yokocho, and whether kneeling on tatami mats or leaning in an alleyway, it's a wonderland for foodies, with around 160,000 restaurants to choose from. If you try nothing else, or can't make up your mind, head for sushi paradise in the stylish setting of Fukuzushi (5-7-8 Roppongi, Minato-ku, +81 03 3402 4116, www.roppongifukuzushi.com), whose origins date back to 1917.

Also try Smoking hot yakitori chicken, ramen noodles and boiled porcine testicles (or maybe not).

800-808

Perfect places in Morocco

800 *Marrakech*
⊞

Founded at the confluence of ancient trade routes, Marrakech has always been rooted in the twin activities of hospitality and trade. In its booming 21st-century incarnation, that means two things: chilling out and shopping. Head to the fantastical central square, Jemaa El Fna, for a nightly carnival of local life; north medina for a thriving network of souks and hagglers; and south medina for the Jewish quarter and the glittering remains of the sultan's palaces and gardens. Stay at Dar les Cigognes (+212 24 38 27 40, www.lescigognes.com).

801 Taza

Head off the tourist trail out of Fes, through steep, rolling hills of brown and velvety green, and you come to Taza, a rather isolated provincial town with stunning views of both the Rif and Middle Atlas mountain ranges. Built as a fortress in the 12th century, you can still wander within medieval city walls and enter its original Andalucian mosque. Nearby is Jbel Tazekka National Park, a rambling wilderness home to the largest cave system in North Africa.
Stay at *Auberge Ain-sahla (+212 61 89 35 87/ www.ainsahla.com).*

802 Tangier

Tangier is a city that has changed hands more times than it cares to remember, and African and European sensibilities battle with each other in its jumble of architecture, ancient alleyways and mixture of coastline and Kasbah. The Grande Mosquée and little cafés in the Petit Socco sedately remain much as they did at the early part of the last century, but a visit to the terrace of the port-side Gran Café de Paris (Place de France, Ville Nouvelle, no phone), and one coffee and pastry's worth of people-watching, leaves you in no doubt that this is a city still very much at the hub of human movement.
Stay at *Riad Tanja (+212 39 33 35 38/ www.riadtanja.com).*

803 Almeln Valley and Tafroute

Trekkers in the Anti Atlas have known about the relaxed, high-altitude town of Tafroute, as well as the landscape that surrounds it (cloud-capped peaks, deep valleys and gorges), for decades. The Almeln Valley is dotted with tiny, thriving villages, but Tafroute is something special, with its spectacular surroundings making it seem cosier and more welcoming than your average Moroccan town. The region is renowned for its almond harvests, which find their way into delicious couscous and tagines.
Stay at *Hotel Les Amandiers (+212 28 80 00 08/ www.hotel-lesamandiers.com).*

804 Asilah

Today one of Morocco's cosiest and charming coastal resorts, Asilah nonetheless possesses a swashbuckling history of Barbary pirates, Riffian rebels and battles on its 15th-century ramparts. The smart and busy Zallaka in the Ville Nouvelle is a hub of decent restaurants and seafront avenues, but you can still get a taste of the romantic past by walking through the Bab Bhar gate into the town's incredibly well-preserved Medina. Casa Garcia (51 Avenue Moulay Hassan ben Mehdi, +212 39 41 74 65) is a small, genuinely beguiling restaurant that knows a lot about the town's speciality food: fish.
Stay at *Berbari (+212 62 58 80 13/ www.berbari.com).*

805 Oualidia

The stretch of azure Atlantic, butterscotch beaches and rugged caramel cliffs between Casablanca and Safi is a haven for wildlife, birds and surfers alike. Oualidia is just one of the unique gems of towns that punctuate the wilderness. Here, a ruined Saadian Kasbah stands sentinel over the ethereal beauty of a crescent-shaped inland lagoon, but the town is most famous for its oysters, which you can sample straight from the water with a dash of sun-kissed lemon. Try a plate of them on ice on the terrace next to the lagoon at eaterie Ostrea, accompanied by a perfect glass of chilled white wine from the Moroccan and French wine list.
Stay at *La Sultana (+212 23 36 65 95/ www.lasultanaoualidia.com).*

806 The Dadés Valley

The Dadés Valley runs between the High Atlas to the north and the Jebel Sarho to the south. Sometimes called 'the Valley of the Kasbahs', dozens of fortress-cities litter the route as a reminder of the civilisation that once flourished here. It's the most barren of the southern valleys, which makes palm-strewn oases like Skoura all the more beautiful, and dramatic, twisting gorges like Dadés and Todra all the more spectacular.
Stay at *Les Jardins de Skoura (+212 24 85 23 24/ www.lesjardinsdeskoura.com).*

807: Chefchaouen, Morocco

807 *Chefchaouen*

♡

Folded high in the inaccessible crags of the Rif Mountains, this remote hideaway has a bewitching, storybook atmosphere to match its fairytale history as a retreat for rebels and disguised European adventurers. Its ancient crafts and diverse cultural heritage have been perfectly preserved, along with its stone-walled streets and impressive Spanish mosque and Kasbah. Try to book a table at Casa Aladin (+212 39 98 90 17), which has a well-executed roll-call of rich and sticky tagines and couscous and a highly romantic atmosphere. **Stay at** *Casa Hassan (+212 39 98 61 53/ www.casahassan.com).*

808 *Ouarzazate*

♀

Ouarzazate is a town primarily known for its on-screen exploits; *Lawrence of Arabia*, the *Asterix* movie and Ridley Scott's *Gladiator* were all filmed here. The town is inhabited mainly by Berbers, who built many of the kasbahs characteristic of the area. Venture out of the town into the biblical landscape of the Draa Valley, however, and you find Morocco in the raw, just a hop, skip and a sand buggy away from the Sahara Desert. **Stay at** *Dar Kamar (+212 24 88 87 33/ www.darkamar.com).*

809-818

Villas in beautiful European settings

809 Villa Belica, Gorenjska, Slovenia

🏃 ♀ 🏊

Book with *Slovenian Retreats (+38 6 40 557 227/www.slovenianretreats.com/belica.php).* Slovenia may be a small country, but with Alpine skiing in the winter, and around 50 kilometres of coastline in which to enjoy the Mediterranean climate in summer, it has plenty of draws. Villa Belica is a lovely accommodation option all year round; from here you can walk to Lake Bohinje's beaches or pick from two ski resorts only ten minutes away by car. Hiking through coniferous forests, bathing in crystalline lakes and endless vineyard routes are further attractions.

810 Villa Cervarolo, Puglia, Italy

🏃

+39 0585 92098/www.merrioncharles.com/villa-pdfs/Merrion-Charles_Trulli%20Cervarolo.pdf. Italy's heel is not quite deserted, but you may go all day without hearing anything but Italian. *Trulli* – traditional Puglian stone houses with cone-shaped roofs – were designed with thick

walls to keep the interiors cool in the baking hot summers. Villa Cervarolo has been adapted to make it a luxury pad befitting a resort in the Caribbean. What's more, there are 800 kilometres of white-sand beaches to explore nearby (if you rent a car), along with endless olive groves and village restaurants tucked into the rocks. Just don't expect to find English on the menu.

811 Villa Markus, Costa Brava, Spain

⚲ ☽

0844 330 3312/www.solmarvillas.com/villa.aspx?reference=VIL463.
The wild coast of Spain lives up to its name; ancient fishing villages saved this part of the Catalan coast from concrete resorts. Make the effort to explore the medieval towns and you will be well rewarded – there are plenty of excellent fish restaurants tucked into cobbled lanes, and delicious tortillas along the beach. Stay in modern luxury at Villa Markus in Tamariu, with two pools to choose from.

812 A holiday villa in the Allgäuer Alps, Bavaria, Germany

☽ ⚐ ♡

+49 8377 97390/www.holiday-rentals.co.uk/p36714.
Germans view hiking like Americans view softball – they love it, and take it very seriously. Overlooking the Allgäuer Alps and Lake

Constance, perched between forest and the pretty village of Wasserburg, is this holiday villa for hire, where there's not much to do but explore the beautiful scenery by foot. The decor may be a little stern, but the area is stunning, and the fact that it remains something of a hidden gem makes it all the more romantic. Not convinced? Plenty of fine Bavarian beer and delicious schnitzel will soon have you thinking otherwise.

813 Villa Claudine, Gozo, Malta

⚲

0800 783 1410/www.meonvillas.co.uk/villa/CV4311.
A tiny archipelago roughly halfway between Italy and Africa, Malta was fought over for 7,000 years – and it shows. Its cuisine and landscape are a loud and eclectic fusion of cultures, while the beaches on the second largest island, Gozo, are often quiet and peaceful. If they do get busy at the height of summer, you can retreat to your private pool at the 300-year-old Villa Claudine – or walk to the market in Victoria where fresh fish of all kinds is sold alongside knickers and beach balls.

814 Finca Malvasia, Lanzarote, Canary Islands

⚲ ☽ ♡

+34 928 173 460/www.fincamalvasia.com.
There are no more Spanish conquerors, Moroccan pirates or fiery volcanic eruptions,

814: Finca Malvasia, Lanzarote

but some farmers still refuse to trade in their camels for tractors in Lanzarote. The volcanoes are now fertile ground for delicious onions and the vineyards carved into craters that produce its Bermejo wine. Enjoy it, with a view of the black mountains and a beautiful sunset, from Finca Malvasia, a family-run vineyard offering four apartments set around a beautifully landscaped pool and spa treatments.

815 Kozle chalet, Borovets, Bulgaria

£ ⚐

www.borovetschalet.com.
Peace at the self-catering Kozle chalet, in the resort of Borovets, is disturbed only by passing goats and the lynx and bear you might hear in the rare and ancient forests of Rila. A frescoed 1,000-year-old monastery, thriving ski resort and beaches at Lake Iskar nearby are all real attractions – and that's without even getting to the food. Head to the town of Samokov for local produce sold in daily markets, or Sofia, barely an hour's drive away, which is said to be the new Prague. Go before everyone else does.

816 Finca Talati, Menorca

⚐ ⚐⚐

0800 074 0122/www.jamesvillas.co.uk/ menorca/mahon/finca-talati-de-dalt-ii-4850.
Punished by Franco for resisting, Menorca was spared the building frenzy of the rest of the Balearics and remains a beautiful, laid-back island with gorgeous, uncrowded beaches. Known for its delicious *queso Mahón* (local cheese with herbs and sea salt) and juniper-berry gin, it's a good spot in which to relax. Stay at Finca Talati, which retains a traditional style, in a rural location not far from the capital, Maó.

817 Casteyre farmhouse, Gascony, France

⚐

+33 5 62 68 95 72/www.gite.com/france/casteyre.
Gascony is France at its best, being the land of the Three Musketeers and the home of foie gras and Armagnac brandy; there's nothing better to do here than dine in medieval villages, stroll around the spa town of Lectoure and explore the countryside. Stay at the 18th-century Casteyre – a stone farmhouse set on a hilltop within four hectares of private land – and survey the valleys and the Spanish Pyrenees from the salt-water pool.

818 Istron Villas, Crete, Greece

♡ ⌂

+44 845 299 7776/www.natureandkind.com/ destinations/country/accommodation/istron-villas.
Along with being a great Greek holiday island and the legendary birthplace of Zeus, Crete wears its remarkable history across its rugged landscape. Stay in luxury at the modern Istron Villas, with a private pool and bayside location; but don't miss out on the nearby archaeological sites, from the Minoan palaces at Gournia and Knossos to the Byzantine monastery at Toplou.

819-827
Watersports

819 *Open-water swimming in Finland*

⚐ ⚐

Swim Trek's 'Finnish Midnight Sun' holiday is a week-long, fully guided swim (around five kilometres a day) through the country's beautiful lakes during the long sunlight summer days. As well as taking dips in remote lakes, you'll also do a bit of walking between visiting each one. In the evening, soothe aching muscles with a traditional sauna.
Swim Trek *01273 739713/www.swimtrek.co.uk.*

820 *Sea kayaking in Scotland*

£ ⚐ ⚐

The five-day 'Sea Kayaking Introduction Course' run by Edinburgh-based Wilderness Scotland takes place several times throughout the year, in the beautiful north-west Highlands on Loch Torridon, and around the coastline of the unspoilt Applecross peninsula. At the end of a tough day perfecting your paddling technique, relax with a wee dram or two before collapsing into bed.
Wilderness Scotland *0131 625 6635/ www.wildernessscotland.com.*

821 *Coasteering in Wales*

£ ⚐ ⚐⚐

The rugged north Pembrokeshire coast lends itself perfectly to the adrenaline-filled sport of coasteering, whose roots date back to the 19th century. The sport essentially involves traversing cliffs and leaping into the sea. The Wicked Liquid Coasteering Break (choose midweek or weekend) run by Pembrokeshire outdoor activity company Preseli Venture is aimed at over-18s, in groups, couples or as individuals. Wetsuits, wetsuit gloves, flotation jackets and helmets are provided, and your guide will encourage you to leap off cliffs, go climbing, explore caves, scramble over rocks and ride waves. Accommodation is in a cosy lodge that sleeps 38 people near the village of Mathry.

Preseli Venture *01348 837709/ www.preseliventure.co.uk.*

822 *Swim with dolphins in Portugal*

Brighton-based agent Responsible Travel organises a range of environmentally friendly holidays, including swimming with wild dolphins in the Azores under the watchful eye of fully trained guides. As well as swimming, the nine-day trip features talks on marine biology and conservation; and if you're up for more activity, there's the option to climb a nearby volcano. You can choose hotel accommodation or opt for self-catering. More marine conservation breaks are available in Thailand, Greece and Mexico; check the website for details.

Responsibletravel.com *www.responsibletravel.com.*

823 *Kitesurfing and windsurfing in Spain*

The pretty town of Tarifa, in the Costa de la Luz part of Cádiz province, is a popular holidaying spot for Spaniards. And due to the converging winds from the east (called the Levante) and the west (called the Poniente), it's one of Europe's best places for kite- and windsurfing – though it's worth noting that the strength of the wind, which can gust up to 100 kilometres per hour, can make it tricky for newcomers to the sports. If you want some tuition, contact Spin Out Tarifa, which also has good-quality equipment for hire, and can organise accommodation. Group kitesurfing lessons start at around €100 per day; group windsurfing lessons from €55 per session.

Spin Out Tarifa Windsport *+34 956 680844/ www.tarifaspinout.com.*

824 *Surf in Hawaii*

Located 2,400 miles off the south-west of the United States in the north Pacific Ocean, the Hawaiian archipelago is a mecca for holidaymakers drawn by the pristine beaches, tropical rainforests and laid-back, multi-ethnic vibe. Seven of the 132 islands are inhabited; the capital, Honolulu, is on O'ahu. Warm waters, blue skies and sunshine mean learning to surf here is nothing short of a dream, whatever your age (some parents enrol their three-year-olds in lessons). There are a number of surf schools to choose from, including the family-run Hawaii Lifeguard Surf Instructors, on the island of Kona (the island is also host to the annual World Ironman Championships in October).

Hawaii Lifeguard Surf Instructors *+1 808 324 0442/www.surflessonshawaii.com.*

825 *Sailing in Turkey*

The warm Mediterranean sun and the calm waters lend themselves very well to messing about on boats. Set Sail, a Suffolk-based tour company, runs the Learning the Ropes course for total novices to sailing. You'll learn how to tie maritime knots, handle a sail, duck under the boom, and what to do if you have a man overboard and other such mishaps. Shipshape fun all round.

Set Sail *01787 310445/www.setsail.co.uk.*

826 *Whitewater rafting in New Zealand*

Charter a chopper to take you whitewater rafting on the west coast of New Zealand's South Island. It's hardcore, for sure, but the five-day rafting adventure on the Karamea River, run by Eco Rafting, is an incredible adrenaline buzz. The trip features a two-day hike into Karamea National Park, white-knuckle rafting at grade 3 and 4 rapids to warm you up, and then grade 5 rapids on the final two days. After that, you can review the rides on video while rewarding your efforts with a beer.

Eco Rafting *+64 21 523 426/ www.ecorafting.co.nz.*

820: Sea kayaking, Scotland

827 *Fly fishing in England*

£ ♡ ⚲

The rolling hills and dry-stone walls of the Yorkshire Dales make a fine backdrop for a gently active day spent fly fishing. There's no shortage of fast-flowing rivers and streams, which are known for their good stocks of trout and grayling. If you're a beginner, take a lesson to get you started. Yorkshire Dales Fly Fishing, based in North Yorkshire, runs a beginner's trout fishing course and a half-day taster course that begins with the basics – including how to use fishing tackle, what flies to use, fishing techniques and how to release the trout once caught. Courses are also available for more experienced anglers. If you're planning to fish independently, you'll need to purchase a day ticket for the river in which you wish to fish. **Yorkshire Dales Fly Fishing** *07761 762660/ www.yorkshire-dales-flyfishing.com.*

828-833

Grand Indian hotels

828 Usha Kiran Palace, Madhya Pradesh

+91 75 1244 4000/www.tajhotels.com.
For some serious pampering, look no further than this historic 120-year-old palace. The 40 rooms range from tastefully minimalist to opulent, and there's no skimping on luxurious touches, such as silk cushions and chaises

longues. For the full regal experience, opt for one of the suites, which boast private terraces with spectacular views, canopied beds and Indian silk furnishings. Walk off your previous night's indulgence with a stroll around the landscaped lawns; or try something more active – the hotel can arrange hot-air ballooning, golf, horseriding and river rafting. If you're looking for total relaxation, the in-house Jiva Spa offers Indian aromatherapy massages, scrubs and wraps.

829 The Imperial India, New Delhi

▦ ♡

+91 11 2334 1234/www.theimperialindia.com.
New Delhi's Imperial exudes sophistication. Stepping into the lobby, after passing the palm trees gracing the entrance, feels like stepping into a private World Heritage Site. Built in 1931, this grand hotel (with 231 rooms and 43 suites) has a romantic, colonial feel, yet its feet are firmly in the 21st century when it comes to mod cons: rooms boast every creature comfort you'd expect from a leading international hotel. Enjoy a G&T in the opulent surrounds of the 1911 bar, before dining in one of the on-site restaurants: the Spice Route serves South-east Asian cuisine; San Gimignano specialises in Italian fare.

830 Fort Tirocol, Goa

⚲

+91 23 6622 7631/www.forttirocol.com.
It's hard to believe that this smart Goan spot in the city of Pernem was once a fort staffed by heavily armed guards. The intimate hotel has just a few guest rooms (two suites and five family rooms, all enjoying sea vistas),

so not only will you receive personal attention, you'll also feel that you have escaped to a peaceful haven far from Goa's sometimes frantic beach scene – with a calming soundtrack of waves. Whether you want to swim, stroll along the sand, enjoy a candlelit supper or take part in one of the yoga classes, staff at this peaceful hotel will ensure your every whim is catered for.

831 Samode Haveli, Jaipur, Rajasthan

+91 14 1263 2370/www.samode.com.
The pink masonry of this impeccably built 150-year-old hotel is very fetching, but that's not the only reason you'll remember your night here. The bijou building is a peaceful retreat from Jaipur's bustling thoroughfares, where you can relax on the veranda with a light afternoon tea and let the friendly staff take care of your every need (ask them to point out the elephant ramp, which was built specially for a marriage ceremony in the 1940s). Rooms are luxuriously decorated and furnished with antiques and old family portraits. Book into the Maharaja and Maharani suites, which have mirrored mosaics and ornaments. Other facilities include a steam room, massage parlour and a swimming pool. And don't miss the opportunity to dine in the spectacularly decorative dining room.

832 Surya Samudra Beach Garden, Kerala

+91 47 1226 7333/www.suryasamudra.com.
A palm-fronded oasis of calm, the tranquil seaside setting of this hotel will not disappoint. Within the resort's 20 acres (in Pulinkudi, southern Kerala) – which include beaches and coconut forests – are just 23 beach houses, so there's plenty of space for guests to spread out and find quiet retreats. By day, stroll through the peaceful gardens and perhaps take a yoga class or two, before settling down with a book before dinner – which is likely to be deliciously fresh seafood. Evenings in South India are magical: gaze out to sea, admire the sunsets and let your worries evaporate while you spend the evening stargazing.

833 Umaid Bhawan Palace, Jodhpur, Rajasthan

+91 29 1251 0101/www.tajhotels.com.
Edwardian architect Henry Lanchester designed this vast grandiose palace. Set in more than 25 acres of gorgeous gardens, he intended it to be a blend of Eastern and Western influences. Completed in 1943, the palace took 15 years to build, and now boasts a whopping 347 rooms; but don't let the size put you off. Inside it's all secret corners and

genteel spaces, with plenty of lavish gilt and exotic murals. If you're in the mood to splurge, stay in the Maharani Suite, which has an impressive marble bath, cracking views over the gardens and smart decor of pink, black, chrome and mirrors. It's part of the Taj chain, so the food is reliably top notch, ranging from an informal coffee shop to smart à la cartes.

834-838
Eco-friendly holidays

Whether you're crashed out on a cargo ship bound for Shanghai, or naked in secret coves on the English coast, there's a lot more to green travel than tree hugging (and sites like www.greenvacationhub.com help you plan with minimal effort.

It may not sound very exciting, but an easy place to start is by **staying at home 834**. With staycations now the new Med, Britons are waking up to the wealth of holiday opportunities to be experienced on our fair isles. And a green holiday at home isn't just about camping in the rain (although even that has moved up a notch, with the advent of the boutique campsite). How about a trip to Bristol, the green capital of Britain and a great destination for weekend breaks? Green travellers can work off Fairtrade food on the many cycling routes, and stay at a climate-conscious hotel. Its cocktail bars may be world class but even the trendiest cafés use locally sourced food, and a trip to Britain's first carbon-neutral restaurant, Bordeaux Quay (www.bordeaux-quay.co.uk), is a must.

Another good option for an eco-friendly break is to take the **train 835**. Catch the Eurostar from London St Pancras in the afternoon for an evening aperitif in Paris; from here, you could continue overnight to Berlin, where you can dine in Germany's first carbon neutral restaurant, Foodorama (www.foodorama.de).

Alternatively, from Paris, hop on the high-speed train to Italy and wake up in Milan for breakfast at 6am, then travel two more hours to Turin in Piedmont, where the Slow Food movement (www.slowfood.it) was born. Say 'ecotourism' and Italians might blink, but one

thing they understand is how to celebrate local cuisine – tastings and fairs all year long will make you glad to have dropped by.

If you're looking for something a bit faster, then head for Spain, where long, slow journeys are now history thanks to the new high-speed train services (book via www.renfe.es/ave). Tour the Prado museum in Madrid, then walk over to its AVE station, where a two-and-a-half-hour train ride will take you to Antoni Gaudi's magical buildings and gardens in Barcelona. The line has cut carbon emissions for travel between the two cities by 83 per cent, reducing air traffic by around half.

Perhaps the greenest of all holidays is a long-distance **walking 836** experience. The most famous tract of the GR5 *grande randonée* (www.grfive.com) from Nice to Lake Geneva is a maze of crystal blue waters and dreamy pastures in the Alps. If you don't have a month, it takes just over a week to trek Ireland's highest mountains along the Kerry Way (www.kerryway.com), and you can get your luggage carried for you; any shorter routes should at least include the Black Valley – named so because its former inhabitants died in the great famine – and the more cheerful traditional farm at Muckross House (www.muckross-house.ie).

If you're desperate to leave Europe, however, consider travelling long-haul by **boat 837**. Board the 'banana boat' (see www.cargoship voyages.co.uk) to the Caribbean or crash out on a cargo ship for two weeks from London to Shanghai, where you can stay at a glamorous carbon-free hotel (www.urbnhotels.com). Old-school sailing ships and expeditions to places like Antarctica often make room for extra passengers as well (see www.freighterworld.com), although comfort, price and duration can vary widely.

All sound too much like hard work? Fly to one of the world's green cities and **offset 838** your carbon emissions instead. Across the pond, the 'Rose City' of Portland, Oregon, is among the greenest cities worldwide (half its energy comes from renewable sources), and with canyons, wine valleys and coasts is effortless fun. In Europe, try the German capital of solar power Frieburg in the Black Forest, or the cycling and wind farm city of Copenhagen, location for the 2009 UN Climate Summit.

Ideas from the expert

839-843

Tourism for All's Brian Seaman suggests five inclusive destinations for disabled travellers.

Trains and planes without wheelchair space, seats too narrow for anyone normal, doors that close too fast for anyone without lightning reflexes... travelling can be a minefield for disabled passengers. Fortunately, though, times have changed in terms of the data available to disabled people when it comes to planning a holiday. There are now more sources of information than ever before, widening the choice of holiday options. And recent EU legislation has encouraged tourism businesses to do more to meet the needs of all users. Operators that offer expert advice about booking an accessible holiday include **Accessible Travel & Leisure** (www.accessible travel.co.uk – the source of much of the text below); **Access Travel** (www.access-travel. co.uk); **Can Be Done** (www.canbedone.co.uk); **Chalfont Line** (www.chalfont-line.co.uk); and **Enable Holidays** (www.enableholidays.com).

839 Mentioned most often among the experts is Tenerife, one of the Canary Islands. The most popular resorts lie along its south coast and have been built around the needs of the holidaymaker, so there's close access from most hotels to clean beaches and a plethora of shops, bars, cafés, restaurants and nightlife. Many of the resorts here, such as Las Americas, Los Cristianos and Adeje, are joined by a wide, long and mostly flat boulevard. This hugs the coast on one side and is bordered by open-air cafés and restaurants on the other, creating an attractive walkway. There are now many accessible properties, including the 'barrier-free' Mar-y-Sol (+34 922 750 540, www.marysol.org) on Los Cristianos.

840 Another good option is Orlando, Florida. Here the American way of life seems to be just right. The locals are friendly and, in a country where service is paramount, very helpful with any mobility needs. Wheelchair-accessible rental cars are available and the theme parks are well adapted to the needs of the less mobile. Florida has gently swaying palms and glorious sunshine, clean beaches with good access and facilities, and there are accessible villas within easy reach of the many attractions, including Villa Ponderosa in Orlando (01757 229607, www.florida-orlando-villa.com).

841 A little over two hours' flight from the UK, Southern Spain's Costa del Sol is one of the most easily accessible holiday destinations in Europe and has much to offer. The resorts revolve around the needs of visitors, so you'll tend to find that shops, bars, cafés and restaurants are all in the immediate area of your hotel, with good pavements, boulevards and road crossings. The Sol Andalusi Health & Spa Resort (+34 952 64 92 92, www.solandalusi.com) offers accessible facilities, including a pool hoist and accessible transport.

842 Boasting some of Europe's cleanest beaches, Cyprus enjoys abundant sunshine and little rainfall, even in winter. This makes it an ideal holiday choice and the hotel accommodation sets a very high standard. Access around the modern international hotels is very good, offering a range of facilities for the less mobile. The wheelchair-accessible Evas Apartments (+357 2632 1881, www. evas-apartments.com) are based here and recommended, as is exploring the island's beautiful interior. It should be noted, however, that much of the countryside, including around the old wine-producing villages and stunning Aphrodite Trail, is pretty rugged.

843 The No.1 destination in the UK for disabled travellers is London – especially as the forthcoming 2012 Olympic and Paralympic Games are being held here. Nowhere in the country can match the scope and innovation of this vast and frenetic metropolis, where you'll find Britain's best nightlife, cultural events, museums, galleries, pubs and restaurants. There are quite a number of accessible hotels in the London area and these are listed on the VisitLondon website (www.visit london.com/accommodation/accessible).

■ Tourism for All 0845 124 9971/ www.tourismforall.org.uk.

844-848
Worldwide yoga retreats

Visit www.yogaholidays.net for information on additional suggestions for yoga-inspired holidays.

844 Sirsasana practice in Italy

茶

Astanga Vinyasa yoga retreats focusing on *sirsasana* – aka the headstand – are held at La Campine, an *eco-masseria* in Italy's Salento region. Nicely decorated apartments, organic food from the property's vegetable garden and a lovely swimming pool all make for a deeply rejuventating break.
YIS *+39 0836 802 108/www.yogainsalento.com.*

845 Breathe deeply in Dahab

£ 茶

Yoga Travel organises yoga holidays in Egypt, Morocco, Turkey and Thailand. In the idyllic Dahab retreat on Egypt's Red Sea coast, daily yoga is taught by highly experienced teachers, and you can also undertake various adventure-type activities. A range of budgets are catered to.
Yoga Travel *01579 320547/www.yogatravel.co.uk/dahab.htm.*

846 Find inner peace in Bhutan

☿ 茶

Practice Ashtanga yoga and *shamatha* sitting meditation in the peaceful Paro valley in Bhutan, South Asia. Learn how to be fully present in the here and now, to fully enjoy the natural surroundings.
Papaya Yoga
www.papayayoga.com/zhiwalingretreats.

847 Sun salutations in the Swiss Alps

☿ 茶

Start the day with asana practice to warm up your muscles for a day of skiing, snowboarding or snow walking. Later, return home for another yoga class to wind down and stretch those aching muscles. This unique retreat, based in the lovely village of Wengen, aims to show how yoga can complement and enhance skiing and other sports.
Yoga Traveller *+353 868517710/www.yogatraveller.com.*

848 Yoga in its spiritual home

£ 茶

For a cheaper, no-frills but authentic yoga retreat in the discipline's homeland, head to India's Surya Thejus Advaita Yoga Centre, near Kaladi in Kerala, where yoga classes are taught by local teachers. Vegetarian satvik food is provided, and rooms are basic but clean.
Book with *www.keralatourismdestinations.com/Hotels.aspx*

849-853
Central Asia: Silk Road holidays

849 Cross Kyrgyzstan on horseback

☿ 茶

Crossing the Tien Shan Mountains in Kyrgyzstan is the ultimate horseback odyssey. The range, whose name translates as the 'Mountains of Heaven', spans approximately 1,500 kilometres and runs from Kazakhstan through Kyrgyzstan into China. As a holiday destination, Kyrgyzstan is wild and unspoilt with rugged peaks and vast, flat plains. The 290-odd kilometre route along the ancient Silk Road from Lake Son Kul to Sari Tash in the south-west of the country takes two weeks and is best suited to intrepid intermediate or advanced horseriders who aren't afraid of roughing it in tents.
Book with *Wild Frontiers (020 7736 3968/www.wildfrontiers.co.uk).*

850 *Travel the Silk Road by train*

♀♡🏠

See some of the most remote parts of Central Asia from the window of a glamorous, specially chartered train; it takes almost a month to travel from Beijing to Moscow. When you're not gazing out of the window trying to spot modern day Marco Polos, you can indulge in sumptuous dinners in the ornate dining car, or sip a G&T in the bar/lounge car. Spend the nights either in hotels or in cabins aboard the train. Highlights include a visit to see the Terracotta Warriors outside Xian, the giant Jiayuguan Fort that has marked the gateway to China for hundreds of years, travelling through the steppes and past mountains in Kazakhstan and a trip to Chorsu bazaar in the Uzbekistan capital, Tashkent.

Book with *Captains Choice (020 8877 1463/ www.captainschoice.co.uk).*

851 *Tashkent to Tehran*

📱🏠

To travel the entire Silk Road (actually a network of interlinking trading routes rather than one road) from Mediterranean Europe to China would take months, but you can get an impression of the ancient traditions – as well as witnessing the influence of the Soviet Union and visiting beautiful Islamic architecture – on an organised tour. Adventure company Explore runs a 19-day trip that takes in two little-visited Central Asian countries and two major Iranian cities. The tour begins in Tashkent, an ancient Uzbek city, and includes time in the bustling city of Samarkand. The journey is an adventure in itself; crossing the Uzbekistan/Turkmenistan border is a time-consuming business that involves patience and a 1.5-kilometre walk – worth it to visit the UNESCO World Heritage Site of Merv in Turkmenistan. In Iran, you'll see impressive mosques and museums in the Islamic holy city of Mashhad, before concluding your trip in the Iranian capital, Tehran.

Book with *Explore (0845 013 1537/ www.explore.co.uk).*

852 *Take a city break in Almaty*

📱

The snow-capped Tien Shan Mountains provide Almaty, Kazakhstan's largest city (the capital, Astana, is in the north), with an impressive backdrop. Located near the border with its poorer neighbour Kyrgyzstan, the city is full of posh European cars driving along the tree-lined boulevards that are lined with aspirational coffee shops and boutiques. Walk around and people-watch in the city centre's Panfilov Park; catch a service in the 56-metre-high wooden Zenkov cathedral, built at the start of the 20th century;

849: Horse riding in Kyrgyzstan

and marvel at the 'golden man', a gold warrior costume displayed in the Central State Museum. **Book with** *Bmi (www.flybmi.com) for flights, and the Marriott Esentai Park (0800 1927 1927/ www.marriott.co.uk) for accommodation.*

853 *Watch the Naadam festival in Mongolia's capital*

Time your trip to the land of Genghis Khan to coincide with the country's greatest sporting spectacle, the annual Naadam festival, consisting of horse racing (horses are central to Mongolian culture), archery and wrestling. The three-day event takes place in mid July in the capital, Ulaan Baatar, and attracts men, women and children from across the country. On the first day, participants dressed as Genghis Khan, the founder of the Mongol empire, parade through the streets. Some 400 horses compete, galloping across the steppe in an awesome sight. Equally entertaining is the eagle festival every October. **Book with** *Panoramic Journeys (01608 811 183/ www.panoramicjourneys.com).*

854-863
Europe's second cities

854 *Valencia, Spain*

Less barmy than Barcelona and more laid-back than Madrid, Valencia is Spain's understated, orange-grove-sprinkled sun-and-culture city break. Just as the Olympics gave Barcelona a facelift back in 1992, so has the City of Arts & Sciences – Valencia's futuristic leisure complex – upgraded the city from backwater to boomtown. By contrast, the historic old town is a well-preserved, car-free amalgam of Baroque, Gothic and Modernista architecture, full of small alleys, honey-coloured stone and shady spots to relax in. Malvarrosa beach is another surprise, a wide expanse of clean white sand, and the cuisine is excellent, too.

Visit during Las Fallas festivities in mid March (www.fallas.com), when Valencia puts on some of the best fireworks displays in the world. **Stay at** *Palau de la Mar (+34 963 162 884/ www.hospes.es).*

855 *Munich, Germany*

Munich embraces just about every German cliché in the book. Old Bavarians in Lederhosen and shaving-brush hats sing in rustic beerhalls, horsing a hulking great Mass of Hacker-Pschorr and wielding a Weisswurst topped and tailed with mustard. It's an oompah image unchanged since the long reign of the Wittelsbachs through most of the last millennium. But away from cliché and history, today's Bavarian capital is dynamic, filled with modern museums, world-class art collections, high-end shopping and adventurous restaurants.

And if you like boisterous tents full of beer, sausages and *Schweinsbraten* (roast pork), get involved in Oktoberfest (www.oktoberfest.de), a massive 16-day Bavarian celebration, from late September. **Stay at** *Advokat Garni (+49 89 216310/ www.hotel-advokat.de).*

856 *Antwerp, Belgium*

Although officially Antwerp is Belgium's second city, its citizens view their hometown as top of the premier league and refuse to concede second place status to that pretender of a capital, Brussels. And they have much to be proud of. Antwerp has seen a magnificent transformation in the past 50 years, from wounded and bombed-out war victim, to the strikingly confident and beautiful city of today. Popular among fashion moguls and art-lovers, Antwerp's cobbled-lane centre is crammed full of antiques shops, designer boutiques and exclusive chocolate outlets where spending-money can be happily squandered.

Visit in July and August to catch Zommer van Antwerpen (www.zva.be), an invigorating performing arts festival that takes place in squares across the city. **Stay at** *Hotel Julien (+32 3 229 0600/ www.hotel-julien.com).*

857 *Rotterdam, Holland*

Long-ignored by Holland's hashish-loving holidayers, this multicultural city is fast becoming recognised as an artist's haven and an architectural inspiration. Bombed to oblivion

during World War II, the city was left in the hands of wacky architects to be pieced back together again. The result is a futuristic skyline that includes some of Europe's most innovative, ingenious and ultramodern designs. To see it all, climb to the top of the Euromast tower and enjoy a full view of the city. September marks the beginning of the cultural season with the De Wereld van Witte de With (www.festivalwww.nl) festival of art and culture.
Stay at *Stroom (+31 102 214 060/ www.stroomrotterdam.nl).*

858 *St Petersburg, Russia*

▦

Once known as Petrograd, then Leningrad, and now 'Russia's window to the West', Peter the Great's imperial capital is also Russia's most elegant and European city. Crammed with tsarist palaces, wonderful museums, neoclassical architecture, rock stars, artists and war veterans, this is a city steeped in history, literature, high culture and dark underground music. The Hermitage is Russia's answer to the Louvre, a must-see collection of art treasures housed in the magnificent Winter Palace that includes early Picassos and a room full of Rembrandts.

Visit in December and January to experience the city in all its icy glory while catching some of the world's most famous stars of classical music and ballet at the Mariinsky Theatre's New Year concerts (www.mariinsky.ru).
Stay at *The Astoria (0800 7666 6667/ +7 812 494 5759/www.thehotelastoria.com).*

859 *Edinburgh, Scotland*

▦♡☼

The 'Athens of the North' is a place of high culture, reincarnated parliaments and the world's most extravagant arts festival. Yet Edinburgh is also one of Europe's most beautiful cities, draped across a series of rocky hills overlooking the sea. In this unique town, cityscape and landscape are one and the same, as cliffs overshadow monuments, castles sit on dormant volcanoes and buildings spread out over grassy hills. From the towering turrets of the sloping historic centre to the tatty souvenir shops of Royal Mile and the impressive boutiques of the Georgian New Town, the city offers a compact array of contrasts that can all be explored by foot.

If you want to avoid the chaos and high room-prices that flood the city during Edinburgh Festival time, visit in Spring for a host of more low-key events (Ceilidh Culture Festival, Edinburgh International Science Festival, Beltane Fire Festival) and, fingers crossed, a few rain-free days (May is one of the driest months).
Stay at *The Howard (0131 274 7402/ www.townhousecompany.com).*

860 *Gothenburg, Sweden*

▦

With barely half a million inhabitants, Gothenburg is doing remarkably well at masquerading as a metropolis. It has no fewer than 25 theatres, 18 museums, four Michelin-starred restaurants and a steady stream of tourists thanks to Ryanair. The No.1 tourist attraction, Liseberg amusement park, draws over three million visitors each year, and the city even beat Barcelona in the contest to host the 19th European Athletics Championships in 2006. Add to that a reputation as the gastronomic capital of Sweden, and 'stuck-up Stockholm' (as Gothenburgers refer to the actual capital) has reason to be worried.

Visit in August for good weather and Göteborgskalaset ('Gothenburg Party'; www.goteborgskalas.com), the biggest city festival in Sweden, with more than 600 concerts and cultural events.
Stay at *Eggers Best Western (+46 31 333 4440/ www.hoteleggers.se).*

861 *Lyon, France*

▦☼♈

Dirty, sprawling, fast, sexy Lyon is like Paris waking up after a hard weekend. It has its beautiful parts – what better place to build a city than at the confluence of two of France's most graceful rivers, the Rhône and the Saône – and its history stretches back to Roman times, but France's second city is best loved for the here and now: for food, fashion and culture. In addition to its Renaissance architecture, Lyon has a thriving arts and nightlife scene, a fine opera house, a slew of museums and monuments, superb shopping and, best of all, some of the country's true gourmet tables.

860: Gothenburg Culture Festival

Visit in December for the Festival of Lights, a candle and lantern tradition that stretches back to 1852. Special concerts and events are held as well as a twinkling procession.
Stay at *Cour des Loges (+33 4 72 77 44 44/ www.courdesloges.com).*

862 *Cork, Ireland*

'The only good thing to come out of Dublin is the road to Cork', is an apparently popular saying among the proud dwellers of Ireland's former 'rebel city'. Sitting on the River Lee, this buzzing place has a burgeoning arts, culture and restaurant scene to rival the country's capital, while those with general disdain for Dublin will tell you it has better retained its traditional Irish charm. In truth, the city is an invigorating mixture of cramped 17th-century alleyways, snug old pubs, top cuisine and modern architectural masterpieces such as the Lewis Glucksman Gallery and the Cork Opera House.

Go in late October, when the city draws in hundreds of musicians and thousands of music fans for the Cork Jazz Festival (www.cork jazzfestival.com).
Stay at *The Imperial (+353 21 4274040/ www.flynnhotels.com).*

863 *Thessaloniki, Greece*

Although Thessaloniki – or Salonica as it's more widely known – may be Greece's second city, it's certainly its capital when it comes to culture. This seafront metropolis, sheltered in a tight nook of the Aegean Sea, offers Roman remains, Byzantine glories, Ottoman alleys and a culinary tradition that makes Athens look like the backwater. Expect a buzzing atmosphere: the waterfront is lined with cafés, the walled old town (and former Turkish quarter) is woven with narrow streets and traditional tavernas and the city's landmark, the enormous white Roman rotunda, is thronged with university students.

Some of the best beaches in the Mediterranean are only an hour's drive away, so why not couple this city break with a summer holiday? For those who prefer the milder months, the city hosts an international film festival in November (www.filmfestival.gr).
Stay at *The Luxembourg (+30 2310 252 600/ www.hotelluxembourg.gr).*

864-868
The best of Egypt

864 *Cairo and Alexandria*

First-time visitors to the sprawling, bustling city of Cairo usually gaze on in wonder at the frenetic activity in the bazaars, the busy streetlife and the Islamic architecture. With approximately 15 million residents, it's Africa's biggest city. It's easy to organise trips to see the Great Pyramid and the Sphinx, as well as the Egyptian Museum that houses Tutankhamun's tomb and its treasures. By contrast, Alexandria, founded in 331 BC, and which occupies a 20-kilometre strip along the Mediterranean coast, is Egypt's second city and feels more cosmopolitan with its colonial-style architecture, beaches and restaurants, not to mention its illustrious ancient past. It's easy to take the train between the two cities.
Book with *Cox & Kings (020 7873 5000/ www.coxandkings.co.uk).*

865 The Red Sea

£ ♀ ♦ ⚘

Stretching from the Suez Canal in the north to
Sudan in the south, the Red Sea is some 1,250
kilometres long and flanked with superb
beaches, mountains and desert. The tranquil
resorts of Marsa Alam, El Quseir and Port
Ghalib on the west coast of the Red Sea east of
Luxor boast beaches, mountain backdrops and
nightlife (largely hotel-based). These resorts
lack the crowds you'll find at other more
popular choices (such as Sharm el Sheikh),
making the area a savvy choice if you're after
a more laid-back vibe. Red Sea diving and
snorkelling is the obvious activity here, but
you can also arrange a Jeep safari to the Eastern
Desert. Be warned: it can get very hot here;
if you prefer cooler climes, opt to visit in the
winter months, when temperatures are in
the mid-20s.
Book with *Thomas Cook (0844 412 5969/*
www.thomascook.com).

866 and 867: Valley of the Kings

866 Luxor

£ 🏠

Luxor, on the east bank of the Nile, has been
attracting visitors for thousands of years.
Built on the site of the ancient Egyptian
capital Thebes, it's home to some of the
world's most important archaeological sights
(be warned that the crowds can be a little
overwhelming). Luxor Temple, founded by
Amenophis III circa 1400 BC, is the city's
most popular attraction; the tombs of the
Valley of the Kings – where Tutankhamun
was buried – are nothing short of impressive.
And if you need a break from the ruins, you
can arrange hot-air ballooning or a one-
day Nile cruise. The best months to visit,
weather-wise, are October to February.
Book with *Discover Egypt (0844 880 0462/*
www.discoveregypt.co.uk).

867 Western Desert

£ ⚘ 🏠

Egypt's Western Desert, which extends to
Libya on the west, Sudan on the south and the
Nile on its east, is a vast expanse that covers
approximately two thirds of the country. It
makes for an adventurous holiday for intrepid
travellers. The only sensible way to get to
see this arid part of Egypt is by booking an
organised trek. The Adventure Company runs
a ten-day Desert Explorer group trip travelling
by camel and Jeep that begins and ends in Cairo
and includes desert camps, visits to empty
desert villages, a trip to the UNESCO World
Heritage Site of the Valley of the Whales to
see 40 million-year-old fossils, the tomb of
Alexander the Great and a donkey ride to
the Valley of the Kings from Luxor.
Book with *The Adventure Company*
(0845 450 0838/www.adventurecompany.co.uk).

868 Mount Sinai

£ ♦ ⚘ 🏠

At 2,285 metres high, an ascent of Mount
Sinai – where Moses received the Ten
Commandments – is not for the faint-hearted,
but it's hard to beat the incredible sense of
achievement and sensational views when you
reach the summit. World Expeditions' 11-day
Sinai Trek begins in Cairo and, after a day
acclimatising and visiting the Pyramids at Giza,
you begin the hiking element. The company

employs Bedouin guides and camels to carry your stuff as you spend five days walking through the surrounding landscape and hills. The hiking culminates with a pre-dawn start – the reward is watching the sunrise from the top of Mount Sinai.

Book with *World Expeditions (0800 0744 135/ www.worldexpeditions.co.uk).*

869-873
The Other Caribbean

869 *Grenada*
♋ �

Isn't that the place that the US invaded in the 1980s? Didn't it get munched by a hurricane a few years ago? Yes, Grenada is used to bad press. But like a fighter on the ropes, it's come out swinging, reinventing itself as the next big thing. The one large island and two small ones in the southeast corner of the Caribbean are undiscovered and rarely visited. But for the smallest independent country in the western hemisphere, this place has a lot to offer, with rainforest scenery, sublime beaches and scuba diving, relaxed villages and friendly locals.

Getting there *Virgin Atlantic (www.virgin-atlantic. com) and British Airways (www.britishairways.com) both operate flights between London and Grenada.*

870 *Isla de la Juventud, Cuba*
♋ � ≋

Cuba's second-largest island lies directly south of Havana. The 'Isle of Youth' is famously friendly and it's easy to get off the beaten track here. Punta Francés is a top scuba-diving spot and there are swathes of wilderness in the southern half of the island. Hotels on Isla de la Juventud are limited, so it's best to use one of the homestays (*casas particulares*) in the capital, Nueva Gerona.

Getting there *Virgin Atlantic flies from London Gatwick to Havana (www.virgin-atlantic.com); from here, take an internal Cubana flight (www.cubana.cu) or a two-hour catamaran from Batabanó.*

871 *Puerto Rico*
♋ � ≋ ♈

Since the embargo on tourism in Cuba, Puerto Rico has been middle-class America's main

870: Cuba

Spanish-Caribbean option. The capital, San Juan, is a vibrant city with a pretty colonial core, and while it has plenty of shopping malls, luxury hotels and glitzy casinos, it also has cool restaurants and great nightlife. In the interior, there are crumbling colonial towns, coffee plantations and tropical rainforests, while the coast is full of dive sites.

Getting there *Virgin Atlantic (www.virgin-atlantic.com) flies from London Gatwick to San Juan, via Antigua.*

872 *Isla Mujeres, Mexico*
♋ ♡

According to Mayan legend, this beautiful little island a short ferry ride from Cancún was used for fertility ceremonies. There are some good seafood and fish restaurants and lovely crushed-coral beaches. Day visitors leave at around 5pm, after which time the place is far calmer – and local shops begin to close. See www.isla-mujeres.net for more information.

Getting there *Express ferries (15 mins) from Puerto Juarez and Gran Puerto Cancún.*

873 *Ambergris Caye, Belize*

It's nowhere near as gritty or edgy as the mainland; instead, this miniature, palm-fronded paradise can be a welcome retreat. Speedboats go from Belize City, and the tiny capital – San Pedro Town – has some great guesthouses, as well as cheesy themed resorts. There isn't much to do but kick back in a hammock, ride around on a golf cart and take the short boat trip out to one of the world's greatest coral reefs for scuba diving or snorkelling.

Getting there *Maya Island Air (+501 223 0734/ www.mayaregional.com) flies daily from Belize. Water taxis to San Pedro run daily.*

874-878
World's safest places (for the travel anxious)

874 *New Hampshire, USA*

The eastern United States is probably the best place in the world to see the annual fall of leaves – a riot of beautiful hues and vibrant foliage – with sleepy New Hampshire officially the safest of all the states, with the lowest crime rate. Stay at Bear Mountain Lodge, a log cabin built in 2005 near Bethlehem. With only nine rooms, the atmosphere and service are intimate and friendly; nearby activities in the surrounding White Mountains include hiking, biking, fishing, skiing and golf.

Bear Mountain Lodge *+1 603 869 2189/ www.bearmountainlodge.net.*

875 *Finland*

Finland is consistently rated as the least corrupt country in the world. Yet in this land of integrity, there is still serious fun to be had. The excellent skiing can be accompanied by dog-sleigh rides and ice fishing, while in summer, the epic days can be spent hiking, cycling or horseback riding, as well as exploring the unique vibrancy of the world's second most northerly capital, Helsinki. The Hotel Haven, in downtown Helsinki, is a comfortable and stylish accommodation option with a sauna and spa; it's also a stone's throw from the city's best restaurants.

Hotel Haven *+358 9 681 930/www.hotelhaven.fi.*

876 *Luxembourg*

The authoritative Mercer global rankings consistently list Luxembourg as the safest country on the planet. Its people live a blessed life, with the highest GDP per head and more Michelin restaurant stars per capita than any other country. As well as fine dining, visit for the ancient castles and verdant hills – all within

878: Copenhagen, Denmark

a very manageable 2,590 square kilometres. The modern and sophisticated Sofitel Lux Le Grand Ducal, in Luxembourg city, is an appropriate pillar of luxury, with two restaurants serving traditional or Italian cuisine.

Sofitel Lux Le Grand *+352 248771/www.sofitel. com/gb/hotel-5555-sofitel-luxembourg-le-grand-ducal/index.shtml.*

877 *The Cotswolds, UK*

The quietly undulating hills of the Cotswolds represent probably the gentlest holiday in the UK. Ancient limestone towns are dispersed among an absurdly English countryside of rolling greenery streaked with dry-stone walls. Sleepy cycle rides and wistful walks can all be had in this calm corner of the country. Painswick is a charming town from which to base your Cotswold explorations, with an excellent accommodation option in Byfield House – one of the friendliest B&Bs in the area. The owners' knowledge of local walks and other sights is unparalleled.

Byfield House *01452 81260/www.byfieldhouse.com.*

878 *Denmark*

The results of astronomical Danish tax revenues are visible in the well-kept parks and public spaces of its capital, Copenhagen; the Botanical Gardens and the garden of the Royal Veterinarian School are some of the best Europe has to offer. The city of effortless European culture also boasts the northern hemisphere's most impressive Opera House. Stay at Somandshjemmet Bethel Hotel, a friendly, comfortable and good-value place in an often eye-wateringly expensive city. It's located right on the Nyhavn, a popular 17th-century canal waterfront lined with bars and cafés.

Somandshjemmet Bethel Hotel *+45 3313 0370/ www.hotel-bethel.dk.*

879-887
Amazing all-inclusives

Forget your prudent self and leave your wallet in your room. Here are nine great all-inclusive resorts that will cater to your every wish.

879 Royal Hideaway Playacar, Mexico

+52 984 873 4500/www.royalhideaway.com.
With five diamond stars and one Michelin-starred chef, this adult-only resort prides itself on personal attention and exceptional service. Relaxation pools dotted around the property are a far cry from splash-ridden social hubs and, when it comes to dining at one of the six gourmet restaurants, you can be sure that there won't be a buffet bar in sight. Situated on one of the Yucatan peninsula's stunning stretches of beachfront, the elegant complex is made up of two- and three-storey villas of Spanish colonial and Mexican design, linked by winding pathways, creeks and waterfalls.

What's included All food and drink (including top shelf alcoholic beverages), 24-hour room service, private concierge service in each villa, all land and non-motorised watersports, DVD library and wireless internet connection. Expect to pay extra for motorised watersports, spa treatments, laundry and airport transfers.

880 Turtle Island, Fiji

0800 028 5938/www.turtlefiji.com.
Along with the rest of the 20 or so volcanic islands of the Yasawa archipelago, Turtle Island was, until recently, an uninhabited and off-limits paradise. Today, this exclusive and eco-friendly island opens its shores to couples – although only 14 at a time. Guests stay in traditional thatched roof bungalows, or *bures*, which overlook private beaches (there are 14 on the island, so one for every couple), tropical gardens or the famous Blue Lagoon, where the movie of the same name was filmed. It's not all lounging around, however, as the crystalline waters and virgin reefs of this area make it the perfect place for snorkelling and scuba diving. Cuisine is top-notch tropical fare.

What's included A fully dedicated 'Bure-mama' concierge, all meals (including à la carte breakfast, afternoon snacks, pre-dinner savouries and gourmet dinners), all beverages (including fine wines and champagne), laundry service and one half-hour Lomi Lomi massage service.

881 Beaches Turks & Caicos Resort

R ᵃⁱᵃ

08000 22 32 33/www.beachesresorts.co.uk.
Beaches manages that rare feat of being both
luxurious and family-friendly. Three resort
'villages', inspired by the architecture of France,
Italy and the Caribbean, come together along
the 12-mile pristine beach of Providenciales on
the islands of Caicos in the West Indies, to make
this a mega-resort of six pools, 16 restaurants
and no-expenses-spared indulgence. The
Sesame Street cast entertain kids throughout
the day, while teens are kept happy with an
Xbox 360 Game Garage and nightly beach
parties; and kids of all ages enjoy the aqua-
themed Pirate's Island playground equipped
with seven rides, a surf simulator and a 650-
foot-long lazy river. Parents can try their
hand at croquet and relax in the spa.
What's included Meals in all 16 restaurants, all
drinks and snacks, watersports (including two
tank dives), airport transfers, entry to Pirate
Island and even wedding ceremonies. Spa
treatments are extra.

882 Guana Island, British Virgins

R ♀♡

+212 482 6247/www.guana.com.
Imagine the Caribbean before it went public.
Once a sugarcane plantation owned by
American Quakers, Guana Island is an 850-
acre privately owned haven of untouched
beaches, lush tropical beauty and 16 discreet
guest rooms. Villas and white-washed cottages
– together with their infinity pools, dining
verandas and hot tubs – hide on hilltops
overlooking the sail-boat studded Caribbean,
while the unique North Beach cottage offers
the ultimate in privacy, with its very own
shore. If you want to meet some of the other
guests, then hop on the hotel beach cart and
head south past the flamingo pond until you
reach White Bay Beach, the resort's main
shoreline and social centre, where all the
pampering, exercising and eating takes
place. Alternatively, candlelit meals can
be arranged on your own villa veranda.
What's Included All packages include three
meals, between-meal refreshments, wine with
lunch and dinner, laundry service, WiFi internet
and unlimited use of sports facilities and non-
motorised watersports. Tax, service charges,
taxi and boat transfers from Beef Island
and additional excursions such as castaway
picnics are not included.

883 Governor's Camp, Kenya

♀

+254 20 273 4000/www.governorscamp.com.
Safaris aren't generally associated with supreme
luxury, but Kenya's Governor's Camp is not your
average huddle of tents. Established in 1972,
when Kenya's colonial governors came to stay,
the camp maintains exceptionally high standards.
Groups of tents make up four different sites, each
located within the heart of the Masai Mara game
reserve. Little Governor's Camp has an extra
special spot right along the River Mara, where
guests can see hippos grazing and elephants
taking a dip from their tent windows. The large
and comfortable marquees, kitted out with
handmade furniture, oil lanterns and verandas,
recreate a Livingstone-esque feel, while flushing
toilets and hot showers seal the deal.
What's included Full-board accommodation,
three game drives per day, tent and laundry
services and transfers to and from the Masai
Mara airstrip. Selected wines, beers and soft
drinks are included in the Little Governor and
Il Moran camps. Park fees, fine wines, spirits
and champagne are extra.

884 Club Med Peisey-Vallandry, France

♀ ⚲

0871 424 4044/www.clubmed.com.
Perched at 1,600 metres in the Tarentaise
Valley, among rocky streams and evergreen
trees, this traditional chalet-resort captures the
authentic spirit of France's Savoy Alps. Typical
stone and wooden architecture blends with the
fir-tree surroundings, while the contemporary
beige and red decor imbue the place with a
warm and friendly brand of luxury. Suites
boast beautiful teak-furnished balconies, from
where the magnificent mountains (including
direct views of Mont Blanc) can be enjoyed
from the safety of sturdy ground. Of the two
restaurants, the Pierra Menta offers the most
authentic dining experience, with mountain
specialities such as fondue and raclette. As for
activities, the 425 kilometres of ski slopes are
your playground, and there are also numerous
activities held inside the hotel as well as indoor
and outdoor heated pools.

What's included Return flights, transfers, full-board meals (served with wine), unlimited beer and soft drinks, bar snacks. Ski passes and group classes are included (as long as you're over four years old), but equipmen hire and insurance are not.

885 Amansala, Tulum, Mexico

♨ ⚲ 🏠
+52 998 185 7428/7426/www.amansala.com.
The Amansala all-inclusive approach is not all about sipping on piña coladas and lounging around under palm trees. The resort hosts two holiday schemes: Bikini Boot Camp and Warrior Week, both of which use the beautiful surroundings, natural supplies of fresh food and inviting climate to compel holidaying boys and girls into an active and balanced lifestyle (Bikini Camp is, despite its name, co-ed, while Warrior Week is a more testosterone-centred affair). Days start bright and early with a beach walk before breakfast, then move on to snorkelling, kayaking, or cycling to the beautiful Mayan ruins of Tulum. After a healthy tropical lunch, you can relax with a Mayan clay treatment before rounding off the day with some meditation and local entertainment. The cabanas where you will eventually rest your head are simple wooden affairs on the beach, but despite the back-to-

basics style, added details such as luxurious linens, plush towels and candles ensure you'll get a good night's sleep.
What's included All meals and drinks, all exercise classes, three excursions, two massages, one full body Mayan clay treatment, kayaking, snorkelling and bike riding. Alcohol is available but not included in the price.

886 Hotel Splendido, Italy

♡ ⚲
+39 0185 267 801/www.hotelsplendido.com.
Suspended in Genoan cliffs and surrounded by flowering gardens, this fine hotel was originally a monastery abandoned by its monks due to constant pirate attacks. Now a luxury retreat of the Orient Express variety, there are no disturbances other than the soothing sounds of the resort's in-house piano player. Dramatic views over the quaint village of Portofino can be enjoyed, cocktail in hand, at the cliffside pool. If you like what you see, why not hop on a complimentary shuttle bus to the hotel's ground-located sister, Splendido Mare, where food and facilities are free for all guests. Inside Hotel Splendido expect grandeur and glamour: marble floors, gilt furniture and Persian rugs.
What's included Various packages to suit couples, 'babymooners' (parents-to-be) and families. Most include breakfast and one other

883: Governor's Camp, Kenya

meal, soft drinks and a few added extras such as a massage or babysitting service.

887 Blackberry Farm, East Tennessee

+1 865 984 8166/www.blackberryfarm.com.
An intimate cottage-based hotel that developed from a family home and farm, this East Tennessee all-inclusive has a wholesome and homely feel that's hard to find in the big resort chains. Surrounded by picket-fenced fields, wild pine forests and the majestic Smoky Mountains, it's perfect for back-to-nature relaxation and open-air excursions. The farm has a live-off-the-land approach, and guests can lend a hand in farming activities or simply enjoy the seasonal produce at either of the inventive (and highly acclaimed) restaurants. Countless fresh-air experiences are on offer, the most traditional of which is fly fishing at nearby Hesse Creek. Unlike the many sun-drenched and beach-based destinations, this Tennessee farm boasts four distinct seasons, each with their own charm.
What's included 'Full American Plan' dining (three gourmet meals plus pantry snacks), backpacks, blankets, trail maps, accommodation and a good dose of Southern hospitality.

888-899
Where to go when

How do you avoid the holiday rush, skip festivals and events that push prices up for rooms and flights, but get the benefit of the local weather and all the pleasures enjoyed by the peak season traveller? Tricky, but possible... the following are savvy ideas to plan your year without getting mobbed by fellow tourists or ripped off by travel agents.

888 *January... Pre-carnival partying in Rio de Janeiro, Brazil*

Catch the shoulder season between New Year and the official Carnaval and go to a samba school in Rio in late January, with breaks on the beach in between classes.
Book with *Jingando Holidays (020 8877 1630/www.jingandoholidays.com).*

889 *February... Beat the winter blues in the Arabian Gulf*

Many winter sunseekers have blown all their savings on Christmas breaks and long-haul odysseys to the southern hemisphere. Why not combine a mid-haul flight (7.5 hours) with an off-peak trip to a luxury resort in Oman, a country that offers travellers green wadis, deserts, stunning beaches, mountains and cities full of ancient architecture and lively souks.
Book with *Shaw Travel (01635 47055/www.shawtravel.co.uk).*

890 *March... Late, cheap skiing in the high Alps*

After pricey February, aim for the upper reaches of the loftier peaks in France, Austria and Italy (the latter is the best value) and enjoy long sunny days and good firm snow for your late skiing fix.
Book with *Iglu (020 8544 6400/www.iglu.com).*

891 *April... Dia de San Jordi, Barcelona*

Warm weather, and seas you can just about swim in before the crowds descend; make sure

889: Oman

23 April falls inside your trip and you can celebrate St George's Day when, historically, Catalan men gave women roses, and women gave men a book to celebrate the occasion. On Barcelona's La Rambla, and all over Catalonia, hundreds of stands flog roses to romantic couples and makeshift bookstalls are set up. The sardana, the national dance, is performed through the day in the Plaça Sant Jaume.

892 May... Pre-summer escape on Mexico's Mayan Riviera

Plan your trip to Cancún before the hurricane season and before Brits come en masse for their summer holidays. The weather will be beautiful. Combine the usual round of swimming and snorkelling with sightseeing at the Mayan ruins – try to see Tulum as well as the more popular Chitzen Itza.
Book with *Asda Travel (www.asda-travel.co.uk).*

893 June... Island retreat in Greece

The schools are still open so this is a good time for a non-family holiday in Greece. There are hundreds of lovely islands; if you choose Crete, you should be able to find a gorgeous villa in which to live out your Magus fantasies.
Book with *Pure Crete (0845 070 1571/ www.purecrete.com).*

894 July... Four UK breaks

Prices for holidays on the Med have been rocketing of late. So why not use the four weekends of this month to do four great staycations? This way you don't use any of your holiday leave, and you get to expand your knowledge of Blighty. We recommend Harlech in Wales, Glencoe in Scotland, Shropshire in England and Belfast in Northern Ireland.

895 August... Great British seaside

Britain has a wealth of beautiful beaches, but a lack of sunny weather sometimes makes it hard to appreciate them. August is probably the best month for enjoying the British coast, but, with schools out for summer, it's also the most popular. If you can't bear the crowds on the

Cornish Riviera, then head to a near deserted beach in Scotland: Calgary and Luskentyre have extraordinary expanses of white sand.

896 September... Autumn in New England

New England – comprised of the north-eastern states of Maine, New Hampshire, Vermont, Massachusetts, Connecticut, New York State and Rhode Island – is beautiful in autumn, with sunny skies and fallen leaves in a riot of hues.

897 October... Icelandic delights

Many travellers head to Iceland to see the awe-inspiring Northern Lights; if you visit in October, you not only have a good chance of seeing them (the best months for viewing them are March, April, September and October), but you can also catch Airwaves (www.iceland airwaves.is), the country's innovative festival of new music, held mid month.

898 November... Post-monsoon India

India's main monsoon period is between June and September, when daily downpours put paid to many travel plans. Avoid this time, and head to this extraordinarily diverse country in November, thereby also avoiding the Christmas and New Year crowds.

899 December... Sun-filled and consumerism-free

A cosy Christmas in Blighty is all well and good, but the mix of commercialism, overindulgence, illness and family bickering often blight the actual point of it. Escape the stress by fleeing to Cuba for the entire month of December. Kick off with the Havana Film Festival (www.habana filmfestival.com) – a two-week showcase of the best of Latin American cinema that creates a noticeable buzz in the capital – and then explore this sunny Caribbean isle known for its rum, cigars, music, picture-perfect beaches – and absence of consumerist culture. New Year is big in Cuba, with 1 January being both the start of the new year and the anniversary of the Revolution. You'll return with a healthy colour that'll help see you through the rest of the winter.

900-909

Tropical paradises

900 *Seychelles*

Think coconut groves, gently lapping waves, stunning sunsets and pretty fish to spot while snorkelling and you've got the Seychelles, a beautiful archipelago of 115 islands in the Indian Ocean. The islands, whichever you select, are ideal if you're feeling overworked and stressed; the pristine beaches, clear blue seas and general laid-back vibe will soothe even the most frazzled office worker. Mahé is the largest and most developed island and a good choice for first-time visitors. Seychelles-specialist Abercrombie & Kent (0845 618 2200, www.abercrombiekent.co.uk) can organise a holiday according to your wishes.

901 Maldives

The Maldives, a string of atolls in the Indian Ocean, south-west of Sri Lanka, top many a list for a dreamy romantic getaway. The 130 villas at exclusive chain One&Only are sumptuous; each has access to a private beach and a pool, a flatscreen TV for when it's too dark to gaze out on to the calm blue sea, espresso- and tea-making machines, a sun terrace, and spacious bathrooms with baths perfect for early evening, pre-dinner wallowing with a glass of champagne. Tropical-themed bedrooms have cosy beds made up with Egyptian bedlinen and there's even a pillow menu to ensure you get a good night's rest after a hard day on the beach.
One&Only *01753 899900/ www.oneandonlyresorts.com.*

902 Uepi Island, Solomon Islands

The Solomon Islands archipelago consists of mountainous, forested volcanic islands to the south-east of Papua New Guinea, and are an adventurous travel destination for anyone looking for a tropical holiday with added oomph. In common with other tropical destinations, the islands can get very humid; most tourists visit during the dry season, which runs from the end of May to the start of December. It's a water-lover's paradise, with gorgeous coral reefs to explore with a snorkel, World War II shipwrecks for intrepid scuba divers, underwater volcanoes, surfing, kayaking and wildlife-watching on Lake Te'Nggano, a UNESCO World Heritage Site.

Uepi Island consists of a rainforest-covered barrier reef with a stunning sandy beach. The Uepi Island Resort has four recently renovated spacious beachfront bungalows with a deck and an all-important hammock.
Uepi Island Resort *+61 3 9787 7904/ www.uepi.com.*

903 Sri Lanka

Sri Lanka is a popular beach holiday destination for good reason – it's got beaches, archaeology, nature and incredibly warm hospitality. Serene Pavilions is a new boutique hotel set in a seven-acre coconut grove on Sri Lanka's west coast. Each of the 12 highly stylish luxurious pavilionshas its own private plunge pool, sitting room, furnished kitchenette, private bar and jacuzzi. The beachside hideaway is only 45 minutes from the capital, Colombo, but feels remote. When not enjoying the swimming pool or gazing dreamily out to sea, you can dine on delicious cuisine such as shrimp and mango salad.
Serene Pavilions *+94 38 229 4447/ www.serenepavilions.com.*

904 Cayman Islands

The exotic Caribbean Cayman Islands are famed for their pristine beaches, romantic sunsets and plush hotels. This tropical paradise is perfect for a relaxing beach holiday, but it's equally suited to family holidays thanks to the calm seas, and nature-watching breaks; keen birders can spot parrots, doves, tricoloured herons, coots, blue-winged teals, rare West Indian whistling ducks and many more. There's a wide accommodation choice but self-catering gives the greatest flexibility; the eight elegant apartments that comprise the beachside Turtle Nest Inn, ten miles from Grand Cayman capital George Town (and the airport), have Spanish-inspired architecture, terraces, whitewashed walls and terracotta tiles. While you're there you can go snorkelling in the crystal-clear sea, take a dip in the freshwater swimming pool, or simply relax on the beach.

905 Jericoacoara, Brazil

Brazil is famous for its beaches, and Jericoacoara, 300 kilometres north of Fortaleza, doesn't disappoint. Some 20 years ago, it was a modest fishing village that had no telephone connection and a rudimentary road system – electricity was only installed in 1998. And although it's grown in size and wealth thanks to international tourism, it's remained relatively undeveloped. But that's to its advantage: the 6,850-hectare National Park of Jericoacoara comprises dunes, lakes, sandy beaches and tranquil seas. But it's not all about nature – recent years have seen Jericoacoara become popular with wind- and kitesurfers, though it's also good for surfing and sandboarding, and you can organise horseriding on the beach.

Pousada Carioca is a small, quiet B&B with a pretty garden (look out for the hummingbirds) and hammocks to relax in after a day of kitesurfing. Breakfasts are healthy, with lots of fruit and home-made coconut bread. **Pousada Carioca** + 55 88 12 75 61/ *www.pousadacarioca.com.*

906 *Borneo*

The northern part of Borneo, an island with exceptional biodiversity, is Malaysian; its southern two-fifths are Indonesian. With pristine jungle, stunning scenery, eye-catching orchids, white-sand beaches and exotic ocean life, Borneo tops the bill for the ultimate adventure-filled tropical holiday. Enticements include staying in a local homestay, spending a night or two in the jungle, chilling on the beach and, of course, watching the wild and endangered orang-utans on the north of the island.

Book with *Intrepid Travel (020 3147 7777/ www.intrepidtravel.com).*

907 *Cocos Islands*

These gorgeous Australian islands in the Indian Ocean, nestled between Sri Lanka and Australia, almost 2,800 kilometres north-west of Perth, are blissfully free of big resorts and chain hotels. Charles Darwin, who was on *The Beagle* when it sailed around the atoll, collected specimens to take back to Kent. Snorkellers, scuba divers and passengers on the glass-bottomed boat can spot colourful fish (around 500 different species), reef sharks and turtles. The islands are also home to many seabirds, including white terns, frigate birds, waders and herons. The tropical climate means sunny days, though there is slightly higher rainfall between March and July. Swim, cycle, fish, walk or simply laze in a hammock.

Stay at *Cocos Cottages (+08 9244 3801/ www.cocos-cottages.cc).*

908 *Barbados*

For glitz, glamour and to see and be seen, Barbados is hard to beat. There's not much modesty here – this island is all about the cash, baby. There's no shortage of accommodation – much of it catering to moneyed lawyers, bankers, movie moguls and honeymooners who enjoy the discreet service the island's renowned for. The uber-luxe Sandpiper is on the beach and its classy rooms and suites are nestled among lush tropical gardens. When you're not watching the armies of gardeners tending to the lawns, you can occupy yourself playing polo or golf, sailing, or taking a refreshing dip in the sea/pool. There's

909: The Eden Project, UK

also the Barbados Wildlife Reserve where you can meet the local green monkeys.
Sandpiper *+246 422 2251/ www.sandpiperbarbados.com.*

909 *The Eden Project, UK*

Who says you need to take a plane to a tropical paradise? Cornwall's greatest tourist attraction started life as a chalk mine. Now its two biomes provide a habitat for two climates. In the tropical rainforest biome – the world's largest conservatory – plants, including mangroves, Fijian ferns, Australian umbrella trees and the endangered bottle palm from Mauritius, thrive in the humid 30-degrees-centigrade-plus temperatures; the cooler Mediterranean biome hosts olive and citrus trees and an array of flora from the world's non-tropical zones, such as cacti common to the Californian desert. There's a big emphasis on sustainability, but in a gently informative way – learn about the Eden Project's involvement in Thailand's Forest Restoration Research Unit or why it's important to source your soy responsibly. Plan to spend at least four hours here to make the most of your visit. The food's also top notch – especially the own-made Cornish pasties. *01726 811911/www.edenproject.com.*

910-919
Awe-inspiring Australia

910 *Exploration... Akadu National Park, Northern Territory*

Alligator Rivers may not be the first place you'd go for a dip but the spectacular waterfalls with dark plunge pools and sparkling beaches beneath are crocodile-free and perfect after a long bushwalk or drive. Countless animal, bird and plant species inhabit the forest and canyons, where 50,000-year-old Aboriginal paintings survive on rocks.

911 *Metropolis... Sydney*

Romantic views, galleries and the Opera House, great bars and excellent shopping all help to

915: Australia's Barossa Valley

make Sydney a world-class city. Make sure the nature tours, gourmet outings and adrenaline boosting adventures around the region leave you time for Bondi Beach, famous for its white sands, parties and sexy surfer boys and chicks.

912 *Surf... Bells beach and the Surf Coast*

Patrick Swayze's quest for the perfect wave in *Point Break* ended on Bells beach on the Surf Coast in Victoria, where the breaks hurl even the best surfers from their boards. The first surfing contest, Rip Curl Pro, was held here, and it's now an annual event every Easter, with a music festival tacked on. Easier breaks and surf schools along the coast also make it a good place to learn.

913 *Road trip... The Great Ocean Road*

The Great Ocean Road follows the limestone cliffs towering above the Southern Ocean for 243 kilometres, above beaches on one side and thick bush on the other. Between romantic sunsets, view the rocky giants of the 12 Apostles, the silent rainforest waterfalls of Great Otway National Park and the wildlife reserve atop the extinct volcano at Tower Hill.

914 *Drama... Kimberley*

The remote western coast's dramatic red cliffs, ancient Aboriginal art and wild rock formations carved into the land are said to be Australia's last wilderness. Endless gorges, creeks and waterfalls can be visited by cruise boat or explored on foot, but for the now infamous *Wolfe Creek* meteorite crater, you'll have to brave the drive.

915 *Wine... vineyards, valleys and Adelaide*

The Barossa Valley is the birthplace of Australia's well-known Jacob's Creek and Wolf Blass labels, but first-class wines are also produced in nearby valleys, where they can be enjoyed with local cheeses, chutneys

and fruits. Chocolate is also a regional speciality. Between tours and tastings, explore Adelaide's cafés, galleries and shops.

916 *Wildlife... Queensland*

Animal-lovers (and their parents) can cuddle koalas and feed the kangaroos at the largest koala sanctuary in the world at Lone Pine, near Brisbane. If your taste for reptiles extends beyond crocodile soup, visit the tropical zoo at Alma Park, where you can pet the crocodiles and snakes. Then meet the fluffy bears, exotic monkeys and fabled dingoes.

917 *History... Alice Springs*

The heart of the Australian outback, this is the land of waterholes and red desert, caterpillar-shaped mountain ranges and rodeos. The Arrernte tribe's historic trails make ideal four-wheel drive and bushwalk territory. Visit the mysterious land formations, including Uluru (Ayers Rock), which have inspired Aboriginal legends and art for thousands of years.

918 *Paradise... The Whitsundays*

A vast tropical paradise of white-sand beaches and turquoise waters, only eight of Whitsunday's 74 islands are inhabited. Sprinkled over the Coral Sea close to the Great Barrier Reef, take a sailing boat to their blue lagoons and hidden coves or try the mesmerising view from the air. In town, explore the markets, boutiques and tasty cuisine.

919 *Rainforest... Skyrail and Caravonica lakes*

The gondola cableway Skyrail (www.skyrail. com.au) runs over the tropical rainforest of Cairns, and stops at Red Peak and Barron Falls on its journey between the colourful village of Kuranda and the Caravonica freshwater lakes, leaving you to explore the innermost depths of the forest. Around Cairns, relax on the beaches, dive at the reefs, venture into the wildlife parks and try out the didgeridoos.

Ideas from the expert

920-929

Chris Galanty from Round the World Experts offers the ultimate globe-spanning trip.

920 Fly to Miami to start the trip off with some hard partying to rid yourself of any pre-trip-related stress. Party at the Mansion Club, Miami Beach; enjoy the city's vibrant art deco architecture; and sample 'floribean' food, a hybrid of Spanish, Caribbean and American cuisine. From here, go overland on a Greyhound bus to Houston (30 hours 55 mins non-stop; www.greyhound.com), and gaze out the window at scenes from the USA's South-eastern states.

921 From Houston, fly to Lima, Peru. Take in the architecture of one of Spanish America's oldest cities. Lima isn't the prettiest of cities but it's home to more than 1,600 balconies from the colonial and early Republican period. Visit the Larco Museum, home to one of the world's largest collections of pre-Columbian art – the museum is also well known for its gallery of pre-Columbian erotic pottery. Then, head to the seaside resort of Cerro Azul and get a surfing lesson.

922 From Lima, travel by bus to Santiago de Chile on the Panamerican highway. In the Chilean capital, climb to the top of Santa Lucia Hill for sweeping views of the city and the snow-capped Andes beyond. Visit the 16th-century Iglesia de San Francisco, the city's oldest church; an art museum is maintained inside, housing some of the most exquisite paintings from the Cuzco School. Ride a hired bike into the lovely Parque Metropolitano San Cristóbal.

923 From Santiago de Chile, fly to Auckland, on New Zealand's North Island. Absolute Tours (www.absolutetours.co.nz) offers a brewery tour that takes you to four local breweries. Then, try your luck at the Sky City Casino. Fans of U2 will want to visit One Tree Hill, which inspired the song of the same name – it's in Cornwall Park, site of a 182-metre-high volcanic peak.

924 Head from Auckland to Christchurch, on the South Island, by rail and ferry. The city is known for its green spaces. Meet a kune kune pig at the Willowbank Wildlife Reserve, and later head for the many cafés and bars downtown. The Canterbury Plains just outside the city are one of the world's best spots for hot-air ballooning.

925 From Christchurch, fly to Sydney for some serious beach action; with more than 50 beaches along Sydney's coastline, from posey Palm Beach in the north to family magnet Cronulla in the south, there's one for every type of beach lover. Catch the Manly Ferry from Circular Quay for great views of the Sydney Opera House and Sydney Harbour Bridge, and enjoy fabulous fusion cuisine in one of the many eateries.

926 Take the train from Sydney to Perth, via Adelaide; the 65-hour (three-night), 4352-kilometre journey passes along the longest stretch of straight track on the planet and takes in the treeless plains of the Nullarbor desert en route. Once you get to Perth, stretch your legs by cycling round the Swan River – bikes can by hired at Langley Park. Then enjoy Perth's fantastic beaches and surfing spots.

927 From Perth, fly to Singapore, where you can enjoy some of the best oriental cuisine in the world. Visit Singapore Zoo at night to spot its amazing collection of nocturnal animals. Ride a rickshaw into Chinatown and view the city from the harbour with an Admiral Cheng Ho Singapore Dinner Cruise.

928 From Singapore, fly to Hong Kong, a city that exudes a special energy. Take the number 15 Bus from Peak to Central to get stunning views of the city; visit the Jade Market in Yau Ma Tei; and, if your timing's right, bet on a horse at the Happy Valley Racecourse.

929 Lastly, fly to Dubai for a surreal and superlative experience to end your trip. See the world's tallest building, the Burj Dubai, and then head to Ski Dubai in the Mall of the Emirates, the world's third largest indoor ski slope, which generates real snow – in one of the world's hottest countries. Then, head back home for a reality check.

■ **Round the World Experts** 0800 707 6010/ www.roundtheworldexperts.co.uk.

930-939
Themed thrills worldwide

930 Discovery Cove, Florida – for all things fishy

+1 407 370 1280/www.discoverycove.com.
With no queues and limited admission, Florida's Discovery Cove, in Orlando, is a refreshing change from the more monstrous breed of amusement park. A series of lagoons, coral reefs and rivers allow a maximum of 1,000 swimmers to have a splash-happy time with all their favourite sea creatures. There's certainly no shortage of activities to immerse yourself in: snorkel among exotic fish at Tropical Reef, paddle with rays at Stingray Shallows or simply soak up the sun by the pristine pools of Serenity Bay. The hands-down highlight of the day is the Dolphin Swim Experience, where small groups have the chance to play and perform tricks with their favourite bottle-nosed friend. Admission isn't cheap but includes everything from food, drink and sunscreen to towels and snorkelling equipment, and even an unlimited two-week pass to the park's mammoth sister, SeaWorld.

931 Six Flags Magic Mountain, Los Angeles – for toe-curling terror

+1 661 255 4100/www.sixflags.com.
If it's G-force thrills you're after, California's Magic Mountain will certainly hit the spot with its imaginative array of gut-wrenching, nausea-inducing attractions. Twist yourself round the seven vertical inversions of Viper, shriek to your heart's content on Scream or soar like your favourite superhero on the Batman-, Superman- and Terminator-themed rides. For those looking for real toe-curling terror, X2 is perhaps the most extreme. Every little detail of this ingenious ride has been thoughtfully designed to scare the living crap out of you. Seats rotate 360 degrees and extend off the track in unexpected ways, while face-down drops push you headfirst into oblivion. Hang on to those handles.

932 Oasys Western Theme Park, Almería – for Clint Eastwood wannabes

+34 950 36 29 31.
It may seem a little random that 30 hectares of Southern Spain should be used as homage to the American Western, but the dry and arid lands of Almería's Tabernas desert were actually where many of the 'spaghettis' were filmed. The now unused film sets make up the park's Old Western Village, a convincing Wild West town complete with a Sheriff's office, Town Square and Saloon (where, yes, they do still serve cold beer). The set comes to life twice a day (or three in summer) when actors dressed as cowboys take part in a gunfight, some rough-looking locals bite the dust and an outlaw gets hanged. Straying from the theme of the Western, the park also includes a slide-equipped pool, a tiger-inhabited safari and plenty of places to snack, drink and eat to your heart's content.

936: Europa Park, Germany

933 LoveLand, Jeju island, South Korea – for sexy statues

♡

+82 64 712 6988/www.jejuloveland.com.

Not your usual ride on the teacups, everything in this one-of-a-kind theme park is sex-related. Walking through the front gates you're greeted by the park's two mascots: Bulkkeuni, a mitten-clad phallus, and Ssaekkeuni, a vagina sporting a floppy hat. Wander a little further to find a massive spurting penis fountain (which rises majestically from a goldfish pond), an interactive sex toy exhibition and a nipple mountain. Even the toilets are adorned with breast handles (for the men) and an erect doorknob (for the ladies). With no rollercoasters in sight, the aptly named Loveland is more hilarious than hair-raising, but it certainly provides punters with some titillating theme park thrills.

934 Legoland, Windsor – building block fun for the little'uns

0871 2222 001/www.legoland.co.uk.

Embrace your inner child and marvel at Miniland's scaled-down reconstructions of London's landmarks. Among the interlocking blocks of Canary Wharf and Millennium Bridge, kids can soar through the skies and sail the seas with over 50 rides and attractions. Rather than getting strapped in and pushed around, the unique feature of this child-centred park is the interactive nature of many of the attractions, such as Laser Raiders (new in 2009) where kids shoot their way through a labyrinth of evil mummies, or Driving School where under-13s cruise around a realistic course of traffic lights, roundabouts and fellow mini-motorists.

935 Wild Wadi, Dubai – for splash-happy sun-lovers

+971 4 348 4444/www.wildwadi.com.

Bursting with 30 state-of-the-art rides and slides, the Arabian-themed Wild Wadi guarantees a wet and wild experience a cut above the rest. Most popular is the Jumeirah Sceirah, a steep and speedy attraction where you fly down a 33-metre drop at 80 kilometres an hour before shooting out through the hollow of a shark-filled aquarium. Summit Surge is another shocker – an uphill ride that blasts swimmers into a pool area before meandering them 170 metres back down again. If you've had adrenaline-overload, Whitewater Wadi is a more leisurely way to spend your day. Kids love the shipwreck and squirting cannons at Juha's Dhow and Lagoon.

936 Europa Park, Rust – for Euro-themed fun

+49 1805 77 66 88/www.europapark.de.

930: Discovery Cove, Florida

Spread over 85 hectares in Germany's south-western corner, Europa Park is the Teutonic equivalent of Disneyland. Unlike your average fairytale-themed fantasylands, Europa Park is quite fittingly split into 13 country-based kingdoms. The lands of Portugal and Scandinavia are home to many of the flumes, rapids and swinging ships while Switzerland, Iceland and France host some fabulous fast speed coasters including Europe's biggest, the Silver Star. England has not been left out of the fun: among Tudor houses and antique merry-go-rounds, those already missing home can hop on a London Bus, hail a ride on a Crazy Taxi or catch a show at the newly built Globe Theatre.

937 Walt Disney World, Florida – for storybook classics

+1 407 939 6244/www.disneyworld.com.
This king of theme parks is the ultimate in holiday heaven or hell, depending on your taste. The four lands that make up the Disney empire are in fact parks in their own right, each with their own admission fee. Crowned by Cinderella's castle, the Magic Kingdom is Disney's classic centrepiece, where cartoon 'celebrities' stroll the grounds and gentle rides such as It's a Small World entertain the youngsters. Animal Kingdom has some stunning live shows that bring animation favourites, such as *Finding Nemo* and the *Lion King*, to life. Catering to older tastes, Epcot has more of a cultural spin, while Disney-MGM is full of TV- and movie-themed rides. As long as you are relatively resilient to queues, nausea and noise, there's plenty to enjoy.

938 Tierra Santa, Buenos Aires – for the religiously pious and the cynically intrigued

+54 11 4784 9551/www.tierrasanta-bsas.com.ar.
Modestly touted by its creators as 'a chance to visit Jerusalem all year round', Tierra Santa is the kind of project that might have been realised had Walt Disney and Billy Graham put their heads together. This Holy Land experience begins with a son-et-lumière extravaganza celebrating the Nativity. As the Angel of the Annunciation descends from a neon-lit sky, locals in Middle Eastern drag herd visitors into the 'world's largest manger'. But the pièce de résistance is the Resurrection – every half hour.

939 Busch Gardens, Florida – for animal-lovers

+1 888 800 5447/www.buschgardens.com.
If you find real animals more exciting than people dressed up as them, Busch Gardens, in Tampa, Florida, is the place for you (although the park admittedly has some of the latter as well). Record-breaking rides and awe-inspiring animals come together in this combination of man-made and live excitement. The Serengeti Plain, home to elephants, zebras and antelopes, can be experienced on rail, by cable car or on foot through one of the park's scenic walkways. For a more up-close encounter, open truck tours allow guests to feed giraffes and come face-to-face with a rhino. The rides are also bestial in nature – SheiKra (one of the world's tallest coasters) plunges its prey down a 90-degree drop, while the sting of the Scorpion ride is in its 360-degree vertical loop.

940-949
Ten useful websites

940 *For city breaks… www.timeout.com/travel*
One of the best sources of information on eating out, nightlife, accommodation, music, cultural attractions and more for cities – from London to Beijing to Vancouver.

941 *For luxury getaways… www.mrandmrssmith.com*
Probably the best site for details of boutique and luxury hotels worldwide.

942 *For world events… www.whatsonwhen.com*
Not a comprehensive events listings site, but it does have a fair amount of information on the larger cultural events.

943 *For comparing prices… www.skyscanner.net*
Fast, user-friendly and clean-looking flight comparison site, which checks no-frills as well as flagships and smarter airlines.

MOULIN ®ROUGE
PARIS

DISCOVER *"FÉERIE"*,
THE SHOW OF THE MOST FAMOUS CABARET IN THE WORLD !

DINNER & SHOW AT 7PM FROM €150 • SHOW AT 9PM: €102, AT 11PM: €92
Montmartre - 82, Boulevard de Clichy - 75018 Paris
Reservations: 33(0)1 53 09 82 82 - www.moulin-rouge.com

944 *For holiday inspiration and advice... www.101holidays.co.uk*

Unsystematic but readable site full of holiday ideas, produced by newspaper travel writers.

945 *For train information... www.seat61.com*

Former station master's fact-filled encyclopaedia; a *Mona Lisa* of a site for trainspotters.

946 *For travel blogs... http://gridskipper.com*

Sites crammed with blogs can be soooo tedious, but this is one of the best anthologies, especially if you're heading to US cities.

947 *For responsible travel... www.responsibletravel.com*

Savvy commercial portal for all the independents offering greener, more ethical travel experiences – with a strong line in adventure travel.

948 *For social and dating trips... www.wayn.com*

Travel-themed meeting arena claiming 15 million users.

949 *For punters reviews... www.tripadvisor.com*

Ugly as sin, but full of stuff if you've got the time out.

950-964
The perfect weekend in Paris

FRIDAY NIGHT

Start your trip at the grandiose **St Pancras International 950**. The 2-hour 15-minute Eurostar journey (01233 617575, www.eurostar.com) will pull in to Gare du Nord before the weekly commuters get back home to Sheffield, while allowing enough time for an early dinner en route. A Leisure Select ticket (not to be confused with Business class) will ensure that you get watered and fed and costs just 20 quid more than the average fare.

Once arrived, make a beeline (via taxi or metro) for the **Latin Quarter 951**, where you'll be staying. The Hotel des Grandes Ecoles (+33 1 43 26 79 23, www.hotel-grandes-ecoles.com) looks like a pastoral cottage, with 51 old-fashioned rooms set in the quiet gardens of this otherwise lively university quarter. Leave your baggage behind (you can unpack later) and join the Parisians for an end of the week party at the techno-spinning Rex (+33 1 42 36 10 96, www.rexclub.com) or La Java (+33 1 42 02 20 52), a historic club where Edith Piaf once performed.

SATURDAY

Wake up to an alfresco breakfast in the leafy gardens of your hotel. Take your time – you've got a busy day of flâneur-inspired behaviour ahead. First up on your walking tour is the **St-Germain-des-Prés** district **952**, the stretch of the Left Bank that used to be Paris's literary and intellectual powerhouse. Verlaine and Rimbaud drank here; later, Sartre, Camus and de Beauvoir scribbled and squabbled, and musicians congregated around Boris Vian in the post-war jazz boom. Wander in a leisurely fashion, taking time to absorb the lingering intellectual air and soak up the smells of café culture.

963: Sacré-Coeur, Montmartre

At the north-western end of the neighbourhood, against the bank of the Seine, is the **Musée d'Orsay 953** (+33 1 45 49 11 11, www.musee-orsay.fr), the first of your unmissable culture stops. Originally a train station and later a theatre, the building now houses a collection of paintings from the fertile art period between 1848 and 1914. Once inside, head straight upstairs. Here you'll find a profusion of paintings by the great Impressionists – Manet, Renoir, Pissarro, Gauguin, Monet, Cézanne – as well as a couple of pieces from Van Gogh, Toulouse-Lautrec's depiction of gaudy lowlife and many more.

From here it's a pleasurable stroll along the quayside to the **Ile de la Cité 954**, the bridging point across the Seine and epicentre of the city. You'll probably be peckish by now, so pop into Maison Berthillon on the adjacent Ile St-Louis (+33 1.4354 3161, www.berthillon-glacier.fr) to try the most celebrated ice-cream in town. The scoops may be small and the price may be high but natural ingredients and delicious flavours have pleased discerning Parisians since the store was opened by Monsieur Berthillon in 1954. Don't worry about getting a full sit-down meal at this point – you'll be snacking again soon and dinner is going to be pricey.

Armed with your sloppy sorbet and fuelled by its sugar load, head across the road for a thorough exploration of the iconic **Cathédral Notre-Dame 955** (+33 1 42 34 56 10, www.cathedraldeparis.com). Commissioned in 1160 and finished in 1334, this Gothic masterpiece took almost 200 years to build. To best appreciate its impressive architecture (which was destroyed during the Revolution, but restored to its former glory in the mid 19th century) walk through the gardens to gaze at the flying buttresses, and take the narrow climb up the north and south towers for a close-up view of the masonry.

After all that walking it's time for some seated touring of the city. Take to the water on the **Batobus Tour Eiffel 956** (+33 8 25 05 01 01, www.batobus.com), a public transport and sightseeing hybrid that cruises down the Seine, pausing at eight hop-on, hop-off stops. From Notre-Dame, float past the Jardin des Plantes botanical garden, before turning back up stream along the Right Bank. Look out for the Hôtel de Ville (city hall) and the iconic glass atrium of the Louvre on your right before sweeping past the imposing gilded dome of the Hôtel des Invalides and finally disembarking

955: Cathédral Notre-Dame

at the world's most famous cast-iron monument, the **Tour Eiffel 957**.

From the Port de la Bourdonnais you'll be able to snap a few classic Eiffel pics while the sun's still out, but don't dawdle too much, you'll be back here for dinner. Instead follow the curve of the Seine, cross at Pont des Invalides and continue along avenue Roosevelt until you hit the magnificent **Champs Elysées 958**, where all of the best high-end stores and Parisian cafés can be found. Walk in the direction of the Arc de Triomphe, stopping about halfway along for a luxury tea break at the prestigious Ladurée (+33 1 40 75 08 75, www.laduree.com). Sit back in the elegant 19th-century-style interior and indulge in tea, fine pastries, macaroons and hot chocolate while looking out on to Paris's favourite fashionable avenue.

With a tummy full of warm beverages and Parisian treats, it's time to head back to the hotel to freshen up for the night-time agenda. For the most efficient journey, take the Paris Métro, a world champion among public transport networks that will get you from A to B before you can say voilà! For dinner you'll be back at the Eiffel for some (literally) high haute cuisine. Perched 123 metres up the tower, **Jules Vernes 959** (+33 1 45 55 61 44, www.tour-eiffel.fr) is a Michelin-starred restaurant that combines adventurous French cuisine with mesmerising views. Dinner here not only gets you sampling some great food, but gives you a top spot up the tower without having to wait in line (the restaurant has a private lift). After eating, take in the vista of the Tour Eiffel one final time as the soaring building lights up with 20,000 flashbulbs in the after-dark hours.

SUNDAY

Start your Sunday bright and early – you're going to need all morning if you want to cover a fair bit of ground at the **Louvre 960** (+33 1 40 20 50 50, www.louvre.fr). If you're heading there by foot, go via Pont Neuf to peer at the grimacing stone faces that line its arches. The palatial art gallery you're looking for is just on the other side, you'll spot it by its glass pyramid roof and by the queue sneaking up to meet you as you step off the bridge. Like Paris's other major museums, this king of galleries is free on the first Sunday of the month, but if you've got a bit of spare cash

(the entrance is around €9) and are prone to claustrophobia, it's probably wiser to avoid this offer. Inside take your pick from 35,000 works of art, eight departments and three wings (Denon, Sully and Richelieu), but by no means attempt to do them all.

After hours of contemplation and concentration, veer towards the **Marais district 961**, where some mindless wandering will weave you between boutiques, museums and bars. Get a well-deserved lunch of hearty French fare at the rustic L'Ambassade d'Auvergne (+33 1 42 72 31 22, www.ambassade-auvergne.com), before checking out the vintage shops along rues Saintonge and Poitou. At some point make sure you stumble across Richard Rogers's **Centre Pompidou 962** – this shouldn't be hard as the 'inside-out' architecture of this museum (air-conditioning pipes, escalators and lifts are all on the outside) make it one of the best-known sights in Paris. Inside, an extensive contemporary art collection is a refreshing complement to the Louvre's classic masterpieces. Alternatively, hang around in the piazza with the street performers and pavement artists to take in the Pompidou in all its exterior glory.

Spend the last hours of the afternoon in the spiralling streets of **Montmartre 963**, a hill-perched village crowned by the extravagant Romano-Byzantine dome of the Sacré-Coeur basilica. Despite the thronging tourists, it's surprisingly easy to fall under the spell of this unabashedly romantic neighbourhood. Climb quiet stairways, peer down narrow alleyways and saunter through bohemian squares before trudging up the steps that lead to the basilica itself. Don't look round until you've reached the peak, then make the top step your pew and watch the sun go down over the Parisian skyline.

If there's time to squeeze in a cocktail, make the short descent to the ever-popular **La Sancerre 964** (+33 1 42 58 08 20) for a final kir royale. Montmarte shows its true colours at night so grab a people-watching spot on the busy terrace for some lasting memories that will keep you entertained on your journey home. From here it's only a short downhill stroll or a quick Métro hop to the Eurostar platforms at the Gare du Nord.

965-969
Spectator holidays

965 *Horseracing... Kentucky Derby*

America's most prestigious horserace is only open to three-year-old thoroughbreds. Americans – Kentuckians especially – spend 12 months preparing for the Kentucky Derby, held on the first Saturday in May, and the weeks leading up to it are filled with lavish parties. It's Louisville's social event of the year, and for owners and trainers much is at stake: the winning horse (or rather, its owner) is given a cool $2 million. On Derby Day itself, some 150,000 spectators flock to the racecourse and many millions tune in to their TVs at home. Whether you choose the grassy infield in the centre of the track (for the most economical tickets) or opt for a pricey Grandstand seat, the chance to soak up such a marvellous mix of social class, age and interests is unrivalled in the race calendar.
www.kentuckyderby.com.
Book with *America As You Like It (020 8742 8299/www.americaasyoulikeit.com).*

966 *Formula 1... Monaco Grand Prix*

Arguably the most prestigious Formula 1 race in the world (www.acm.mc), and certainly the most glitzy, attracting countless celebrities and billionaires as eager to show off their riches as they are to watch the cars race round the twisting narrow streets of Monte Carlo and La Condamine. The most thrilling vantage point is the circuit's tight Portier corner, just before the tunnel. The most economical way to see this spectacle, held each May, is to get a ticket to the Secteur Rocher, a hill above the last corner to the west of the circuit – take binoculars if you choose to stand here. If you're considering a package, check where you'll be seated before booking – not all seats have views of a big-screen TV.
Book with *Bespoke Events (0131 653 6009/ www.bespokeevents.co.uk).*

967 *Sailing... Sydney to Hobart Yacht Race*

The Sydney to Hobart race (www.rolexsydney hobart.com), which takes place on Boxing Day, is the southern hemisphere's most thrilling yacht race, attracting competitors from around the

965: Kentucky Derby

world. The boats must cross the Tasman Sea and the notoriously windy Bass Strait. When the race was first held in the mid 20th century, the boats were all timber and not specifically designed to race. Over the last 60-odd years technology has advanced and today's yachts are lightweight high-performance vessels built with kevlar and other man-made materials. The start of the race attracts thousands of spectators, who flock to Sydney's striking harbour to see the yachts set sail; whether you're on a spectator boat or standing on the shore, the buzz of the crowds and the hum of the helicopters overhead are electric. The end of the race in Hobart is just as exciting, as you watch the elation on the faces of the winning crew members as they pull into Tasmania's historic port.

Book with *Trailfinders (0845 058 5858/ www.trailfinders.com).*

968 *Tests of strength... Highland Games*

£ ⚄ ⌚

Originally, the Highland Games would have been a way to determine the strongest men. They would have competed against one another to test their strength and bravado in preparation for battle. The modern games, which involve a mix of physical contests alongside displays such as Highland dancing and races for children, were established in the 1820s. Going to see the Highland Games now is an entertaining blend of contests such as tug-of-war, wrestling, throwing the hammer, with traditional cultural and social elements such as piping. One of the largest games is the Braemar Gathering (www.braemar gathering.org), held on the first Saturday in September; there's always a great atmosphere – helped along with plenty of ales and whisky.

Book with *Highland Explorer Tours (0131 558 3738/www.highlandexplorertours.com).*

969 *Cycling... Tour de France*

£ ⌚

This annual, long-distance cycle road race attracts some 12 to 15 million spectators every July, and is sensational to watch. But this team-based race is gruelling for the riders, particularly when they reach the steep Alpine stages. The Tour (www.letour.fr) takes three weeks, and is largely held along the roads in France, which are always lined with cheering crowds, though some stages are held in surrounding countries. Until the 1950s, the race always started and finished in Paris, but since then it's started elsewhere. The American Lance Armstrong has won the individual title seven times.

Book with *Sporting Tours (0161 703 8161/ www.sportingtours.co.uk).*

970-974
Middle Eastern promises

970 *Tour Israel's kibbutzim*

Israel may be more in the news than it'd like, but an open mind (and firmly sealed lips) will leave even the worst cynics speechless before the tide of history and meeting of three great monotheistic religions. Sleep in its agricultural communities, the kibbutzim (see www. superstar.co.uk/tours/kibbutz-touring.html), travelling from the legendary Lake of Galilee, where Jesus grew up and made miracles (though their wine doesn't come from water these days), to his final march down the Via Dolorosa in Jerusalem. Best to do it by car rather than the more uncomfortable camel ride now, though.

Book with *Superstar Holidays (020 7121 1500/ www.superstar.co.uk/tours).*

971 *Trek to Jordan's Petra*

One of the new Seven Wonders of the World, the Rose city of Petra is the final stop on a nine-day tour worthy of Indiana Jones's last crusade. From the land of jackals and wildcats, falcons and wolves in the Dana Nature Reserve, you'll be led to a Bedouin track dotted with black nomadic tents, past waterfalls and fragrant date palms. A full day is spent exploring the Rose city, founded in the sixth century BC by the Nabateans and eventually lost during the Roman Empire – not to be rediscovered until 1812; its tombs, temples and façade are miraculously intact.

Book with *On the Go Tours (020 7371 1113/ www.onthegotours.com).*

972 *Journey through time in Lebanon*

Tiny Lebanon's great history unfolded under the influence of Greeks, Romans and Arabs and its capital has risen to notoriety as the Paris of the East. Starting at Byblos, the trading hub of the Bronze Age, you'll move on to Tripoli's two great mosques, its Crusader castle and Belmont Abbey. A day in Beirut won't be enough, but you'll have time to soak up the art galleries, the cafés and taste its vibrant evenings – you can always go back. End at the coastal cities of Tyre and Sidon.

Book with *Barebones Tours (01722 713800/ www.barebonestours.co.uk).*

973 *Explore Syria*

From Damascus to Aleppo, the bustle of this modern, efficient nation is as noisy as its 700 dead but perfectly preserved cities are silent, abandoned after the Byzantine Empire fell to the Arabs. Then there's the castle of Crac des Chevaliers, once the headquarters of the

971: Petra, Jordan

Knights Hospitallers, the great desert emporium of Palmyra and the ancient Al-Hamidiyeh Souk in Damascus. Best of all, there's Aleppo, a labyrinth of bazaars, mosques and possibly the best mezze in Syria, still thriving after 4,000 years.

Book with *Martin Randall (020 8742 3355/ www.martinrandall.com).*

974 *Have fun in Tel Aviv*

Tel Aviv is a city that never sleeps, its pulse racing with the mingling of people at all hours. What it lacks in historical sites it more than makes up for in nightlife, with pumping discos, fantastic food and beach resorts where you can lie in the sand or leap for a volleyball. You won't remember where you are until you see the signs for the 'Separate Beach', with bathing days for men and women (but never both); and then you'll forget all about it again at the gay beach a few steps away.

Book with *Issta Direct (020 8202 0800/ www.isstadirect.com).*

975-979

Stay for free... well, almost

975 *Homestays*
£

Like a B&B but with a more intimate, family vibe, homestays are catching on. Cuba, if not the inventor of this sort of accommodation, has perfected it. Stay at one of the many *casas particulares* (private homes) and you'll meet local people, see the reality of their kitchens and living rooms (a combination of ancient Soviet household items and ancient Spanish antiques is common) and be able to talk freely (often) about Castro and *el comunismo*. Visit www.casaparticularcuba.org for more info. One city we strongly recommend for homestays is New York, not least because hotels there are so darn expensive. As reputable agencies carefully select their host families and guests are obliged to pay a set (yet usually reasonable) rate, this

accommodation alternative lessens the risk factor and offers visitors the security and peace of mind of a paid-for service – as well as the possibility of insider tips from NYC natives. Good agencies to try are Sara's New York Homestay (+1 212 564 5979, www.sarahomestay.com) and New York Homestay (+1 206 201 2085, www.newyorkhomestay.com). Homestays are also a great way to learn a language – so definitely consider them if heading to, say, Guatemala or Salamanca, for Spanish lessons.

976 *House-swapping*
£

The general gist here is that you offer up your humble UK home in return for another family abode wherever you're heading (with the most options in the USA, Canada and Australia). No, you never meet your happy home-swappers and yes, it's a bit of a gamble, but in general the emphasis on good communication between members and the mutual nature of the scheme mean that you won't end up in a trailer park in North Carolina. The first step is to join a home exchange network. Most charge a yearly membership fee, but it's worth shopping around to compare prices and the number of homeswap options in your preferred area. Agencies to check out include Home Base Holidays (www.homebase-hols.com), Home Exchange (www.homeexchange.com) and Home Xchange Vacation (www.homexchangevacation.com). The website www.newyork.craigslist.org has its own home-swapping section for the Big Apple under the Housing classifieds.

977 *Couchsurfing*
£

Based on the same sense of open hospitality as the houseswap, the difference with this budget option is that your holiday home host will be staying put when you come to visit. The nature and quality of your stay therefore rest largely on the host in question; some provide company as well as couches and take it upon themselves to be your guide and guru for the duration of your stay, while other homeowners may simply show you to your sofa and leave you to it. The former is, in fact, more likely to be true as the CouchSurfing Project (www.couchsurfing.com), by far the biggest network of this kind, encourages cultural involvement and interaction, so it's probable that you'll be making friends as well as free trips. With hundreds of New York members willing to open their homes to travelling unknowns, this may well be the perfect cheap trip option for those who are keen to meet locals and are not too preoccupied with privacy. Unlike the homestay and the homeswap, both the membership and hospitality are free, although the idea is that you'll one day return the favour, if not to your host then to another couch-searching surfer.

978 *Hostelling*
£

Time was when the word 'hostel' meant, in Britain, bunk beds, dorms, scouts and warming up beans, and everywhere else, cockroaches, cold showers and toilets beyond hope. But, in parallel with the rise of the boutique and spa hotel and the ever-expanding world of luxury, hostels have risen to the challenge and many offer hotel comforts under another name. Also, as many occupy refurbished historic buildings, you often get rooms of character and a good location; the YHA hostel Railway Square (www.yha.com.au/hostels/details.cfm?hostelid=

215) in Sydney, Australia, is one of our faves. Useful sites include the two strong global portals www.hostelworld.com and www.hostelbookers.com; Latin American network www.hosteltrail.com; and the YHA affiliated Hostelling International (www.hihostels.com).

979 *Discounted rooms*
£

Travel out of season, book late and/or be willing to take whatever is thrown at you, and you can scoop lovely accommodation at a seriously discounted rate. General websites such as www.laterooms.com, www.lastminute.com and www.expedia.com are always worth a look, and you may get flight and car-hire deals too. The big chains, such as French company Accor (www.accorhotels.com) and the Alan Partridge-esque Premier Inn (www.premierinn.com) and Travelodge (www.travelodge.co.uk), have competitive rates too. But it's not all Lenny Henry and his rubber ducky – cool can be cut price too. Consider the Hoxton Hotel (www.hoxtonhotels.com), in one of London's coolest (or most poseur-infested, depends who you speak to) districts; it offers rooms for £1 a night every once in a while. You just have to check the site regularly and book fast.

978: Railway Square hostel, Sydney

980-989

Coastal retreats in the UK

980 Scarista House, Isle of Harris

£ ♞ ♡ ☼

Not many beaches in Britain can be said to have really white sand, but Luskentyre on the Isle of Harris does, and it's shot through with rivulets of sea water that sparkle in a hundred hues of blue and bright white light. Framed by the hills of the Outer Hebrides, all the elements combine to create arguably Britain's most beautiful views. The alien topography goes back three billion years – here are rocks two-thirds as old as the earth itself. The five characterful rooms in converted Georgian manse Scarista House have cosy rugs and warm colours, while the Neolithic-inspired Blue Reef Cottages are a good bet if you fancy spending a week gazing at the stars from your own private sauna and jacuzzi.

Stay at *Scarista House (01859 550238/ www.scaristahouse.com) or Blue Reef Cottages (01859 550370/www.stay-hebrides.com).*

981 Landmark Trust, Lundy

£ ♞ ♦ ♔ ⚲ ☼

The Landmark Trust owns this three-mile-long granite island in the middle of the Bristol Channel, so there are no hotels, no fish and chip shops and definitely no kiss-me-quick hats. Instead, there's a pub, a shop, miles of coastal walks, wild cliffs for climbing fans, a nature reserve for diving fans, and wildlife galore both on- and off-shore – including Silka deer, Lundy ponies, Soay sheep, dolphins, seals and basking sharks. Stay in one of the Landmark Trust's 23 self-catering options on the island, which include a lighthouse, a castle or, for loners, a converted pigsty that sleeps one.

Landmark Trust *(01628 825925/ www.landmarktrust.org.uk).*

982 The Place at Camber Sands, East Sussex

£ ♞ ♔ ⚲ ☼

Hidden behind a mountain of golden dunes, Camber Sands in East Sussex is an awesome sight, a vast, windswept expanse of soft, sandy beach that goes on for miles – seven of them no less – and boasts an impressive half-a-mile width at low tide. Come here for a gorgeous sunset walk in the gentle surf, or to hunker down behind a windbreak, or to ride your horse, fly your kite or act out your *Lawrence of Arabia* fantasies at the quieter western end of the beach. For a more *Carry On Follow that Camel* feel (the film was shot here), stick to the eastern end.

The Place at Camber Sands is the best accommodation option – an affordable, family-friendly motel-style boutique hotel with a great café/brasserie.

Stay at *The Place at Camber Sands (01797 225057/www.theplacecambersands.co.uk).*

983 The Cley Windmill, Norfolk

£ ♞ ♦ ☼

On the north coast of Norfolk, Holkham gets all the lyrical prose and weekend supplements' praise for its undoubtedly stunning expanse of sandy beach backed by pine woods and dunes. But if you want to get away from the London set, head east. A few miles will bring you to Blakeney and Cley-next-the-Sea, connected by a three-mile sand and shingle spit from which you can venture out to see the seals at Blakeney Point. Windswept marshes, sea and sand as far as the eye can see make this an atmospheric spot.

The Cley Windmill has lovely tower rooms accessed by ladders and filled with colourful rugs and patterns aplenty, offering a welcome change from muted boutiquey tones.

Stay at *The Cley Windmill (01263 740209/ www.cleywindmill.co.uk).*

984 The Seabreeze, Devon

£ ♞ ☼

Slapton Sands isn't actually sandy, but it's still a beach that's worth spending a few days exploring, especially if you're looking for some solitude on this beautiful stretch of packed-to-the-gills Devonshire coast. Caught between the fast-encroaching sea on one side and a huge freshwater lake on the other, the vulnerable, three-mile-long shingle bar is distinguished by its calm beauty and relative peace. Stay at the Seabreeze, where you can hear the sea gently slapping the shingle from rustic blue-and-white painted rooms that will make you think you're on a Greek island –

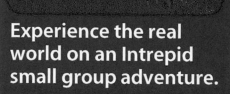

though outbreaks of *Mamma Mia* might offend the smoothie-sipping guests at the excellent terrace café.

Stay at *The Seabreeze (01548 580697/ www.seabreezebreaks.com).*

985 Primrose Valley Hotel, Cornwall

£ ♀ ◔

It's as old as the hills that rise steeply from it, but the ageing hipsters' Cornwall town of St Ives still has plenty of draws: two terrific art galleries, picturesque cobbled streets, pubs that serve scrumpy strong enough to make you fall over after a leisurely pint and, of course, one of the loveliest bays in Britain.

The Primrose Valley Hotel on Porthminster beach has airy, bright rooms with light modern furniture, good art and, best of all, sparkling sea views.

Stay at *Primrose Valley Hotel (01736 794939/ www.primroseonline.co.uk).*

986 Stackpole Inn, Pembrokeshire

£ ♀ ♡ ◔

Choosing just one Welsh beach location is an obvious insult to this country's stunning coastline, so we'll make our selection a good one. Barafundle Bay on the Pembrokeshire coast is utterly spellbinding, a perfect metaphor for a country steeped in folklore and magic. You have to walk along a cliff path from nearby Stackpole Quay and through a stone archway to find it, but once you do, you'll be transported to another world. Stay at the outwardly twee, inwardly cool Stackpole Inn, a 17th-century coaching inn that also does great food.

Stay at *The Stackpole Inn (01646 672324/ www.stackpoleinn.co.uk).*

987 Beach Court, Northumberland

£ ♀ ◔ 🏛

A good beach needs some element of drama, and they don't come much more dramatic than the towering Bamburgh Castle looming from its craggy perch over the Northumberland coast. More drama is close by at Holy Island, accessed by a low-tide causeway leading to the ancient Lindisfarne Priory and even more golden, deserted beaches.

The guesthouses at Bamburgh village all make decent accommodation options; or, better still, book in to the lovely Beach Court, right on the seafront at Beadnell, a few miles south

984: Slapton Sands, Devon

along the coast. Expansive sea views are guaranteed from the wide, wide window seats of all three first-floor rooms.

Stay at *Beach Court (01665 720225/ www.beachcourt.com).*

988 Mallondene, West Sussex

£ ♀ ᛞᛞ ☺

With not one but two fabulous beach cafés designed by leading British architects – the West Beach Café by Asif Khan and the undulating, sculptural East Beach Café by Thomas Heatherwick – Littlehampton is fast becoming a foodie haven, and once you've eaten your fill of the excellent fish and chips at the former, or more sophisticated dishes at the latter, you can enjoy one of the area's most beautiful, quietest beaches. Or head out of town to explore Rick Mather's much-lauded new Towner Gallery in nearby Eastbourne.

Stay in one of the two sea-view rooms at the dinky Mallondene guesthouse, where owners Jenny and Gabrielle will make you feel like you're in your home rather than theirs. Alternatively, the small, very pretty Slindon campsite, set in the orchards of the National Trust-owned Slindon Estate between Arundel and Chichester, offers beautiful views across the coastal plain of West Sussex.

Stay at *Mallondene (01903 77538/ www.mallondene.co.uk) or Slindon campsite (01243 814387).*

989 Priory Bay, Isle of Wight

♀ ♡ ᛞᛞ ☺

As you'd expect of an old-fashioned island with an Enid Blyton vibe, the Isle of Wight has some exceptionally pretty beaches, and one of the nicest is also one of its most wild and secluded. Priory Bay near Sandview on the eastern side of the island is wild, untamed and accessed via the 70-acre estate of the sumptuous Priory Bay hotel that backs on to it; there's even an oyster bar from which to enjoy the views. Take advantage of the hotel's generous special packages on its website for a stay in the hotel proper, or share a self-catering cottage with friends.

Stay at *Priory Bay (01983 613146/ www.priorybay.co.uk).*

988: Littlehampton

FISH & CHIPS

990-999

And now for something completely different...

990 Chase an eclipse

◊♡

There's something about cosmic, myth-laden, uniquely dramatic events that moves our very being. Increasingly, travellers tired of the obvious are making their way to precise locations on earth to be there at the very moment when an eclipse takes place. These come in lunar and solar form, and can be partial or total. Which is the best? Well, a total solar normally does the job. You'll need the dark glasses, of course, and a GPS is handy so you can record just where you were and geotag your photos. When darkness strikes, the birds stop singing and, for a brief moment nature is out of joint. In recent years there have been memorable solar eclipses in the Russian Altai region (great because it's generally cloud-free) and off the coast of China.

991 Hide away on Scotland's St Kilda

ৎ ◊♡

It's July, the sun is shining and the seas, even around Britain, are a few degrees warmer. Just when everyone else is boarding packed aeroplanes to join massed ranks of tourists all over the beaches of the Med, get yourself off to the unique archipelago of St Kilda. It's the remotest spot in the British Isles, lying 41 miles west of Benbecula in Scotland's Outer Hebrides, and the islands' stunning high cliffs form north-western Europe's most important seabird breeding area. Since the evacuation of the native population in 1930, the archipelago – a UNESCO World Heritage Site – has been managed by the National Trust for Scotland, Scottish Natural Heritage and the Ministry of Defence, who work together to protect St Kilda's natural habitats and marine environment (its waters are crystal clear, making it one of Britain's best diving spots).

It's not easy to reach St Kilda; many people visit as part of a cruise, or you can take chartered boats from Mallaig and Oban, with journey times varying between eight and 14 hours.
www.kilda.org.uk.

992 Go to the end of the line on the Baikal–Amur Railway

The Trans-Siberian Railway, while epic and exciting, is ultra-familiar to seasoned travellers. Our friends have done it. Dozens of posh tour operators offer it. You can do it when you retire. To impress even the coolest trainspotter, head to Irkutsk to ride the Baikal–Amur line (often referred to as the BAM). Construction of the 4,324-kilometre-long broad-gauge track, laid on top of Siberian permafrost, was begun in the 1930s by Gulag workers but only completed in 1991. It connects Irkutsk with the empty wastes north of Lake Baikal, passing through dozens of remote villages before arriving at the Pacific Ocean in Vladivostok. Highlights of the trip include Irkutsk, the 'Paris of Siberia', a giant sculpture of a *Worker with a Sledge Hammer* and the ruins of deserted Gulags – and, of course, before you get on you should toast your trip with a finger of neat vodka beside beautiful Baikal.
Book with *Explore (0845 013 1537/ www.explore.co.uk).*

993 Join an expedition

◊ ⚐

You don't have to be Scott, Amundsen or Fogle to do something extraordinary. The Edwardian Heroic Age's great divide between Them and Us, and the mid 20th century's equally invidious worship of the Professional Scientific Researcher are now generally regarded as self-aggrandising codswallop. It's still not easy to blag your way to the US base at the South Pole or meet natives in the unmapped reaches of Amazonia, but there serious-ish expeditions that ordinary travellers can join. Raleigh International started out organising expeditions for young people, but has now expanded to encourage people of all ages to take up the challenge of self-funded (through sponsorship) expeditions in the charity's core destinations of Borneo, Costa Rica, Nicaragua or India – as both a way to increase personal empowerment, and to make a difference in the world by helping disadvantaged communities.
Raleigh International *020 7183 1270/ www.raleighinternational.org.*

994 Do the ultimate detox

Many holidays seem to be about causing us as much physical damage as possible, whether it's popping pills on a clubbing break, eating three lobsters a day aboard a cruise ship, or just pushing our filtering organs to the limit on oily, spicy food and rich wine. If your last few holidays have been less than models of health and moderation, it may be time for some serious plumbing, and there are plenty of holidays designed to help you de-stress and detox. One of the best established and extreme is Thailand's Spa Samui Resort on the island of Ko Samui. Comprised of 24 air-conditioned bungalows, tropical gardens, a spa and pool, its seven-day 'Clean-Me-Out' programme aims to purify the bloodstream and colon through fasting (no solid foods are consumed); by taking diluted fruit juices, enemas and herbal intestinal cleansers to clear out the colon; and through light exercise and therapies such as yoga and massage. Toxins, mucous and debris that your body has been building up for years are flushed out, and by the end – as long as you don't cheat – you'll hopefully have increased energy, fewer aches and ailments, clearer skin and improved vitality.

Spa Samui Resort *+66 77 424 666/ www.thespasresorts.net.*

995 *Look out for mistakes at North Korea's Mass Games*

What most impressed those who saw the opening of the 2008 Beijing Olympic Games was the co-ordination and elegance of the massed dance routines. Well, compared to the Mass Games at North Korea's Airang festival, the Chinese effort was a ragbag of St Vitus dancers at a dress rehearsal. It takes old-school hardcore Communism and a closed society to really train people to behave. North Korea's amazing spectacle, devised by politicians to help the little people celebrate the birthday of Kim Il Sung and, later, Kim Jong Il, involves tens of thousands of loyal citizens moving and chanting in unison; to the spectator, it looks like something very natural, one whole body moving

seamlessly through complex steps and patterns, but requires huge amounts of individual strength and, above all, concentration from the quasi-robotic performers. With only a few hundred visitors a year, North Korea is still out-there, and the Mass Games is its FA Cup, Derby Day, Henley and Christmas all rolled into one. **Who goes there?** *Koryotours (+86 10 6416 7544/ www.koryogroup.com).*

996 *Surprise yourself*

Brochures, websites, TV shows, guidebooks, illustrated atlases, this book… we are all keenly aware that we're overloaded with information, yet we still gobble up as much as we can before we set off on our travels. Why not approach your next holiday with some of the gusto of the early explorers and just spin a globe, point a finger and *go* there? Or, take a no-frills, no-hotel-booked flight to somewhere you're deeply curious (or wholly ignorant) about. Haiti? Congo? Guam? Cameroon? Paraguay? Cardiff? Are they even on your 'to do' list? Travelling with no preparation (apart from perhaps checking the Foreign & Commonwealth Travel website, www.fco.gov. uk/travel, to prevent you from walking into a war zone) is perhaps the only way to really feel the buzz of a place. You may do well to go alone on such a trip: it's probably the only way to expose yourself fully to the people and place, and get outside all those comfort zones that dilute and dampen your experiences.

997 *Learn ninja skills in Japan*

Black Tomato, a company that seeks out cutting-edge travel experiences for the brave and the adventurous, offers a week-long trip that's bound to get hearts racing among fans of films such as *Kill Bill* and *Crouching Tiger, Hidden Dragon*: a trip to Tokyo to learn the ancient skills of the ninja – the legendary disgraced Samurai warriors who decided to train independently of a master rather than committing *harakiri* (dying with honour). Lessons with one of Japan's renowned martial arts masters are arranged for you in Tokyo, as well as classes in the much gentler Zen skills of calligraphy, origami and *ikebana*

(flower arranging) – which all help to train the mind. You'll also get to experience one of the world's most exciting, forward-looking and, at the same time, traditional cities.
Black Tomato *020 7426 9888/ www.blacktomato.co.uk.*

998 *Stay at home*

Argentinian author Julio Cortázar wrote a whole story about how to walk up a flight of stairs. The London-based School of Life – a sort of cod university and vehicle for philosopher Alain de Botton and his pals – has come up with a whole package for holidaying in your living room. But, what do you actually need for a holiday that takes you nowhere? Let's say a decent holiday for one costs around £500. This means you can buy the best bottle of wine you've ever had, three new books, a new T-shirt (holiday attire is useful to keep up the illusion), some delicious deli grub and pay the heating bill even if you crank the thermostat up to Tropical. That's the basics. For the holiday element, dedicate your time to lounging in the garden, napping and reading, scribbling a journal or postcards-to-self, avoiding household tasks and mobile phone appeals, sunning yourself or cloudspotting (listening out for jets just to give your brain its airport fix) – and do make sure to take taxis when you go to the supermarket; holidays should not be spent on public transport. Internet means you can hook up with new friends all over the world, and flick through the *CIA Factbook* to get juicy, if hawkish, takes on all the places you'd love to visit. The world – at home – is an oyster, and, while we're at it, buy some of them too… See www.holidaysfromhome.co.uk for inspiration.

999 *Go somewhere with a friend or relative*

Life moves on. Relationships fragment and dissipate. One group of friends is replaced by another. Families decide – one day, at random – that it's no longer necessary to travel together. But travel can be an opportunity to reconnect with a friend or parent or sibling and, contrary to received wisdom, can be a wonderful experience; even if it is sometimes trying, it will be an opportunity to bond, reflect and take time out. The best trips for this sort of long-view experience are overland epics – a big railway journey across Australia, a slow drive across Patagonia, a boat to Greenland, say – providing plenty of time to chat, slow down, and indulge in a bit of 'do you remember?' therapy. The new milieu may be just what the relationship needed to boost it – and if that sounds like a bit of free astrology, then so be it.

1000

See the ultimate sunset

Rio de Janeiro

There are lots of contenders for places to go to see the 'ultimate sunset' (Santorini in Greece and Goa in India are two often mentioned), but Rio de Janeiro in Brazil is certainly high up the list. The dramatic, sweeping vista from the Corcovado (meaning 'hunchback') hill viewpoint, where the iconic, 39.6-metre art deco statue of Christ the Redeemer stands, is truly breathtaking, taking in the Tijuca Forest National Park as well as the city's sparkling lights and Sugarloaf Mountain. Christ's outstretched arms appear to embrace the socially-divided city – known for its hedonistic beaches and carnival, but also its urban crime and favelas (shantytowns) – uniting it in a moment of true beauty. Seeing the sun set behind the hills will have you wanting to chase it around the globe and travel some more.

Scotland

Northern Ireland

Republic of Ireland

England

Wales

Great Britain & Ireland

Numbers given are ideas numbers, not page numbers.

England

2, 19, 22, 23, 24, 62, 66, 67, 83, 139, 140, 141, 142, 151, 152, 153, 155, 156, 157, 158, 159, 190, 210, 211, 212, 213, 214, 215, 216, 217, 224, 227, 252, 320, 322, 332, 360, 363, 364, 365, 366, 367, 368, 369, 384, 386, 432, 440, 456, 475, 498, 502, 510-519, 520, 521, 522, 538, 539, 540, 541, 545, 546, 547, 572, 601, 612, 613, 626, 632, 650, 664, 674, 691, 692, 694, 697, 699, 738, 740, 743, 761, 766, 768, 769, 827, 843, 877, 894, 909, 924, 981, 982, 983, 984, 985, 987, 988, 989

Scotland

69, 159, 221, 222, 223, 321, 333, 361, 429, 440, 457, 542, 601, 606, 611, 614, 615, 616, 617, 618, 619, 629, 693, 703, 717, 718, 719, 720, 765, 820, 859, 894, 958, 980, 991

Wales

56, 150, 154, 219, 220, 362, 448, 543, 610, 621, 695, 696, 767, 821, 894, 986

Northern Ireland

358, 359, 544, 894

Republic of Ireland

163, 179, 218, 353, 354, 355, 356, 357, 380, 484, 600, 763, 836, 862

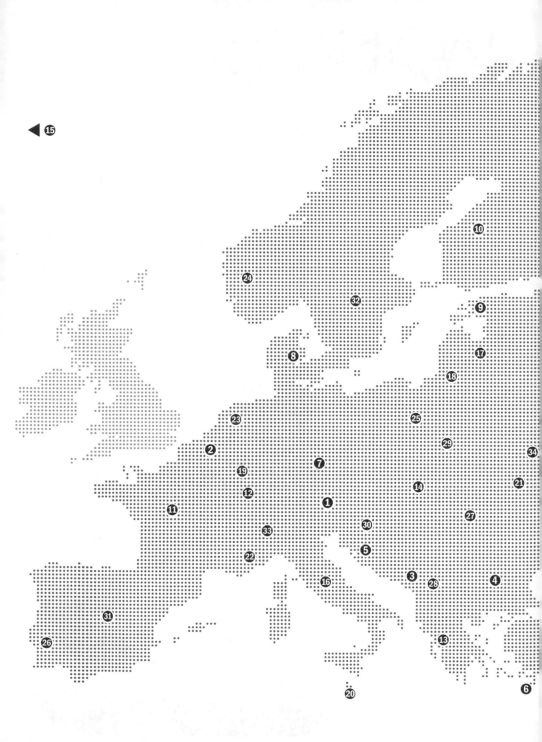

Europe

❶ Austria
22, 49, 180, 254, 334, 420, 443, 549, 550, 554, 890

❷ Belgium
20, 23, 64, 191, 251, 372, 378, 856

❸ Bosnia and Herzegovina 196

❹ Bulgaria
22, 109, 183, 495, 815

❺ Croatia
46, 105, 323, 473, 493, 622, 725-732, 759

❻ Cyprus
120-129, 387, 497, 842

❼ Czech Republic
80, 194, 226, 250, 454

❽ Denmark
17, 70, 138, 267, 838, 878

❾ Estonia
84

❿ Finland
188, 330, 422, 451, 819, 875

⓫ France
22, 24, 41, 68, 104, 113, 118, 136, 143, 164, 182, 257, 274, 280, 307, 370, 373, 374, 375, 376, 377, 379, 388, 419, 428, 430, 445, 447, 449, 488, 503, 523, 548, 551, 553, 607, 609, 625, 667, 670, 722, 745, 758, 773, 817, 835, 836, 861, 884, 890, 940-954, 959

⓬ Germany
9, 22, 23, 100, 192, 253, 255, 371, 443, 470, 506, 702, 723, 812, 835, 838, 855, 926

⓭ Greece
50, 111, 114, 281-290, 402, 411, 662, 762, 818, 863, 893

⓮ Hungary
22, 195, 225

⓯ Iceland
60, 65, 336, 423, 496, 897

⓰ Italy
6, 14, 47, 85-94, 103, 107, 115, 135, 143, 146, 147, 162, 175, 187, 259, 266, 277, 305, 382, 385, 452, 476, 602, 628, 652, 721, 793, 810, 835, 844, 886, 890

⓱ Latvia
82

⓲ Lithuania
193, 494

⓳ Luxembourg
876

⓴ Malta
117, 326, 412, 478, 813

㉑ Moldova
499

㉒ Monaco
956

㉓ Netherlands
63, 264, 446, 472, 857

㉔ Norway
27, 309, 421, 677, 711

㉕ Poland
23, 119

㉖ Portugal
106, 116, 275, 327, 560, 780-784, 822

㉗ Romania
189, 198

㉘ Serbia
22

㉙ Slovakia
480

㉚ Slovenia
184, 809

㉛ Spain
24, 44, 61, 81-101, 102, 108, 112, 134, 145, 173, 228, 230-239, 279, 381, 410, 414, 460-469, 474, 477, 555, 579, 620, 633, 654, 668, 764, 774, 798, 811, 814, 816, 823, 835, 839, 841, 854, 891, 922

㉜ Sweden
27, 324, 427, 532, 860

㉝ Switzerland
45, 133, 143, 185, 428, 552, 747, 836, 847

㉞ Ukraine
169

The Americas

❶ Alaska 525

❷ Argentina
1, 74, 273, 438, 455, 526, 605, 785, 786, 788, 789, 790, 792, 928

❸ Bahamas 307

❹ Barbados
754, 908

❺ Belize
79, 406, 413, 733, 873

❻ Brazil
7, 75, 165, 203, 261, 268, 404, 479, 483, 530, 563, 582, 624, 669, 888, 905, 1000

❼ Canada
25, 181, 270, 401, 425, 630, 671, 742, 751

❽ Cayman Islands 900

❾ Chile
59, 76, 132, 209, 272, 438, 705, 710, 787, 790, 791

❿ Colombia
72, 655, 736

⓫ Costa Rica
409, 700

⓬ Cuba
441, 603, 870, 899

⓭ Dominican Republic
558

⓮ Ecuador
71, 679

⓯ Grenada
757, 869

⓰ Guana Island 882

⓱ Guatemala 78, 408

⓲ Jamaica 178

⓳ Mexico
77, 166, 206, 310-319, 508, 564, 657, 663, 795, 872, 879, 885, 892

⓴ Peru
73, 262, 509, 642, 708, 712

㉑ Puerto Rico
271, 871

㉒ St Barth's 665

㉓ St Lucia 407, 753

㉔ Suriname 293

㉕ Turks & Caicos Islands 881

㉖ USA
3, 4, 10, 12, 21, 54, 130, 137, 160, 161, 170, 207, 208, 229, 276, 331, 338-342, 383, 389, 415, 417, 424, 439, 442, 458, 471, 501, 565-571, 574, 580, 583, 623, 631, 634, 641, 651, 678, 680-689, 707, 714, 749, 750, 752, 756, 775, 796, 824, 838, 840, 874, 887, 896, 920, 921, 927, 929, 955

㉗ Venezuela
746

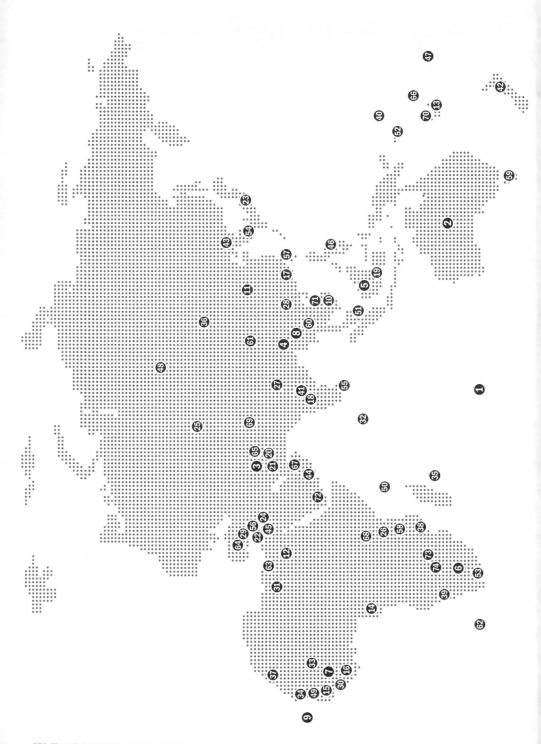

Rest of the world

(1) *Antarctic*
57, 301, 437, 837

(2) *Australia*
16, 30, 43, 200, 205, 265, 278, 416, 453, 529, 604, 635, 709, 755, 907, 910-919, 957

(3) *Azerbaijan* 294

(4) *Bhutan* 846

(5) *Borneo*
204, 245, 246, 675, 906

(6) *Botswana*
96, 98, 706

(7) *Burkina Faso*
295

(8) *Burma* 658

(9) *Cabo Verde* 350

(10) *Cambodia*
18, 244, 507

(11) *China*
58, 256, 291, 426, 505, 598, 704, 794, 837, 850

(12) *Egypt*
490, 500, 557, 716, 734, 845, 864-868

(13) *Fiji* 308, 880

(14) *Gabon*
99, 349

(15) *Gambia*
346, 559, 760

(16) *Ghana* 348

(17) *Hong Kong*
581

(18) *India*
28, 51, 176, 306, 504, 575, 608, 636, 643, 676, 797, 828-833, 848, 898

(19) *Indonesia*
666, 737

(20) *Iran* 535, 851

(21) *Iraq* 659

(22) *Israel*
459, 970, 974

(23) *Japan*
5, 15, 29, 172, 186, 260, 400, 595, 627, 799, 997

(24) *Jordan* 971

(25) *Kazakhstan*
291, 852

(26) *Kenya*
52, 97, 482, 638, 673, 883

(27) *Kyrgyzstan*
849

(28) *Laos* 242

(29) *Lebanon*
561, 972

(30) *Liberia* 433

(31) *Libya*
335, 343, 344

(32) *Maldives, The*
661, 901

(33) *Mali* 345

(34) *Mauritania* 292

(35) *Mauritius* 748

(36) *Mongolia*
291, 599, 853

(37) *Morocco*
24, 171, 258, 325, 343, 524, 556, 653, 701, 759, 800-808, 845

(38) *Mozambique*
527

(39) *Namibia* 98, 351

(40) *Nauru*
299

(41) *Nepal*
209, 485

(42) *New Zealand*
48, 55, 148, 168, 202, 390-399, 672, 772, 826

(43) *North Korea*
995

(44) *Oman*
329, 537, 889

(45) *Palestinian National Authority*
337

(46) *Philippines*
597

(47) *Polynesia*
263

(48) *Russia*
23, 291, 300, 434, 850, 858, 990

(49) *Senegal* 347

(50) *Seychelles*
660, 904

(51) *Singapore* 578

(52) *Solomon Islands*
902

(53) *South Africa*
26, 96, 149, 177, 352, 418, 562

(54) *South Korea*
596, 923

(55) *Sri Lanka*
528, 903

(56) *Syria* 11, 973

(57) *Taiwan* 594

(58) *Tanzania*
42, 52, 637, 638

(59) *Tasmania*
957

(60) *Thailand*
18, 53, 131, 241, 248, 249, 403, 436, 645-649, 735, 739, 845, 994

(61) *Tibet*
209

(62) *Tristan da Cunha* 297

(63) *Tunisia*
167, 492

(64) *Turkey*
8, 22, 31-40, 110, 144, 199, 405, 450, 491, 497, 724, 759, 825, 845

(65) *Turkmenistan*
851

(66) *Tuvalu*
296

(67) *UAE*
13, 533, 534, 536, 577, 925

(68) *Uganda* 95

(69) *Uzbekistan* 851

(70) *Vanuatu* 269

(71) *Vietnam*
174, 240, 243, 713

(72) *Yemen*
298, 656

(73) *Zambia*
98, 201, 531

(74) *Zimbabwe*
201

Planning your trip

GET INFORMED

General advice

www.fco.gov.uk/en/travel-and-living-abroad
The Foreign & Commonwealth Office (FCO) provides reasonably up-to-date information about the political, crime and health issues of every country. Call 0845 850 2829 (24hrs, seven days a week) or email traveladvicepublicenquiries@fco.gov.uk.
www.cia.gov/library/publications/the-world-factbook
The *CIA World Factbook* is an up-to-date guidebook to '266 world entities' (goonspeak for countries) and a source of interesting, albeit sometimes hawkish, analyses as well as facts and stats.

Travel and tourism organisations

There are several tourism bodies that regulate travel operators and promote responsible tourism. It is advisable to travel with tour operators approved by the likes of ABTA and AITO, as these will provide compensation in the event of a tour firm, airline or travel agent going bankrupt.

www.abta.com
The Association of British Travel Agents (ABTA) represents more than 5,000 travel agents and 800 tour operators – including the two largest UK travel firms, Thomas Cook Group and TUI (which, combined, handle about 90 per cent of UK package-holiday bookings).

www.aito.com
The Association of Independent Tour Operators (AITO) is a respected body, representing some 140 small- to medium-sized specialist tour operators selling holidays that offer 100 per cent financial protection abroad. For advice, call 020 8744 9280.

www.traveltrust.co.uk
The Travel Trust Association represents 370 independent travel companies and provides financial protection for all members.

www.atol.org.uk
The organisation Air Travel Organisers Licensing (ATOL) protects consumer money in the event of a flight operator going bust.

www.the-psa.co.uk
The Passenger Shipping Association (PSA) represents 14 ferry operators and dozens of cruise-ship operators.

Ethical issues

Before travelling, you may want to consult NGOs and charities about the ethics of your planned trip.

Burma Campaign (www.burmacampaign.org.uk)
Working for human rights, democracy and development in Burma, this organisation has the latest on Aung San Suu Kyi and the ethics and effects of travel to and in Burma.

Amnesty International (www.amnesty.org.uk)
Amnesty's website provides a comprehensive guide to state terrorism around the world, often in countries where tourism is a vital part of the economy.

Tourism Concern (www.tourismconcern.org.uk)
The only NGO in Europe campaigning against exploitation in the global tourism industry.

Tourism for All (www.tourismforall.org.uk)
A national charity dedicated to 'standards of world-class tourism that are welcoming to all'.

Holiday Travel Watch (www.holidaytravelwatch.com)
General website covering all sorts of consumer issues for those planning to travel.

UK regional/metropolitan tourist boards

England
020 7578 1400/
www.visitengland.com (corporate)/
www.enjoyengland.com (consumer).

Scotland
0845 22 55 121/www.visitscotland.co.uk.

Wales
08708 300 306/www.visitwales.co.uk.

Northern Ireland +44 (0)28 9023 1221/
www.discovernorthernireland.com.

Birmingham
0121 202 5115/www.visitbirmingham.com.

Brighton
0906 711 2255/www.visitbrighton.com.

Ideas from the expert

Chris Moss, Travel Editor of Time Out magazine and Editor of this book, shares his 20 killer trip-planning tips.

1 Check your passport well in advance of travel, especially if you're going to need a visa. Some governments require a certain number of months validity for entry. Ordering passports at short notice is punitively expensive.

2 Consider picking up your hire-car in the centre of town instead of at the airport. You can save on hefty rental taxes this way.

3 Check your mobile phone account to see what the overseas roaming costs are; it may be cheaper to buy a local SIM card. Note that data costs are likely to be high – look for free wireless.

4 Check voucher sites such as www.my vouchercodes.co.uk and www.discount vouchers.co.uk, which often have car hire, hotel and attraction discounts. You can usually get up to eight per cent cashback on car rental and hotels if you go via a cashback site such as www.quidco.com or www.moneysavingexpert.com.

5 Never let any of your bank cards out of your sight. ATM fraud is a common problem for travellers. Take your bank's emergency international telephone number when you travel.

6 When booking a hotel on an online discount site, be sure to call it and see if staff can equal the price. If so, book direct. You'll have better cancellation rights plus they're more likely to give you a good room.

7 Join one or more frequent-flier schemes. You'll have to work out where you're most likely to be heading for the next few years before joining one, but it could pay: you can get free flights, upgrades, better seats and you'll be welcomed on board as an official club member.

8 Upgrades and lies: there's a lot of tosh told about getting upgrades, but if you want to try and blag a business-class seat, dress smart, be polite and don't try any 'do you know who I am' nonsense. Being tall helps.

9 Fly in style. If you hate the whole economy cattle-truck experience, but don't have the readies to fly business, ease your pains by having a decent, light meal and a good glass of wine at the airport, get some slippers and a soft eyemask, and invest in noise-reduction headphones (jetlag is caused by engine noise as much as time difference).

10 If you're going short-haul, why not fly using only carry-on luggage? It can save you heaps of time as you skip jauntily past the carousels and you'll probably find yourself packing with more care and intelligence.

12 Pay for flights and holidays using a credit card as, under Section 75 of the Consumer Credit Act, your money (over £100 and under £30,000) is guaranteed if the tour firm or airline goes out of business (and they do!).

13 If you're lucky enough to be a student get yourself an International Student Identity Card; these are internationally recognised and will get you discounts on museums, transport and more. See www.isic.org or contact STA Travel (www.statravel.co.uk).

14 Check if the airports you're using charge departure tax; if they do, it will likely have to be paid with the exact cash, which can be a nasty surprise when you're at the airport heading home – and you've just spent all your local currency on quirky gifts.

15 Heading somewhere where crime is an issue? Forget cash or travellers cheques and get yourself a prepaid cashcard. It's a safe and convenient way to carry money, and they're becoming widely accepted (get a well-known one such as the STA Cashcard).

16 Buy rail and bus passes before you leave; they're usually aimed at foreign visitors and are often more expensive once you get there. Buying rail passes for places such as Japan and Korea before you leave can save you heaps of money.

17 Some premium credit/charge cards accounts, such as the AmEx Platinum chargecard offer annual travel insurance for you, your partner and your family, as well as extra perks such as airport and Eurostar lounge access and car-hire insurance.

18 The Post Office charges zero commission for foreign currency. If you have time, buy your currency online using Travelex's (www.travelex. co.uk) 'buy online and collect at airport' deal.

19 Learn 20 words of the local language – it's worth a million hand signals and will almost always get you better treatment.

20 Don't overplan – at least half the pleasure of travelling is the fun of the unknown.

FOR MORE INSPIRATION...

As well as this book, Time Out publishes over 100 guides to destinations around the world, including traditional guidebooks and holiday inspiration compilations. We also publish 30 magazines and visitors guides, many of which are in English. So, if you're heading to New York, Dubai, Sydney, Buenos Aires or Cape Town, among other cities, look out for our logo.

In addition to our City Guides and Shortlists, the following Time Out books should help you plan the perfect break.

Adventure!

Our big book of 38 active and adventurous trips around the world.

Flight-free Europe

How to get from here to 30 destinations, from Jersey to Marrakech and the Polar Circle, without using planes.

Great Train Journeys

Time Out's homage to the greatest trains and the long and wonderful railway lines that encircle the planet from Tibet to Tokyo to the North York Moors.

World's Greatest Cities

Our lavishly photographed portrait of 75 metropolises.

Perfect Places series

Our new range of guides that focus on the standout destinations in a country and take you to the loveliest hotels, restaurants and landscapes in each. The series includes:

Perfect Places in Argentina & Uruguay
Perfect Places in Britain
Perfect Places in France
Perfect Places in Italy
Perfect Places in Morocco

www.timeout.com/travel

Finally, don't forget our website where you can explore all our city guides and top 20 lists, as well as features from the Travel section of London's Time Out magazine, for free!

Bristol
0333 321 0101/www.visitbristol.co.uk.

Edinburgh
0845 2255 121/www.edinburgh.org.

Glasgow
0141 566 0800/www.seeglasgow.com.

Isle of Man
01624 686801/www.visitisleofman.com.

Isle of Wight
01983 813 813/www.islandbreaks.co.uk.

Liverpool
0844 870 0123/www.visitliverpool.com.

London
08701 566 366/www.visitlondon.com.

Manchester
0871 222 8223/www.visitmanchester.com.

Portsmouth
023 9282 6722/www.visitportsmouth.co.uk.

Major foreign tourist boards with offices in the UK

Australia
020 7438 4600/www.tourism.australia.com.

Austria
0845 101 1818/www.austria.info.

Brazil
020 7399 9000/www.brazil.org.uk/tourism.

Canada
0870 380 0070/www.canada.travel.

China
020 7373 0888/www.cnto.org.uk.

Denmark
020 7259 5958/www.visitdenmark.com.

France
09068 244123/www.franceguide.com.

Germany
020 7317 0908/www.germany-tourism.co.uk.

Greece
020 7495 9300/www.visitgreece.gr/
www.gnto.co.uk.

Hong Kong
020 7533 7100/www.discoverhongkong.com.

India
020 7437 3677/www.incredibleindia.org.

Ireland
0808 234 2009/www.discoverireland.com.

Italy
020 7408 1254/www.italiantouristboard.co.uk.

Japan
020 7398 5678/www.seejapan.co.uk.

Mexico
0800 1111 2266/www.visitmexico.com.

New Zealand
no phone/www.newzealand.com.

Norway
020 7389 8800/www.visitnorway.com.

Poland
08700 675010/www.polandtour.org.

Portugal
0845 355 1212/www.visitportugal.com.

Singapore
020 7484 2701/www.visitsingapore.com.

Russia
020 7495 7570/www.visitrussia.org.uk.

South Africa
0870 155 0044/www.southafrica.net.

Spain
020 7486 8077/www.spain.info/uk.

Sweden
020 7108 6168/www.visitsweden.com.

Switzerland
0800 1002 0030/www.myswitzerland.com.

Thailand
0870 900 2007/www.tourismthailand.co.uk.

Turkey
020 7839 7778/www.gototurkey.co.uk.

USA (most popular states):
Visit USA Association
0870 777 2213/www.visitusa.org.uk.

California
020 7257 6180/http://visitcalifornia.co.uk.

Florida
020 7932 2406/www.visitflorida.com/uk.

Los Angeles
020 7318 9555/www.discoverlosangeles.com.

New York
020 7629 6891/www.nylovesu.co.uk.

Texas
020 7367 0963/www.traveltex.com.

HEALTH

The FCO estimates that an air ambulance from the East Coast of the USA back to the UK costs between £35,000-£45,000 (figures from FirstAssist Services Ltd). It is, then, clear that all travel should be backed up with an insurance policy. The best ones cover health, emergency assistance (with a 24-hour hotline), personal liability (in case you injure someone else or

damage property), lost and stolen possessions, cancellation or curtailment (cutting short) your holiday, and any extras you might require, such as cover for dangerous sports. See www.fco.gov.uk/en/travel-and-living-abroad/staying-safe/travel-insurance for full details. The website www.nhs.uk/healthcareabroad is also useful.

European Health Insurance Card (EHIC)

If you're a UK resident, you are entitled to medical treatment that becomes necessary, at reduced cost or sometimes free, when temporarily visiting a European Union (EU) country, Iceland, Liechtenstein, Norway or Switzerland. Only treatment provided under the state scheme is covered. However, to obtain treatment you will need to take a European Health Insurance Card (EHIC) with you. Please note: not all UK residents are covered in Denmark, Iceland, Liechtenstein, Norway or Switzerland. Apply and find out more at wsw.ehic.org.uk.

Vaccinations

The US NHS travel health website www.fitfortravel.nhs.uk/home.aspx, with its easy-to-use map-based guide to jabs and general health matters, is useful for travellers on both sides of the border.

INSURANCE

New FSA regulations mean it's become too costly and time-consuming for most tour firms to offer insurance directly. That said, many operators require customers to take out insurance before travelling. In addition to providing cover for medical emergences, insurance schemes can protect travellers against the following: loss of money and personal effects; personal accident; delayed baggage; travel interruption and travel delay. There may be optional extensions, such as loss of passport and legal expenses.

Check with your broker before you travel if intend to carry a lot of expensive photographic equipment, as many policies only cover inexpensive cameras. Always report crimes to local police agencies as insurance firms will require an official document as proof of loss.

Travel insurance covers you when you're travelling within the UK or abroad, either for specific trips or on an annual basis to cover all trips during the year. The policies typically cover medical expenses, loss of baggage and loss of deposit, and pay compensation for travel delays. Policies are also available to cover business travel.

Annual policies have become more popular with the growing trend to take more than one holiday a year.

OFFSETTING & GREEN TRAVEL

www.responsibletravel.com
The portal of Responsible Travel, which acts as an agent for many of the greener UK tour operators and also as a platform for green tourism awards.

www.treesforcities.org
Charity working with local communities on tree planting and landscaping projects, and also Time Out's partner for carbon offsetting.

www.greentraveller.co.uk
Green hotel guide.

www.greenhotels.com
US-based company surveying hotels for green credentials.

www.ecotourism.org
Portal of the so-called International Ecotourism Society, a non-profit organisation dedicated to promoting ecotourism.

www.sustainabletravelinternational.org
Another self-appointed watchdog.

WEBSITES (MISCELLANEOUS)

As well as the top ten travel websites listed on p249-251, we also recommend the following:

www.lonelyplanet.com/thorntree/
Online community of travellers who swap ideas and advice.

www.flightmapping.com
Useful guide to 'who flies where' for all flights out of the UK and Ireland.

www.seat61.com
Comprehensive railway timetable website.

CHEAP FLIGHTS

Main UK low-cost carriers

Bmibaby www.bmibaby.com.
Eastern Airways www.easternairways.com.
Easyjet www.easyjet.com.
Flybe www.flybe.com.
Jet 2 www.jet2.com.
Ryanair www.ryanair.com.

General websites:

www.attitudetravel.com/lowcostairlines/ europe/#map
A list and map of the now burgeoning European budget airline scene.
www.momondo.com
www.skyscanner.net
www.mobissimo.com
And these specific airlines:
www.airasia.com (UK-SE Asia)
www.jetlite.com (India domestic)
www.opodo.com (Not no-frills but useful for comparing the major airlines)

Advertisers' Index

Regione Lombardia	IFC
DoSomethingDifferent.com	6
Carbon Neutral	8
Trees for Cities	56
Oxfam	74
Turismo Madrid	78
Moulin Rouge	250
Intrepid Travel	260
Primrose Valley Hotel	260
Insure and Go	260